Praise for

Committed to Victory:
The Kentucky Home Front during World War II

"Thoroughly researched and employing a wealth of sources from across the Commonwealth, *Committed to Victory* offers a comprehensive examination of Kentucky's World War II home front. Offering an impressive array of economic and demographic detail as well as personal stories, this work charts the remarkable effects of the war on Kentucky. Arising from the devastation of the Great Depression, the World War II home front offered new opportunities for all Kentuckians regardless of race or gender. *Committed to Victory,* however, also recognizes that not every development was purely positive. Consensus was not automatic. Despite the demands for labor that allowed for the economic advancement of blacks and women, for example, they both felt the strains of gender and racial discrimination. Price controls, rationing, and wage levels caused their share of conflicts. Further, while the state may have experienced 'politics as usual,' many Kentuckians— both as families and as individuals—felt the strains of global conflict. Fortunately, however, Kentucky's home front mobilization contributed significantly to the country's success in World War II. In the end, given its balance, its inclusiveness, and its comprehensiveness, this work makes a tremendous contribution to Kentucky's twentieth-century story."
—Thomas Kiffmeyer, associate professor of history, Morehead State University

"Richard Holl's work is an important addition to the existing literature on the state-level home front during World War II that weaves complex issues into a cohesive story of how Kentucky contributed to the United States war effort. His careful analysis of the economic, political, and social developments that affected Kentucky during the early 1940s adds to our national understanding of how the war affected the lives of people

on the home front and how they adjusted to the stress and change of wartime experiences."
—Jerry Sanson, Louisiana State University at Alexandria

"Deeply researched and clearly written, *Committed to Victory* provides a wide-ranging and detailed account of Kentucky's society, economy, and politics during World War II, one that effectively includes national perspectives and illuminating individual stories. The book is a valuable addition to the literature on the World War II home front and thus to our understanding of the war's impact on the United States."
—John W. Jeffries, author of *Wartime America: The World War II Home Front*

"A very informative and interesting look at a fascinating yet frightening era in the history of the state, nation, and world. Holl has produced an interesting, well-written, well-researched, and detailed account of the traumatic years of World War II on the American home front, and most especially in the Bluegrass State."
—Nancy Baird, professor emerita, special collections library, Western Kentucky University

Committed to Victory

COMMITTED TO
VICTORY

The Kentucky Home Front during World War II

RICHARD E. HOLL

UNIVERSITY PRESS OF KENTUCKY

Scholarly publisher for the Commonwealth,
serving Bellarmine University, Berea College, Centre College of Kentucky, Eastern
Kentucky University, The Filson Historical Society, Georgetown College,
Kentucky Historical Society, Kentucky State University, Morehead State
University, Murray State University, Northern Kentucky University, Transylvania
University, University of Kentucky, University of Louisville, and Western
Kentucky University.

Editorial and Sales Offices: The University Press of Kentucky
663 South Limestone Street, Lexington, Kentucky 40508-4008
www.kentuckypress.com

Library of Congress Cataloging-in-Publication Data

Holl, Richard E., 1960-
  Committed to victory : the Kentucky home front in World War II / Richard E.
Holl.
    pages cm. — (Topics in Kentucky history)
  Includes bibliographical references and index.
  ISBN 978-0-8131-6563-9 (hardcover : alk. paper) —
  ISBN 978-0-8131-6565-3 (pdf) — ISBN 978-0-8131-6564-6 (epub)
  1. World War, 1939-1945—Kentucky. 2. Kentucky—Social conditions—
20th century. 3. Kentucky—History—20th century. 4. United States—Social
conditions—1933-1945. I. Title.
  D769.85.K4H65 2015
  940.53'769—dc23   2015020383

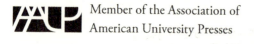

To Jody,
with love

Contents

Introduction   1

1. Kentucky War Plants and Weapons   9

2. Ralph, Rosie, and Labor-Management Relations   49

3. Food for Freedom   79

4. Rationing, Price Controls, and the Black Market   107

5. Politics as Usual   129

6. Kentucky on Guard   157

7. A Black Man's Place and a New Place for Blacks   181

8. Choosing to Go: Migration, Identity, and Social Change   211

9. Loved Ones   235

10. Rupp on the Rise and Rubinstein's Wine:
    Entertainment in a Barbaric Age   263

Conclusion   297

Acknowledgments   315

Notes   317

Bibliography   359

Index   381

Introduction

In 1997, Lowell H. Harrison and James C. Klotter published *A New History of Kentucky*. Since then, this book has become the standard account of Kentucky's past. One part of Harrison and Klotter's extensive bibliography, on sources related to the comings and goings inside the commonwealth during World War II, concludes with the observation that a "full study of the Kentucky home front remains much needed." *Committed to Victory* is intended both to fill this gap and to serve as a new starting point for additional work on the history of modern Kentucky.[1]

In 1939, Kentucky remained a place that was largely rural and agricultural. Farms and hamlets dotted the countryside. Prices for tobacco, cows, and other agricultural commodities interested most Kentuckians, as did news about meetings of farm organizations and better ways to raise crops and livestock. Except for Louisville and a few much smaller towns, little industry existed in the Bluegrass State, and even in the "Falls City" economic activity was scant compared to earlier, flush times.[2]

By then almost a decade long, the Great Depression lingered in Kentucky. The ongoing struggle to find jobs and better incomes took priority over other matters for many thousands of Kentuckians. The January 5, 1939, edition of the *Jackson Times* noted that in "spite of . . . vast (federal government) spending for relief, in spite of improvement in business, little if any dent has been made in the number of the unemployed." A mix of frustration and apathy gripped the commonwealth, because it appeared that there was no end in sight to the economic slump.[3]

Kentuckians endorsed President Franklin D. Roosevelt's "New Deal." The unprecedented severity of the Great Depression convinced them that government assistance was both needed and acceptable. Emergency relief payments helped many Kentuckians after the Depression started; agricultural subsidies supported the crucial tobacco industry; the Works Progress Administration gave some unemployed Kentuckians jobs; and old age pensions covered their retirement. Most Kentuckians supported big government before World War II broke out.[4]

1

On the eve of World War II, Kentucky politics was known for its boisterousness. Democrats held the upper hand over the Republicans in the commonwealth. Normally the winner of the Democratic party primary captured the general election, which in many cases was a mere formality. Under these circumstances, factionalism within the Democratic party was both pronounced and heated. Governor Albert Benjamin Chandler, whose nickname was "Happy," headed the dominant part of the Democratic party in 1939, but he always faced opposition. Chandlerites battled anti-Chandlerites to the finish. Sometimes Republicans won office, though often this happened only because the enmity between various Democrats created an opening. Liberal doses of patronage and out-and-out corruption seasoned the mixture. Politicians rewarded supporters with jobs, while nepotism, vote buying, ballot box stuffing, and other illegal practices thrived.[5]

Before World War II, Kentucky society expected that women would be wives and mothers. Married women catered to their husbands and raised the children. Though a small minority of females worked outside the home, this was not the Kentucky ideal. Necessity most often forced women into the labor force, where they held such traditionally female jobs as maids, secretaries, and teachers. A small number worked in Kentucky industry, but they made less money than men in the same positions and were true pioneers. A woman's place was still small, with forays into college and new vocations frowned upon.[6]

African Americans fared less well than white women. Blacks suffered under segregation in Kentucky, forced by the system to attend separate but inferior schools while they were barred from public parks and many stores and restaurants. African Americans—like white women—worked in traditional areas (performing general labor and domestic service) and knew that better-paying jobs were closed off to them. Kentucky whites subordinated blacks and treated them as inferiors. Blacks chafed under white supremacy; groups like the National Association for the Advancement of Colored People and the Kentucky Negro Education Association challenged the racial status quo but had not yet made much progress prior to World War II.[7]

In February 1939, Kentuckians viewed foreign affairs as a lesser concern than the Depression, the approaching spring planting season, and the upcoming gubernatorial race. Though many knew that Germany had taken over Austria and Czechoslovakia, and Japan had swallowed a part of China, Kentuckians remained optimistic about America's chances to avoid European and Asian hostilities. The *Park City Daily News* of south central Kentucky captured the prevailing sentiment well when it observed that "war is still hated and despised in this country as in no other."[8]

Then German dictator Adolf Hitler struck, sending German tanks crashing into Poland on September 1, 1939. Some minor, ineffectual diplomacy ensued. On September 3, Britain and France declared war against Germany. Having violated an earlier promise not to seize more land, Hitler's aggression had led to war in Europe. The *Jackson Times* reacted to the armed conflict in Poland by reemphasizing its position that peace was far better than war and noting the tragedy of another world war only a quarter-century after the first began.[9]

Surprised by the sudden outbreak of European war, Kentuckians clung to their belief that the United States should stay out of the conflict. Kentucky representatives in Washington, DC, as well as the people at home supported President Roosevelt's cash-and-carry and lend-lease programs. This way Britain could obtain American arms and munitions to fight Germany without the involvement of U.S. troops. Roosevelt also recalled the old World War I National Defense Advisory Commission (NDAC), which was dominated by industrial interests. FDR wanted NDAC to work with the military to see that the nation had troops, machines, and weapons ready should the United States become an active participant in the war. Kentuckians backed Roosevelt's "aid short of war" program and prudent war preparedness measures but did not want to put American soldiers and sailors in places where they might be harmed.[10]

Meanwhile, the trouble between the United States and Japan grew more serious. The crux of the dispute was China. Japan had invaded that country in 1937, and the United States wanted the Japanese to withdraw. When Japan refused to leave, the Roosevelt administration applied additional pressure by shutting off the flow of American oil to Japan. Even after the embargo, Kentuckians thought that the United States would sidestep war. Diplomacy could be counted upon to resolve tensions between the United States and the Empire of the Rising Sun.

The oil cutoff left Japan with only eighteen months of oil in reserve. The Japanese leadership found itself facing an unpalatable choice: give up

Chinese territory to get back American oil or take additional oil land in east Asia to make up for the loss of the American supply. Japan chose the latter course, with a strike at Pearl Harbor designed to buy time should the United States retaliate.[11]

The Japanese attack on Pearl Harbor destroyed any illusions of peace Kentuckians may have still held. At dawn on December 7, 1941, 183 Japanese torpedo and dive-bombers, escorted by fighter planes, descended on Battleship Row, dropping their deadly weapons. Unprepared American servicemen returned fire, but to little avail. The Japanese sunk five U.S. battleships and damaged others. Lesser vessels went down. Two thousand five hundred sailors and civilians perished. The days of American neutrality and isolationist strength ended in a most emphatic way, as the United States plunged head over heels into the global conflict.[12]

Kentuckians demanded retribution. Many noted that the Japanese pounced "while peace negotiations were underway." Lizzie Watts of Leatherwood, in the eastern Kentucky mountains, said that many people in her hollow "hated the Japanese" while others merely wished to teach them a lesson. The *Herald News* of Hodgenville, in central Kentucky, opined that the United States must become the workshop, supply arsenal, and food store of the Allies. "If we do that well all will be well." Victory took precedence over everything else at this point, not least of all because Kentuckians knew that ours "is a just cause."[13]

World War II changed the Kentucky economy dramatically. Manufacture of wartime goods took precedence over the making of peacetime goods, since the American Army and Navy required all manner of arms and munitions to defeat the enemy. While Kentucky did not produce nearly as many war goods as Michigan, Texas, or even Tennessee, it did make critical goods, such as industrial alcohol and synthetic rubber, which the United States desperately needed. The Bluegrass State was therefore a valuable cog in the American war machine. So much new military production along with the draft and maintenance of the essential civilian economy restored economic health to the commonwealth after ten years of depression. The state unemployment rate fell from 1940 to 1944, by which time everybody who wanted a job could find one. In a very real sense, the return of prosperity represented an unintended but immensely welcome by-product of the war effort.[14]

A related point is worth making. Although Kentucky certainly made great headway in absolute economic terms from 1939 to 1945, it only managed to tread water compared to other Southern states. Kentucky left World War II in approximately the same economic position that it entered the conflict relative to the South as a whole: namely, just above Arkansas and Mississippi but below the rest. Indeed, Florida, Texas, and Louisiana (among others) pulled further ahead of Kentucky when it came to overall economic activity and personal income.[15]

Like plant and equipment used to fashion weapons, labor proved indispensable to the construction of FDR's "arsenal of democracy." Kentucky workers of both genders and all races benefited from the creation of a plethora of wartime jobs. Though the movement of many females into wartime industrial work has attracted great attention, and rightfully so, it must be remembered that Ralph the Riveter contributed far more hours and products to the overall war effort than Rosie the Riveter. Ralph is an unsung hero of the Kentucky and American home fronts.

World War II recast Kentucky society, unleashing forces of change that only became more apparent over ensuing decades. Having secured better jobs during the war, and a taste of the good life, many women and African Americans resisted giving these things up, and some actively began the pursuit of social advancement. Black servicemen came home from fighting the enemies of life and liberty determined to see that the race reap its share of the freedoms that American public relations men extolled throughout the conflict. Segregation and inequality would no longer do; newly militant African American veterans lent their considerable energies to the burgeoning effort to dismantle Jim Crow. Many women, too, decided to keep their jobs once the war ended. Some of them possessed a keener appreciation of the lack of economic and educational opportunities available to Kentucky women before the war. If they did not organize to combat sexism themselves, the examples they set inspired their daughters and granddaughters to speak up, step out, and win a fairer share of American abundance. The war influenced both the Kentucky civil rights movement and the Kentucky women's liberation movement.

Massive wartime migration contributed to the new postwar face of Kentucky, as did the loss of thousands of servicemen in the various European and Asian battles of this most ruinous of all wars. Hundreds of thousands of persons moved from the Kentucky countryside to cities inside and outside Kentucky. The cities and towns were the usual location of war production centers; the jobs were there, and the people followed. Louisville welcomed the most newcomers among all Kentucky locales, but people also traveled to places like Richmond, Ashland, Paducah, Elizabethtown, and Lexington. Other Kentuckians left the state entirely for the airplane and tank assembly lines of Detroit, Michigan; the shipyards of Newport News, Virginia; the machine shops of Cincinnati, Ohio; and other destinations. As combat deaths increased, pockets of grief spread across all regions of the commonwealth and relatives and friends mourned. World War II may still have been "the good war" for some folks, but not for those who lost loved ones. The war left Kentucky a more urban, industrial place while it accelerated the chronic loss of human capital.

Kentucky politics carried on pretty much as usual through World War II into the postwar period. No elections were postponed due to the emergency. Successful Democratic party politicians and successful Republican party politicians distributed patronage in the old tried-and-true manner. Party factionalism remained a constant, as did the use of corrupt methods to achieve electoral triumphs. The Chandlerites ran the State House from 1939 to 1943. A rare Republican victory in a gubernatorial contest followed as well as substantial Republican gains in both houses of the state legislature in 1944, but the Democrats quickly reasserted themselves and ended up in an even stronger position than customary. Anti-Chandlerite Democrats took control of the governor's mansion in 1947, but "Happy" himself returned to power in 1955.

Although wartime conditions brought little change to state politics, Kentuckians thought more highly of the federal government after the war than before it. While the New Deal helped Kentuckians mitigate the problems of unemployment and poverty, the wartime American state achieved victory over barbaric and deceitful foes who challenged the American way of life and the restoration of prosperity. Nothing could be better than those results, and the credibility of the federal government with most Kentuckians reached new heights by 1945. Big government moved into the postwar period with added strength and confidence, and its opponents in the Bluegrass State found it impossible to roll back.

In about half a decade, World War II transformed Kentucky. Victory over the Axis brought Kentuckians immense satisfaction and reinforced the notion that America was a force for good in the world. Production of the various implements of war lifted a feeble economy to unprecedented heights, generating full employment and higher incomes for the people of the commonwealth. Urban areas of Kentucky gained population and skilled workers at the expense of rural areas due to wartime migration patterns. Since federal government orchestration of the war effort yielded salutary results, Kentuckians reaffirmed their support for a large, activist state capable of regulating the national economy and brokering deals between powerful special interests. African Americans and women registered significant economic gains during the war and made greater social progress later. All in all, World War II propelled Kentucky along new historical pathways, leaving the state a fundamentally different place, but one that would not have to wait long before confronting fresh challenges.

1

Kentucky War Plants and Weapons

Axis aggression during the late 1930s profoundly affected the thinking of Kentuckians. Kentuckians grew to despise German leader Adolf Hitler, viewing him as a growing threat to the peace they enjoyed. Given Hitler's misbehavior, most particularly the use of force against weaker nations, the people of the commonwealth embraced the official American policy of preparedness for the possibility of war even as they hoped that war would not engulf the United States. When war did come, thrust on Americans by the Japanese bombing of U.S. vessels docked at Pearl Harbor, Kentucky businesses and workers committed themselves wholeheartedly to construction of war plants and mass production of war goods. Victory over the Axis and the return of peace could not be achieved without a myriad of weapons.

Hitler's rise to power in Germany went against all the odds. A corporal during the First World War, Hitler headed a fringe political party in the early 1920s called the National Socialists (or Nazis). After the failure of the Beer Hall Putsch, an effort by the National Socialists to overthrow the Weimar Republic, Hitler ended up in jail. Released in 1924, he rebuilt the National Socialist party over the next half-dozen years and made it a force in German politics. Hitler's ultranationalism, attacks on the Versailles Treaty, and mesmerizing oratory earned him the support of many Germans. In 1933, he ascended to the chancellorship of Germany. Shortly thereafter, he crushed his political opposition, establishing a dictatorship. Secure now as *der Fuehrer*, Hitler eyed European land that he intended to incorporate into a greater Germany.

If Kentuckians were not concerned about Hitler in the beginning, he got their attention soon enough. Remilitarization of the Rhineland by the German army in violation of the Versailles Treaty did not bother Kentuckians much. The Rhineland was German territory, after all, and it was an ocean away. German absorption of Austria in March 1939 may have turned a few more heads, but a deep desire for peace overshadowed the Anschluss. The Munich conference and the subsequent cession of a part of Czechoslovakia called the Sudetenland to Germany made Hitler's lust for land clear to Kentuckians, though many shared British prime minister Neville Chamberlain's faith that Germany now possessed all the land it wanted and would go no further.

Czechoslovakia's ultimate fate and events surrounding Poland proved to Kentuckians that Hitler could never be trusted and that American involvement in another European war could not be ruled out. In March 1939, Germany swallowed what remained of Czechoslovakia. In September 1939, Hitler launched a massive military strike against Poland, resulting in British and French declarations of war against the Third Reich. Only a little more than twenty years after World War I ended, World War II began.

Newspapers across the commonwealth reported these momentous events, and their editorials captured the sentiments of the people of Kentucky. The *Jackson Times* responded to the German seizure of Moravia and Bohemia by noting that the "ex–house painter had deliberately violated every promise and guarantee, written and verbal, he had made [at Munich]." The *Times* characterized the feelings "in this country" as ones "of anger and disgust." The *Richmond Daily Register* insisted that the German takeover of every bit of Czechoslovakia proved that Hitler "will never be appeased, and will continue to covet the territory and property of other nations until death lays him low or the armies of other nations stop him." According to the *Madisonville Messenger,* Hitler's decision to hurl tanks, planes, and infantry against Poland, along with continuation of the Asian war, revealed that "maddogs [are] again loose in the world."[1]

Under these circumstances, Kentuckian endorsed both U.S. neutrality and military-industrial preparedness. In late 1939, Kentuckians most emphatically did not want to send their sons overseas to fight and die, even though sympathies for the British and French ran strong. Kentuckians hoped against hope that the United States would stay out of the global fracas and that it would end quickly. Realities being what they were, however, the people supported sensible measures to ready industry and the military for whatever might come. The prevailing belief was that it would be foolish to "sit back and do nothing until the enemy stands at our borders." As the *Richmond Daily Register* asserted, the moment for "self-defense is here, now."[2]

President Franklin D. Roosevelt responded to the unsettled circumstances of the day by setting up the War Resources Board (WRB) in August 1939, between Germany's acquisition of Czechoslovakia and its invasion of Poland. FDR wanted an assessment of earlier plans related to industrial mobilization of the United States for war, and improved communication between government and business. Hostilities between the New Deal administration and big business over such matters as collective bargaining, welfare, and taxation had been pronounced just a few short years earlier, and the president did not want lingering ill feelings to get in the way of contingency planning for war. Roosevelt had to mend fences with the "economic royalists" to better prepare the country should the worst come to pass. The establishment of the WRB let Roosevelt double-check earlier industrial mobilization planning and court an important segment of the business community. Edward R. Stettinius Jr., Roosevelt's pick for WRB chairman, came from General Motors and United States Steel Corporation. A liberal businessman, with sympathy for New Deal social goals, Stettinius also possessed a wide array of friendships and acquaintances throughout American business. FDR knew he could count on "Stett" and a few others like him to appease key industrialists and ultimately bring them on board for the weapons push, should it be vital to do so.[3]

The WRB issued its final report in October 1939. Stettinius and the other corporate liberals on the board had scrutinized the World War I War Industries Board and studied the various Industrial Mobilization Plans of the 1920s and 1930s. They praised the Industrial Mobilization Plan of 1939, the latest in the line, characterizing it as "a decided advance in the field of national preparedness and adequate plans for defense." They accepted the need, during an emergency, for a War Resources Administration (WRA), one-man leadership, and the commodity committee–war service committee interlock, all reminiscent of the 1917–1918 War Industries Board experience. Without doubt, the commodity committee–war service committee interface would permit the WRA to "provide point of contact between government and industry." This connection was essential because only industry possessed the managerial skills and intricate hands-on production expertise required to meet monumental military demand in the midst of a modern, global conflict.[4]

Roosevelt's reaction to the War Resources Board report can best be described as circumspect. FDR thanked board members for "exceedingly good work." His confidence in Stettinius increased. Nevertheless, Roosevelt decided not to act on the WRB report quickly or even to make it public. After all, the United States was still at peace, and the War Resources Administration was to be called into service only after the issuance of a declaration of war. More to the point, labor and agriculture did not like the influence of big business on the report, and isolationists were leery of it. Believing it to be too controversial in nature, FDR made the expedient decision to shelve the WRB report; but that did not mean that it was forgotten.[5]

The War Resources Administration was never established. The WRB recommendation, however, did not go for naught. In late May 1940 Roosevelt announced the recall of the Great War's National Defense Advisory Commission (NDAC) and in succeeding years created the Office of Production Management (OPM) and the War Production Board (WPB). Each new agency more closely resembled the War Resources Administration than the last. The WPB, which took form just after the attack on Pearl Harbor, was essentially the WRA by another name. Each organizational overhaul brought the country closer to the old War Industries Board (WIB) until an equivalent came into being. The WPB (like the WIB) functioned as a temporary, ends-oriented federal agency with overarching economic power, a single chief, and the requisite linkages between federal commodity committees and semiprivate war service committees. The War Production Board furthered wartime planning and production by providing a conduit between federal supervisory personnel, who had the tax money to construct massive war plants, and big business managers, who operated these plants. The military brass participated, too, pressing their point of view on total arms and munitions requirements, distribution of scarce materials, and profits for business. The fact that the

NDAC, the OPM, and the WPB played vital roles from the preparedness period through the war itself is indicative of the ultimate triumph of the state-building approach of the corporate liberals and military planners. Roosevelt buried the War Resources Board report only to unearth it later, brush it off, and implement it. Small business, big labor, and agricultural interests were not pleased by this development, but could not stop it.[6]

The War Department acted swiftly to get a better handle on national defense supplies, dispatching sealed envelopes to businesses in all states to be opened only in case of emergency. Ninety manufacturing plants throughout Kentucky received such letters—fifty-four in the Louisville area and thirty-six throughout the rest of the state. The Army accounted for eighty-eight of the letters and the Navy for two. The War Department sent the orders to Kentucky firms that it believed could "fill them promptly and efficiently with the least disturbance to private industry." X-ray apparatus, radio tubes, machine tools, ammunition components, and powder and explosives were known to be items the government wanted from Kentucky if the time came.[7]

Though the Kentucky companies selected for the possibility of defense work were not known at the time, speculation centered on two firms. The Kelley-Koett Manufacturing Company of Covington had supplied all the portable x-ray equipment that was put to such good use by American Army medical personnel in France during World War I, so it was the natural choice to perform that job again should the call come. Ken-Rad Company of Owensboro specialized in vacuum tubes for radio sets; it also seemed to be a good bet. If the United States ever became involved in the expanding European and Asian wars, these kinds of products and many, many others would be required. War Department officials behaved in a proactive manner to see to it that the needs of soldiers and sailors would be satisfied.[8]

European hostilities ignited an economic boomlet in Kentucky. In September and October 1939, various industries began to surge, including transportation, coal, steel, clothing, shipbuilding, aircraft, and automobiles. The Louisville & Nashville (L&N) Railroad added 2,100 workers across its system from September 12 to October 1, many of them in Louisville and other Kentucky locations. The Illinois Central Railroad, which ran through far western Kentucky, declared that it would spend

$8 million on new equipment, such as diesel electric and switching loco-
motives, box cars, and coal cars. The Baltimore & Ohio, Chesapeake &
Ohio, and Southern Railroads announced expansion plans. Anticipating
increased demand for their product from Europe, coal companies rehired
old employees and brought on new ones. Coal mining surged in the Elkhorn, Harlan, and Hazard areas, as well as in western Kentucky, and hundreds of men returned to the fields. In Ashland, the American Rolling
Mill Company (ARMCO) upped its production of steel. Textile factories
received new orders. Heavy backlogs developed for ships and airplanes.
Increases in employment became inevitable in those areas. Even the Ford
Motor Company plant in Louisville benefited from war-induced stimulus, seeing its staff catapult from 150 in August 1939 to 714 by September 5. From the very inception of the European war, Kentucky's economy
grew. The Great Depression continued, but its grip on the state weakened
and better days lay ahead.[9]

Kentucky's economic recovery actually began before the European
war, but news of the fighting accelerated it. Expansion of the railroad,
coal, and steel industries continued through the remainder of 1939 into
1940 and beyond. The L&N registered gross earnings of just above $88
million in 1939. This figure increased to $98 million in 1940 and $119
million in 1941. Over the same period, the freight carried by the railroad jumped from just above 42 million tons to over 58 million tons.
The L&N made its gains in large part because defense plants and military installations opened near its lines and established forts and camps
grew. With expectations high for increased demand and prices for coal
following the attack on Poland, coal production ratcheted upward, as did
employment. The amount of coal mined in Kentucky increased from 42.3
million tons in 1939 to 54 million tons in 1941. Employment in state coal
mines passed 52,000 men and kept rising. By 1941, ARMCO started
construction of a new blast furnace to meet the growing clamor for steel.
Responding to war in Europe and Asia, as well as to Roosevelt's industrial
and military preparedness program, Kentucky's transportation network
became more extensive, and the output of raw materials burgeoned. These
developments helped pave the way for additional Kentucky war production before Pearl Harbor and a much larger volume after it.[10]

Given events abroad and at home, the military bases of Kentucky expanded. Located south of Louisville, Fort Knox received word in late June 1940 from the War Department that it would become the home of the nation's Army Armor Center. The center included an armor school and the staff and equipment necessary to form new armored divisions and tank battalions. By early 1942, the armor school possessed the capability of graduating 1,440 officers and 22,000 enlisted men annually. The number of graduates only rose thereafter. From its origin at Fort Knox, the armored force mushroomed from almost nothing to sixteen armored divisions and over 100 separate tank battalions and mechanized cavalry squadrons by 1945. As officers, enlisted men, tanks, and the rest arrived at the base, the number of buildings multiplied. Fort Knox had 864 buildings in 1940 and 3,820 by 1943. Land acquisitions during the war doubled the size of the base to almost 107,000 acres in parts of Hardin, Meade, and Bullitt counties. Bowman Field in Louisville became an Army Air Corps training base by August 1940. Fort Thomas in northern Kentucky, which overlooked the Ohio River, served as an army induction center from September 1940 to June 1944. At its height, the installation processed approximately 3,000 recruits per week.[11]

As Kentucky's economy gradually regained strength, and the first steps were taken to put the American military on a war-ready footing, the success of Germany's spring 1940 blitzkrieg compelled President Roosevelt to resuscitate the National Defense Advisory Commission. On May 26, 1940, while Allied forces in France still reeled under heavy Nazi assault, Roosevelt informed Americans that he intended "calling on men now engaged in private industry to help . . . in carrying out" the defense program, and that the public would "hear more of this in a few days." On May 28, the president activated the NDAC with a mission to "expedite the provision of supplies and munitions to the armed forces." A temporary, emergency agency, sure to be retired once any war was won, the NDAC attacked the federal government's lack of capacity to gear the economy for war by harnessing corporate liberal expertise and connections to carry out private production of weapons and other war-related items, which would then be purchased by the Army and Navy. An experiment in public-private planning and intelligent collaboration, the NDAC prepared the way for similar but larger and more meaningful efforts after 1940.[12]

The structure of the National Defense Advisory Commission was

Photograph taken by a Japanese bomber pilot of the devastation inflicted on American naval ships at Pearl Harbor on December 7, 1941. (Courtesy of the Library of Congress.)

unique. Seven members sat on the NDAC, one each for raw materials, production, labor, agriculture, consumers, transportation, and prices. In June 1940, Roosevelt appointed a Coordinator of National Defense Purchases, putting him on par with the various commissioners. Although these eight people came from many walks of life and represented diverse interests, three were most significant because they were best positioned to make use of the assets of corporate America: Industrial Materials Commissioner Edward Stettinius Jr., Production Commissioner William Knudsen, and Coordinator of National Defense Purchases Donald Nelson. Stettinius, who had done good service for Roosevelt as head of the War Resources Board seven months earlier, returned. A handsome, affable, white-haired fellow, he continued to use his many connections throughout American business to good effect. Stettinius's job was to amass essential raw materials so that the finished defense products could be made. Industrialists nationwide considered General Motors president Knudsen the top production man in the nation. Once the chief assistant to Henry Ford at Ford Motor Company, he now ran the day-to-day affairs of GM. As a member of the NDAC, he planned for future defense production and sought ways to eliminate any bottlenecks that arose. Knudsen envisioned construction of wholly new defense plants, expansion of some existing plants, and conversion of plants not engaged in peace work to war work. Nelson, executive vice president of Sears, Roebuck, and Company in civilian life, would see to the purchase and distribution of defense goods. A perfectionist who, it was said, pursued information "like a dentist after an ailing tooth," Nelson preferred the use of patience, tact, and diplomacy rather than brute force to get results. Stettinius, Knudsen, and Nelson worked together to better coordinate the national economy so that the military would get all the weapons and other goods it needed to meet any challenge.[13]

The National Defense Advisory Commission issued various public pronouncements. Every American citizen was encouraged to think about preparedness and to do what they could to help. Scrap drives designed to increase stockpiles of valuable metals such as aluminum were encouraged. The NDAC's Production Department stressed again the need for businesses to convert peacetime plants to war work where feasible. Some Kentucky companies responded to this emphasis by devoting thought to the kinds of war goods they might manufacture. Roosevelt delegated the authority to clear defense contracts of $500,000 or more to Knudsen and Nelson, who took into account site location before granting approval. Given this power, firms often consulted with the two businessmen-bureaucrats about good places to establish arms and munitions plants, and their orders sometimes affected Kentucky.[14]

Kentucky was well situated geographically to get war work. At the beginning of the conflict, the federal government required that defense plants be located at least two hundred miles from any coastline or international boundary. Additional advantages would be taken into account, but this stipulation was a must, and Kentucky met it. Senators Alben Barkley and Albert B. "Happy" Chandler and the various U.S. representatives from the commonwealth immediately lobbied Roosevelt, the War Department, the NDAC, and Congress for a fair share of defense contracts and facilities.[15]

Louisville's attractions for defense work far surpassed those of any other place in Kentucky. Louisville's advantages included an abundance of land, greater availability of labor than any other place in the commonwealth, ready availability of managerial talent, a fine railroad network, and copious amounts of water. Its signal distinction, however, may well have been close proximity to the greatest concentration of distilleries in the country. Bourbon whiskey was no prerequisite for war work, but the conversion of such plants to production of industrial alcohol would be a huge plus. Both smokeless powder and synthetic rubber (immensely important war goods) required a certain amount of industrial alcohol to make, and Louisville could get that ingredient more easily and more cheaply than any big city in the United States.

From mid-1940 forward, signs of war industry in the Louisville area multiplied. Groundbreaking took place for a huge smokeless powder plant, followed by a naval gun plant and a bag-loading plant. This activity only started the ball rolling. Ranked twenty-fourth in the United States in terms of population according to the 1940 census, Louisville ultimately became the eighteenth largest center of war production in the country while generating well over one-half of all war-related output in the state. As time passed, other parts of the commonwealth experienced defense construction and the eventual appearance of many types of war-related facilities. New plants generally appeared first, since they took so long to build and were so crucial to meeting the most pressing needs of the nation should it be drawn into the world war. Conversion of established Kentucky plants to war work usually occurred later—often after the United States declared war on Japan. Factory conversion generally took less time than building an industrial facility from scratch.[16]

Rumors about an E. I. du Pont de Nemours and Company defense facility to be located near Louisville began to circulate sometime during the spring of 1940. Locals noticed C. V. Atwell, a Wilmington, Delaware, real estate operator, taking options on land in the Indiana suburbs of Louisville. Louisvillians guessed that DuPont wanted to open a nylon factory there. Soon thereafter everyone learned that a DuPont plant was indeed coming and that it would actually make smokeless powder, a brown, granular substance that the military employed as a propellant charge to hurl projectiles such as bullets, shells, and rockets.[17]

A small part of the Charlestown, Indiana, smokeless powder plant operating through the night. (Courtesy of the Hagley Museum and Library.)

The Army Ordnance Department, with the permission of Production Commissioner Knudsen, selected a site about twelve miles from Louisville—Charlestown, Indiana—for the proposed smokeless powder plant. Five thousand acres of land were purchased from a relatively small number of private owners who had lived in that area. The availability of relatively cheap land, skilled labor from nearby Louisville, water from the Ohio River, and especially the distilleries made this location attractive. The government would pay for the plant and own it, contracting with DuPont to build and operate it.

Estimates of the cost of the smokeless powder plant, the number of workers needed, and the ultimate output proved to be well short of the mark. A $20 million price tag when construction began in late August 1940 rose to almost $110 million by the time new production lines and other expansions were finished in June 1942. The number of construction workers required to build the various facilities grew from an initial projection of 10,000 to a high of 28,000. Upon completion, the Charlestown operation included some eight hundred buildings, twenty-four gates for in-and-out car and rail traffic, fourteen miles of fence to surround the place, and eighty miles of railroad track connecting it to outside locations. The plant hit a peak of 9,000 permanent workers, up from the 5,000 originally anticipated. At first, planners pegged maximum production of smokeless powder at 600,000 pounds per day. During October 1942, the plant actually made 28,734,481 pounds—an average of almost 1 million pounds per day. The Charlestown smokeless powder plant was the largest of its kind in the world, immediately tripling total U.S. output of smokeless propellant for American arms, and it could not have succeeded without Kentucky labor, construction materials, and production ingredients. From beginning to end, the Charlestown powder plant constituted a joint enterprise of Indiana and Kentucky.[18]

The same thing could be said for the other two facilities of what came to be known as the Indiana Army Ammunition Plant. Kentuckians found work not only at the smokeless powder plant, but also at the adjacent powder bag plant and the rocket propellant plant. Louisville firms received preferential treatment on subcontracts related to the complex as a whole, and the economic benefit to the Louisville area from the entire complex far exceeded original expectations.[19]

Located just to the southwest of the powder plant, the bag-loading plant included eight lines for loading smokeless powder into silk bags. The smokeless powder, of course, came from the powder plant to the bag plant, where it was properly packaged. Just the right amount of powder went into each bag. The more powder a bag held, the greater the distance it would throw an artillery shell when ignited. The less powder in the bag, the shorter the distance traveled by the shell. All told, the bag-loading plant stretched out over 3,000 acres, cost nearly $14 million in the beginning and more later, and employed some 6,500 permanent "high-type, semi-skilled" workers.[20]

Goodyear Engineering Corporation, a subsidiary of Goodyear Tire and Rubber Company, equipped and operated the bag plant for the federal government. Goodyear's chairman, P. W. Litchfield, ran the new corporation himself rather than delegating authority to an underling. Litchfield underscored the importance of the budding relationship between big business and the federal government when he issued the following statement: "In this hour of national emergency, the Government is calling upon the resourcefulness and versatility of large corporations which are skilled in the technique of mass production. We have accepted our particular assignment and will devote every ounce of effort to provide a smooth and efficient plant."[21]

DuPont later agreed to construct and run a 2,700-acre rocket propellant plant near the powder and bag plants. Work started in November 1944. Two-thirds of the plant had been built when V-J day arrived and the War Department canceled the contract. A small amount of double-base rocket propellant was actually made over a five-week stretch, but output was halted with the defeat of Japan, and the three-line rocket plant never reached completion.[22]

Unlike the powder plant, the bag plant, and the rocket propellant plant, the naval gun plant occupied territory inside Kentucky. On November 29, 1940, the Navy Department announced that a 135-acre site on the outskirts of Louisville had been selected for the new gun plant. The *Courier-Journal* pinpointed its location south of Douglas Park and adjacent to the L&N Strawberry Yards.[23]

Officially known as the Louisville Naval Ordnance Station, the gun plant specialized in the manufacture of gun mounts and torpedo tubes. It also assembled big naval guns, using parts shipped to the plant from Detroit, Michigan, and Canton, Ohio. Upon passing muster, the mounts, tubes, guns, and other products were then sent to naval vessels for final installation. J. G. White Engineering Corporation of New York City held the main construction contract from the government, but subcontracted heavily with Louisville firms. Westinghouse Electric & Manufacturing Company operated the naval gun plant after its erection. Groundbreaking occurred on January 29, 1941, with actual production beginning in May. The Louisville naval gun plant continued operations until the Westinghouse contract ended in 1946.[24]

Louisville also appealed to proponents of American air power. A large, capable woodworking industry existed in the Falls City area by the early 1940s, which drew the Curtiss-Wright Corporation to Standiford Field. Curtiss-Wright constructed a $12 million airplane assembly facility there, while Mengel Company added a subassembly plant. The partnership of Curtiss-Wright and Mengel resulted in the employment of several thousand people and the addition of many C-46 Commandos to the Army Air Force. The C-46 was a wooden cargo plane capable of transporting freight and paratroopers to desired locations, and saw valuable service in the Pacific area against the Japanese.[25]

Next to the Louisville metropolitan area, western Kentucky received the most new, large war plants. An Axis strike there was deemed highly unlikely. Plenty of land, labor, and raw materials were available. Senator Alben Barkley, a powerhouse in Washington, DC, lobbied hard and effectively for his homeland. Henderson, Graves, and McCracken counties each obtained sizable munitions operations that benefited the war effort and regional economy handsomely.

In early March 1941, news spread throughout Henderson County that a $15 million ammonia plant would be constructed on the western side of the town of Henderson. The size of the plant would be 766 acres. Construction of the facility began almost immediately, with ammonia production beginning in September 1942. Atmospheric Nitrogen Corporation of Allied Chemical & Dye Corporation built and operated the plant. The ammonia went into the manufacture of nitric acid for the explosives industry. At peak operation, the Henderson plant employed some 500 workers. Given the amount of war work in the vicinity, the government built both a 100-bed hospital, with cutting edge x-ray and operating equipment, and a health center in Henderson.[26]

A Navy shell-loading plant opened about the same time as the ammonia plant. Located in Graves County, in the small hamlet of Viola, the Navy plant employed 3,000 workers to fill antiaircraft, incendiary, and tracer shells with powder. Workers manned machines, pulling levers that slid the shells underneath and poured in the powder. Pulling a second lever tamped the powder down, while activating a conveyor belt transported the shells to another building, where the detonator was attached. Production of the shells commenced on September 23, 1942. I. B. Clark, the National Fireworks Company plant manager, reported that by early November, Viola shells had reached the U.S. Navy in the Pacific Theater and were already being deployed with excellent results against the Japanese.[27]

Residents of McCracken County closely scrutinized the erection of war plants in Louisville, Henderson, and other places. They desired war work, too. Expectations abounded that Senator Barkley would bring the bacon home to Paducah, where he lived when not in Washington, DC. In the beginning, the locals were disappointed, though Barkley and other Kentucky representatives delivered in the end.

The hopes of Paducahans soared when they learned in early 1941 that their town was in the running for a $15 million aluminum plant to be constructed by the Reynolds Metal Company. Army planes required large amounts of aluminum. Other war goods needed this metal as well. Senator Barkley, Senator Chandler, and Reynolds executives had met to discuss Paducah as the site for the aluminum plant, and progress resulted. Unfortunately for the Purchase area, the plan fell apart when it was ascertained that the Kentucky Utilities Company could not provide sufficient electricity for the operation within the established time frame of four months. Given this reality, the National Defense Advisory Commission nixed the Paducah aluminum plant, moving it to Sheffield, Alabama, instead. Frustrated McCracken County inhabitants could only shake their heads.[28]

Barkley and western Kentucky politicians persisted despite the setback. Small-scale war contracts went to a number of firms in McCracken County. Construction began on the Paducah airport, a facility designed to help improve the air transport system of a nation at war. Dedication of the airport took place on November 8, 1942. The big breakthrough finally came with the announcement that a very large explosives plant would be located on a site just outside of Paducah.[29]

The War Department named the explosives plant the Kentucky Ordnance Works (KOW). The facility occupied about 16,000 acres of land nine miles west of Paducah. It took six thousand workers to build the complex, which included chemical buildings, a box factory, a steam plant, a cafeteria, water and sewer systems, a hospital, a laundry, and its own railroad network. A minimum of 1,200 workers kept the place operating. The plant produced more trinitrotoluene, commonly known as TNT, than any other facility in the world at that time.[30]

Contrary to public perception, the value of TNT actually derived most from its inherent stability. TNT flakes could be poured into various types of projectiles—such as shells and bombs—without great danger.

Precisely because of its relative lack of volatility, TNT became a good base for more powerful and dangerous explosives. A 50-50 mix of TNT and pentaerythritol tetranitrate (PETN), for instance, yields pentolite, which the United States used extensively in detonators and hand grenades. A 70-30 mix of tetryl with TNT produced tetrytol, used for mines and demolition. The great sensitivity of PETN and tetryl caused the Americans and the Allies in general to combine them with TNT for safety reasons. The TNT plant near Paducah therefore contributed significantly to the American stock of many different types of explosives.[31]

American efforts to supply Great Britain with munitions intensified after the fall of France to Nazi Germany on June 22, 1940. President Roosevelt had already established a cash-and-carry policy, whereby Britain could procure American munitions by converting British pounds to U.S. dollars, paying for the war materials, and transporting the goods home in its own ships. On December 29, 1940, FDR underlined the urgent need for greater assistance to Britain against its enemies. Speaking over the radio to a national audience, he declared that Britain must get American tanks, airplanes, guns, and ships so that Nazi tyranny could be stopped. This approach offered the best chance for keeping American boys out of the fray. With passage of the Lend-Lease Act in March 1941, the volume of munitions to England increased dramatically. Seven billion dollars' worth of war material flowed to Britain, with more delivered after that.[32]

Dire circumstances for the Allies also necessitated another American organizational response. In January 1941, FDR replaced the National Defense Advisory Commission with a stronger, more efficient agency called the Office of Production Management. NDAC's leaders and much of its personnel transferred to OPM, which increased stockpiles of essential materials such as steel, aluminum, and copper while facilitating construction of new war plants and conversion of old ones. The automobile industry, for instance, scaled back production of passenger cars and trucks under an OPM directive, turning out its first military jeeps and tanks before the year ended. OPM also introduced a priorities system, handing out tickets to companies based on the value of what they were going to produce. Defense goods received the highest priority, followed by certain essential civilian goods. When the priorities system faltered, due to material shortages and the distribution of so many high-priority tickets that lower-priority ticket holders got no material at all, OPM made a decent start on an improved allocation approach. Existing national stocks of materials and goods were divided among various claimants, with Army and Navy requirements fulfilled ahead of any others. Roosevelt installed William Knudsen, production commissioner for the NDAC, as director general of OPM; Donald Nelson handled OPM's Purchases Department; Edward Stettinius got the thorny job as chief of the Priorities Department. FDR retained the services of each of these businessmen turned administration officials because they possessed a combination of ability, knowledge, and connections available to him nowhere else.[33]

From then on, events moved more quickly. OPM experienced a priorities backlog, given the huge demand for priority assignments from the Army, the Navy, the Maritime Commission, and corporations. Donald Nelson and his colleagues at Sears, Roebuck streamlined the process, greatly reducing the problem. Roosevelt took Stettinius out of OPM, making the steel executive head of the Office of Lend-Lease Administration. To protect war goods going to Britain, Roosevelt provided U.S. Navy escort by autumn 1941. After that, U.S. and German vessels occasionally skirmished with each other in the Atlantic. By that time, U.S. military aid to Britain was greater than ever before, fighting between U.S. destroyers and German submarines had claimed American lives, and OPM's exertions put the nation's economy close to where it needed to be to effectively wage total war.[34]

Japan struck Pearl Harbor on December 7, 1941, catapulting the United States into war and putting it at an immediate naval disadvantage. Soon thereafter, the Japanese seized British, French, and Dutch holdings in the Far East. The Japanese plan called for the establishment of an enhanced Pacific empire strong enough to hold off an American counterattack. Roosevelt, of course, expressed his outrage at the dastardly attack on American territory, expressing absolute confidence that the United States would prevail in the end. The Japanese assault on Pearl Harbor put the United States on the Allied side against the Axis, and Americans demanded retribution.[35]

A greater sense of urgency gripped the nation and its people after Japan belted Hawaii. Federal officials, businessmen, ordinary citizens, and soldiers worked harder. The Office of Production Management gave way to the War Production Board (WPB), which was to exercise "general responsibility" over an American economy now engaged in total war. Raw-materials production climbed. Scrap drives supplemented the expanding output of steel, aluminum, synthetic rubber, and other vital war ingredients. New military camps and depots sprang into existence in Kentucky. Conversion of civilian plants and equipment to wartime purposes accelerated. Many parts of the Bluegrass State performed war work, making and delivering items to the military ranging from the mundane to the sublime.[36]

President Roosevelt created the War Production Board to better balance civilian and military needs for raw materials, finished goods, and human capital. After distinguishing himself with the OPM, Donald Nelson received the nod to head the WPB. Under Nelson's leadership, the War Production Board integrated competing civilian and military mobilization structures; established annual, maximum war production totals; and solved the raw-materials problem by implementation of the Controlled Materials Plan (CMP). Through the CMP, the total amount of steel, aluminum, and copper was divided among major claimants, including the Army and Navy. The claimants then distributed their cut of the materials to contractors, who split up what they had among subcontractors. Kentucky businesses, like those in every other state in the Union, were significantly affected by the Controlled Materials Plan. The WPB's greatest value derived from the fact that it ultimately compelled the military to accede to a lower level of war production than it wanted, a level that did not threaten the American economy with collapse, yet one that allowed the Services to receive more than enough weapons from companies large and small to win the war. Nelson, who has often been portrayed as "soft" for the various concessions he made to the military, got the big job done more than well enough in the end. A somewhat unlikely champion of small business and labor, Nelson lost his position as WPB chief just before the end of the war because of opposition from the largest corporations; he became a political liability for FDR. Nelson's departure reflected the triumph of a type of public-private partnership dominated by big businessmen with more conservative ways than his own, and by the generals. The military-industrial complex reached a new, higher stage of development by 1945, which in modified form still exists today.[37]

Donald Nelson (left), Executive Director of the Supply Priorities and Allocation Board, confers with Leon Henderson, head of the Office of Price Administration, September 12, 1941. President Roosevelt named Nelson chairman of the War Production Board in January 1942, with general responsibility over the American economy and a specific mandate to see to it that the U.S. military had all the arms and munitions it required to achieve victory over the Axis. (Courtesy of the Library of Congress.)

The American war machine burned through vast amounts of raw materials. Kentucky contributed a growing volume of coal from 1942 into 1945. The eastern and western coalfields hummed with activity. The commonwealth also provided its share of that most critical of all war materials, steel, and huge quantities of synthetic rubber.

The American Rolling Mill Company (ARMCO) had located a steel plant in Ashland years before the war began. In February 1941, ARMCO announced its decision to build a new $5 million blast furnace at that site, which would more than double its current output of steel. European conflict and the American defense buildup inspired this move. ARMCO executives discovered that it was easy to mix patriotism and profits.[38]

Completed in 1942, the Bellefonte furnace produced 1,000 tons of steel per day. Most went into various types of war production. The Bellefonte operation included the furnace itself, whose height was greater than 200 feet, plus a 400,000-ton ore storage yard and a railroad yard capable of holding 200 cars. Each day's output required 1,950 tons of iron ore, 935 tons of coke, 485 tons of limestone, and 125 tons of mill scale and open-hearth slag. Altogether, the Ashland steel operation generated at least 2 billion pounds of steel for the U.S. war effort—perhaps more.[39]

Along with coal and steel, the United States required rubber for a successful war effort. Japanese gains in the Far East following the attack on

Pearl Harbor cut the United States off from 90 percent of its prewar supply of natural rubber. Development of a high-volume synthetic rubber industry became imperative under these circumstances. Ultimately, companies such as DuPont and Goodrich helped meet this challenge by producing tremendous amounts of various synthetic rubbers—indispensable inputs for the output of many wartime goods.[40]

Kentucky played a dominant role in the creation of a large, wartime American synthetic rubber industry. Not surprisingly, Louisville was at the center of activity. Indeed, a part of west Louisville, which included Bell's Lane, received the nickname "Rubbertown" because it became home to several synthetic rubber plants whose combined, coordinated operations significantly bolstered the overall stock of American synthetic rubbers.[41]

DuPont and National Carbide Corporation set up shop first. In June 1941, DuPont began construction of its synthetic rubber plant in west Louisville. Neoprene was the specific type of synthetic rubber that would be made there. Since neoprene requires acetylene gas, National Carbide Corporation appeared almost simultaneously. National Carbide's major product was calcium carbide, a mix of coke and lime, which when combined with water produces acetylene gas. Simply put, National Carbide shipped calcium carbide to DuPont, and DuPont added the water to make the gas. The one plant could not operate without the other.[42]

The Defense Plant Corporation (DPC) of the federal government also got into the act. DPC helped expand DuPont's synthetic rubber plant in 1942, supplying the capital to quadruple production. DuPont's staff continued to operate the plant. Indeed, it increased output still further.[43]

Though neoprene was only one of several synthetic rubbers used by the United States during World War II, and it was far from the most common form, its unique characteristics lent itself to certain important applications. A relatively costly synthetic rubber, and not so easily made as some others, it went into specialty items that required relatively small amounts of the material. Exposure suits for aviators, carburetor diaphragms for airplane motors, hoses, tubes, and thousands of molded articles for airplanes, tanks, and ships required neoprene. From December 1, 1941, to August 31, 1945, DuPont's synthetic rubber plant at Louisville produced 229,245,000 pounds of the stuff.[44]

A picture of the
DuPont neoprene
plant in Louisville.
(Courtesy of the
Hagley Museum
and Library.)

A step along the way
in the manufacture
of neoprene.
(Courtesy of the
Hagley Museum
and Library.)

B. F. Goodrich Company, National Synthetic Rubber Company, and Carbide and Carbon Chemical Company followed DuPont and National Carbide into Rubbertown. Goodrich, which became the single largest maker of artificial rubber in the United States by the end of the war, and National Synthetic Rubber churned out a form of synthetic rubber called Buna-S. Carbide and Carbon Chemical Company manufactured butadiene, Buna-S's key ingredient. Buna-S also required industrial alcohol. The American synthetic rubber industry produced much more Buna-S during World War II than any other type of synthetic rubber; indeed, it constituted 86 percent of all synthetic rubber made during this period. The vast majority of U.S. military and combat tires during the war contained more Buna-S than any other material, hence its great value.[45]

Louisville's contribution to the American synthetic rubber supply was truly impressive. So, too, was the team effort of local officials, private chemical companies, and the U.S. government. In 1944 alone, Louisville's synthetic rubber facilities generated 195,000 tons of synthetic rubber. This figure represented over one-quarter of the entire American synthetic rubber output for that year. Blessed by the nearby concentration of Kentucky distilleries, the "Falls City" had become the largest producer of synthetic rubber in the nation, ahead of such places as Akron, Pittsburgh, and Houston.[46]

Scrap drives throughout Kentucky resulted in the collection of massive amounts of raw materials vital for the effective functioning of the American war machine. Great piles of old aluminum, rubber, tin, iron, steel, and other substances appeared, which were processed and then shaped into arms and munitions. Scrap of many kinds added appreciably to U.S. stockpiles of the inputs necessary to generate finished war goods such as tires, airplanes, battleships, and tanks.

Kentuckians participated in a multitude of scrap drives, which were carried out from the preparedness period through the end of World War II. The citizens exhibited great enthusiasm, especially during the first year after the Japanese savaged Pearl Harbor. They wanted revenge, and scrap donations gave them one way to get it. Philip Hutti of Louisville, a ninety-year-old stonecutter, contributed fifty pounds of old tools to Uncle Sam's scrap heap "to make bullets for those Japs and Germans." Many Kentuckians shared Hutti's sentiment.[47]

A nationwide aluminum scrap drive took place during the summer of 1941. With the help of some three thousand Boy Scouts and seventy-five civic-minded clubs, Louisville raised some 30,000 pounds of aluminum in this campaign. Owensboro chipped in with 6,750 pounds. The Lions Club at Bowling Green and the Hopkinsville Boy Scouts contributed more old aluminum. In December, Clark County added ten truckloads of aluminum to the war effort.[48]

The year following Pearl Harbor, 1942, witnessed much greater activity. From June 15 to June 21 of that year, Kentuckians handed over 3,600,000 pounds of scrap rubber to the federal government's Rubber Reserve Company. The old rubber came from many sources, including worn-out tires, hoses, and toys. In one case, a dismantled player piano yielded several pounds of rubber tubing for the cause. A Louisville scrap tin drive during the first half of August 1942 depended most on housewives, who could both donate and collect tin cans. The Coca-Cola Bottling Company threw in an additional 6,000 pounds of the metal. The total amount of tin collected in this drive came to at least 16,000 pounds.[49]

A truly gigantic American scrap metal drive unfolded in October 1942. Kentucky set the bar high, announcing that it would raise 285 million pounds of scrap metal, or the equivalent of 100 pounds of scrap metal for every man, woman, and child living in the commonwealth. Governor Keen Johnson noted the importance of the drive for the war effort, saying it is "as impossible to make steel without scrap as it is to make a mint julep without mint." With the War Production Board urging the states on, and Johnson in full accord with the push, Kentuckians distinguished themselves. Louisville turned in miles of old iron yard fences. Ashland residents sorted through numerous junkyards and automobile graveyards for salvageable metals. One Kentucky girl gave all her metal toys away, saving only her miniature stove. Jefferson County, having the largest population of any county in Kentucky, contributed the most scrap in absolute terms, but sparsely populated Powell County led the way in per capita terms by bringing in an amazing 566.5 pounds of metal per person. Altogether, Kentucky surrendered almost 327 million pounds of scrap metal to the U.S. government, a figure that far exceeded the original ambitious objective.[50]

Other items received attention, too. The WPB called on women everywhere, including Kentucky, to save kitchen grease and to give up their hosiery. Kitchen grease contained glycerin, an ingredient used in manufacturing dynamite. Hosiery was made of either silk or the new synthetic known as nylon; both materials could be used to fashion powder bags and parachutes. Mignon Doran, a grand lady originally from Graves County, remembered well the willing sacrifice of her silk stockings for the boys at war. Though men were required to do without garters and suspenders, one senses that this was not as distressing for them as the absence of corsets, girdles, and stockings was for women.[51]

After collection of the rubber, various metals, grease, and other substances, the items had to be handled in the appropriate manner and ultimately transformed into war goods. Centers were established in towns such as Louisville, Lexington, and Paducah as points to pool the materials. Federal agencies such as the Rubber Reserve Company, the Metals Reserve Company, and the procurement office of the U.S. Treasury disposed of the great piles by funneling materials to private companies that performed every sort of chore, from cutting up the metal to assembling an aircraft carrier. Mansbach Metal Company of Ashland and firms like it bought up scrap metals from sellers, cut the metals up, and performed basic processing. In cooperation with the WPB and other relevant federal agencies, Mansbach shipped these materials to companies that fashioned them into useful implements of war.[52]

Conservation of existing materials accompanied new production and collection of scrap. Governor Johnson expected Kentuckians to get the most wear possible out of tires, cars, clothing, and other products they possessed at the time of U.S. entry into the war. Rationing of tires was inevitable, given the loss of natural rubber from Asia. Regular gasoline was not in short supply, but was rationed anyway to ensure that citizens drove their cars fewer miles. This approach reduced the loss of rubber from tires, as did Johnson's announcement that the state speed limit be set at a maximum of 40 miles per hour. Later, it was reduced to 35 miles per hour. Large numbers of people began to retread old tires for further use. An early version of carpooling came into vogue, as war workers at the Charlestown, Indiana, war facilities and such Louisville locations as DuPont Neoprene, B. F. Goodrich, National Carbide, Vogt Manufacturing, and the Mengel Company joined in on the plan. Stretching limited resources as far as they could go became the order of the day.[53]

This poster implores Americans to contribute scrap materials such as iron, tin, and rubber for the U.S. war effort. (Courtesy of the Library of Congress.)

American entry into the war resulted in the establishment of new military installations in Kentucky, which joined Fort Knox and Fort Nelson. Camp Breckinridge and Camp Campbell appeared only a little over six months after Pearl Harbor. At about the same time, the Lexington Signal Depot and the Blue Grass Ordnance Depot began operations. The training of soldiers and the storing and shipment of war goods, like the manufacture of arms and munitions, were begun in many Bluegrass State locations.

Herbert F. Hoffman, a young soldier in charge of a construction unit, played a part in the erection of Camp Breckinridge. Hoffman marveled at the rapid pace of building, proudly noting that the place in western Kentucky "was a pasture field and 150 days later we let 14,000 troops in." Camp Breckinridge stretched across almost 36,000 acres of land in three counties, and the sergeants and other Army personnel there ultimately trained 30,000 infantry recruits for the rigors of battle.[54]

Camp Campbell, located sixteen miles south of Hopkinsville in parts of Kentucky and Tennessee, opened in July 1942 to train men for armored divisions and to test tanks. The camp produced the 12th and 14th Armored Divisions, U.S. Army. The 20th Armored Division served at Camp Campbell, providing basic training for tankers who would take the spots of other tankers already stationed overseas. All told, the staff at Camp Campbell trained and deployed more than 25 percent of all armored soldiers who fought in the Army's armored divisions during World War II. Camp Campbell supplemented the work of Fort Knox in the realm of tank warfare.[55]

The U.S. Army needed facilities to hold ammunition and other supplies until the time was right to transport them to army bases, where they could be disseminated to the troops. The Lexington Signal Depot and the Blue Grass Ordnance Depot were such places. Both installations began their work in 1942, continuing throughout the war and into peacetime.

Construction of the various structures at the Lexington Signal Depot commenced on July 1, 1941, with operations beginning in late May 1942. The Depot encompassed 782 acres in the eastern section of Fayette County, complete with an administration building, eight 130,000-square-foot brick warehouses, a power plant, a motor pool, and forty temporary buildings. The warehouses, of course, held the ammo and other supplies that flowed in and out of the Depot. Research and development also took place here. A new, more sensitive type of radar equipment and an enhanced fingerprinting technique resulted from work done at the Signal Depot.[56]

A much larger facility, known officially as the Blue Grass Ordnance Depot (BGOD), occupied some 15,000 acres near Richmond, Kentucky. The BGOD featured hundreds of "igloos" for storing, processing, and issuing ammunition of many types. Artillery and tank shells came and went, moving out to key army bases throughout the Ohio Valley. Amped-up rounds containing mustard gas arrived, though mercifully this exotic killer was not used during World War II. Some 6,500 civilian workers and a lesser number of soldiers constructed this vast complex, which far exceeded the Lexington Signal Depot in magnitude but could not rival the size of the mammoth propellant complex around Charlestown, Indiana. The permanent workforce of the BGOD reached its peak at 3,800 in 1943. Central Kentucky and eastern Kentucky received a tremendous economic boost from this base.[57]

Like Uncle Sam, private enterprise picked up the pace after the United States declared war on Japan. During the preparedness period, some businesses threw themselves into defense work with abandon while others hedged. Corporations, especially large ones, tended toward the status quo: they preferred to do their normal work even as the country edged closer to war because change involved risk. Lingering animosities toward New Deal economic and social policy interfered from time to time with the establishment of productive business-government partnerships. After the Japanese wrecked Pearl Harbor, cooperation improved. Even *Nation's Business,* formerly a bitter foe of the Roosevelt administration, rejected whatever "finagling" businessmen had engaged in during preparedness, convinced now that all industrialists and manufacturers "found their hearts in their (war) jobs."[58]

Corporate executives throughout the Commonwealth converted their factories and other productive assets to the manufacture of war goods. Often their decisions were voluntary. In a few instances, the long arm of federal power gave them no choice. Looking back after the passage of a half-century, John A. Hillerich III, chairman of the board of Louisville's Hillerich & Bradsby Company, said, "Everyone associated with manufacturing had to look to the government. How do you want us to respond with our company? It's a national emergency. We are here to do what you need done, and that's how our company and all the other companies responded to this national effort." A. P. Cochran, president of the Falls

City Cochran Foil Company, added more candidly that, "while we would naturally prefer to operate on our regular business, we will . . . do our bit in aiding the defense of our country." Patriotism influenced Kentucky executives, as did sheer necessity and profit considerations.[59]

The truth is that the federal government compensated corporate America very well for going along with the war effort. Secretary of War Henry Stimson once observed famously that "if you are going . . . to war . . . in a capitalist country you have got to let business make money out of the process or business won't work." Guided by this principle, the War Department furnished firms everywhere with cost-plus contracts—guaranteeing good profits to businesses that converted to war production. Other inducements were offered as well. In the case of Hillerich & Bradsby, for instance, the government provided the company with the specialized equipment it needed to manufacture rifle stocks, and all of it came without charge. Companies in Kentucky helped provide the stock of arms and munitions essential to pursuit of victory over the Axis and in return earned a considerable financial reward.[60]

Central Kentucky, northern Kentucky, western Kentucky, and eastern Kentucky witnessed the movement of business plants and equipment away from civilian production to wartime production. The conversion of business from peace to war throughout the "old Kentucky home" provided the American military with a range of items from jeeps to jeans to components of the atomic bomb. The sheer diversity of war goods made in the Bluegrass State proved astounding.

Central Kentucky, not surprisingly, generated the greatest amount of conversion activities. Louisville dominated the process. Frankfort, Lexington, Mt. Sterling, and other places in the Bluegrass region turned out war-related goods in smaller amounts.

Ford Motor Company's plant in Louisville, located at 1400 South Western Parkway, was already fifteen years old in 1941. Situated on a 22.5-acre site, the plant was originally set up for one thousand workers and production of four hundred vehicles a day. It made the Model A, then V-8 engines. When WPB chairman Nelson issued a February 1942 order to the auto industry not to build any more civilian vehicles "for the duration," the Louisville facility turned entirely to the production of the new quarter-ton 4x4 truck known as the jeep. The first Army jeep rolled off the assembly line at the Louisville plant in May 1942. Ultimately, this Kentucky plant produced 93,389 jeeps for military use by war's end. No less an authority than Supreme Allied Commander Dwight D. Eisenhower labeled the multipurpose jeep as one of the four weapons that proved most valuable in winning the war, classing it with the atomic bomb, the C-47 transport plane, and the bazooka.[61]

Many other Louisville and Louisville-area concerns contributed to the American war machine by adding to their normal production or by switching over entirely to war production. Hillerich & Bradsby continued to make baseball bats throughout World War II while accepting government contracts to fashion billy clubs and rifle stocks for M-1 carbines. Reynolds Metal Company shaped aluminum airplane parts for assembly plants throughout the United States. The Henry Vogt Company constructed boilers for use in Maritime Commission vessels. Tube Turns, Incorporated, sent welding fittings to virtually all of America's shipyards. The Jeffersonville Boat & Machine Company built submarine chasers and landing craft for amphibious operations. On and on it went.[62]

Central Kentucky's great distilleries converted to war work, abandoning bourbon whiskey and other drinks for industrial alcohol. Whiskey and other potable spirits were most emphatically not necessities when fighting a war against powerful and cruel enemies. Scarce resources dictated that the manufacture of luxuries be scaled back or eliminated. Under these circumstances, it only made sense for Kentucky distilleries to convert production from bourbon and other liquors to industrial alcohol—which the American war machine absolutely, positively had to have.

Lewis S. Rosenstiel, president of Schenley Distillers Corporation, the nation's second largest distiller, understood this truth well. Before 1940 was out, Rosenstiel initiated gradual conversion of facilities from the manufacture of drinkable alcohol to industrial alcohol. By late September 1942, Schenley operations at Louisville, Lexington, Frankfort, and Covington had produced their last barrel of whiskey and from then on made only industrial alcohol for the war effort. (Industrial alcohol differed from potable alcohol by the addition of methyl alcohol and benzene, making it unfit to drink, and by the use of a higher cooking temperature to raise the proof to 190.)[63]

Other distillers completed conversion to industrial alcohol at about the same time. From October 1942 to October 1944, Kentucky's fifty-seven distilleries, clustered in the Bluegrass region, made 244 million gallons of industrial alcohol. This quantity proved to be roughly three times greater than the amount of drinkable alcohol that might have been produced over the same span without the war. Kentucky distillers wisely chose to pursue this course, thereby avoiding extinction and maximizing profits while doing their part to help win the war.[64]

Industrial alcohol was so valuable because it went into a myriad of wartime goods. Buna-S required butadiene, a substance synthesized from high-proof industrial alcohol. Smokeless powder, like the type made at Charlestown, depended on industrial alcohol as well: the alcohol acted as a solvent to remove water from the powder. After the solvent was removed and the powder dried, it was ready to go. When industrial alcohol was added to gasoline, it boosted the octane level. American fighter planes were powered by such high-octane fuel. Other products that employed industrial alcohol in one way or another included gas masks, life vests, hoses, and footwear.[65]

Franklin County's war industry included industrial alcohol, textiles, and precision parts for various kinds of bombs. George T. Stagg Distillery in Frankfort made both industrial alcohol and dried grain food for military use. The Union Underwear Company fashioned shorts for the armed forces, ultimately shipping more than 50 million pairs to the nation's fighting men. George W. Gayle & Son, which had a long tradition of making the finest hand-crafted, original fishing reels and the artisanal and machining skills indispensable to the task, performed the most intriguing work of any Kentucky firm during the war. Gayle & Son graduated from work on the firing mechanism of ocean mines to shaping components for use in some unknown, mystery product, which later turned out to be the atomic bomb. Though Gayle & Son was only one of many companies involved in the nuclear project, it did contribute to the manufacture of the superweapon that brought World War II to an abrupt close.[66]

Other central Kentucky towns did what they could to provide for the vast needs of the Army, Navy, and air forces. In 1942, the Irving Air Chute Company of Lexington opened a new factory on Versailles Road to manufacture parachutes for airmen. The Cowden Manufacturing Company of Mt. Sterling converted its plant and equipment to turn out dungarees for the Navy. Approximately 150 employees and 100 machines cut and stitched cloth together, churning out 2,400 pairs of dungarees daily by mid-January 1945. Centers of war production, whether big or small, new or converted, dotted all regions of Kentucky by this time.[67]

Converted plants and shops of many varieties could be found in northern Kentucky. Almost every business operation in that area that employed machine tools for one product or another turned to war work. A sizable military output resulted.

The Wadsworth Watchcase Company of Dayton made all kinds of watchcases before the conflict, ranging from the smallest watchcase for a women's wristwatch to the largest watchcase for a railroad conductor. When the war came, Waddy's used its machines, tools, and dies to shape military parts such as shell casings and radio components. Wadsworth also built machine guns. Employment at the plant, which included expert die-makers and designers, peaked at 1,350 workers in 1943. The fact that Waddy's worked so much with gold watchcases before World War II, and needed to conserve this precious material lest it hemorrhage money, meant that precision was of utmost importance, and its workers exhibited that same attitude of perfectionism toward the manufacture of war goods. The Wadsworth Watchcase Company ultimately produced millions of parts for the military during the war.[68]

Other northern Kentucky firms pitched in, too. Monarch Tool and Manufacturing Company of Covington, maker of coin devices for jukeboxes, parts for automobiles, and specialty valves, turned out aircraft, bombsight, and munitions parts during the war. Stewart Iron Works Company of Covington, which made wrought-iron fence normally, shifted to portable landing equipment for the air force at this dangerous moment in our history. Andrews Steel Company, located in Newport and Wilder, forged steel sheets, shell casings, and other products, including machine guns, for military consumption.[69]

Western Kentucky firms involved in the great productive effort included Ken-Rad Company, Cumberland Manufacturing Company, and International Shoe Company. Ken-Rad of Owensboro appeared on the earliest War Department list of manufacturing concerns in Kentucky that possessed the wherewithal to fulfill defense orders reliably. The mili-

These people buy
a battleship
every week!

Meet John S_____ and Mary D_____. John works at an electronics plant on Long Island, and makes $85 a week. Almost 16% of it goes into War Bonds.

Mary has been driving rivets into bombers at an airplane plant on the West Coast. She makes $55 a week, and puts 14% of it into War Bonds.

John and Mary are typical of more than 27 million Americans on the Payroll Savings Plan who, every single month, put half a BILLION dollars into War Bonds. That's enough to buy one of those hundred-million-dollar battleships every week, with enough money for an aircraft carrier and three or four cruisers left over.

In addition, John and Mary and the other people on the Payroll Plan have been among the biggest buyers of *extra* Bonds in every War Loan Drive.

They've financed a good share of our war effort all by themselves, and they've tucked away billions of dollars in savings that are going to come in mighty handy for both them and their country later on.

When this war is won, and we start giving credit where credit is due, don't forget John and Mary. After the fighting men, they deserve a place at the top. They've earned it.

YOU'VE BACKED THE ATTACK

—NOW SPEED THE VICTORY!

6
the
WAR LOAN

Ralph the Riveter and Rosie the Riveter got the big war production job done. (Courtesy of the Hagley Museum and Library.)

tary needed radio tubes, and Ken-Rad supplied a good many of them. Indeed, the demand was such that Ken-Rad opened up a branch factory in Bowling Green in 1943 to augment its output of radio tubes and other equipment. Modern Welding Company and Glenmore Distillery Company, both of which also operated out of Owensboro, were also active in the war effort. Modern Welding used metals to construct buoys and buoy moorings for the Navy. Glenmore Distillery, like distilleries elsewhere in the state, brewed industrial alcohol, which found its way into the manufacture of powder in the powder plants of Memphis, Tennessee. Cumberland Manufacturing Company of Princeton, Kentucky, produced flannel shirts for military use, while Paducah's International Shoe Company plant made thousands of pairs of shoes for Army nurses.[70]

Though much of rugged eastern Kentucky lacked industry, it experienced a small degree of conversion and the odd defense contract here and there. Ashland Oil Company capitalized on its existing Ashland refinery, adding more facilities to it, in order to make 100-octane aviation gasoline. Using this type of gas, American fighter pilots had the edge over their German counterparts. The McGlore Stove Company of Bell County cut planks from white oak to make the sides of barrels. Any planks that were defective were set afire, then covered with dirt to bring about slow combustion. This process yielded charcoal, which could be used to purify water. Charcoal was also employed in black-powder production and in the manufacture of gas masks.[71]

Inevitably, the appearance of so many new and converted war facilities in Kentucky generated significant, sometimes unwanted, consequences. Overcrowding in urban areas and pollution resulted from large-scale production of arms and munitions. The Indiana suburbs of Louisville experienced the greatest degree of industrial overcrowding, followed by downtown Louisville. Paducah and the Lexington-Richmond-Winchester triangle grappled with congestion, too, though it was not as severe in those places. The presence of so many defense workers and soldiers led to higher prices and rents for housing and periodic housing shortages. Sometimes troops on leave could not find accommodations at all. Infrastructure was strained. Overcrowding proved to be a serious and complex problem for Kentucky's major war production centers.

Charlestown, Jeffersonville, and New Albany, all towns in the section of Indiana just across the Ohio River from Louisville, grew fastest and felt the most strain. Because of the erection of the smokeless powder plant and the bag plant, Charlestown's population soared from roughly 900 people in February 1940 to over 4,500 people a year later. This type of expansion meant that construction on a sewage disposal plant had to be halted and the whole project redesigned and expanded to meet the needs of so many new arrivals to the town. There were simply not enough living spaces in Charlestown to keep up with demand, despite frantic efforts to make up the difference. Mrs. B. H. Backus, proprietress of the Residence Hotel, added a sixteen-room annex and partitioned existing rooms so that she could cram forty-two men into the complex. Donald and Edward Laughlin operated a bunk-bed establishment, which leased out rooms for sleeping men on daytime and nighttime shifts. Nineteen camps, with some 375 trailers, served Charlestown by December 1940, and more trailers came later. The federal government provided 250 housing units early on and more after that. Homeowners in Charlestown leased out rooms in their houses. Even with all this activity, men looking for places to stay often had to go elsewhere. School enrollment rose by 25 percent in Charlestown, then 50 percent, then more. The community knew it needed new public school facilities, but how to fund them became an issue. A day-care facility for children would have been nice, too. Crime increased around the town, and more automobile accidents occurred. Charlestown, albeit on a much smaller scale, began to resemble Detroit, Michigan, or Los Angeles, California. Jeffersonville and New Albany witnessed similar, if smaller, problems. The housing shortage in that area was pronounced. Rents jumped by 22.3 percent from May 1941 to February 1942. The creation of so many jobs, and the production of arms to aid the war effort, was offset to some extent by the adverse consequences of unrestrained growth, and the gravity of that situation was heaviest in the Indiana part of the Louisville metropolitan area.[72]

Downtown Louisville adjusted to the war boom with less difficulty than its Indiana outposts. The population of the Falls City rose during the conflict, but not as steeply as in a place like Charlestown. Demand for living spaces of all types increased, but not to the extent that it did in Floyd and Clark counties, Indiana. The result was that the housing situation in Louisville from 1941 through 1945 was tight, but not critical. Experts debated whether or not an actual housing shortage existed; some said yes and others no. Realtors believed that the overall stock of housing was adequate, while government officials and social settlement workers asserted that there was a shortage. A Works Progress Administration (WPA) survey at the end of 1941 estimated that Louisville had 92,000 dwelling units and that 99 percent of them were occupied. The WPA predicted an initial shortage of about 2,000 units by the end of January 1942, which was certainly reason for concern. Nevertheless, during the period that Jeffersonville-Albany rents increased by 22.3 percent, the figure for Louisville was just 8 percent.[73]

Income and price considerations, not surprisingly, meant a great deal. War workers who received high wages and incomes obviously had an easier time finding a suitable place to live than war workers who made lower wages and incomes. Prices for houses and rents for apartments had to be taken into account. The lower the price or rent, given decent conditions, the better. So it was that there were plenty of Louisville properties available for families at $75 per month rent but a "decided lack" of properties at $35 per month. As always, the details determined financial decisions and, in many cases, whether a shortage existed or not. There were shortages in some categories of Louisville housing but not in others, and the particulars often proved decisive.[74]

Overcrowding in Paducah owed to the establishment of the Kentucky Ordnance Works nearby and to an influx of Camp Tyson, Tennessee, soldiers on weekends. By mid-1942, 6,000 men labored each day to help construct the TNT plant and between 600 to 800 soldiers arrived each Friday and Saturday for entertainment. Finding housing, or even a bare sleeping place, for these people tested the ingenuity of Paducah authorities.[75]

For the Lexington-Richmond-Winchester corridor, the story was much the same. The appearance of the Avon Signal Depot, the Blue Grass Ordnance Depot, and the expansion of various companies due to war work made it a struggle to house workers and troops. Hundreds, if not thousands, of apartments and houses were needed. Some were found, through partitioning or add-ons, and others were wholly new constructions. Shortages appeared at points, were rectified, and appeared again.[76]

Realtors, homeowners, apartment landlords, the federal government, and troop support organizations provided housing for those who needed it, but the circumstances in Kentucky were such that wartime shortages never disappeared completely, and some people were dissatisfied with the accommodations they did get. Unfortunately, private interests came out against federal housing because they said it was not needed. In reality, they were afraid that Uncle Sam would become a competitor and they did not think that fair or right. The federal government did provide apartment housing in the commonwealth, but it was always limited. Realtors fought against it, and conservative representatives in Washington, DC, did not want to see New Deal social experimentation under the guise of wartime exigency. By 1942, 1,600 units of government housing were available in Louisville and 250 units each for Charlestown and New Albany. Those numbers grew slowly over time. The United Service Organizations (USO) also offered soldiers rooms to rent. Despite all these sources, the number of available living spaces was never quite enough.[77]

Founded in February 1942, the United Service Organizations proliferated during World War II. Over 3,000 USO centers opened up before the war ended. The individual USO provided recreational activities to GIs, doing everything in its power to bolster morale. Some USOs, as indicated before, set up sleeping quarters for soldiers on leave. The USO became a "home away from home."[78]

Cities and towns in Kentucky with World War II USOs included Louisville, Radcliff, Elizabethtown, and Paducah. A total of thirty-seven USO centers came into being in the Bluegrass State in twenty-three towns. The Louisville Service Club began operations on March 15, 1941, one of the first of its type in the nation. "Wholesome amusement," such as that available from reading rooms and dances, attracted the soldiers and kept many away from prostitutes. Local girls sometimes came in and danced with the troops, which was especially appealing to them. This USO also featured warm showers and clean, decent beds at reasonable rates in a 150-bed dormitory. In just two months, 6,326 soldiers registered at the Falls City USO and countless others later. Thomas Dewey, New York City District Attorney and chairman of the campaign committee of the United Service Organizations for National Defense, after visiting the Louisville USO proclaimed that it could be a model for the rest of the country. On January 31, 1942, and February 1, 1942, respectively, the Radcliff and Elizabethtown USOs were dedicated, although they did not open for the GIs until January 1943. Their purpose was to "ease the emotional strain of soldiers 'ripped up' from home and transplanted into the intensive training for army life." In Paducah, a shortage of hotels resulted in some visiting soldiers "staying on the streets all night or in all-night beer places." This sort of thing struck many Paducahans as unacceptable, leading to the establishment of a USO there with beds. Just the same, a lack of suitable sleeping quarters always left a few American soldiers in Kentucky on park benches overnight, and too many war workers ended up in subpar habitations or with wasteful commutes.[79]

Pollution and related health hazards for workers went hand in hand with industrial mobilization for war. As defense production gave way to war production in Kentucky, industrial activity soared and so did the amount of air pollution and water pollution. Though few workers worried about it at the time, consumed as they were by the need for money and by the goal of defeating the Axis, contact with a number of dangerous substances on the shop floor threatened their long-term physical well-being. Due to the passage of two-thirds of a century, much less cultural awareness of the environmental impact on health then than now, and the extreme difficulties of establishing a direct causal link between workplace toxins and sickness or death, it is impossible to precisely quantify the ill effects that resulted from exposure of Kentucky's World War II laborers to harmful chemicals, but it is obvious that adverse physiological results eventually took place.

Butadiene, the crucial ingredient in the manufacture of Buna-S synthetic rubber, fouled the air while posing perhaps the gravest threat to human health of all the wartime home front chemicals. An invisible gas, butadiene possesses a mild gasoline-like odor. Some of it spewed into the atmosphere in the production process at various Rubbertown plants in Louisville. Butadiene is now known to be a carcinogen (a fact that was not known in the early 1940s), and the U.S. Environmental Protection Agency recognizes it as such. The best science indicates that there is a convincing link between butadiene and leukemia, and significant though lesser evidence for a link between butadiene and various respiratory, bladder, and stomach cancers. Workers at the Carbide and Carbon Chemical Company and other facilities in Louisville inhaled this gas, and it is likely that a percentage of them paid the price later.

A study does exist for a butadiene plant at Port Neches, Texas, which began operations during World War II and is still open today. This study shows that butadiene levels in the air outside the plant were "far above safety standards." Probably not coincidentally, twenty-six students at nearby Port Neches–Groves High School developed cases of leukemia, lymphoma, and related cancers between 1963 and 1993, resulting in at least fourteen deaths. These numbers are much higher than would normally be expected for any high school over the same period. Other deaths around Port Neches from cancer caused by excessive exposure to butadiene almost assuredly occurred before 1963, though that is not the focus of this study. During World War II, Carbide and Carbon Chemical Company in Louisville used the same production process for butadiene that was employed at the Port Neches facility, while Louisville as a whole generated more Buna-S than the little Texas town. The chance that the number of war production–related cancers and deaths in and around Louisville after the war exceeded that for Port Neches in absolute terms is high, though the question of per capita incidence is open for debate.[80]

Kentucky's groundwater, surface water, and land were contaminated in various ways. Trinitrotoluene (TNT) stored in lagoons at the Blue Grass Ordnance Depot near Richmond seeped into groundwater in a concentration that caused concern decades later, forcing soil removal in the 1980s. At the Kentucky Ordnance Works near Paducah, the situation was more serious. Even after KOW shut down in the mid-1940s and disposal efforts took place, chunks of TNT littered a portion of the old grounds. As of the year 2000, this area had been fenced off, but pieces of the explosive could still be found. Gary Chisholm of the U.S. Army Corps of Engineers noted that the TNT is "pretty stable" but would ignite if heated. Chisholm said, "You just don't want kids or hunters picking the stuff up or walking home with it." Arsenic levels in the soil remain high at the KOW site, too.[81]

Lessons can be drawn from the environmental experience of World War II. Peggy Terry, who worked at the naval shell loading plant at Viola, once observed that the tetryl used there "turned us orange. Just as orange as orange. Our hair was streaked orange. Our hands, our face, our neck just turned orange, even our eyeballs. We never questioned. None of us ever asked, what is this? Is this harmful? We simply didn't think about it. That was just one of the conditions of the job." Luckily for Peggy and the others exposed to tetryl, it turns out that this chemical is relatively harmless. Butadiene and vinyl chloride (an ingredient used in making certain plastics), however, are not benign. They are now certified cancer-causing agents. The necessities of war overrode concern for the health of war workers. Soldiers and workers were expendable, at least in low numbers. Massive war production in Kentucky from 1941 to 1945 generated more pollutants than in any earlier four-year span of the commonwealth's history, with the added consequence that an unknown number of wartime factory workers must have sickened and died in later years.[82]

Economic rejuvenation more than counterbalanced overcrowding and environmental strain. Kentucky's economy rebounded from the Great Depression during the war years, becoming healthy again. Plenty of jobs opened up and incomes rose. Kentuckians welcomed the return of economic strength, and then unprecedented prosperity, with open arms.

The commonwealth's economy grew dramatically in absolute terms, though in a comparative sense the results were less impressive. About 240 more coal mines operated in the state at the end of 1941 than at the beginning of the year. January 1942 retail sales for Louisville were 100 percent higher than they had been in January 1940. The state government collected $486 million in tax revenue during 1943—a record figure that exceeded the previous year's take by $148 million. At the close of business on December 30, 1944, Mt. Sterling bank deposits topped $6.6 million, up $1.8 million from the preceding year. From June 1940 to September 1945, Kentucky received more than $1.06 billion in wartime federal government contracts. No wonder that unemployment almost vanished, citizens longed for an end to rationing so they could spend more of the cash they had accumulated, and the state government wallowed in a veritable ocean of black ink. Compared to other Southern states, however, the picture was less rosy. Kentucky placed tenth out of the thirteen states of the South in the dollar value of wartime federal government contracts, beating out only Mississippi, Arkansas, and South Carolina. Kentucky still ranked as one of the poorer states in the Union, though Kentuckians found considerable solace in the increased income and purchasing power that the war brought them.[83]

Germany and Japan were finally defeated in 1945. After a difficult crossing from England to Normandy, the Americans and British made halting progress through France into western Germany. Russian forces swept into Germany from the opposite direction. Hitler killed himself rather than fall into Allied hands, a victim of his own hunger for power and domination. The Third Reich surrendered unconditionally to the Allies on May 7. Atomic bombs dropped on Hiroshima and Nagasaki in early August compelled Japanese capitulation. The fighting ended.

By this time, Kentucky's contribution to the American military machine during the war could be quantified. Distilleries in the commonwealth produced well over 250 million gallons of industrial alcohol. Louisville companies made almost 200,000 tons of synthetic rubber in 1944 alone. The Charlestown, Indiana, smokeless powder complex churned out over 1 billion pounds of smokeless powder, a large part of it made by Kentuckians. Kentucky manufactured one-sixth of the total output of U.S. jeeps during the wartime period. TNT, cargo planes, M-1 rifle stocks, big guns for battleships, landing craft, and precision parts for conventional and nuclear bombs rolled off assembly lines. Though Kentucky entered World War II as a predominantly rural state with a relatively small population, it supplied crucial raw materials for the war effort, and in the process beat out sixteen other states and the District of Columbia in the provision of combat equipment.[84]

Well before Pearl Harbor, President Franklin D. Roosevelt called on America to become "the great arsenal of democracy." Kentucky performed its share of the heavy lifting needed to achieve Roosevelt's goal. The output of industrial alcohol, synthetic rubber, and smokeless powder from the commonwealth, even if everything else was subtracted, guaranteed that outcome. Kentuckians participated in the various scrap drives of the war with fervor in the beginning and determination throughout, providing inputs indispensable to weapons output. The various discomforts associated with rapid industrial mobilization for war, such as overcrowding and environmental damage, proved to be relatively minor. Many people experienced positive feelings from the return of economic prosperity, which ended the pain caused by the Great Depression. Victory over Germany and Japan added significantly to the ranks of Kentuckians who accepted big government and lauded the virtues of corporate America. Organizational concepts, such as rationality, order, regularity, expertise, and efficiency, already significant before the war, bulked larger after it. The advance of organizational society in Kentucky, as in America, continued.

2

Ralph, Rosie, and Labor-Management Relations

Production of arms and munitions for the war effort required labor as well as management. War workers in Kentucky factories performed jobs of many sorts, and their output was prodigious. Be the workers men or women, white or black, in the aircraft industry, shell manufacture, or some other field, the value of what they did proved immense. Patriotism compelled industrial workers to give it their all on the assembly line, and unions renounced the strike for the duration of the conflict. While occasional strikes did occur in World War II Kentucky despite the no-strike pledge, most turned out to be small and short-lived. Even the most threatening of all the strikes, orchestrated by United Mine Workers of America leader John L. Lewis in the soft coal fields of the eastern United States, did not substantially impair the flow of weapons to U.S. soldiers in Europe and Asia, though it did lead to a backlash against the American union movement. As the war proceeded, Kentucky women claimed a large number of new jobs, many of them in traditionally male areas such as manufacturing. The novelty of this situation obscured the vast contributions of white male war workers, who did not get enough credit then or now, while it challenged the traditional sexual division of labor in America. In the end, victory over the Axis was achieved, and labor was one of many groups that helped bring about the salutary result.

Various organizations offered Kentucky men and women training so they could carry out war work effectively. During the preparedness period, and for a while after U.S. entry into the war, the National Youth Administration of the federal government and the Kentucky Department of Vocational Education were most involved in the training effort. After that, the War Manpower Commission in conjunction with the United States Employment Service funneled war workers to Kentucky employers.

The National Youth Administration (NYA) emerged out of the New Deal. The NYA found part-time work for high-school and college students as a means of keeping them in school and out of the regular employment market. Organized on a state-by-state basis, the National Youth Administration was one of many anti-Depression programs of the 1930s. By 1940, the NYA responded to an improving national economy and an increasingly dangerous climate in foreign affairs by seizing on the opportunity to prepare young people for defense jobs. By the summer of 1942, the NYA had redirected all its resources to training new war production workers. This was a way to maintain agency relevance, indeed the very existence of the organization, in an environment quite different from the one in which it was born.[1]

The National Youth Administration divided Kentucky into six war production training centers. The state office and one training center were situated in Louisville. Ashland, London, Vine Grove, Bowling Green, and Mayfield received the other training centers. Through these centers, the NYA built and ran forty-two training and work experience shops capable of turning out almost 1,000 new war workers a month. The young men and women learned about machine-shop operation, arc and gas welding, woodworking, radio equipment, and allied industrial pursuits. From December 7, 1941, to August 1942, the NYA trained more than 5,000 Kentuckians for factory jobs in industrial areas, and that number continued to rise.[2]

Ralph Woods, director of vocational education for the state of Kentucky, noted that at least 25,000 Kentuckians underwent training for work in national defense industries from July 1, 1941, to July 1, 1942. The 1941–1942 program concentrated on machine-tool work and aircraft production. The courses, reported the *Courier-Journal*, were "expanded to meet the needs of industries both in and out of Kentucky."[3]

After Congress eliminated the National Youth Administration in 1943, insisting that it had outlived its usefulness, Kentucky employers secured war workers by going through the War Manpower Commission–United States Employment Service structure. The War Manpower Commission (WMC) dealt with the overall American labor supply, including civilian and military workers. It acted as a supervisory body. The United States Employment Service (USES), with the WMC's blessing, placed qualified war workers with industrial firms. Every effort was made to insure that labor went to the companies that needed it most, and significant progress resulted. By November 1942, WMC designated thirty-two industries and services "essential" for war effort. Workers in these areas could not go to another job without a certificate of separation and referral from the United States Employment Service. This approach reduced "job-shopping" by the workers themselves and "pirating" of help by outside companies. The WMC employee stabilization plan went into effect in Louisville before any other city in the United States, then was used successfully elsewhere. Labor turnover and the resultant loss of man-days were reduced substantially. A. J. Johnson, manager of the USES Hazard office, also made it clear that "any [hiring] barriers against [women and blacks] must be broken down, if we are to produce the necessary equipment." The point was unmistakable: every available source of labor must be fully tapped, and disruptions of all sorts avoided.[4]

Given the stress on inclusivity and the dictates of total war, the number of war workers in Kentucky swelled, peaking at 197,000 in May 1944. Approximately 137,000 of the 197,000 jobs went to men and 60,000 to women. Kentucky whites and Kentucky blacks labored in the scattered war plants of central, western, and eastern Kentucky. Every major industry of the Bluegrass State, from coal mining to railroads and automobiles, was represented.[5]

Kentucky's white males prior to Pearl Harbor found the most work in agriculture, manufacturing, and mining. While agriculture was connected to the war effort because civilians and soldiers must have food, manufacturing and coal mining moved front and center in the massive effort to mobilize industry and make weapons. About one of every five white males in the commonwealth toiled in these crucial areas, and these individuals helped more than any other group in Kentucky to make war production a grand success.[6]

Relegated to the background by the understandable attention given to female workers, especially the riveters, welders, and others in industrial areas, a host of white men in Kentucky contributed heavily to the produc-

"Free labor will win." The United States employed free labor to construct weapons and to produce essential civilian goods. Workers received an hourly wage. Germany, on the other hand, often resorted to the use of slave labor. (Courtesy of the Library of Congress.)

tion feat and to the defeat of the Axis. When the total number of women doing war work reached its height in Kentucky in 1944, two-thirds or slightly more of all war workers were still men. These virtually anonymous male war workers included Herman Roberts, Shelby Burns, Creighton Newton, James W. Settle, and Millard Bennett. Each man's story sheds light on the wartime labor experience.[7]

Herman Roberts began his employment with Ford Motor Car Company in the fall of 1944. Roberts worked in the chassis department at the Louisville plant, helping turn out jeeps. He soon joined United Automobile Workers (UAW) Local 862, the union there. In his capacities as a worker and union representative, Roberts learned much about the production of military vehicles and the wartime interaction between Ford and the UAW.[8]

Ford's Louisville operation assembled almost 100,000 jeeps from 1942 to 1945. It also produced bomb carriers—olive green, camouflaged trucks specially designed to carry bombs and other explosives. Roberts watched as these vehicles were put together, road-tested, dismantled, crated, and shipped out to where they were needed. Although he only worked with the chassis, attaching related parts to the rectangular frame, he took pride in the finished products and their value for the war effort.[9]

Workers at the Ford plant during the war handled the workload without great strain. War Department orders for jeeps and bomb carriers proved manageable enough. Those items did not require major alterations in assembly-line techniques: the changes that were made were relatively simple ones. Labor and management at Ford got along well during this period, in large part due to the payment of union wages and company receipt of cost-plus contracts from the federal government. Since Ford was insured a nice profit, there was little incentive to crack down on the help. Roberts noted that "everything was good at that time . . . we didn't have to work hard in those days. We . . . put in eight hours," and that was that. As for the UAW local, it "almost had its way" with the company.[10]

Shelby Burns hailed from Springfield, Kentucky. Born in 1908, Shelby was a farmer for many years in the Springfield area. He left for Louisville in 1942 to find war work, securing a job with the Tube Turns Company. At Tube Turns, he was part of a five-man team that ran a 10-inch National Company upsetter forge. This gigantic piece of equipment, which was the size of a three-room house, shaped airplane engine parts for American bomber planes.[11]

Day after day, Shelby traveled to the Tube Turns location on 28th and Broadway in Louisville. He grabbed a tail pole, a long instrument that permitted him to place a hot piece of aluminum into the upsetter forge. The dies would close, then move from side to side, crushing the aluminum into the correct shapes for the airplane engine. Then the dies opened, causing the forged pieces (now a cylinder head) to fall out the bottom of the machine onto a conveyor. Other workers took a number of different parts, including the cylinder head, and fitted them together to make a complete engine. Final work was done at a machine shop.[12]

Burns and his coworkers on the huge forge produced many cylinder heads for B-25 and B-29 bombers. The cylinder head was essentially the top portion of the B-25 or B-29 engine. It sat above the cylinder, forming a combustion chamber, where the fuel burned. The B-25 Mitchell, a medium bomber, possessed two engines and thirty-six cylinders. The B-29 Superfortress, the heaviest bomber the United States used during World War II, came equipped with four engines and a grand total of seventy-two cylinders. Neither plane could run at all without accompanying cylinder heads of the type that Burns and others made at Tube Turns.[13]

The worth of Burns's work is obvious. The B-25 was perhaps the most popular and famous American medium bomber of World War II. This aircraft saw action in the Atlantic and Pacific theaters, performing well in both. B-25 bombs sank enemy ships and destroyed enemy submarines. The B-29 is even more well known, indeed legendary. Flying from the Mariana Islands and from Iwo Jima, the superfortresses engaged in saturation bombing of many Japanese cities, including Tokyo.[14]

Industry after industry used white, male labor from Kentucky. Creighton Newton manned the assembly line for General Shoe Company in Frankfort, then became an assembly line inspector before going off to war. After washing out of Army Air Corps training school, James W. Settle of Louisville worked many different civilian jobs throughout the conflict. Settle started as a riveter in the B-24 bomber wing assembly department for Consolidated Aircraft Corporation in San Diego, California. He moved on to Curtiss-Wright Technical Institute, serving as an instructor in the Aircraft Engine Overhaul Section. There Settle showed students how to disassemble, repair, and reassemble large radial aircraft engines. Returning to Consolidated Airways, he inspected B-24s to make sure that all engine parts were in order, and eventually refitted bombers for cargo and transport purposes. Refitting required removal of bomb-racks and bomb-bay doors and installation of a deck complete with removable passenger seats and specialized equipment for tying down freight. Millard Bennett, Joe McCarthy, and Sandy Woolridge hailed from the white working class of Kentucky. Each of them performed uncomplicated physical labor for the Louisville & Nashville Railroad, such as clearing tracks of debris, painting signs attached to freight cars, sweeping floors, and vacuuming the fabric covering of seats. The white, male labor force of the commonwealth handled jobs ranging from the most basic of all tasks to enormously complicated undertakings.[15]

Though historians have often overlooked Kentucky's white, male war labor force, it was a tremendous asset. Depending upon the time frame, 67 percent to 82 percent of all war workers in the state were white males. When the war started, white males possessed the industrial training, expertise, and experience that so many women lacked, and the men passed it on to the women. The federal government recognized the great value of the white male workforce, not least of all by granting deferments from the military draft to many of these skilled individuals (Shelby Burns, for example, fell into this category). By this route, a significant part of Kentucky's white male labor force remained intact as the war dragged on. The value of these workers was simply too high to give them up.[16]

Black males comprised only 3.7 percent of Kentucky's population in 1940, so it is not surprising that this group supplied only a tiny fraction of the commonwealth's war workers. Other factors that limited the contribution of black males to war production included a weak presence in manufacturing areas prior to the war, discrimination based on color, and the military draft. The upshot is that African American male employment in Kentucky war industry (including coal mining and the railroad industry) peaked at approximately 12,000.[17]

Of 50,000 nonwhite male employees in Kentucky in 1940 (almost all of them black), 15,199 held agricultural jobs, 5,755 were in the wholesale and retail trade, 5,459 in coal mining, 3,967 in manufacturing, and 1,966 with railroads. The exigencies of war led to gains for black males in manufacturing and railroads, while a substantial amount of work remained in the coal fields. Just the same, the number of black workers in any field was never that large given the diminutive base numbers of 1940–1941. Moreover, black males found it harder to secure work than white males, often received lower wages for doing the same job, and found it far more difficult to obtain promotions.[18]

By 1942–1943 Uncle Sam urged everyone, no matter their race, sex, or age, to join the ranks of war industry if they did not owe military service. The black men of Kentucky needed the work and responded well to the challenge. African American Rufus Stout resigned his teaching post to take a job as assistant personnel manager at National Carbide Company in Louisville. Other black men worked at National Carbide as well, producing calcium carbide, which went into the making of neoprene for pontoon boats, ship fittings, airplane fittings, and more. A black man remembered only as "Preacher" toiled alongside Shelby Burns and three other whites on Tube Turns's upsetter forge, transforming aluminum into cylinder heads for B-25s and B-29s. Roughly 1,000 black coal miners worked at U.S. Steel Company's Lynch operation during the war, including Alfonso Simms. International Harvester's Benham mine employed black miners. Woolford Griffey was one, becoming the first African Amer-

ican promoted to mine foreman by the industrial giant. The Louisville &
Nashville Railroad hired quite a few black men. Unfortunately, the L&N
offered the blacks menial, low-paying jobs for the vast part. B. H. Whittaker, a coach cleaner, filled depleted water tanks and emptied trash recep-
tacles. L. Beauchamp, a coach cleaner as well, vacuumed coach seats and
swept floors. Their jobs were no different from that of poor white men like
Sandy Woolridge. Hillious Harris, another black L&N employee, served
as a storeroom attendant, dispensing parts and equipment to other workers who needed them. The federal government welcomed every little bit
of labor, and the black males of the Bluegrass State overcame significant
impediments to help out.[19]

Next to white men, white women held the most wartime jobs in Kentucky. Over 50,000 white females performed war work of various kinds
throughout the commonwealth by 1944. The women of the airplane
industry stood out, but females also made powder bags, shells of various kinds, parachutes, and many more items. Indeed, "Rosie the Riveter"
became a wartime icon, and the addition of so many female workers to
the Kentucky labor force marked a dramatic break with the past.[20]

Just before the war, 122,947 white females were employed in Kentucky. Of that number, 26,590 worked in the wholesale and retail trade,
16,365 as domestic servants, and 8,283 in the clothing industry. Only
2,043 white women worked in machinery, automobile, and transportation equipment jobs.[21]

With the arrival of war, the labor situation changed more rapidly than
before. Whatever surplus of workers remained from the Great Depression
was soon exhausted, and by 1943 a labor shortage had broken out in Kentucky. A combination of the military draft, which deprived industry of a
huge number of workers, and increasing demand for arms and munitions
led the state to this perilous situation. Unemployed white women became
the largest single pool of available labor, and the federal government
launched a publicity campaign urging full use of this valuable resource.[22]

"Rosie the Riveter" sprang into existence at this point. A creation of
song and picture, Rosie became the prototypical female war worker. She
was strong and capable. She could do any war job that came along expertly.
A government-commissioned poster showed Rosie as a fit, dark-haired
woman with a red and white bandanna and a blue shirt. Her demeanor is

serious, and she exudes competence. Rosie and her sisters could clearly do the big war production job, helping to bring fathers, husbands, and brothers home sooner rather than later.[23]

Kentucky's white women proved that they were up to the challenge. Rose Will Monroe, Edna Winstead, Dorothy Louise Powell, Mildred Harris, Anna McDevitt, Peggy Terry, Virginia Burns, and thousands more like them made their presence felt. They performed their war jobs well, meeting the high standard set by the government and industry.

Rose Will Monroe became a celebrity during World War II. Out of 6 million new women war workers in the United States, the public most associated the character of Rosie the Riveter with Kentucky's Monroe. She was *the* Rosie, not just *a* Rosie.

Rose Monroe's story might have come out of some fantastic novel, but all of it was true. Monroe, a native of Pulaski County, was born in 1920. She married young and had two children by the time war broke out. Her husband was killed in an automobile accident in 1942, and soon thereafter the Monroes left for Ypsilanti, Michigan. Rose found work at the Ford plant there, securing a position as a riveter. She helped assemble B-24 and B-29 bombers. One day, Hollywood actor Walter Pidgeon came to the plant to shoot scenes designed to sell war bonds and set his eyes upon Rose. She reminded him of the curly-haired, trim lady with the red bandanna in the famous poster that the government had just put out. When Pidgeon learned her name really was Rose, it seemed too good to be true. Pidgeon asked Rose Will Monroe to star in promotional films as "Rosie the Riveter" and she said yes. Monroe went on to do short films shown between Hollywood features and a commercial film. As daughter Vickie Jarvis remarked later, "Mom happened to be at the right place at the right time." Rose Will Monroe's fame owed to good fortune, and vast numbers of Americans identified this Kentuckian more than any other individual as the wartime heroine of the U.S. production effort.[24]

Edna Winstead and Dorothy Louise Powell did not garner the attention Rose Monroe attracted, but they performed equally important work. Winstead, who hailed from Dixon, a small western Kentucky community, toiled with other women at an airplane factory. "We made airplane wings for the B-47s," she recalled. "We ran the riveting machine, that's what we did." Powell, then only seventeen or eighteen years old, took a

Kentuckian Rose Will Monroe, the real-life embodiment of Rosie the Riveter. (Courtesy of Vickie Croston.)

B-24 bombers
("Liberators"), one of
the types of plane Rose
Will Monroe worked
on, pouring off the
assembly line at the
Willow Run bomber
plant near Detroit,
Michigan. (Courtesy
of the Library of
Congress.)

position as a welder for Curtiss-Wright in Louisville. She used a torch to join together metal parts of the C-46 Commando, a twin-engine cargo aircraft. Winstead and Powell, like Monroe, moved into occupations that had once been reserved exclusively for males and proved that they could get the job done right. Barriers that had once blocked the advance of women were falling, and they would be difficult, if not impossible, to resurrect even when peacetime returned.[25]

The experiences of Edna Winstead and Dorothy Powell tell us even more about the female workers of the World War II era. Winstead notes that the women received uniforms when they took jobs. She remembered coveralls, shirts, and pants. She also said that "you didn't wear them out—oh, no. Women just didn't wear pants." When you "went out on the street you had your dress on." After Dorothy Powell quit high school in Louisville, her mother insisted that she go to work. Seventeen or eighteen was old enough to get a job if you dropped out of school. Women workers had a crucial role to play in war production, but society expected them to retain their femininity outside the factory; and their motivations for working were far more varied than just patriotism, a desire to bring family home, or money.[26]

Mildred Harris, too, secured work in the military aircraft industry. In 1943, Harris commuted six days a week from Providence, Kentucky, to the Republic Aviation plant in Evansville, Indiana. Once at the plant, she carried out her responsibilities as an inspector for the Army Air Force. Harris's main duty was to make sure that Republic Aviation's part checkers did their job correctly as they sorted through newly received P-47 fighter components. Another aspect of the job was to pull parts out of trucks or bins on a random basis and compare them to blueprints. If several pieces of equipment lined up with the blueprint, then the inspector moved on to the next truckload or bin of parts. If a part failed to line up with the blueprint or was broken, Harris returned it to the plant. The company did a good job, so the vast majority of parts passed muster.[27]

Mildred Harris spent most of her time in the Evansville plant with receiving. For six months or so she worked in shipping, the department responsible for mailing spare parts for the P-47 Thunderbolts to all areas of the world that required them. The outgoing packages were thoroughly waterproofed to protect them from potential damage and loaded onto boxcars to start their journey. Harris learned a lot about the art of stacking and distributing weight safely during her time with the Army Air Force.[28]

Anna McDevitt, Peggy Terry, and Virginia Burns performed basic munitions work. McDevitt, of Louisville, took a job at the nearby Charlestown bag plant, "making ammunition for my brothers to use." Peggy Terry of Paducah traveled to the Navy's shell-loading plant at Viola, where she operated a machine that loaded large projectiles with just the right amount of powder. Virginia Burns, of Springfield, like her brother Shelby, worked at Tube Turns, where she ran a little press that shaped 40-millimeter shell casings for four-barrel antiaircraft guns. One fateful day, Virginia lost two fingers on her left hand when it became caught in the press. Hospitalized, she recovered in due time and returned to Tube Turns.[29]

Women from Kentucky moved into a large number of occupations that were formerly the exclusive or nearly exclusive domain of men. Females not only took positions as riveters, welders, and shell makers; they also worked with other types of war materiel and in civilian posts normally associated with men. The Hub Tool Company of Lexington hired women early on to fashion precision tools for producing aircraft motors. The Irving Air Chute Company, also of Lexington, used female employees to make parachutes. Kathleen Stone of Louisville took a job as a draftsman in the Engineering Department of the Naval Ordnance

Plant, where she kept the electrical layouts up to date. Maude Christian, from Wyoming originally, came to Louisville and then got a job as a butcher at the Fort Knox commissary. Patsie Porter of Stearns, Kentucky, helped out her dad at Porter's Garage, holding down a job as a gas station attendant. Among other tasks, Patsie put piston rings in pistons and patches on the inner tubes of tires using a little electric vulcanizer. Several Lexington women did similar work, dispensing gasoline, putting air in tires and water in batteries, and changing oil. Women served as guards at the Avon Signal Depot, watching out for potential sabotage. Larry Smith, president of the Lexington Yellow Cab Company, declared that maintaining "the firm's high standard of operation" would have been impossible "without employing competent women to fill these vacancies." Smith stressed over and over again the great worth of his lady taxi drivers and announced that he was "more than pleased with the way women are carrying out their new duties."[30]

In Kentucky, black females constituted a far smaller pool of labor than did white males and white females. Even black male employees outnumbered black female employees by almost two to one just before official U.S. entry into World War II. In 1940, Kentucky companies and households employed just 26,000 black women, and most of them toiled in the personal services area. Domestic service alone (household maids) accounted for almost 20,000 of these jobs—or just less than 77 percent. Hotels, other lodging places, and restaurants hired much smaller numbers of black women. By comparison to white males, white females, and even black men, black women found themselves clustered in one low-paying area where the work was often demeaning. Vocational opportunities for African American women were decidedly limited in the commonwealth before the war.[31]

Once war came, black women became the very symbol of the old adage "Last hired, first fired." Only after the rapidly swelling economy sucked up all other readily available pools of labor did Kentucky companies engaged in war production deign to bring aboard black females. It really was not until 1943 that black women managed to secure much work in war plants. After that, African American females proved vulnerable to layoffs because they lacked seniority and because white-dominated American society demanded that they make way for returning servicemen.[32]

Black women greatly desired war work, but they had to wait. Belatedly, they made progress. From 1943 to 1945, black females obtained many war-related jobs. A trend developed wherein the women moved from domestic service to better-paying work on military airplanes and in the munitions realm. This development, in turn, allowed others like them to get household work. Black women found more work in both the war production and civilian sectors during the conflict.

Margaret Peyton Lutes Hayden, an African American Rosie, worked at Curtiss-Wright in Louisville from August 30, 1943, to 1945. Margaret enjoyed her job as a riveter. She liked using her hands and putting a plane together. Seeing the final product gratified her, as did the realization that she was making a difference in the war effort.[33]

Nova Hays Downs held three jobs during the war. This black woman lived in Leitchfield, the seat of Grayson County. Because Leitchfield "didn't have any factories or anyplace to work really," Nova traveled to Louisville. Unable to secure a defense job in the beginning, she worked at Capitol Cleaners during 1941–1942. From there, she switched to Beatty-Cummins, a firm that hired her to make 20-millimeter shells for the Navy. Her last wartime job was at Curtiss-Wright, cutting metal skin for C-46s and attaching it with rivets to the airplane body. Nova worked because her family needed more money than her husband, John, could make alone.[34]

Other black females from Kentucky who worked in one capacity or another during World War II included Everylee Ashby, Fannie Lane, and Elizabeth Lawson. Everylee Ashby took jobs at the Charlestown powder plant and Reynolds Metals Company. At Reynolds, she inserted tubes inside big guns. She enjoyed this task, she recalled, "'cause it had a rhythm to it." The pay was a plus, and she pointed out that all the employees "went to the same restroom." Fannie Lane worked at the bag plant near Charlestown, filling 1,300 bags a day. Elizabeth Lawson cared for her two young children during the war while performing part-time jobs as a cooking assistant and cleaner. Hearing about the Japanese strike on Pearl Harbor, Elizabeth thought immediately about her brother-in-law, who was in the Navy. She did not like to dwell on the grisly aspects of the war; instead, she just "stayed busy." Lawson wanted the United States to win the war quickly and "to bring those boys back home."[35]

Women of both races in Kentucky made economic gains during

World War II, although inequality and discrimination persisted. Entry into fields formerly reserved for men and the sheer number of new, available jobs were remarkable. Along with these jobs, of course, came good incomes and a sense of fulfillment from tasks well done. Just the same, women often encountered preexisting negative attitudes and unfair practices.

Statistics reveal a lot about the changing work environment. From 1940 to 1950, the number of white female employees in the state jumped from 122,947 to 180,372, an increase of 47 percent. The gain in employment over that decade was much greater than that from 1930 to 1940 and far above increases for earlier decades. The war greatly accelerated the process whereby white females expanded their numbers in the Kentucky workforce. Though not all of the 1950 jobs can be attributed to wartime beginnings, many were connected to that conflict one way or another. Unlike white women, black females actually lost about 90 jobs from 1940 to 1950, but that figure requires additional explanation. Since the total black female population decreased by a higher percentage during this time than the percentage decrease in jobs for black females, it can be argued that Kentucky's black females were actually slightly better off economically in 1950 than 1940. Moreover, the percentage of black women who were in domestic service fell dramatically, from 77 percent in 1940 to 54 percent in 1950. This decrease indicates a sustained movement of some black females from private household work to better jobs in other areas. The number of all women in manufacturing machinery positions (except electrical machinery) leaped from 231 in 1940 to 865 in 1950. An increase from 1,640 to 3,762 female workers was seen in the electrical machinery field over the same interval. Quantitative and qualitative progress occurred, though the benefits proved far greater for white women than black women.[36]

A daunting array of impediments did not prevent Kentucky females from achieving occupational and economic advancement. Women received about two-thirds of the pay that men got for doing the same types of manufacturing jobs. Western Union employed women to deliver telegrams in Lexington, but they received only "a commission for each message delivered" while messenger boys earned an hourly wage. The wage gave the boys more money than the commissions gave the women.

One Lexington woman who worked at a Standard Oil station remembered that female customers actually gave her a harder time than the male customers did. The women would stop by and ask for Joe. The female gas station attendant would reply, "Am I not as good as Joe?" And the answer was, "No, you're not." Patsie Porter reported that a lot of men who stopped at the filling station in Stearns stared at her "goggle-eyed"; they did not believe she could do the job. African American Nova Downs experienced sexual harassment at Beatty-Cummins. Her boss—she could not remember his name—asked her out on a date even though he knew she was married. Nova said no, so he put her on a harder job for about two weeks before returning her to her former position. This punishment made Nova mad, but she decided not to complain, and nothing else bad happened to her. Even before the war ended, when production cutbacks started, women lost their jobs at twice the rate of men. Although Nova Downs and many others remained in the workforce, a large number of women who wished to keep their positions forfeited them to returning soldiers. As these examples show, women were able to overcome some of the obstacles they faced during and after the war, but by no means all of them. Given gender bias and other relevant adverse circumstances, Rosie's accomplishments appear even more impressive.[37]

Kentucky male and female workers joined labor unions in record numbers during World War II. The United Automobile Workers–American Federation of Labor (UAW-AFL) represented 3,300 workers at Ken-Rad, 90 percent of them females. The United Automobile Workers–Congress of Industrial Organizations (UAW-CIO) stood behind the 1,275 men at the Ford plant in Louisville. Aluminum workers at the Reynolds Metals Company belonged to the AFL, as did the employees at thirteen Louisville-area lumber mills. The CIO maintained a presence at Jeffboat in Jeffersonville, Indiana. Close to 20,000 coal miners in mountainous eastern Kentucky had cast their lot with the United Mine Workers (UMW) and revered UMW head John L. Lewis. Kentucky was home to a significant and growing union movement, one that wartime circumstances buoyed.[38]

National union leaders, such as the AFL's William Green and UMW chief Lewis, entered into an agreement with the federal government shortly after Pearl Harbor, and this agreement helped shape the experience of Kentucky unionists throughout the war. Driven by a complex mix of patriotism and pragmatism, Green, Lewis, and the others agreed that their members would not go out on strike for the duration of the war. Acceptance of the no-strike pledge came with the understanding that management would not engage in lockouts and that the Roosevelt administration still fully endorsed collective bargaining rights under the National Labor Relations Act. Additionally, labor received an equal voice with management and the public on the newly created National War Labor Board (NWLB), a federal entity designed to settle labor-management disputes before they could disrupt war production. Union members in Kentucky did not quibble with the no-strike promise but expected fair collective bargaining practices when disagreements arose with the company as well as an even-handed approach from the National War Labor Board. Subsequent NWLB endorsement of the "maintenance of membership" principle, wherein a person who took a job with a firm under a union contract automatically became a union member, offered significant reassurance to unionists. In the end, NWLB sided with labor on some occasions and management on others.[39]

Kentucky unions generally adhered to the no-strike pledge. Union members provided a great deal of work, and few labor disturbances occurred. In 1942, union workers in the commonwealth performed $250 million in construction work alone, setting records for speedy completion of a variety of projects. Later years witnessed the same kind of effort. All told, strikes led to the loss of far less than 1 percent of all man-days of labor. DuPont reported that in all its war-related operations in the United States, which included the Louisville neoprene plant and the Charlestown smokeless powder plant, less than one-fiftieth of 1 percent of man-days were forfeited due to all causes combined. The great outpouring of jeeps, radio tubes, landing craft, synthetic rubber, smokeless powder, and much more from Kentucky attests to the reliability of union labor. Unionists showed up for work day after day, year after year, and performed their jobs well. Production was high and victory over the enemy achieved.[40]

Governor Keen Johnson appreciated the commitment of Kentucky workers to victory. Johnson let it be known over and over again that the workers of his state were doing a commendable job, even as he condemned anyone who might think about a walkout. In April 1943, Governor Johnson declared, "I delight in the fact that not since Pearl Harbor

Hitler had a problem—American labor! (Courtesy of the Hagley Museum and Library.)

has there been a serious strike in a Kentucky industry . . . engaged in war production."[41]

Kentucky, of course, experienced some strikes during the war despite the no-strike pledge; given human nature, strikes were all but inevitable. From time to time, union workers got fed up with inadequate wages or dangerous conditions or a combination of both. Other factors entered the equation as well. Strikes occasionally resulted from frustration and anger. Work stoppages took place in Kentucky in the tin, meat, aluminum, railroad, lumber, woodworking, airplane, electronics, radio, and coal mining industries from 1941 to 1945. Almost all were brief, unauthorized ventures that ended after workers asserted themselves and blew off some steam. Only the Ken-Rad seizure and the bituminous coal strike (discussed below) proved serious, though neither did any real damage to the national war production effort.

Examples of relatively small, short-lived strikes or similar labor disturbances can be found. Workers at the Louisville Tin & Stove Company left their jobs making powder containers for the Indiana Ordnance Works in October 1941. The workers returned on October 27, 1941, after a satisfactory agreement was reached with the company. A checkoff system, whereby the company subtracted union dues and other assessments from an employee's wages after said employee signed an authorization, replaced an earlier requirement mandating that 75 percent of all workers at the plant be union members. Additionally, union president Ernest Ford and recording secretary Sherman Bowling were rehired by the company after being discharged for supposedly taking off too much time from work to attend the annual state labor convention. These provisions proved sufficient for the men to resume their work. In another action, in early August 1942, about 130 meat cutters went on strike at Armour Creameries in Louisville, returned to work the next day, and struck again the day after that. The meat cutters' unhappiness stemmed from the matter of overtime pay. Armour Creameries characterized the work stoppage as an "outlaw wildcat" walkout and noted that the plant was back in operation by August 3. A dispute between the American Federation of Labor and the Congress of Industrial Organizations over which group should be the sole bargaining agent for workers at eleven Reynolds Metal Company plants led to the termination of sixty striking workers who backed the CIO. Reynolds officials claimed that the CIO men engaged in an "outlaw strike," while Secretary Edward H. Weyler of the Kentucky State Federation of Labor maintained that the existing contract between the AFL and Reynolds called for no strikes and permitted the discharge of striking workers who impaired war production. Weyler stressed, too, that AFL workers put in additional hours to make up for the CIO strikers, with the end result being that production had not "slackened." In March 1944, a Firestone Tire and Rubber Company subsidiary that had taken over operation of the Blue Grass Ordnance Depot axed fifty truck drivers who refused to load and unload their vehicles. Just the same, storage and distribution activities continued without a hiccup.[42]

A greater threat to war production materialized when the management and employees of the Ken-Rad Company could not agree on a range of issues. An impasse developed, centering on wage rates and the length of probation for new hires. With a strike in the offing, which would have had the effect of depriving the United States of desperately needed radio and radar capabilities, President Roosevelt ordered the U.S. Army to take over Ken-Rad and run its operations. The nation could not do without the various radio and radar sending and receiving tubes that Ken-Rad made, and no replacement supplier existed.[43]

The crisis arose largely because Ken-Rad owner Roy Burlew flatly rejected the National War Labor Board's determination that his workers receive wage increases retroactive to September 4, 1942. Burlew contended that the retroactive payments were so large that they would bankrupt the company. He refused to budge on the matter at all. The workers, fully aware of the NWLB ruling in their favor, grew more agitated as time went on and their wages did not go up. The workers decided to go on strike on April 14, 1944, if government intervention was not forthcoming. The Army seized the Ken-Rad plant at Owensboro just hours before the strike would have commenced. Burlew's stubbornness and fervent desire to cut costs led to an action that the War Department really did not want to take.[44]

The Army, aided by the Ken-Rad plant manager and by nonstriking Ken-Rad employees, directed operations at the Owensboro facility from April 14, 1944, to May 25, 1944. Keeping production up was imperative. Colonel Carroll Badeau saw to it that the output of various kinds of tubes remained high. Badeau's analysis of Ken-Rad operations revealed that interconnections between the Owensboro plant and other Ken-Rad plants in Bowling Green, Kentucky, and various out-of-state locations were such that the main plant could not operate without the feeder plants. The Army therefore took over all the Ken-Rad plants.

Burlew sued Badeau, as the War Department representative. The suit claimed Badeau had acted unlawfully to enforce an illegal NWLB order—an order that was not "fair and equitable" under section 7 of the War Labor Disputes Act. Burlew also alleged that his due-process rights had been violated and requested an end to Army possession of the Ken-Rad plant. After a hearing, a judge of the U.S. District Court for the Western District of Kentucky ruled that the takeover was legal and the complaint was dismissed. Burlew did not appeal the decision.[45]

Having had his day in court, Burlew turned belatedly to additional negotiations with the United Automobile Workers–American Federation of Labor Local 783, the representative of the Ken-Rad workers. This time the two parties reached a consensus. They agreed on retroactive pay for Ken-Rad workers still on the job and for Ken-Rad workers who had left for military service, but denied such pay to Ken-Rad workers who had gone on to other civilian jobs sometime before the date of the final settlement. Probationary pay, sometimes called learners' pay, was set at eighty-four days rather than the forty-five days mandated by the National War Labor Board. These concessions saved Burlew a considerable amount of money, though the UAW-AFL became the accepted bargaining agent not only for the main plant but for the feeder plants as well. That result would not have taken place outside of this accord. Thus, both parties got something of value.

Both management and labor, of course, had executed an end-run around the original National War Labor Board decision. Since the NWLB was supreme when it came to arbitration between employers and employees, it might have scuttled the new arrangements. Instead, the board ratified the Burlew–UAW-AFL agreement because the principle of collective bargaining was more important than strict enforcement of every detail of every order it made.

From the perspective of Roosevelt and the War Department, the most important result of the Ken-Rad episode was that the production of radio tubes and radar tubes at Ken-Rad continued at a good clip under Army control. When the Army left, turning back Ken-Rad to Burlew and top management in late May 1944, output was actually higher than it had been before the specter of a strike and the Army's intervention. Wartime operations at Ken-Rad continued for as long as they were necessary and the servicemen had their radios and radar equipment.[46]

The bituminous coal strike of 1943 constituted the single greatest exception to labor's no-strike pledge in Kentucky and can be properly understood only with reference to formidable unionist John L. Lewis. Facing dangerous conditions in and around the mines, along with a decline in overall purchasing power as the war progressed, America's coal miners demanded more money. Ahead of UMW president Lewis in the beginning, miners exhibited a militancy surpassing that of any other type of worker. In jeopardy of being left behind by the rank and file, Lewis bolted to the front and took charge. Now spearheading the drive for increased pay, Lewis ran headlong into entrenched opposition from the government and coal company operators. A massive coal strike resulted, sweeping through Alabama, Kentucky, Indiana, Ohio, and Pennsylvania. After much hue and cry over the space of many tension-filled months, Lewis's United Mine Workers emerged victorious. Kentucky miners and those in other states received greater compensation, although it came with plenty of adverse public opinion and burgeoning political opposition in the U.S. Congress. An antiunion trend, which was already under way, accelerated greatly.

Lewis's role in the bituminous coal strike was crucial. Though surprised initially by the advanced position taken by members of the UMW, he reasserted his leadership in short order and, as was his nature, took the bull by the horns. Alone among major American labor leaders, Lewis deliberately flouted government authority by authorizing a major strike in the midst of a war that had to be won. It was as if he took a sledgehammer to the no-strike promise and shattered it along its fault lines.

John Llewellyn Lewis came to the coal fields honestly. Lewis's parents traveled to the United States from Welsh mining towns. John himself abandoned public school in the seventh grade, going to work in a coal mine at age fifteen. Joining the United Mine Workers of America, he rose through the ranks over decades to attain the presidency in 1920. A strong, pugnacious man with huge, bushy eyebrows, a bulldog chin, and a uniquely compelling oratorical style, Lewis led the UMW for the next four decades. Along the way, he became chief founder of the Congress of Industrial Organizations. In 1942, he took the UMW out of the CIO. By 1943, Lewis challenged President Franklin D. Roosevelt, the National War Labor Board, and coal company executives by ordering his beloved miners out on strike several times. He gave these commands despite the fact that war was on and coal was indispensable to the American war machine. Motivated by the sure and certain knowledge that his men were having a hard time supporting their families and that they were losing more ground with each passing day, and by his own ambition and lust for power, Lewis could not accept the status quo.[47]

In truth, the miners' case was a good one. Explosions, cave-ins, and other grim happenings claimed the lives of Kentucky miners during each year of the war. Prices of goods they bought rose faster than their wages; what money the miners possessed did not go as far as it once had, and it bought fewer and fewer goods with each passing year. As long as their incomes stayed the same, their pain and anxiety increased. These facts caused the miners to advocate strong action against their enemies.

Lewis gave the miners what they wanted. He strenuously argued their case before the government, asserting that they were on the side of justice. He demanded a $2-per-day wage increase for the men. He would not give in, no matter what forces stood against him. His sincerity, forcefulness, even his stridency endeared him to the UMW rank and file. They loved him, and he loved them.[48]

The National War Labor Board was a big problem. The chief federal agency for arbitration of labor-management disputes, it ruled against the UMW request for a $2-per-day hike in the pay of each miner. Earlier, the NWLB had adopted the "Little Steel" formula. It permitted workers up to a 15 percent increase in wages from January 1, 1941, forward. Unfortunately, the UMW had already secured a 16 percent increase within this time frame but before the "Little Steel" formula went into effect or even was announced. The NWLB interpretation was that the UMW already had its pay boost and was therefore ineligible for another one. This decision aroused the particular ire of Lewis, who, as historian David M. Kennedy noted, "sought as much to loosen the

NWLB's stranglehold over labor relations as to put more money in miners' pockets." If the NWLB decision was not overturned, the UMW workers were stuck with their existing wage rate for the rest of the war.[49] The bituminous coal strike commenced in late April 1943. It continued into early May with flare-ups in June, late October, and early November. Across the nation, over 500,000 coal miners struck. The *Courier-Journal* estimated that, by June 4, 46,000 of 60,000 coal miners in Kentucky were refusing to work. A mix of UMW-endorsed strikes and unauthorized walkouts took place. Millions of tons of coal that might have been dug for the war effort remained in the ground. As coal stocks diminished, some steel production was lost and railroads reduced their hours of operation. The bituminous coal strike endangered the output of war goods and the distribution of these items.[50]

President Roosevelt and Governor Johnson chastised Lewis and to a lesser extent the UMW. Roosevelt said the strike hurt national defense and was not conducive to victory over the Axis. He declared that the UMW could not be allowed to operate outside NWLB machinery and procedures. If the miners got an increase in wages over and above 15 percent, then the "Little Steel" formula would be undermined and unions in other industries might strike. Such a wage hike would also increase the risk of inflation, something FDR did not want at all. For his part, Governor Johnson found the strike repugnant, insisting that no labor group had the right to impair the war effort. He promised Roosevelt full cooperation in efforts to deal with the labor disruption. Unlike governors in some other states, Johnson resisted any impulse to remove the occupational deferments of striking miners so that they could be punished by the draft. If Washington wanted to do that, fine, but Johnson would leave that decision to Selective Service officials in the nation's capital.[51]

The Kentucky press blasted John L. Lewis. The *Courier-Journal* of Louisville asserted that Lewis pursued "high-handed" tactics and that the walkout was "indefensible" at a time when the nation depended upon a growing fuel supply to whip the Axis. The *Herald-Leader* of Lexington stressed that the Lewis strikes "have done untold damage." The *Harlan Daily Enterprise* estimated that the bituminous coal strikes "called by John L. Lewis . . . cost 35,000,000 tons of coal output." This estimate was too high—perhaps half as much output was forfeited—and experts agreed that the loss did not appreciably affect the overall war effort, but the very thought of it made many folks see red. Lewis's name was mud. Kentucky papers viewed John L. Lewis with varying degrees of hostility, contempt, and disgust.[52]

In the end, Lewis withstood the flak and he won. Even though Roosevelt took over the mines on more than one occasion, directing Secretary of the Interior Harold Ickes and the U.S. Army to run them and insure coal production, these interventions did not last long. It was difficult to see how government officials and soldiers could run the mines effectively over the long duration without so many experienced miners. Additionally, Roosevelt was sympathetic to labor in general, and labor was part of his ruling coalition, even if he disagreed with the UMW in this specific instance. So Roosevelt eventually gave in to the miners. Ickes was instructed to cut a deal with Lewis, and it was consummated. The agreement of November 3, 1943, granted the UMW portal-to-portal pay, reduced the workers' lunch period by fifteen minutes in return for fifteen more minutes of work and the wages that went with that effort, and made other, more minor adjustments. Technically the deal did not violate the "Little Steel" formula because it did not raise the hourly wage of the workers: instead they just "worked" longer; but it did result in about a $2

United Mine Workers President John L. Lewis leaves the White House after speaking with President Roosevelt in 1939. Lewis steered the UMW to victory during the 1943 coal strike. (Courtesy of the Library of Congress.)

increase in income for workers each day. Everyone knew that Lewis and the UMW defeated Roosevelt and the NWLB. Given the narrow margin of Republican Simeon Willis's victory over Democrat J. Lyter Donaldson in the November 1943 gubernatorial race in Kentucky, voter retaliation against the "favoritism" FDR supposedly showed Lewis may well have been one of several factors in turning the tide against Donaldson.[53]

Other results of the bituminous coal strike are clearer. The American people, including Kentuckians, disliked Lewis heartily before the strike. They hated him after it. One poll revealed that 87 percent of all respondents had an "unfavorable opinion" of him a little over a month into the strike. About the only people who supported Lewis were the miners who gained from his actions. It should also be noted that the venom directed toward Lewis by the general public and like-minded politicians exacerbated the antiunion trend already visible in the nation. An angry U.S. Congress, upset by such a serious strike in the midst of a just war and by other strikes that Lewis's success stimulated, struck back at big labor with a vengeance, passing antilabor laws and other measures that threw the whole American union movement on the defensive at the very moment when it reached its greatest height. What was good for Lewis and the UMW was not necessarily good for the entire union movement. Corporatist arrangements formulated at this point and afterward gave big business much greater clout then big labor. If Lewis calculated that this was going to happen anyway and he might as well do what he could for himself and his miners, then he made a wise, though cynical, choice. If, however, he believed equality between labor and business in the important agencies of the federal government was still attainable, he miscalculated. One suspects that the former view won out in his mind.[54]

Labor sustained one heavy blow after another from the time of the bituminous coal strike through passage of the Taft-Hartley Act in 1947, leaving it clearly subordinate to big business and without the hopes it once nurtured for equality through a tripartite arrangement of the federal government, unions, and corporations. With labor's great march forward during the New Deal and the early World War II period, a few intellectuals and some labor leaders opined that big labor would overtake big business as the greatest power within America's political economy. With 30 percent of the workforce unionized, dues payments at an all-time high,

Secretary of the Interior Harold Ickes (left) and "Brain Truster" Tommy Corcoran leaving the White House after a conference with President Roosevelt in 1938. Later, Ickes would joust with Lewis during the 1943 coal strike. (Courtesy of the Library of Congress.)

and Roosevelt administration support, a new day seemed about to dawn. This kind of thinking turned out to be wildly premature. It downplayed the traditional American attachment to managerial capitalism, powerful connections between business owners and politicians in Congress, and the intrinsic conservatism of the vast majority of the American people. When John L. Lewis violated the no-strike pledge, he gave encouragement to powerful forces determined to check labor's advance and reverse it.

Backed by a large part of the public, Congress retaliated against Lewis, the UMW, indeed the entire American labor movement. The Smith-Connally Act of June 1943 permitted the president to take over any war plant or industry that would not go along with rulings of the National War Labor Board. Another provision stated that a union must announce a strike before undertaking it and wait thirty days before beginning the strike. Union political contributions to participants in federal elections were banned. The Employment Act of 1946 mandated only that the federal government try to maximize employment through planning, deficit spending, and other means; Congress deleted original prolabor language calling for an explicit pledge of government to achieve full employment. The Taft-Hartley Act of 1947 banned the closed shop, where a company was required to hire only union members. Taft-Hartley also called for an eighty-day cooling-off period before a strike affecting national security commenced and reinstated the ban on union political contributions to candidates in federal elections. A particularly noxious part of the law forbade foremen and certain kinds of supervisors from receiving labor protections. By this device, the intermediary positions between management and labor were turned in management's direction. Congressional statute during the late-war and immediate postwar period pushed labor back and left it shackled.[55]

Corporate management cheered these legislative developments and helped make them happen. Management's strategy included lobbying Congress for advantage and making successful efforts to pigeonhole trade unions. Too often, unions settled for institutional security and benefits for their members while losing sight of broader social objectives. Winning a wage increase here and there for the workers, a company pension plan, or perhaps a new, improved grievance procedure, labor leaders forgot about the fact that the lion's share of workers in the United States remained unorganized or that the maldistribution of income remained great. Larger matters of industrial democracy and social justice received too little attention after 1945.

Business-dominated corporatism prevailed in the United States. Equality between big business and big labor proved to be a pipe dream. President Harry Truman established a tripartite organization in late 1945 called the National Wage Stabilization Board (NWSB). Truman intended to transfer arbitration and other functions of the NWLB to the new agency, but the NWSB never gained any traction. With the demise of the Office of Price Administration and the end of price controls in 1946, tripartite efforts ground almost to a halt and amounted to little in the end. Big business, working with public opinion averse to unionism and with a conservative Congress, denied labor an equal place in American corporatism. Managers of oligopolistic corporations retained control over product, design, place and pace of production, prices, and other crucial matters. In northern Europe, particularly in Britain and Scandinavia during the 1960s, unions helped negotiate national wage and price controls designed to redistribute income or fight inflation. They had a powerful political presence that went along with real economic power. They fought for social justice. In the United States, unions were weaker, and these kinds of advances either did not happen or never got very far.[56]

In retrospect, industrial labor contributed just as much to victory over the Axis as management. Kentucky factory workers built cargo planes, fighter aircraft, landing ships, jeeps, and many other kinds of war-related goods. White male workers within the commonwealth received little acknowledgment then and historians have paid scant attention to them since, but they performed far more war work than any other group while passing on their knowledge to inexperienced operatives. Ralph the Riveter preceded Rosie and supported her. The addition of Kentucky women to the wartime labor force supplied a valuable extra increment of help, thereby shortening the war and saving lives. Society embraced "Rosie" during the war, but resisted her postwar vocational aspirations. Union leaders, with the notable exception of John L. Lewis, kept the no-strike pledge they gave to the government. Authorized and unauthorized strikes in Kentucky were infrequent and not too costly, though the Bluegrass State probably experienced more labor unrest than the average state because of its heavy involvement with the coal industry and the UMW-inspired bituminous coal strike. Antiunionism in Kentucky, like that in America as a whole, grew tremendously in response to the 1943 coal strike, resulting in the passage of antilabor laws. Big labor as a whole suffered, exiting the war less powerful than it would have been without the big coal shutdown and additional wartime labor disturbances of 1944–1945. Since then, the business-government partnership and the military-industrial complex have only grown stronger, while the labor union movement has waned and is currently struggling just to remain relevant.

3

Food for Freedom

Food, like managerial skill, industrial labor, and weapons, was indispensable to the overall American war effort. Victory over the Axis could not be obtained without enough to eat for American soldiers, civilians, and the Allies generally. Kentucky farmers produced a considerable amount of corn, beef, garden vegetables, fruits, tobacco, and other products for the Allied cause. Enhanced demand for crops and livestock boosted farm prices, which led to the long-awaited return of prosperity for the commonwealth's farmers. With so many men away in the armed services and women increasingly working in war plants, a serious agricultural labor shortage developed by 1943, which might have derailed the burgeoning war food supply program had farm owners not reacted so quickly and imaginatively to the problem. They found ways to get the help they needed from boys, old women, prisoners of war, and others, thus enabling them to reap the bounty of the land. More food per person was available for American troops and civilians during World War II than in World War I, while the British, the Russians, and other comrades in arms benefited significantly at certain points from American surpluses. Kentucky farmers contributed their share to achieve this impressive record, proving that they did as much as other groups to achieve wartime goals.

After World War I, Kentucky agriculture entered a deep slump. Without wartime European demand for American foodstuffs, overproduction reasserted itself. The price for Kentucky tobacco sank from 34 cents per pound in 1919 to 13 cents per pound in 1920. Corn, wheat, and hog prices also suffered. Low prices acted as a disincentive to the commonwealth's farmers, who cut the amount of land under cultivation only to find that prices and income remained low. Despite the much-ballyhooed prosperity of America in the Roaring Twenties, the agricultural community of Kentucky found itself mired in depression throughout this period, and it hurt.[1]

This regrettable state of affairs continued into the 1930s without abatement until President Franklin D. Roosevelt took over the White House and initiated the New Deal. Roosevelt insisted that only the federal government possessed the resources to end the Great Depression. He created big government in the United States to bring about economic and social improvement. The Agricultural Adjustment Administration (AAA) was a New Deal agency designed to attack farm problems. The AAA persuaded farmers to scale back the amount of crops and livestock in production in return for a price at or above the one set by the free market. Under the Tobacco Control Act of 1934, for instance, the tobacco farmer agreed to limit production of leaf and therefore received a parity price. If the market yielded a lower price per pound than parity, the federal government promised to make up the difference. Under this scheme, Kentucky tobacco growers cut their harvest by 28 percent in 1936, but their overall income rose by several million dollars. Likewise, the slaughter of 48,000 hogs resulted paradoxically in greater income for hog farmers. Progress, however, was not uniform. Bumper tobacco crops in 1937 and 1939 depressed tobacco prices and revenue. The average price for tobacco in 1939 stood at just 17 cents per pound, up only 4 cents per pound from the disastrous 1920 price. New Deal agricultural policy led to greater stability on the Kentucky farm and somewhat more money, but the overall situation was still relatively poor.[2]

European war altered the American farm equation fundamentally. President Roosevelt made it clear that American national security and such American values as freedom demanded a British victory over the Germans. To facilitate this outcome, the Roosevelt administration performed an about-face on national farm policy. Old efforts to reduce supply and boost prices gave way to a thoroughgoing emphasis on increased agricultural output and price control. After all, the growing U.S. Army and Navy required more food, as did the people of America's foremost ally, Great Britain. With American grain and meat, as well as American machines and guns, Britain might prevail over Germany without the sacrifice of American soldiers. American plenty, specifically greater and greater amounts of food directed to the proper places, became a key to U.S. preparation for war even if war itself should not materialize—as well as a possible means to skirt the conflict entirely.[3]

The U.S. Department of Agriculture (USDA), with an early assist from the Agriculture Department of the National Defense Advisory Commission (NDAC), ran the War Food Supply Program. The USDA had been concerned with levels of agricultural production since its inception in the late nineteenth century, and it certainly possessed the organizational capacity necessary to achieve the revised national goal of significantly higher food production accompanied by relatively stable prices. Secretary of Agriculture Claude Wickard and his subordinates immediately understood the strategic importance of food to British victory over the Nazis and therefore to the triumph of freedom over tyranny. The USDA quickly coined the slogan "Food for Freedom" as a way to communicate one of Roosevelt's central messages about the international conflict to the American people.[4]

As described earlier, President Roosevelt revived the National Defense Advisory Commission, an old World War I body, in late May 1940. Roosevelt stated that the NDAC would facilitate the flow of supplies and munitions to the U.S. armed forces. Though FDR's main objective was undoubtedly to extend an olive branch to big businessmen, who landed the most significant posts in the new agency and whose experience and connections were indispensable to military mobilization, he also recognized that the Army and Navy needed milk, bread, and beef. It followed that one of the seven NDAC commissioners, former Agricultural Adjustment Administrator Chester Davis, represented agriculture. Davis and Secretary Wickard were on the same team.[5]

The USDA and the NDAC worked together to augment production on farms across America. In 1940, Wickard and Davis became allies in the quest to save steel and other crucial raw materials for agriculture so that a decent stock of tractors, harvesting machines, sprayers, dusters, and other farm equipment would be available. The natural tendency of the generals, and to lesser extent industrialists, was to hog crucial materials without giving much thought to other interests vital to the overall preparedness program. Wickard and Davis fought to insure that farmers got an adequate amount of resources (such as metals and fertilizers) so that they were in a position to funnel foodstuffs not only to the servicemen but also to civilians and America's allies.[6]

As time passed, the USDA, the NDAC, and other federal agencies and authorities increasingly emphasized the "Food for Freedom " angle. Vice President Henry Wallace, formerly Secretary of Agriculture, proclaimed that America must be not only the arsenal of democracy but also the "larder" of democracy. Alben Barkley, Kentucky's senior senator as well as U.S. Senate Majority Leader, seconded Wallace. Barkley and others encouraged Kentucky farmers to increase crop production of many types in order to assist the American preparedness program. The notion was that increasing the amount of food available would boost the U.S. effort to overcome Axis aggression. The Agricultural Adjustment Administration urged all American farmers to grow more food so that surpluses could be sent to England, an approach in line with the Food for Freedom program. Shortly thereafter, Edward Stettinius Jr., head of the Office of Lend-Lease Administration, agreed with the AAA that the program must include American allies such as Britain and Russia.[7]

America entered 1941 with agricultural surpluses built during the Great Depression and a keen appreciation for Britain's role in the struggle against totalitarianism. With passage of the Lend-Lease Act in late March, the United States made a strenuous effort to transport foodstuffs to its embattled ally. R. M. Evans, a high-ranking official in the AAA, said, "Food from America is arriving in England in ever increasing amounts . . . and it is being used to the very best advantage." Evans quoted British Minister of Labour Ernest Bevin as saying that receiving enough additional American proteins—such as meat and eggs—would allow Britain "to increase production in our war factories 15 to 20 percent in thirty days." In 1941, lend-lease provided Britain with 29.1 percent of its food. It is no exaggeration to say that American foodstuffs dispelled British hunger and allowed Britain to concentrate more heavily on the production of arms and munitions.[8] Progress toward Allied victory surely occurred.

Formulation of annual U.S. agricultural production goals, of course, fell to the USDA. Contacts already existed between the Agriculture Department, officials from all of the states, and county extension agents. Experts of all kinds gave their input. Taking into account overall demand

National Defense Advisory Commission members Edward R. Stettinius Jr. (left) and Sidney Hillman talk outside the White House, May 1940. Stettinius went on to become Lend-Lease Administrator and ultimately U.S. Secretary of State. (Courtesy of the Library of Congress.)

for American food at home and abroad, along with potential expansion of American agriculture and limitations on available resources for machinery and other assets, production goal committees within the Department of Agriculture set targets for a host of significant crops and animals. Almost all of the targets called for higher output to meet war needs. The annual production goals for 1942 mandated that American farmers raise production of milk and burley tobacco by 7 percent, corn by 8 percent, chickens by 10 percent, eggs by 13 percent, hogs by 14 percent, and soybeans by a whopping 54 percent. The USDA asked for a 12 percent reduction in wheat production. The Agriculture Department clearly wanted more proteins and oils and must have believed that some resources devoted to growing wheat could better be used in other ways.[9]

Production goals changed over time. Revisions were based on altered circumstances, which might be related either to additional mouths to feed abroad as the Allies took enemy territory or to crop and livestock numbers at home. The variables were numerous and often hard to pin down. To cite just one example, when American hog production soared well beyond the target figure by mid-year 1943, authorities moved as quickly as they could to reduce hog numbers. Like every other agency concerned at some level with requirements, USDA ran into trouble with the military. The problem was that the armed forces could not or would not provide the Agriculture Department with a list of overall needs for various types of food, leaving the USDA guessing about total requirements. Nevertheless, goals were established for grains, dairy products, meats, fruits, and vegetables, and the total output of food for most constituencies was satisfactory or better. American servicemen, civilians at home, and Allied armies got what they needed or more.[10]

Kentucky responded well to the USDA's War Food Supply program, though differences between the Mountains, Bluegrass, Pennyrile, Western Coal Fields, and Purchase areas could be discerned. In general, state farmers worked hard to give the federal government what it wanted, and they succeeded. Amply motivated by the opportunity for profits after two decades of hardship and by love of country, they plowed their fields with renewed vigor, adding a few acres here and there, while giving every encouragement to farm animals to reproduce. Farmers throughout the commonwealth applied more nitrogen and potash to the soil to raise the yield per acre, and the acquisition of many more tractors during the war made an even bigger difference than the use of fertilizers. Farm production and farm income expanded nicely as the years passed.

On October 18, 1941, the Kentucky Agricultural Defense Board let it be known that Kentucky farmers strongly supported the USDA's Food for Freedom drive. State farmers were already hard at work, toiling diligently to expand the supply of dairy products and meats. Kentucky farmers expected to produce an additional 27,648,000 gallons of milk along with 122,544,000 eggs. They also anticipated the sale of 21,127,000 pounds of beef and veal beyond what they would have marketed under normal circumstances. Farmers knew that their cash receipts were about to rise and that they were helping the preparedness effort. Moreover, this burst of activity was just the beginning.[11]

During 1942 and 1943, the Department of Agriculture stressed certain foodstuffs even more than in 1941. The USDA constantly repeated the refrain for more milk, more eggs, more meat, and more garden vegetables. Civilians and allied troops depended upon proteins and the vitamins from green and yellow vegetables for the energy that allowed them to make weapons and fight enemies. Every effort had to be exerted to see that they got proper nutrition. Indeed, the USDA put out another slogan, shouting to the masses, "Food Will Win the War and Write the Peace." A Kroger store in Lexington put up a sign starkly announcing, "Meat Is a War Weapon."[12]

Farmers in every region of Kentucky involved themselves with the Food for Freedom endeavor, especially after the Japanese strike against Pearl Harbor transformed it into a "Food for Victory" struggle. Blessed with lots of flat land and fine soil, the Pennyrile and Bluegrass regions led the way. The Western Coal Field, Purchase, and Mountains regions followed, supplementing the agricultural output of the more favored areas. Kentucky alone possessed more good land than some European nations, and the state also boasted hundreds of thousands of farmers, many of them endowed with an entrepreneurial spirit. Much-needed additional capital for equipment and fertilizer came from the federal government, where the U.S. Commodity Credit Corporation loaned money to the commonwealth's farmers and Congress enhanced agricultural subsidies. A 1942 law resulted in farm prices hovering at 110 percent of parity. Given these advantages, Kentucky farmers surmounted such obstacles as the severe labor shortages of 1943 and 1944 on the way to record- or near-record-setting output levels for tobacco, cattle, hogs, and other goods. Granted that Kentucky could not hope to match the agricultural exploits of Iowa, California, Texas, or even North Carolina, farmers from the commonwealth performed their war jobs creditably and did raise more crops than such states as Tennessee, South Carolina, Florida, Alabama, and Louisiana.[13]

Characterized by level land, good soil, and comparatively large farms, the Pennyrile (located in south-central and part of western Kentucky) entered the preparedness and wartime periods well positioned to meet certain basic objectives of the U.S. War Food program. Commercial farms were the norm in this region, and area farmers enthusiastically expanded operations from 1940 to 1945, doing more than their share to feed civilians and soldiers. Corn, tobacco, small grains, and legume hays were the chief crops. The primary livestock included cattle for dairy and meat, along with hogs. All categories experienced growth at some point during World War II, while the total output and value of farm products in this region reached new heights by the end of the conflict.[14]

Agricultural production and results for Muhlenberg County proved rather typical of the Pennyrile during the war. Corn production in Muhlenberg County rose from 594,973 bushels in 1940 to 707,243 bushels in 1945, a jump of almost 19 percent. Given that the price of corn ratcheted upward, too, the value of the corn harvested soared from $399,922 in 1940 to $873,044 in 1945. Most of this corn went to feed livestock, only a small amount to people. Tobacco, including both burley and dark varieties, took second place in terms of value, behind only corn. Muhlenberg tobacco was worth just $176,638 in 1940, but the figure for 1945 stood at a princely $594,734. The production totals for 1940 and 1945 were 1,650,825 pounds and 2,287,438 pounds respectively. Notable increases also occurred for lespedeza hay, clover timothy hay, and alfalfa. In keeping with USDA priorities, the Muhlenberg soybean harvest more than quadrupled from 1940 to 1945, while sales of cattle and calves and hogs and pigs rose 86 percent and 63 percent respectively. Higher numbers of sheep, lambs, chickens, and chicken eggs were bought. The USDA demanded more feed grain, proteins, and oils, and Muhlenberg County rendered considerable assistance.[15]

The Bluegrass region covers the central part of Kentucky. Meadowlands here have rich, fertile soil, but some steep hills exist that are less productive, and there are even some cliffs. Large and small farms coexist. Burley tobacco, corn, hay, wheat, cattle, sheep, hogs, and poultry were the major farm products during World War II. Next to the Pennyrile, the Bluegrass possessed the best combination of terrain and soil for wartime agricultural purposes.[16]

Boyle and Fleming counties illustrate well enough the dynamics of the Bluegrass agricultural experience during a time of total war. Boyle County is situated in the Inner Bluegrass area, while Fleming County occupies a portion of the Outer Bluegrass. Statistics reveal that both counties served the Food for Freedom campaign with distinction. Not surprisingly, burley tobacco, corn, and cattle dominated in both places. Burley tobacco proved to be the single most valuable farm product by far. Burley alone accounted for 52 percent of the total value of all crops harvested in Boyle County in 1939; by 1944 that figure had increased to 65 percent. In Fleming County, the numbers for the same years were 58 percent and 69 percent respectively. Large amounts of corn and clover timothy hay were also grown in these counties to feed livestock. Cattle and hogs for consumption were raised in significant numbers. In 1944 alone, Boyle County cattlemen sold almost 10,000 cattle and calves, while the number in Fleming County passed 14,000. The total value of all crops and livestock sold in the two counties rose sharply, from $3.4 million in 1939 to $8.8 million in 1944.[17]

Bounded on the north by the Ohio River and partially enclosed by the Pennyrile, the Western Coal Fields are a place of hills and bottom lands. Soil on the uplands is poor and productivity low, but the soil on the bottoms can be exploited well by farmers, assuming they use proper draining methods. Small farms predominated here in 1939, and tobacco, corn, cattle, and hogs were the major farm products.[18]

Grayson County extends farthest east of all the Western Coal Field counties. Its topography consists of hills, the Rough and Nolin rivers, and numerous streams. When the European war broke out, Grayson County's top three crops were corn, lespedeza hay, and burley tobacco, in that order. Wartime circumstances, including prices, reshuffled the deck. The value of Grayson County burley tobacco increased eightfold from 1939 to 1944, skyrocketing from $106,968 to $847,888. By the time the war ended, burley receipts left lespedeza far behind and ran neck and neck with corn. The total value of crops harvested here jumped from less than $1 million to over $2.5 million from 1939 to 1944. The value of all livestock sold, cattle being most significant, rose from approximately $600,000 to more than $1.5 million over the same five-year span.[19]

The Jackson Purchase is located in the far western part of Kentucky. Like the Western Coal Fields, the soil is best along the waterways and lower elevations, while the soil of the upland areas is not as productive. Unlike the rest of Kentucky, the Purchase grew cotton on a regular basis, and the emphasis on tobacco was weaker than in the Bluegrass and Pennyrile.[20]

Fulton County is the most southwest county in the Jackson Purchase, with an extensive border on the Mississippi River. The value of cotton and cotton seed there amounted to over $600,000 in 1939, more than the worth of any other crop. Corn for grain was second, worth $419,500; tobacco was only $22,101. By 1945, the value of cotton alone reached more than $1 million, while corn actually passed cotton by with a slightly higher value. The reason for this change is that the number of acres devoted to cotton fell at the same time that the number of acres given over to corn rose. This adjustment, in turn, bore a relation to a greater need for corn (to feed meat animals) than for clothing. The trend toward less cotton and more corn prevailed in the United States generally as well as in Kentucky, and the USDA generally set increases in production of meat at a higher percentage than those for cotton. More evidence that Fulton County tailored its agricultural output to USDA goals and the nutritional needs of the troops can be found in a 153 percent increase in the number of bushels of sweet potatoes grown from 1939 to 1944. (The sweet potato, it should be noted, is often ranked as the most nutritious vegetable of all because of its complex carbohydrates, dietary fiber, protein, vitamins A and C, iron, and calcium.) Overall, the value of farm products in Fulton County advanced from about $1.5 million in 1940 to $3.4 million in 1945. Nontobacco counties, as well as tobacco counties, proved capable of making great headway during the war.[21]

The Mountains, the last major region of the state, are located in the far eastern portion of Kentucky. Given the extremely rough topography, thin soil, small farms, and lack of equipment, the difficulty of farming in this area was obvious. Nature handicapped farmers here, and the Mountains gave up less foodstuffs for the preparedness and war efforts than any region of the commonwealth. Just the same, some food was grown here for civilians and the military.[22]

Knox and Bell counties are situated in the southeastern part of Kentucky's Appalachian range. Taken together, they reveal the basic contours of the Mountains region's agricultural experience during the Food for Freedom campaign. The total value of farm products in Bell County actually declined by 2.8 percent between 1940 and 1945, from $416,874 to

$405,106. Knox County, by contrast, experienced a dramatic increase in the total value of crops and livestock sold, which escalated from $251,828 in 1939 to $628,473 in 1944. Though the aggregates in both counties depended heavily on corn for grain, certain kinds of hay, and white potatoes, the superior performance of Knox County derived mainly from the fact that its terrain is much less rugged than that of Bell. Although both counties are almost identical in land area, Knox had 64 percent of its acreage in farmland, compared to just 20 percent for Bell. Not all mountainous areas are the same, so production of foodstuffs varied widely across the Mountain counties. Nevertheless, the Mountains as a whole could not match the other regions of Kentucky when it came to total food output.[23]

As can be determined from these snapshots of various Kentucky regions and counties, the effect of the war on Kentucky agriculture was overwhelmingly, though not universally, positive. Kentucky farmers in every region benefited from higher prices for farm products generated by greater demand at home and abroad. Many farmers, though not all, responded to wartime stimuli by applying more machinery and fertilizer to existing acreage, increasing acreage under cultivation, or both. The number of tractors on all Kentucky farms rose from 11,927 on April 1, 1940, to 24,409 on January 1, 1945. Nitrogen-based fertilizers applied to Kentucky soil increased from 2,124 tons in 1940 to 6,435 tons in 1944, while the amount of potash went up from 3,347 tons to 8,689 tons over the same interval. Larger decreases in the weight of phosphoric acid spread over the land, however, meant that the total weight of all fertilizers employed from 1940 to 1945 actually fell. Yet the combination of a highly motivated labor force, new equipment such as tractors, and adequate amounts of fertilizer brought higher per acre yields for tobacco and some other crops. Demand for crops and livestock in general remained strong throughout these years, and so too did prices and farm income. Indeed, the income of all state farmers more than doubled from 1940 to 1945. The bottom line is that Kentucky farmers left the war much better off economically than when they entered it.[24]

Wartime reinforced tobacco's place as the undisputed king of Kentucky agriculture. In county after county, tobacco brought home more money to farmers during the conflict than any other single farm good, be it crop or animal. In some counties, like Fleming and Boyle, it will be recalled that burley tobacco proved more valuable than all other crops combined. In Carroll County, in northern Kentucky, 744 of the 833 farms raised tobacco as the primary or sole crop. Many other counties in the Pennyrile and Bluegrass regions compiled similarly impressive numbers. From 1941 to 1945, Kentucky ranked second among all the states in tobacco production, and it actually cut slightly into North Carolina's lead.[25]

One element in the tobacco equation of great significance remained the same during the war, while others changed. A lot of tobacco could still be grown on a relatively small piece of land, and the cash return could be sizable. The major difference of the wartime period was that government limits on acreage coupled with additional demand for the leaf boosted the price of burley tobacco from 16 cents per pound in 1939 to 45 cents per pound in 1943. Dark tobaccos averaged roughly a dime less per pound than burley. With the near trebling of prices and an increase in total tobacco land statewide, from 361,005 acres to 372,438 acres, the value of all tobacco harvested shot up from just over $50 million to $180 million during this four-year interval. Little wonder then that an unidentified letter writer to the *Carrollton (KY) News-Democrat* in 1944 waxed eloquently that tobacco would "pay off the mortgage, if there still is one, buy a used car or a new one after the war is over, purchase the winter's needs and maybe still be able to take a few war bonds on the side."[26]

Kentucky farmers were not the only people with a strong connection to tobacco. Smokers of all sorts craved their cigarettes. A 75 percent increase in consumption of cigarettes between 1939 and 1945 came from three principal sources: women, who were smoking in greater numbers than ever before, perhaps to reduce stress from war work or from the often-agonizing wait for loved ones to come home safe from the battlefield; teenagers, whose rate of smoking ticked upward, spurred in part by less supervision from parents who had been called into the armed services or who worked; and soldiers in Europe and Asia, who received millions and millions of free cigarettes. The military brass deemed it imperative to get GIs their smokes to maintain good morale. Only Coca-Cola, among all specialized products ingested by the soldiers, rivaled cigarettes in the affection it commanded from the generals. By the later part of the war,

Tobacco hung near Jackson, Kentucky, in late 1940. (Courtesy of the Library of Congress.)

C-rations and K-rations for the troops came with accessory packs containing cigarettes, and much of the tobacco in them came from the Bluegrass State. Each soldier got some type of meat, perhaps a vegetable or pasta or crackers, and a powdered drink along with nine cigarettes. Indeed, the fighting men smoked such popular brands as Camels, Chesterfields, Lucky Strikes, and Philip Morris, whereas civilians in Kentucky had to make do with off-brands such as Rameses or Pacayunes. Given demand from all sources, a cigarette shortage in the United States actually broke out by 1944–1945, which ended only after V-E Day.

Like cigarettes, chewing tobacco made its way overseas. Scott Tobacco Company of Bowling Green and other concerns shipped "tobacco twist"—a special type of chewing tobacco resembling short pieces of thin rope—to the South Pacific, where it was used to pay New Guineans and other islanders for services rendered to the U.S. military during the conflict. Tobacco twist proved to be so valuable that the U.S. government deemed it an "essential war industry."[27]

Hemp, a cash crop like tobacco, made a comeback of sorts during

World War II. At the encouragement of the U.S. government, some Kentucky farmers grew excited about the prospect of hemp production and profits. One expert, Professor E. J. Kinney of the University of Kentucky College of Agriculture, anticipated a $5 million annual income from hemp. Hopes ran high as *cannabis sativa* returned to Kentucky in a big way.[28]

During the early nineteenth century, hemp beat out every other crop in Kentucky as a moneymaker. In 1831, for example, exports from the Bluegrass State to other places amounted to $2,750,000, and hemp and hempen goods accounted for $750,000 of the total—more than tobacco, corn, or wheat. Eighteen factories employing 1,000 workers existed in Fayette County alone by 1838, transforming hemp fibers into rope and bagging. Though price fluctuated, the fibers often fetched $100 a ton or more. Hemp growers rightfully insisted that their crop was more lucrative than any other grown in the commonwealth.[29]

Hemp's decline took place during and after the Civil War. Jute replaced hemp as the material of choice for cotton bags in the South, and Manila abacà from Asia proved better than hemp for rope. Ships began using wire rigging rather than fiber and then were driven by steam and did not need any sail rope at all. The market for Kentucky hemp almost dried up.[30]

As World War II approached, very few Kentuckians still planted and harvested hemp. Federal regulation, such as the Marijuana Tax Act of 1937, hurt. Though hemp was not technically illegal to grow, it required the purchase of a license, and the red tape made the endeavor so burdensome that farmers were not willing to bother with it. In 1939, only four farms in Kentucky still grew hemp. Once a top cash crop, hemp had become a mere agricultural curiosity.[31]

This situation changed radically after the Japanese military captured the Philippine Islands and other parts of the Far East in the wake of the assault against Pearl Harbor. The United States found that it could no longer obtain Manila abacà and jute from that part of the world. The Agriculture Department, the Defense Plant Corporation, and the Commodity Credit Corporation (CCC) launched an extensive program to resurrect the old American hemp-for-fibers industry. The USDA publicized the great need for American rope, cordage, and bagging. The Defense Plant Corporation paid for construction of rope and bagging mills. The

CCC guaranteed farmers who undertook the challenge of growing hemp $8 per bushel for all recleaned seed, while the market generated a price of 30 cents per pound for fiber. Given these incentives, the Internal Revenue Service issued 8,000 permits to grow hemp, and a goodly portion of these went to Kentucky farmers.[32]

Kentucky played a key role in the federal hemp program. Bluegrass farmers grew hemp seed, which was then transported to Corn Belt states and planted in the soil there. Iowa, Wisconsin, Illinois, and Kansas were too far north for hemp plants to reach full maturity and bear seeds, but they possessed lots of space to cultivate immature plants and therefore the fiber needed to make up for the loss of Asian markets. While Kentuckians did grow some hemp fiber during the war, seed production was deemed more important. The U.S. government requested that Kentucky plant and harvest at least 36,000 acres of hemp for seed in 1942.[33]

Senator Albert B. "Happy" Chandler announced that as many as ten hemp-breaking mills might be erected in central and western Kentucky as part of the government hemp program. A plant for cleaning fiber appeared near Winchester, though nothing like the multitude of facilities Chandler suggested at the beginning were actually developed. The Winchester plant operated in 1943 and processed only one hemp crop before closing.[34]

Hemp activity in Kentucky was greatest in 1943 and 1944. Farmers grew hemp in central, western, and even eastern Kentucky. Turner Dunlap of Fayette County noted that the eight- or nine-foot-high hemp plants were cut down and left where they fell to rot. "So you rot the pith away from the outside surface," he said, "which makes the string. And it was an interesting process and a very difficult thing to do." G. H. McMurtrey of Henderson, Kentucky, said that the guaranteed federal price took "80 percent or more of the risk out of growing hemp seed." In 1943, McMurtrey's 243-acre farm averaged up to twenty bushels of hemp per acre. Farmers at Cope's Branch in Breathitt County threshed hemp in late November 1943. So it went. While the hemp plant and seeds never yielded $5 million a year in income, cash receipts for 1943 reached $3.4 million and in 1944 made almost $800,000.[35]

Once the United States recaptured the Philippines and other nearby areas in late 1944, it did not take long for the flow of manila and jute to resume. By 1945, the need for an American hemp program no longer existed and it was shut down. Without government financial support, Kentucky hemp growers abandoned the crop as they had once before, and hemp buildings were sold as war surplus.[36]

The U.S. hemp program proved to be expensive and in the end unnecessary. The government spent $30 million on the program, the return to Kentucky farmers did not meet initial expectations, and hemp surpluses built up in Uncle Sam's storehouses. Even so, the fruits of the program did provide insurance in case additional fiber was needed, and nobody could be certain in 1942–1943 that the war would end as soon as 1945. While the government synthetic rubber program—which also emerged out of the Japanese takeover of Far Eastern land and resources—proved wildly successful during the war and reaped immense benefits afterward, the federal hemp program turned out to be a short-lived, rather unsatisfying experiment.[37]

Kentucky corn, hay, wheat, and even commodities as seemingly insignificant as milkweed pods addressed additional requirements of the overall war effort. Corn, the top crop in Knox, Grayson, Muhlenberg, and a number of other counties, went mainly to feed livestock. Cattle, hogs, and chickens received this food to fatten them up for slaughter. Meat production therefore depended a good deal on corn production. Farmers also fed lespedeza hay to cattle and sheep. From 1940 to 1945, Muhlenberg County lespedeza production advanced from 7,684 tons to 16,244 tons. Wheat was raised largely for human consumption, being the key ingredient to make bread, pasta, and crackers. Wheat output for Muhlenberg County leaped from approximately 65,000 bushels in 1940 to 169,000 bushels in 1945. Even in Grayson County, where the soil was not as good as it was in Muhlenberg, wheat production over roughly the same span increased from 31,685 bushels to 52,124 bushels. Milkweed pods were desirable because fibers could be extracted from them and used to stuff mattresses and sleeping bags for military use.[38]

Victory gardens appeared in every part of Kentucky during the war. These gardens met the needs of Kentucky civilians for yellow, green, and leafy vegetables, nutritious foods that would not have been available without these small plots. Since the U.S. military and lend-lease took 35 percent of the most important canned vegetables in 1942 and over 50 percent of all commercially canned vegetables in 1943, the only way to make

The U.S. government urged all Americans who could to plant a victory garden. These vegetables and fruits were necessary for civilian consumption since a large amount of canned vegetables went overseas to help feed the troops. (Courtesy of the Library of Congress.)

up the difference was for farmers and nonfarm homeowners with a little extra land to devote the space to raising squash, broccoli, cucumbers, peas, tomatoes, kale, spinach, lettuce, and other edibles.[39]

In 1942, the Victory Garden program started to gain real momentum. At the urging of the USDA, the Office of War Information, and the Office of Civilian Defense, thousands of Kentuckians found a spot on the farm, the lawn, vacant lots, or other places; cleared away the grass; and buried seeds to grow vegetables and fruits. Food for good health, freedom, and victory were constant themes. The idea was to "beet the enemy."[40]

President Roosevelt created the War Food Administration (WFA) in 1943 to direct all activities concerned with food production and distribution. Though the WFA was designated as a subsidiary of the USDA, its chief reported directly to FDR rather than to Secretary Wickard. Chester Davis, formerly NDAC Agriculture Commissioner, headed the WFA for a short time, then was replaced by Marvin Jones. Wickard and Jones might have clashed, given the unusual chain of command, but the two developed a good relationship. The War Food Administration Victory Garden drive highlighted the accumulation of home vegetables to lessen demand for commercially grown vegetables. The burden on the transportation system could also be eased by local production of beans, peas, tomatoes, turnips, greens, and other vitamin-laden vegetables. Like most wartime agencies, the WFA got the job done.[41]

In Kentucky, the College of Agriculture and Home Economics at the University of Kentucky established a "Victory Home Food Production" program. The state program dovetailed nicely with the overarching national program. The Victory Home Food Production program stressed that every farm family have a victory garden and that farm families should raise at least 75 percent of their own food. An effort was made to reach as many farm families as possible through county meetings and thirty-three district conferences.[42]

Victory gardens soon dotted the Kentucky landscape. In Louisville, a six-acre victory garden took over a portion of the old Ohio Street municipal dump. The garden supplied fresh vegetables to families on relief, freeing up other food for use by soldiers. Clarence and Dean Whalen of Cynthiana, in Harrison County, raised a victory garden. Virgie Wells, a granddaughter, still recalls fondly "the good meals Grandma and my mother cooked from the garden." Other victory gardens materialized in Lexington, Owensboro, and Ashland. The list of places was endless. Kentuckians embraced victory gardens as a way to contribute to the civilian food supply and win the war. Besides, victory gardens became fashionable.[43]

In the end, the federal and state victory garden programs succeeded marvelously. Nationwide, up to 40 percent of U.S. vegetables came from victory gardens at the height of the effort. In Kentucky, by Thanksgiving Day 1943 farmers and nonfarmers managed to stockpile at least 1,242,924 gallons of brined vegetables and 2,846,764 pounds of dehydrated or dried fruits and vegetables, as well as 4,511,942 bushels of potatoes, root crops, and apples. These figures do not count other types of foodstuffs associated with the campaign. When these additional foods are taken into account, the amount of home-produced and -conserved food totaled more than 86 million quarts. Dean Thomas P. Cooper, the head of UK's College of Agriculture and Home Economics, summed up the results of the Kentucky program well: "This gigantic food reserve represents the united efforts of Kentucky . . . people in this time of great emergency. It shows what can be done when all forces cooperate. Farmers, county agencies, [government officials], civic groups and citizens did a magnificent job."[44]

Kentucky livestock, like crops, provided the home front, soldiers, and American allies with food essential to achievement of victory. Cattle were most important. Hogs, sheep, and chickens contributed as well. The USDA War Food Supply campaign repeatedly promoted meat as an excellent source of protein and overall nutritional value for soldiers. Meat gave the troops energy to defeat the foes of democracy and the opponents of basic human rights.

In Kentucky, Hereford and Angus cattle had gained popularity before the 1930s. These stout, muscular breeds were raised for their meat. Their numbers continued to grow during the war, given the high demand for various cuts of beef. Some Kentucky meat went into the rations of the GIs.[45]

Dairy cows roamed Kentucky, too. They gave milk to farmers, who sold it to wholesalers, retailers, and the military. Milk contained protein for muscle growth and repair, calcium for bones and teeth, and potassium for healthy cell function.

Cattle production increased significantly in Kentucky during the war,

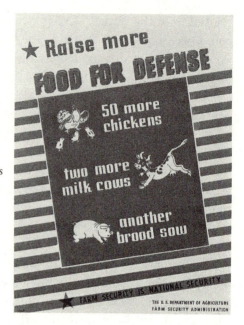

"Raise more food for defense." Increased food production became a major theme of the war years, since civilians, American fighters, and the Allies needed meat and other nutritious foods. (Courtesy of the Library of Congress.)

and so did sales. In Bracken County, in the north-central part of the state, 3,460 calves and cattle were sold in 1939; but in 1944 that number reached 6,375. The value of all cattle and calves in Bracken County more than doubled over the same years. In Muhlenberg County, the number of cattle and calves sold stood at 3,751 in 1940; yet by 1945 the total was almost 7,000. The value in the earlier year for all cattle and calves was $284,836; in the latter year, $699,111. Even Bell County, which experienced a decline in the overall value of farm products during the war—a rare occurrence—witnessed a small increase in the number of cattle and calves sold during the first half of the 1940s. County after county after county racked up favorable statistics. Kentucky cattlemen experienced terrific improvement in their cash receipts as the war years passed.[46]

Bill Goodman, from the Elizabethtown area in Hardin County, worked with his father on the family farm for the decade and a half before World War II began. Bill got his training as a cattleman while he was just a kid. He remembers the high cattle prices and prosperity of the war years, though he did go off to the U.S. Marines for a spell. A romantic, Bill chooses not to focus on the ultimate fate of his animals or even the bottom line. Watching young calves bolt through the fields, "worrying their mothers ragged," has always been his favorite part of the business.[47]

Hogs, sheep, and chickens augmented the wartime meat supply. The number of pigs and hogs sold in Fulton, Boyle, and Knox counties, for instance, swelled from 33,233 in 1939 to 43,560 in 1944. While the number of sheep purchased by buyers from the same three counties was up by a smaller amount than hogs, lamb and mutton helped diversify the diet of soldiers and civilians alike. Moreover, Kentucky agreed to supply U.S. Army Air Force pilots with the lamb pelts they needed to insulate trousers, jackets, boots, mittens, and helmets for high-altitude flights. These pelts provided great warmth to the flyers, an absolute necessity since temperatures at a height of 25,000 feet frequently hit 20 to 30 degrees below zero. As for chickens, the number of chickens in Kentucky reached its apogee at over 14 million birds in 1944. The amount of chicken flesh and eggs consumed from this number of chickens simply boggles the mind. The worth of Kentucky livestock to the war effort, like Kentucky crops, was gigantic.[48]

"Food for Freedom" was more than simply a slogan; it illuminated a fundamental difference between the Axis powers and the Allied powers. The Axis, one U.S. government publication noted, utilized "starvation to beat conquered peoples into submission." Nazi Germany went furthest, killing Greeks by sheer indifference to their need for sustenance and working enslaved Slavs to death. It subjected the Jews to slow starvation and to death by poison-gas chambers disguised as showers. By contrast, the Allies built, "with food, new power to throw against the Axis" while making friends by feeding liberated peoples. The distinction between the Allied side and the Axis side, between what was right and what was wrong, could hardly have been drawn any sharper.[49]

Roy F. Hendrickson, deputy director of the United Nations Relief and Rehabilitation Administration, put it well. "American food is one of the most powerful resources on our side in this global struggle. On all fronts, on every ocean and every continent, American food is being employed as a major element in the grand strategy of the United Nations. American food helped Britain hang on through the dark autumn of 1940. American food helped the Red Army turn the tide at Stalingrad. American food was at El Alamein, at Casablanca and at Sicily. These great battles were easier and cheaper in lives because we brought food with us. The enemy had taken it away." Hendrickson also noted that every nation retrieved from Germany (and he might well have added Japan) put a greater responsibility on the United States to provide sustenance to the multitudes until they could get back on their feet. American food made a major difference in triumph over the Axis, though it can never be quantified exactly.[50]

On a lighter note, Americans were seen by Europeans and Asians as a people of plenty. The British, who had it better in the end than the Germans, Japanese, and many other nationalities, marveled at the American GIs arriving in their nation. "We had never seen anything like it," wrote one commentator. "Massive, well-fed men marching sloppily through our streets with enormous bottoms waggling." U.S. soldiers gave away Hershey chocolates and sticks of chewing gum to British children. They talked of representative government and the Bill of Rights, but for many of the people the Americans met, their lifestyle "seemed mainly to consist of enormous amounts to eat." America's war, unlike that anywhere else, was at least partly about the renewal of prosperity and reaffirmation of the blessings of abundance. No wonder at all that Governor Keen Johnson, Governor Simeon Willis, and other state and national officials praised Kentucky farmers for their many contributions to the larder of democracy.[51]

A grave threat to the U.S. War Food Supply Program materialized by 1943, threatening to derail the vast enterprise just as it really began to hum. Given the military draft, the pull of higher-paying jobs in domestic war plants, and the demand for larger and larger amounts of foodstuffs, a serious shortage of agricultural workers struck many states, including Kentucky. The labor shortfall imperiled the federal Food for Freedom effort, and it called for a quick solution. Horace Cleveland, farm placement supervisor for the U.S. Employment Service (USES), speaking before a meeting of the Kentucky Horticultural Society, confessed that "we don't have the answer" to the farm labor problem, and "as far as I know no one has, but if we work together we can find that answer."[52]

Government officials like Cleveland, farmers throughout Kentucky, and their organizations devoted great attention to the situation. They beat the bushes, ferreting out every conceivable source of farm labor, be it large or small. Bluegrass politicians helped, too. Before the war concluded, farmers in the state relied on military deferments, rejects for military service, females of every age, high school boys, industrial workers, migrants, convicts, and Axis prisoners of war to bring in crops before they rotted.

In alliance with the USES, the War Manpower Commission made clear to everyone that the lack of agricultural help had to be addressed. On March 6, 1943, the WMC ordered "local draft boards . . . to keep farm workers in deferred classifications—even if the quotas for the armed forces cannot be met." Governor Johnson's plea to the U.S. Selective Service for liberalization of Kentucky farm deferments, particularly for tobacco farmers, had already been favorably received. A point had been reached where the unfolding farm crisis took priority over military service. The U.S. Army was big enough and strong enough already, whereas the acute nature of the Kentucky labor situation required immediate action. Exemptions from military service for reasons of necessity or health (4-Fs) retained a core agricultural labor force for Kentucky, with no further erosion allowed.[53]

The Woman's Land Army supplied much-needed additional labor to Kentucky farmers. Thousands, perhaps tens of thousands, of Kentucky women replaced able-bodied men taken by the draft in the fields. Farm agent John W. Irvine reported in August 1944 that many females of the Land Army helped bring in crops and did other farm work in Greenup County. "There was no other way to get the farm work done," he said, "with nearby war plants taking most of the men."[54]

An inspirational story out of this same place, Greenup County, bears repeating. County Agent Irvine could not find any men to thresh some local wheat. Four women joined him to do the chore. One was eighty-year-old Mrs. C. Sparks, who picked up heavy wheat bundles and threw them on the feeder's table as Irvine fed them into the thresher. Sparks's example shows how so many people joined together to help win the war.[55]

Authorities called high school boys and girls, industrial workers, migrants, and convicts into agricultural service. Paducah junior and senior high school students, with an average of C or higher in their classes and the permission of their parents, were excused from classes to pick strawberries in the spring of 1943. The boys and girls were encouraged to work with USES, so that the agency could send the names of the youthful workers to the various schools to insure that they were not playing hooky. Students might work the whole strawberry season, thus escaping final exams, or return to classes if they felt the farm work was too taxing. H. L. Smith, superintendent of the Paducah Board of Education, stated, "We are doing our best to cooperate with the fruit growers of this section in working out their labor problem." Bourbon County junior and senior boys were also released from school to do war work. In the town of Paris, Hansley Mills employees left the textile factory to assist in the tobacco harvest. John H. Perry's Owen County agricultural estate brought in migrant workers from the island of Nassau to grow and harvest corn, cucumbers, cabbage, tomatoes, broccoli, and peppers. The state government suspended a law decreeing that prison convicts serve at least half of their sentences up to ten years' time. If these convicts were first offenders jailed for relatively minor offenses, State Commissioner of Welfare W. A. Frost received the power to parole them to do farm work. Hundreds of parolees, perhaps thousands, took advantage of this option and contributed to the available pool of agricultural labor. The bodies available to do farm work multiplied.[56]

Of all the new sources of farm labor, surely the most unusual and interesting were the Axis prisoners of war. The appearance of so many POWs in Kentucky alarmed the public at first, but the farmers soon jumped on the opportunity to put these men to work. The vast majority of them were Germans, who had been captured in places like North Africa and shipped to the United States for safekeeping. Once the Office of the Provost Marshal General—the War Department agency in charge of the national POW program—decided to shift its policy from merely containing the captives to actively working them, Kentucky farmers met the requirements to get them and POWs harvested many varieties of crops.[57]

Of the 10,000 German POWs in Kentucky, at least 3,000 performed agricultural labor around branch camps, which were offshoots of the base camps located at Fort Knox, Camp Breckinridge, and Camp Campbell. Henry County farmers acquired German prisoner-workers from the Eminence, Kentucky, branch camp. Since POWs cost the farmers only $3.20 for an eight-hour day, compared to $7.50 for a local worker, prisoners were bargains despite their inexperience. The Eminence POWs harvested tobacco, brought in corn, baled hay, scattered grain, filled silos, and even dug ditches. All told, Eminence POWs contributed 6,843 man-days of labor to the local economy during September-October 1944. Events unfolded in a similar way at the Maysville branch camp. John Dixon Perrine, only nine years old at the time, recalled that the 300 Germans in the Limestone Park stockade drew spectators. "People would drive by just to see them. They were a curiosity and didn't cause a lot of problems." POWs from the Maysville installation put in 4,170 man-days in the fall of 1944, cutting, hanging, and drying tobacco. In Owensboro, POWs harvested wheat, strawberries, apples, hemp, and—most of all—tobacco.[58]

Some bumps arose along the way. Because the U.S. government followed the terms of the 1929 Geneva Convention, which mandated humane treatment of prisoners, a number of Americans felt that the German captives were being coddled. Kentucky labor unions complained that POW labor depressed wage rates and kept jobs away from Americans, including returning veterans. These charges proved baseless, as the War Manpower Commission always made sure that insufficient civilian help was available in a certain area before permitting POWs to work. Kentucky farmers understood only too well that they needed Germans precisely because Americans were not around.[59]

Farmers acknowledged the significant aid the POWs gave them. POWs were largely responsible for saving the 1944 tobacco crop in Henry County, which was valued at $3,090,000—up from $2,800,000 the year before. Indeed, prisoners of war helped in many central Kentucky locations to get the $125,000,000 burley crop in the barns before it suffered damage. S. Headley Shouse, a Fayette County employer, noted that "you couldn't expect these prisoners to go down the rows suckering tobacco like veteran farmhands, but they are doing alright." Kentucky tobacco farmers and those who grew grain and fruits owed the ex–German soldiers a lot.[60]

Kentuckians reacted favorably to the POWs. They came to like these fellows, and many POWs developed a good relationship with the farmers. The German prisoners of war worked hard enough and well enough and they resembled clean-cut, handsome American boys—except it should not be forgotten that a few possessed souls corrupted by Nazi political and racial doctrines.[61]

Statistics reveal the magnitude of Kentucky farm production during World War II and tell us about the compensation level for Kentucky farmers. From 1939 to 1945, tobacco growers in the state produced about 3,000 million pounds of tobacco. Output of wheat doubled from 1940 to 1945. Soybeans harvested for the beans rose by 246 percent over the same period. Although corn production fell slightly during the course of the war, its value in 1944 was almost $35 million more than in 1940 because of the higher price per bushel. Cattlemen witnessed the dollar value of their cattle and calves expand from $42 million in 1940 to $80 million in 1944. Dairymen sold about 300 million pounds more milk in 1945 than they did in 1940. The total value of all crops and livestock in the possession of Kentucky farmers increased from $242 million in 1940 to $523 million in 1945. Farm earnings more than doubled from 1940 to 1945, starting at $145 million, ending at $392 million. While total agricultural output in the commonwealth increased appreciably during World War II, farm income rose even faster. Kentucky farmers met the basic wartime objectives set by the USDA, earning a king's ransom in the process.[62]

The American War Food Supply Program was undoubtedly a success, though a few caveats must be voiced. Kentucky farmers and those in other states grew an enormous amount of food for the U.S. military, civilians, the Allies, and some of the neediest people around the world. The war was won. Yet the program was not without its flaws. Prices for farm goods of many types became excessive, which hurt the government anti-inflation program while transferring tremendous wealth from consumers to farmers. The price of burley tobacco in Kentucky, to cite just one example, ballooned by 181 percent from 1939 to 1945. This kind of return to farmers, when industrial workers were generally limited to a 15 percent gain in wages, was also patently unfair. Another imperfection resulted from the misallocation of scarce resources to hogs, sweet corn, and hemp while soybeans, milk, and eggs should have received even greater emphasis. A plausible case can be constructed that farmers in Kentucky and the other states could, with a few basic adjustments, have generated even more food than they did, and that world hunger and starvation in the latter stages of the war and immediate postwar period might then have been diminished even further. The weakness in this argument is that President Roosevelt and his advisers always ranked military triumph above social concerns. Unconditional surrender of the German and Japanese military forces and establishment of progressive governments in both nations took priority over feeding all the hungry peoples of the world.[63]

Like Kentucky industrial workers, Kentucky farmers put their muscles, sinew, and sweat into the national quest to vanquish the foes of freedom, and the final result was positive. Aided by modern science and technology, in the form of chemical fertilizers and tractors with internal-combustion engines, farmers of the commonwealth raised a huge amount of food, which helped satisfy the caloric and nutritional needs of American civilians, the U.S. military, Allied armies, and some—though not all—liberated peoples. In the middle of this unprecedented food drive, a labor crunch brought up the ghastly specter of rotting crops and reduced production. Farm leaders and farm owners responded by employing white male farmers released from military service, women, and more exotic types of labor to prevent nature's bounty from going to waste during the last critical harvest seasons of the war. Instead, Kentucky meats, vegetables, fruits, and cigarettes flowed to American, British, Russian, and Chinese soldiers, who used them to defeat German and Japanese totalitarianism. In this way, country farmers and city gardeners of Kentucky contributed to the preservation of Allied forces and the noble ideas for which they fought.

4

Rationing, Price Controls, and the Black Market

Though production for the military took precedence inside Kentucky during World War II, other economic and institutional developments of the period deserve attention. Reconfiguration of the national economy to achieve wartime goals, as we have seen, required the establishment of new federal agencies such as the War Production Board (WPB) and the Office of Price Administration (OPA). The OPA's fight against inflation led to greater regulation, and some Kentuckians resisted the new rules. Distribution of scarce goods became more equitable and prices were restrained, but an extensive black market came into being. Vast expenditures on the part of the U.S. government to finance the war effort were only made possible by increases in taxation and borrowing. Kentuckians complained about higher taxes but purchased war bonds enthusiastically. The Allies—ultimately well fortified with tanks, ships, planes, and food provided by a stronger American state—ultimately compelled German and Japanese surrender with comparatively little sacrifice required of Kentuckians at home. Indeed, wartime spending generated recovery from the Great Depression, and Kentuckians faced greatly enhanced economic prospects after the attainment of victory.

Before the twentieth century, America's central government was small and unobtrusive. The state, which can be defined as a political community possessing its own territory and the ability to make laws, consisted of relatively few organs and a correspondingly small number of workers. As defined by the Constitution, the structure of government included three branches—the executive, the legislative, and the judicial. Checks and balances within the fundamental law prevented any one branch from taking over another, and no one person—not even the chief executive—could become a tyrant. Liberty was safeguarded by the division of power and by the Bill of Rights. Kentuckians expected the federal government to behave constructively without exceeding its constitutional bounds. Federal officials were to maintain law and order at home, distribute the mail, and defend the United States from its enemies. Little else should be attempted.

Like their counterparts in other states, Kentucky businessmen believed that the federal government should leave the economy alone. Any governmental intrusions into the economic realm bothered them, and regulatory agencies were anathema. Milton Hannibal Smith, president of the Louisville & Nashville Railroad, the most powerful corporation in the commonwealth, especially hated federal interference. One of the leading foes of the Interstate Commerce Commission in the country, Smith rejected the right of that agency to uphold "reasonable and just (railroad) rates" and reveled when it was humbled by the courts and by his colleagues.[1]

Much to the dismay of the various supporters of limited government, the Progressive movement of the early twentieth century embraced statism. The notion that the central government could help the disadvantaged, be they children hurt on the job or small businesses oppressed by large corporations, came into vogue. New laws and agencies appeared, which were intended to achieve goals such as a reduction in the use of child labor, establishment of the eight-hour day for individual workers, and curtailment of a host of corporate abuses. Yet the Progressive impulse eventually receded, and the Republican ascendancy of the 1920s insured a retreat toward small government and the old laissez-faire business philosophy.

Only the massive unemployment and suffering spawned by the Great Depression changed the basic relationship between the U.S. government and the American people. Democrat Franklin D. Roosevelt swept into power in 1932 when economic collapse convinced the American people that continued reliance on the free market amounted to folly. Roosevelt's great contribution to American state building was the creation of truly big government in the United States, capable of producing more bureaucratic goods and services than ever before in its history. So many alphabet-soup agencies appeared to fight economic collapse that it proved hard to keep track. They provided so much in the way of jobs, roads, bridges, dams, airports, electricity, labor supports, agricultural subsidies, and welfare checks that it dazzled some folks and shocked others. Nevertheless, big government was here to stay and took a leading role in the maintenance of national economic health through fiscal policy, monetary policy, and other types of regulation.[2]

Initially leery of an overgreat state, which might impinge upon their liberties, Kentuckians grew familiar with New Deal programs over time. The Social Security Act of 1935 brought them unemployment insurance, old-age pensions, and other kinds of welfare. The National Labor Relations Act granted unions the right to bargain collectively with management for higher wages and other benefits. The Tobacco Control Act generated additional revenue for tobacco farmers. The Tennessee Valley Authority (TVA) lit many Kentucky homes for the first time, and on it went. Kentuckians deemed these programs largely positive, though the New Deal state lacked a powerful central planning body, agencies often competed against one another, services were sometimes duplicated, and red tape abounded. As historian James Klotter makes clear, the greatest change wrought by FDR's New Deal for the commonwealth may well have been that the people came to accept big government as a beneficial force in their lives.[3]

The state expanded still further during World War II. The New Deal was consolidated, and the military sector of government swelled to vast proportions. The loss of a few New Deal agencies meant little or nothing compared to the growth experienced by the War Department, the Navy Department, the Army, and the Navy. Other bodies appeared, too. Public-private linkages became much more extensive. Older power centers lodged in the branches of the federal establishment persevered, while new power centers arose in the civilian and military sectors of the state. The clash of competing interests sometimes proved deafening. The complexity of the overall mix increased tremendously. A much bigger, somewhat more capable, though rather ill-coordinated federal colossus had now taken shape.[4]

Though the New Deal ended by 1940, many of President Roosevelt's agencies continued to operate well past the war. The TVA, the National Labor Relations Board, the Social Security Board, the Civil Aeronautics

Board, and the Securities and Exchange Commission are just some of the more prominent examples. With the return of a degree of national economic health by 1943, Congress phased out the Civilian Conservation Corps, the Works Progress Administration, and the National Youth Administration. Unemployment was almost gone, so they were no longer needed. A solid New Deal core remained.[5]

Preparedness and war dictated that the size of the military establishment balloon. In 1942, the War Department moved from its old quarters in a hodgepodge of government and private buildings to the Pentagon, an impressive new facility. The number of War Department and Navy Department employees rose dramatically. An Army that numbered just 200,000 troops in 1939 counted 8,300,000 by May of 1945. The Navy jumped from 160,000 officers and enlisted men on December 7, 1941, to 3,380,000 at war's end.[6]

Because of a lack of expertise about industrial mobilization within the government, Roosevelt created a host of temporary, emergency bodies, staffed by prominent corporate executives, to redress the problem. The War Resources Board appeared, followed by the National Defense Advisory Commission, the Office of Production Management, and the War Production Board. Other agencies, such as the Office of Price Administration, accompanied them. These agencies and their corporate leaders connected the American state to the trade associations and business enterprises across the country that could fill War Department and Navy Department needs for all types of arms and munitions. A public-private matrix of federal agencies, military organizations, and companies took shape, and mobilization proceeded. Never a seamless process, the system did manage to get soldiers and sailors the arms and munitions they needed in time for battle.[7]

State building greatly affected Kentucky. Military and civil agencies of the federal government reached into the commonwealth, repeatedly touching its citizenry. The draft spirited away many Kentuckians. The defense buildup prior to Pearl Harbor, then war itself, led to the expansion of military sites within the Bluegrass State. War Production Board and Office of Price Administration rulings influenced the lives of every Kentuckian.

Kentuckians entered the armed services in one of two ways: either they volunteered or they were drafted. El Hannen Stacy, who lived near Jackson, Kentucky, joined the U.S. Army on July 16, 1940. Embarrassed by the mere thought that the government might have to force him to join the service, Stacy averted that outcome by willingly signing up for duty. After traveling to Fort Thomas, Kentucky, he left for Fort Jackson, South Carolina. There he received his initial field training. An infantryman, he was wounded in Europe and ultimately received an honorable discharge. Philip Ardery, like El Hannen Stacy, made a decision to serve long before Pearl Harbor. Ardery, of Paris, Kentucky, attended the University of Kentucky. He graduated with a Bachelor of Arts degree in 1935 along with a commission as second lieutenant, Infantry Reserve. After flight training in Lincoln, Nebraska, he flew heavy bombers over Germany during the war. Bombs from his B-24 Liberator took their toll on German industry, and Ardery returned home safely. William E. Barber of West Liberty joined the Marines because he wanted to serve with "the best." In late 1940 Congress and the War Department compelled other men to fight by implementing the first peacetime draft in U.S. history. Most Kentuckians found themselves in the military via the draft. Frank F. Mathias, of Carlisle, proved typical. Mathias was drafted in 1943, trained at Fort Benning, Georgia, and experienced combat in the Pacific at Bougainville and in the Philippine Islands. Altogether, 307,000 Kentuckians participated in the American military during the war. That figure constituted about 2 percent of the nation's military manpower. Most of these men survived the conflict, but about 8,000 unlucky souls perished and a smaller number became prisoners of war.[8]

Army facilities dotted the commonwealth; even the Navy was noticeable for those Kentuckians who lived along parts of the Ohio River. Fort Knox flourished. As we have seen, buildings at this base more than quadrupled from 1940 to 1943. The land area of the post doubled, stretching across three counties. Fort Campbell and Camp Breckinridge were constructed during 1942. Located on the Kentucky-Tennessee border south of Hopkinsville, Fort Campbell served as a training ground for various armored divisions of the U.S. Army. Camp Breckinridge, positioned between Morganfield and Henderson in the northern part of western Kentucky, housed and trained approximately 30,000 infantry recruits through February 1946. Richmond became home to the Blue Grass Ord-

nance Depot, which employed up to 3,800 workers to process ammunition and other supplies. The U.S. Army Signal Corps operation appeared
at Avon, just east of Lexington. Bowman Field in Louisville burgeoned,
adding an Army Air Corps training field. The Kentucky Ordnance Works
in Paducah was yet another large military depot, this one in far western
Kentucky. Louisvillians and others who passed through Kentucky's major
metropolis glimpsed activity across the river at Jeffersonville, Indiana's
Howard Shipyards, which had been purchased by the Navy and made
landing craft. War-related activities were not hard to find.[9]

War Production Board decisions impacted Kentucky in significant
ways. After the American declaration of war against Japan, President
Roosevelt needed a stronger industrial mobilization agency. In January
1942, FDR replaced the Supply, Priorities, and Allocation Board–OPM
duo with the War Production Board. The WPB exercised "general responsibility" over the national economy. It set priorities. This power permitted the WPB a large measure of control over raw materials and finished
goods. Since the agency ultimately divided existing stores of steel, aluminum, and copper among claimants such as the Army, the Navy, the
Maritime Commission, and the Office of Lend-Lease Administration, it
indirectly determined the number of contractors and subcontractors each
agency used and the size of the respective arms and ammo orders. The
Army, for instance, could not exceed its share of critical materials and
therefore had to issue a limited, if large, number of contracts to firms big
and small in the various states. Kentucky businesses, like businesses across
the United States, were affected by this method of operation. The WPB's
authority over the civilian sector was just as profound. The Board stopped
production of nonessential civilian goods as a means to further industrial
conversion and military output. In 1942, it banned the production of passenger cars for the duration, forcing automobile plants such as the Ford
operation in Louisville to make army jeeps or tanks. Refrigerators, other
household appliances, and lawn mowers could not be made. Some 400
items composed the list of off-limit items. By July 1, 1942, 29 percent of
the prewar production of consumer durable goods had been ended. Kentucky companies and the Kentucky people had never seen anything quite
like this before.[10]

Though Kentuckians could not get around War Production Board actions, Office of Price Administration regulations proved even more pervasive and irritating. President Roosevelt had never forgotten the damaging inflation of World War I. He would not let that sort of thing happen under his watch. Thus, he created the Office of Price Administration in August 1941, and it became an independent agency in January 1942. The OPA's job was to keep the inflation rate down so that the general price level did not undermine wartime economic performance. To accomplish its mission, the OPA administered the federal rationing program and set price and wage ceilings. Most Kentuckians accepted OPA regulations as a part of the sacrifice needed to win the war. A sizable minority resented the OPA's telling them that they could not buy more than the prescribed amount of certain products when they had extra money in their pockets for the first time since before the Great Depression. Sellers complained about maximum prices and workers about wage limits. An extensive black market for rationed goods took shape in the commonwealth, reflecting public discontent.[11]

Federal regulation of the free market was a no-brainer. During war, demand for essential goods often exceeds supply, and prices rise. Sometimes prices can increase dramatically. Under these circumstances, when the free market is in operation, wealthier people snap up scarce products whereas poorer people cannot afford them. Eventually the market will distribute available goods, but the end result is unsatisfactory in the midst of a conflict. The working class, precisely the same folks who make up the bulk of the military and the majority of workers in weapons plants, lose out, with disastrous effects on morale. Simply put, this is an untenable position from which to proceed when victory over an enemy is your goal. Moreover, high inflation decreases overall civilian purchasing power while it increases the debt of the central government. It follows that a free market must sometimes be put aside during wartime; more government control over the national economy becomes an absolute necessity. This imperative led to the establishment of temporary, ends-oriented agencies like the OPA and from there to the equitable but circumscribed distribution of scarce goods to American consumers and the erection of price and wage controls.[12]

Rationing began only a month or so after American entry into the war. In January 1942, tires were rationed to save scarce rubber for military

"Share the meat." Rationing of meat for stores and restaurants had already begun by 1942. (Courtesy of the Library of Congress.)

purposes. By December 1, 1942, gasoline, coffee, and coal oil joined rubber on the OPA list. Other rationed goods included meat, sugar, butter, shoes, and canned foods. Office of Price Administration chief Leon Henderson, an economist and a stalwart New Dealer, vowed to keep inflation in check and to fairly apportion goods that were short.[13]

Rationing alone, even when coupled with taxation, would not keep prices at bay. As prices began to creep up, the OPA moved forward with price controls. Its General Maximum Price Regulation of April 1942 set price ceilings for merchants at the highest price they had charged for goods during the previous month. These prices held for the rest of the war, despite any and all criticism. Roosevelt helped out when he issued his "hold the line" order on prices and wages in April 1943.[14]

Wage controls materialized, too. In July 1942, the National War Labor Board (NWLB) decreed that hourly wage increases were permissible if they had not exceeded 15 percent in the period from January 1, 1941, to May 1942. Furthermore, the maximum wage increase for any worker could not total more than that 15 percent over the remaining part of the war. OPA worked hard to uphold the NWLB ruling, and with a full set of controls in place inflation slowed. The consumer price index showed an increase of approximately 25 percent from 1939 to 1943, but in the last two years of the war the rise amounted to only 4 percent.[15]

The Office of Price Administration achieved its great goals. It tamed inflation while it spread out available goods rather evenly. Henderson and his successors had considerable resources at their disposal to get the job done. Over 63,000 paid workers and some 235,000 volunteers staffed the Washington, DC, headquarters and regional and local offices. Literally thousands of local price and rationing boards conducted business. George H. Goodman served as Kentucky director of the OPA. As of November 8, 1942, 136 ration boards operated in cities and towns across the Bluegrass State, dealing with tire rationing, price ceilings of various types, and other matters. OPA price executive Robert D. Haun, a University of Kentucky accounting professor, explained that his particular group acted "to determine the propriety of prices set by merchants and pass upon appeals for revisions in the price schedules at the retail level." Haun emphasized that "the people of this state understand the need for price control and the merchants themselves want to co-operate." He did acknowledge some "inclination to disregard the law" but made it clear that a sizable majority of Kentuckians supported the OPA's program.[16]

Professor Haun's pronouncement about public and business compliance with OPA regulations was more or less true. Most Kentucky consumers, approximately 75 to 80 percent, abided by federal price ceilings. A smaller percentage of businesses, though still a majority, respected them. Still, a surprisingly large number of people and firms opted to participate in the black market. The situation in Kentucky proved particularly egregious when it came to gasoline, used cars, and whiskey.[17]

A black market is a place where scarce goods are bought and sold secretly. After the Japanese attacked Pearl Harbor, the United States found itself cut off from sources of supply in the Far East. Goods such as natural rubber could not be imported. War also dictated a shift from civilian consumption to military production, which resulted in other shortages.

By December 1942, in addition to rubber, shortages of meat, fats, oils, dairy products, and canned foods were seen. The WPB and the OPA implemented home-front rationing and price controls to conserve scarce goods and to maintain price stability. Military demand continued to escalate, intensifying the shortages at home. Consumers had jobs and more income than before but could not get all the goods they wanted. A significant minority resorted to the black market, paying sellers a higher price than normal to obtain desirable goods.[18]

In many cases, hoarding preceded black-market activity. Buying up as much of a good as possible before it went on the OPA ration list was not illegal but certainly could be classified as unethical. Occurrences of this type in Kentucky were not infrequent. A good example occurred in Owensboro, where customers stormed grocery stores just before meat rationing was scheduled to go into effect on March 28, 1943. The buyers left shelves almost bare. When rationing officially commenced two days later, one grocer reported, "I couldn't even give you enough meat for a 10-cent hamburger." A restaurant operator lamented, "If we don't get more meat we'll either have to serve all-vegetable meals or close our doors." Meat availability in Owensboro did improve later that week and over the next month, but spot shortages plagued Kentucky for the rest of the war and even for a short interval after the war. Gas hoarding and sugar hoarding caused concerns, too, and several other items were hoarded at least occasionally.[19]

Kentuckians routinely violated price controls, though one would think that the patriotic nature of World War II might well have mitigated against such behavior. Thousands permitted greed or circumstances to get the better of them. John W. Lewis of Hiram, in Harlan County, sold a used truck at more than the OPA ceiling price. Lewis admitted his guilt, settling the case by paying a fine of $29.49. The Lexington district office of the OPA learned that Allen Hall of Flemingsburg also received an over-ceiling price for his old vehicle. Hall made the case go away by coughing up $51.68 to the U.S. Treasury. A. F. Blanton of Ashland, a trucker, unloaded 4,561 bushels of yellow and white corn at seven cents a bushel above the maximum price. Blanton paid $319.39 to resolve the matter. Several individuals acknowledged buying gasoline from a Stanford service station without using the legally required ration coupons. Even children were aware of rule-breaking. Eileen Wooton Sandlin Ingram remembers that her grandmother, Laura Gay York, "occasionally sent my mother hose or lard from Buckhorn to Frankfort—this was a black market thing." Other violations were never discovered at all. A rather large number of Kentuckians embraced the notion that cheating was acceptable under certain conditions, though it should be noted again that the majority frowned upon such rationalization.[20]

Wrongdoing by Kentucky businessmen proved more serious than that perpetrated by other individuals. Companies, owners, and managers broke federal law with seeming impunity. They employed different dodges along the way. Stores routinely charged over-ceiling prices. Upgrades, wherein a low-quality product was assigned a price reserved for a high-quality product, became a common practice. Tie-ins, which involved the sale of goods at the established ceiling price provided that buyers also purchase some other good that they may not want, happened just as often. Counterfeited gas ration coupons appeared in vast numbers. An automobile ring and whiskey scams attracted the notice of the OPA, the Federal Bureau of Investigation, and local police forces. In a time of war, where sacrifice and good conduct might have been expected from Kentucky business to achieve victory over a determined enemy, a disturbing amount of crooked activity transpired.[21]

Business violations of OPA price ceilings happened all over the state. No region was exempt, while the transgressions themselves ranged from small and seemingly insignificant to gigantic. Bates & Moore of Darfork, in eastern Kentucky, sold various types of food at above ceiling prices. The price panel of the Hazard war price and rationing board agreed that Bates & Moore should be assessed treble damages for breaking the law. Even so, the company's fine amounted to all of $25. Art Rott, a Covington grocer, did not keep proper records concerning rationed commodities and overdrew his ration bank account. The OPA ruled that Rott could not sell any type of rationed good for thirty days. After that, he had to follow the rules or his next punishment would be more severe. While these infractions may seem trivial, grocers across Kentucky were implicated time and time again in schemes to overcharge customers or with failure to follow OPA regulations. R. H. Raibert, assistant secretary of the Kentucky Retail Food Dealers' Association, conceded that "in many cases patrons offered and . . . storekeepers accepted higher than ceiling prices for scarce commodities." Certainly storekeepers also fixed prices at unlawfully high levels and compelled customers to pay these rates. In central Kentucky, turkey producers got 39 cents a pound for their birds when the ceiling was set at 35 cents per pound. An audit revealed that Georgetown grocer L. C. Kemper's sugar inventory was 4,133 pounds short. OPA's Lexington office forced bicycle and toy dealers to refund the difference between ceiling prices and what was actually charged to buyers. In western Kentucky, Clete W. Youngblood, a Paducah merchant, sold many electric irons at over-ceiling prices. The OPA hauled Youngblood in front of a federal district court judge, who fined him $1,000 and gave him a suspended jail sentence of six months.[22]

When Kentucky OPA director George Goodman heard Raibert's statement about grocers taking illegal sums of money for foodstuffs, he reacted in a predictable manner. Goodman acknowledged that this sort of thing happened, "but we don't know who the people are. If Mr. Raibert knows who they are, he should tell us." Goodman and hundreds of his subordinates across the state fought an uphill battle against criminal activity large and small. If the sudden rush of lawbreaking by individuals and small businesses was not bad enough, organized crime and big business made it far worse.[23]

The black market in gasoline reached epic proportions. In 1944, black-market gasoline transactions within the United States totaled approximately 2.5 million gallons of gas a day. In December of that year, federal verification centers collected almost 2 million counterfeit gas coupons. With so much money to be made selling gasoline illegally, the appearance of crime syndicates should not have surprised anyone.[24]

Perhaps the largest single operation of this kind followed the Atlantic and Pacific coasts, penetrating into the interior of the nation by way of the Mississippi River. According to the Office of Price Administration, this organization of gasoline crooks amassed $1 billion of profit each and every month from the sale of counterfeit gas coupons. Organized crime furnished skilled counterfeiters, who found it simpler to fake gas coupons than federal reserve notes. In some cases, the crooks stole the kind of paper that was used to make gas coupons and imitated the real coupons so effectively that it became nearly impossible to detect them. Other fraudulent coupons, of course, lacked the quality of the best and could be spotted.[25]

Kentucky played a part in the far-flung counterfeit gas coupon scam. Although counterfeiting was most extensive in the big cities of the East and West coasts, counterfeit gas coupons circulated in far western Kentucky river towns such as Hickman, Columbus, and Wickliffe. Phony gasoline coupons manufactured by the mob passed to wholesalers, who in turn distributed them to gas station dealers and individuals. Transgressors understood fully that they broke the law but excused themselves by voicing their opinion that the supply of gasoline for military and civilian uses was sufficient; that being the case, they hurt nobody by dispensing gas illegally.[26]

Kentucky OPA director Goodman underscored the selfish, fallacious thinking at play here. Gasoline itself was not short, he pointed out. Gasoline was rationed "on a mileage basis to save rubber," whose scarcity nobody disputed. OPA officials in Kentucky worked hard to enforce gas rationing, warning anyone who violated the regulations that they subjected themselves to fines and/or imprisonment. Consumers needed their ration books to purchase gasoline, and gas retailers were obliged to register their supply—and any additional supplies—with the local ration board. In December 1944, the sheer volume of counterfeiting became great enough that the OPA moved away from spot checks of gas ration coupons to examination of all gas ration coupons accepted by dealers.[27]

Like the counterfeiting of gas ration coupons, the black market in used cars was substantial. After the War Production Board prohibited the manufacture of new cars, the demand for used cars increased dramatically. The OPA set price ceilings on different types of old cars to contain inflationary pressures. Under these conditions, the purchase of used cars at over-ceiling prices could not be stopped. Former OPA administrator Leon Henderson disclosed that the national black market in used cars amounted to "approximately a million cars a year, one fourth of the total annual turnover." Overcharges normally ran from $100 to $400 per vehicle.[28]

Some Kentuckians participated in the automobile black market. John W. Lewis of Hiram and Allen Hall of Flemingsburg exchanged their old trucks for more money than the OPA allowed, although they did not get away with it. Daniel Boone Razor Jr. of Mount Sterling recalls that the black market was a big thing, especially when it came to newer cars, which fetched premium prices on the street. A thirty-one-person used-car ring, which included Kentuckians as well as some people from southern Illinois and Detroit, Michigan, acquired used cars, which they then sold at higher than ceiling prices. This operation involved all of Kentucky, and the autos changed hands in a variety of locales across the country. Unlawful behavior related to used-car transactions was not uncommon in the Bluegrass State during the war.[29]

Whiskey entered the Kentucky black market after the government ordered production of beverage spirits stopped in October 1942. Supposedly the distillers possessed enough whiskey on hand to last for five years, but unforeseen, increased consumption of that liquor nearly exhausted the stock by mid-1944. Both the demand and the high price for whiskey encouraged misbehavior by large distillers, retailers, and moonshiners. As with the case of the automobile black market, most Kentuckians refused to become involved with the liquor black market, but offenders received lots of adverse publicity.[30]

U.S. Representative Andrew Jackson May (D-Kentucky) grew concerned about the whiskey situation. May's investigation revealed that large distilleries in the Bluegrass State were buying up small distilleries at "fabulous and fictitious prices." He concluded that these mergers took place so that the big distillers, already oligopolists, could grab an even larger piece of the overall market. What is more, the big distilleries snapped up barrel after barrel of aged whiskey stored in the small distilleries, which was subsequently sold at over-ceiling prices or advertised as premium whiskey (at the high OPA price) when in reality it was lower quality. May pointed the finger at the "big four"—McKesson and Roberts, National Distillery, American Distillery, and Schenley—saying that each firm conducted itself in a predatory, illegal manner. The congressman characterized their activities as "a flagrant and inexcusable violation of the anti-inflation program." Whether May's charges were true or not, the OPA opened an investigation and threatened the Kentucky distillers with large fines unless they quickly conformed to government regulations.

Convictions were commonplace. The Lafayette Drug Company of Lexington, a retail concern, pled guilty to nine counts of selling distilled spirits—including whiskey—at prices which exceeded the ceiling by 25 percent to 75 percent. It paid a $500 fine. Other box stores, located in Lexington, Louisville, Owensboro, and elsewhere, also engaged in this type of illicit activity. Top OPA enforcement officer Marshall Clinard concluded that whiskey wholesalers and retailers in Kentucky (and other states) committed numerous "serious violations," including setting prices above OPA maximums, making bogus upgrades, and forcing tie-ins.[31]

Big money could be made through all types of alcohol sales. Even before 1944–1945, moonshining picked up in the eastern Kentucky mountains. The number of stills and the amount of "white lightning" produced and sold rose appreciably. Federal revenuer Hollis Gibson remembered the burst of illegal activity that occurred in Knott County, Perry County, and Breathitt County. When the military drafted revenuers, it only became harder to catch moonshiners. Kentucky lawmen seized just 1,484 stills from 1941 to 1945, making 4,624 arrests in the process. Over half a million gallons of whiskey were appropriated, which barely dented Kentucky moonshine operations. Most moonshiners escaped detection and prosecution, selling large quantities of booze inside and outside the mountains. Elizabeth Lawson, from Lexington, said her town "was full of bootleggers and moonshine in those days."[32]

Although the responsibilities of the Office of Price Administration were immense, it persevered. A large organization, the OPA still lacked the manpower it needed to fully enforce rationing and price controls. In 1944, fewer than fifty OPA enforcement officials worked in all of Kentucky. That figure translated into about one enforcer for every 40,000 Kentuckians. Little wonder that a significant number of Kentucky companies and individuals got away with wrongdoing. Of course, violations of OPA regulations occurred in every state. In Wyoming, the editor of a Laramie newspaper noted that "too many of us have connived to get steaks and extra gasoline." It was the same everywhere, which shows that selfishness never goes out of season, even when the best of causes is at stake. Criticism of the OPA in Kentucky declined after its regulations became more familiar and the inflation rate never got out of hand. While the Kentucky OPA sometimes resembled a sieve, it performed a thankless job with dedication and muddled through in the end.[33]

Inflation remained the bogeyman of the wartime economy. Though price increases were ultimately checked, President Roosevelt was always on alert. Roosevelt not only embraced rationing and various types of price controls, he wanted to pay for the war largely through increased taxation rather than by borrowing. Higher taxes would effectively stem inflation by relieving corporations and individuals of disposable income. They would have less money to invest and consume, and would then cut back on economic activity, thus preventing the economy from overheating. FDR saw inflation as the major economic threat to the war effort and fought hard against it.[34]

Congress, backed by public opinion, resisted Roosevelt's plan for wartime finance. Tax increases, even for the national good, proved unpopular, and an increasingly large body of Republicans and conservative Democrats in Congress stood in Roosevelt's way. After 1940, Congress refused to give FDR anything close to the tax revenue he sought. The president's revenue goals were slashed repeatedly. In 1944, for the first time in American history, Congress overrode a presidential veto of a revenue bill. This fight even cost Roosevelt Senate majority leader Alben Barkley (D-Kentucky), who resigned in the midst of the brouhaha.[35]

As it turned out, total wartime spending amounted to something over $300 billion, and taxation paid for a little less than half of that sum. The most significant change in the tax system for Kentuckians was that a larger percentage of citizens paid personal income taxes by the end of the war than before it. By 1945, most full-time workers paid income taxes, and the tax rate was up. Kentucky corporations paid a larger amount in taxes, too. Sin taxes, always a more palatable target for politicians than any other kind of tax, soared. The excise tax on distilled spirits alone jumped from $4 a gallon in 1941 to $9 a gallon in 1945, a 125 percent increase. If Roosevelt had had his way, tax collections by the federal government would have been even higher as a way to defuse inflation and minimize the national debt.[36]

Borrowing accounted for the rest of wartime spending, about 55 percent. The U.S. Treasury Department handled the program. Seven War Loan drives and one Victory Loan drive, launched between November 1942 and December 1945, garnered the federal government almost $157 billion in bond sales. About one-quarter of the money came from individuals, including both adults and children. Eleven-year-old Sylvia Clark

Seventh War Loan drive: "Now all together." Official U.S. Treasury poster from 1945, urging Americans to loan more money to the U.S. government for the purpose of bringing the fight to a successful conclusion. (Of the six men hoisting the U.S. flag at Iwo Jima, Kentuckian Franklin Sousley is the relatively tall, thin man second from the left.) (Courtesy of the Library of Congress.)

bought war stamps and bonds to support the war effort. "You saved a little," she recalled, "and your mother gave you some." The lion's share of bond purchases emanated from banks, savings and loan companies, insurance companies, and state and local governments. The Treasury used motion picture stars and comic strip characters (such as Batman, Superman, and Dick Tracy) to spur purchases. The people who bought various types of bonds and certificates eventually made back the principal plus 1.8 percent interest—a small return for the investor and a bargain for the government. Bond sales, like taxation, worked against inflation. While higher taxes decreased individual buying, reducing effective demand, bond purchases took money out of the economy over the short run. The result was a cooling effect on the national economy during the war years and a big burst of spending during the postwar era.[37]

Kentucky politicians heavily promoted the national bond campaign. Governor Keen Johnson and Highway Department chief J. Lyter Donaldson established a payroll deduction plan for state employees who were interested in buying war bonds. Donaldson suggested Highway Department workers "authorize 10 per cent of [their] monthly pay . . . [for] war bonds." On one occasion, Governor Johnson bet Nebraska governor Dwight Griswold that Kentucky would outperform Nebraska in the latest war bond drive. Johnson put up a purebred Kentucky lamb against a Nebraska hog. After Kentucky won, Griswold apparently reneged, but Johnson had the satisfaction of knowing that the commonwealth had put the Cornhusker State to shame.[38]

Kentucky contributed more than its fair share to the Treasury Department bond campaign. Desirous of getting "a crack" at Hitler and Hirohito, Kentuckians purchased a grand total of $687 million in Series E, F, and G savings bonds from 1941 to 1946. Kentucky ranked twenty-ninth out of the forty-eight existing states in E bond sales. It placed higher in the F and G category, coming in at nineteenth. This showing was quite respectable for a state with a relatively small population and little wealth. The patriotism of Kentuckians, of course, had never been in doubt.[39]

A monumental by-product of federal spending to win the war was the gradual return of economic health to the nation and to Kentucky. As British economist John Maynard Keynes had theorized, vast governmental spending had the effect of boosting the economy until it reached full employment. Keynes held that an economy in depression suffered from insufficient consumer spending and business investment. Only the government could step in and make up the difference. New Deal expenditures were too small to generate recovery from depression, but wartime spending reached the gigantic proportions necessary to push aggregate demand to an optimal level. Everyone who wanted a job eventually found one—either in the military, in war plants, or in the essential civilian sector. The unemployment level nationwide dropped from 17 percent in 1939, when the Fortune Magazine Roundtable characterized chronic joblessness as the foremost problem in the country, to just over 1 percent in 1944. American involvement in the worldwide conflict bore out Keynesian economics: the American people—including Kentuckians—enjoyed a higher standard of living by 1943 than they had in 1939, and the Great Depression was a thing of the past.[40]

Kentucky and the other states were fortunate. No significant Axis attack ever materialized. If the Germans or the Japanese had managed to strike the states on any kind of consistent, sustained basis, economic progress would have been impaired. As it turned out, this never happened, and the United States witnessed economic advance from 1940 to 1945 and beyond.

Indications of economic improvement within Kentucky were not hard to find. Indeed, statistic after statistic told the same story. So, too, did eyewitnesses to wartime events. Kentucky moved away from the Great Depression steadily, reached an extraordinarily high level of employment by 1943–1944, and achieved a measure of prosperity before the war concluded. After the war was over, Kentucky experienced even greater prosperity.

Unemployment in Kentucky declined significantly over a five-year stretch, until nearly everybody who wanted a job had one. In 1940, the U.S. unemployment rate stood at 14.4 percent, with Kentucky at 15.1 percent. The Depression still reigned. After that, as government spending kicked in, the Kentucky unemployment rate fell from 10.4 percent in 1941 to a low of 1.3 percent in 1944. Reflecting a decrease in government defense spending thereafter, the 1945 figure edged up to 2 percent. The Kentucky figures were excellent, but were just above the national average throughout this period.[41]

As one would expect, state unemployment outlays plunged as the job-less found positions. The Kentucky Unemployment Compensation Commission announced that unemployment relief payments reached a new monthly low of just $85,445 for February 1943. Only 9,817 Kentuckians received unemployment checks that month, a drop of 20.3 percent from January. These totals continued to go down until 1944.[42]

Kentuckians found work in numerous fields. Aside from the military, jobs became available with railroad, coal, and steel companies. Employment on the Louisville & Nashville Railroad, for instance, moved upward from 28,000 in 1939 to 34,303 in 1945. The horse racing industry expanded as the need for a break from war-induced anxieties grew. Tobacco farmers required help, especially with war-related labor shortages, hiring just about any able-bodied person they could find. On and on it went.[43]

Rationing and much greater employment led to substantial increases in savings among the people of Kentucky. Since certain goods, such as new automobiles, were not available at all by 1942, and other items could be purchased only in limited amounts, consumption was less than it might have been. At the same time, the number of Kentuckians with jobs rose appreciably, as did income. Raises, overtime pay, and—most of all—longer hours led to larger paychecks. Money accumulated in people's hands, but limitations existed on spending. Savings grew by leaps and bounds. Kentuckians added tens of millions of dollars to their bank accounts. In a related vein, the total assets of state-chartered banks and trust companies set an all-time high as of June 30, 1944, reaching almost $579 million. This amount represented an increase of $101 million over the preceding twelve months. Just as telling, the bulk of bank earnings assets now came in the form of investment securities rather than loans.[44]

A booming economy, of course, left Kentuckians with substantially higher per capita income as well as a marked increase in total income. Per capita income shot upward from $317 in 1940 to $990 in 1948. Likewise, total income in Kentucky lunged ahead from $908 million for 1940 to $2,788 million for 1948. Even taking into account inflation, real per capita income and real total income advanced rapidly through the war and the immediate postwar period. Kentucky's people possessed much greater wealth than they did before the conflict started, though it should be recalled that many other Southern states fared as well or better economically than the commonwealth.[45]

Kentuckians who lived through the war knew that it benefited them financially. One way or another, individuals secured work before or after Pearl Harbor, accumulated savings, and emerged from the conflict with greater purchasing power. While they could not spend as much as they wanted during the war, they were still better off than before and made up for lost time as soon as rationing ended and consumer durable goods became available again. After Allied victory was achieved, passenger cars were reintroduced, and sales of these vehicles skyrocketed. A higher standard of living for most Kentuckians yielded a record number of new-car purchases. In Jefferson County alone the number of registered motor vehicles rose from 89,000 in 1940 to nearly 150,000 a decade later. Von Watts, Hollis Gibson, and Daniel Boone Razor Sr. were among many, many Kentuckians who raced to buy cars once they reappeared.[46]

When war broke out, Von and Lizzie Watts were a young married couple who resided in Leatherwood, a tiny eastern Kentucky community located in Breathitt County. A draftee, Von Watts fought against the Germans in France as an antiaircraft artillery man. Watts traversed Omaha Beach a day or two after D-Day and later found himself in the thick of the Battle of the Bulge. He sent home part of his Army pay, while Lizzie collected rent from boarders to make a few extra bucks. In the immediate postwar period, Von and Lizzie Watts had more money than ever before and could afford to buy a shiny, new black Ford pickup truck. It was their first car.[47]

Hollis Gibson lived in Hindman, Kentucky, when the United States declared war on Japan. Three months later Hollis was drafted by the Army, left his work as an Alcohol, Tobacco, and Firearms agent, and was sent to Mexico. His military job there was to try to talk draft dodgers into returning to the United States. Hollis and his subordinates, he recalled, "never got a one to go back," but stayed at it until the war was over. A cushy assignment indeed; Hollis really lucked out. More to the point, said Hollis, his wife, Helen, "went where I went," and the two of them lived cheaply. Expenditures at camp PXs saved them money. In 1947, the Gibsons used savings from the war to buy a Ford for private use. Hollis already had access to a "company car," his ATF vehicle.[48]

Daniel Boone Razor Sr., of Mount Sterling, Kentucky, earned his daily bread as a tobacco farmer. With the tobacco price way up during the war, and family income higher thereafter, Razor purchased a 1947 model Chevrolet two-door coupe, which was painted yellow. Though he had owned used cars during the Great Depression, this Chevrolet was his first new car and was really intended for his son. Daniel Boone Razor Jr. used the coupe to commute to Lexington, where he attended classes at the University of Kentucky. The coupe also came in handy as his "courting car." Dan must have been a pretty good driver, because he met Elaine in 1947 and married her in 1950.[49]

The political economy of the United States during World War II was complex and dynamic. The federal government regulated the national economy more forcefully than ever before. Implementation of rationing, price controls, and wage controls took place, which was in keeping with a greater degree of statist regimentation. While the state did not always plan well, it generated more than enough goods and services to achieve victory over the Axis without a debilitating inflationary spiral. Along the way, most Kentuckians complied with War Production Board and Office of Price Administration regulations, although a significant minority resorted to the black market; sacrifice and selfishness commingled. Rejuvenation of Kentucky's economy resulted from unprecedented government spending on arms and munitions, which was financed by higher taxes and war bonds. Kentucky reached the brink of prosperity before V-E Day, passing beyond that point when the government finally terminated rationing and then Kentuckians could buy all the cars, steaks, and butter that their new-found wealth allowed.

5

Politics as Usual

Kentucky politics proceeded along normal lines from 1939 to 1945, despite the intrusion of World War II. The Constitution of 1891 remained in effect, mandating gubernatorial elections every four years while prohibiting a governor from succeeding himself. Democrat Keen Johnson became Kentucky's first wartime governor, followed by Republican Simeon Willis. Johnson and Willis balanced state budgets and expanded services in a cautious, sensible fashion. They handled war-related responsibilities, including financial expenditures, largely by going through regular legislative channels. A few new wartime bodies did appear, but not many. Factional strife—especially between Chandlerites and anti-Chandlerites within the dominant Democratic party—played a significant part in determining election results, though other factors were at work, too. An intensively partisan, pluralistic brand of representative government flourished in Kentucky even as totalitarianism threatened democratic institutions everywhere in the world.

Apparently Kentuckians never entertained the possibility that partisan politics be suspended for the sake of unity during the fight. Perhaps the concept of "one man, one vote" and other democratic principles meant too much to them, or maybe some people valued patronage too highly to give up a chance at the spoils. In any case, politics as usual carried on.[1]

The 1939 race for governor played out against the backdrop of previous events. By early to mid-1935, deep divisions troubled the Democratic party of Kentucky. Governor Ruby Laffoon and Logan County political boss Thomas Rhea headed one Democratic faction, while Lieutenant Governor Albert Benjamin "Happy" Chandler emerged as the leader of another. Political ambitions, loyalty considerations, and a clash of personalities had brought disunity to the Democratic party.

Happy Chandler stood squarely in the center of the storm. As lieutenant governor, he had broken with Governor Laffoon over issues such
as the chief executive's support for a new state sales tax. Chandler wanted
to be the next governor, and he cared little about Laffoon's program or
feelings. Laffoon, naturally enough, saw Chandler as disloyal and inordi-
nately ambitious. The two men butted heads often, and their feud reached
its climax when Laffoon left the state on a political trip during the first
part of 1935. "Happy" Chandler, now acting governor, employed his temporary executive power to convene an extraordinary session of the state
legislature. The legislature passed a law requiring a primary (rather than
simply a party convention) to choose a candidate for governor. This legislation benefited Chandler, who believed that he was much more likely to
gain the Democratic nod to run for governor under the new system than
the old one. All Laffoon could do once he returned home was to rebuke
Chandler and establish a double primary system, which would necessi-
tate a second primary if none of the candidates in the first primary race
received a majority of votes.[2]

The double primary law set the stage for what happened next. Rhea—
Governor Laffoon's Highway Commissioner and pick to succeed him—
nipped Chandler in the first 1935 Democratic primary for governor, but
obtained only a plurality of votes. In the second primary, Chandler turned
the table, beating Rhea and securing the Democratic nomination. Laffoon
and Rhea would neither forget this painful setback nor forgive Chandler.[3]

Matters deteriorated from there. Still smarting over their primary
defeat, Laffoon and Rhea supported Republican candidate King Swope
against Chandler in the 1935 general election. Chandler won the governorship anyway, but bad blood remained. The Chandler faction of the
Democratic party and the anti-Chandler faction of the Democratic party,
headed by Laffoon and Rhea, despised each other more after the election
than before, and their animosities only deepened over time.[4]

Another election campaign influenced the Kentucky political landscape of 1939. In 1938, Governor Chandler made an ill-advised decision
to run against incumbent Senator Alben Barkley in the Democratic primary for the U.S. Senate. Nothing better illustrates Chandler's chutz-
pah, or that he was a young man in a big hurry. Beating Senate Majority
Leader Barkley, who commanded a powerful political following in Ken-

Former governor and then U.S. senator Albert Benjamin "Happy" Chandler (at left) presents Vice President John Nance Garner with a gift of Kentucky chewing tobacco, 1940. Chandler dominated the most prominent faction of the Kentucky Democratic party from the late 1930s through the 1950s. (Courtesy of the Library of Congress.)

tucky and could count on President Franklin D. Roosevelt's active support, was a monumental challenge, but Happy seemed to just shrug it off. After all, he was a popular standing governor who had never lost an election, and he did not foresee that happening now. The people spoke otherwise; Chandler had bitten off more than he could chew and suffered a resounding defeat at the polls. From that point forward, Chandler saw "Old Alben" as his political and personal enemy, and Barkley joined Laffoon and Rhea on the other side of state Democratic party politics.[5]

Given these developments, the 1939 contest for governor figured to be an exciting one, and it did not disappoint. Keen Johnson squared off against John Y. Brown Sr. in a rambunctious battle for the Democratic

Senator Alben Barkley (left) shaking hands with Senator Alexander Wiley (R-Wisconsin) in 1940. (Courtesy of the Library of Congress.)

nomination. A quieter Republican primary pitted King Swope against John Sherman Cooper. The two survivors would meet in the November general election.[6]

Kentucky voters understood quite well where Keen Johnson and John Y. Brown fit into the factional politics of that day. Though once on opposite sides of the Democratic party, Governor Chandler and Lieutenant Governor Johnson mended fences in the late 1930s. Johnson proved himself to be a loyal Chandler subordinate and approved of Chandler's program to reduce the size of the state's debt. Johnson also endorsed Chandler's plan to renovate state hospitals and prisons. Brown, a former member of the U.S. House of Representatives, received strong support from the Barkley-Rhea-Laffoon camp. Brown advocated a larger role for state government, which he envisioned providing additional services for Kentucky citizens.[7]

Keen Johnson kicked off his primary campaign with speeches in June and July of 1939. He announced that if elected governor he would be frugal with the people's money. The state debt, though smaller than before, remained and needed to be paid off. Keeping budgetary constraints in mind, he would also do what he could for education and increase pensions for the elderly. At Somerset Johnson stressed his experience as lieutenant governor and told the audience that he knew "the financial limitations of the State as well as its needs. I know what I am going to do as governor and that is more than my opponent does."[8]

John Y. Brown fired back. He declared that the current administration, of which Johnson was a part, engaged in a variety of corrupt practices. State jobs went to people with political connections rather than ability. State employees were forced to accept assessments, where a part of their hard-earned paycheck went to the Chandler faction of the Democratic party. Brown said it was past time to end "the system of assessing state employes for political or private use."[9] Like Johnson, Brown believed in aid to education and higher old-age pensions. The difference was that he had staked out these positions earlier than his opponent and favored greater funding. A "me, too" approach by Johnson would not do. Most importantly, Brown portrayed himself as the true disciple of Roosevelt's New Deal. Johnson, he said, was the candidate of the "anti–New Deal, anti-Roosevelt Liberty League crowd."[10]

Throughout the Democratic primary season, the same issues appeared and reappeared. Education and old-age pensions attracted the most attention. The New Deal credentials of both candidates, or lack thereof, received considerable scrutiny, as did the subject of political corruption. The Congress of Industrial Organizations became a major bone of contention. A matter of lesser interest, though of concern to many farmers, involved the stance of the candidates on tobacco pricing.

Since education claimed roughly one-half of all the revenue that flowed into state coffers, it was a perennial topic of political discourse. Brown pledged to raise average spending per student in the public schools from $12.12 to $15.00, a substantial boost. He also favored higher pay for teachers. Johnson replied that these kinds of increases, while nice in theory, were not possible. The money simply did not exist for such big hikes unless taxes were raised, and Johnson rejected that course out of hand. The state must make do with its current level of revenue.[11]

Old-age pensions provoked controversy. Congressman Brown and his allies promised senior citizens old-age pension checks of $30 per month. Their rhetoric implied that every senior citizen would get the full $30, no matter what. In early August 1939, speaking over WHAS microphones in Louisville just before primary election day, Senator Barkley said, "When I voted for $30-a-month pensions in the Senate of the United States, I thought it meant $30 and not $8 or $4 or $3. John Young Brown has pledged himself to see to it that Kentucky meets this obligation completely."[12] Lieutenant Governor Johnson explained that his opponents knew better. Every elderly person in Kentucky deserved the pension check entitled to them under federal and state laws. But $30 per month represented the maximum amount possible; the vast majority would receive less. Rather than misleading our worthy elderly, Johnson let it be known that Brown and Barkley should stick to the facts.[13]

One part of Brown's strategy for victory involved President Roosevelt, who was popular in Kentucky. Brown repeatedly depicted himself as the real New Dealer in this race and Johnson as a pretender. In reality, Brown did exhibit a greater affinity for big government and social activism than Johnson. Barkley, a key Roosevelt lieutenant, Rhea, and others reinforced the New Deal theme. They told Democratic voters in the state that a Brown triumph would also be a Roosevelt–New Deal triumph. If Brown could ride Roosevelt's coattails to a victory over Johnson he would be only too happy to do so.[14]

Keen Johnson did experience some anxious moments on this score, undoubtedly remembering the 1938 U.S. Senate race. FDR visited Kentucky soil then, letting everyone know that he favored Barkley over Chandler. Barkley then won by a landslide. A Roosevelt nod to Brown, perhaps at the behest of Old Alben himself, worried Johnson. Relief arrived in the form of a Roosevelt declaration of neutrality; the president would not back either candidate for the Democratic gubernatorial nomination.[15]

Johnson and Brown swapped charges of misbehavior along the campaign trail. Both candidates alleged that the other was guilty of political infidelity, and each castigated his opponent for the use of graft. Brown took Johnson to task for first opposing Chandler, then supporting him. Johnson reminded Brown that he had once attacked Tom Rhea for spending money on burgoo parties that should have gone to pay depositors of a failed Russellville bank. Similarly, Brown had rebuked Ruby Laffoon for selling his Madisonville house to the state for twice what it was worth. Johnson thought it passing strange that Brown now occupied the same political bed as Rhea and Laffoon. Even worse, of course, Brown compatriots Rhea and Laffoon had committed heresy in 1935 when they turned their backs on the Democratic party to support Republican King Swope. Johnson knew that true Democrats would not back party traitors. Supposedly unethical acts, too, supplied grist for the political mill. After noting that he intended to run a clean government, free of political manipulation, Johnson stated that Kentuckians "can hardly expect a millennium at the hands of the creators of head-chopping, weed-cutting and 'highway-manship.'" The shot at Rhea, whom Johnson labeled the "chief apostle of political spoils and assessments," was unmistakable. Brown countered by reiterating his belief in a "civil service approach" to government, repudiating the old patronage system. Concluding with a rhetorical flourish, Brown declared that the "present system of the state administration of padding payrolls with useless employees before elections" was nothing less than a "political dictatorship and destructive to Democracy."[16]

Opinions about the Congress of Industrial Organizations (CIO) and its controversial leader, John L. Lewis, influenced the Democratic primary. Lewis, one of the founders of the CIO, also headed the United Mine Workers of America (UMW). An aggressive, sometimes belligerent trade unionist, his personality and militancy brought him the love of some Kentucky workers—especially in the Eastern Kentucky coal mines—and the hatred of management. Since average Kentuckians embraced conservative principles, most people in the commonwealth came to dislike Lewis more and more as the years passed. Seeking to exploit the anti-Lewis, anti-CIO sentiment, Keen Johnson asserted that Lewis and the CIO were the "chief sponsors of the candidacy of my opponent." Most people knew that Brown served as a lawyer for the UMW, so it did not seem to be that much of a stretch to say that he was a pawn of the CIO. This issue hurt Brown.[17]

Farmers did not seem to like Brown much, either. Brown tried to make hay by playing upon his experience on the farm as a boy. Told that the youthful Brown rose at two o'clock in the morning every day to perform his chores, farmers deemed this predictable because he was "just the type to get up an hour or two ahead of anybody else and do all the crowing himself and wake up the roosters." The real problem with Brown for farmers, however, was not so much that he liked attention or took credit that he did not really deserve. Years before, while in the U.S. Congress, Brown had voted against an amendment to the first Agricultural Adjustment Administration bill, which called for raising the parity price of tobacco from 10 cents per pound to 16 cents per pound. When queried about this, Brown answered that he was "not interested in the parity

price of tobacco." All other Kentucky congressmen supported the amendment and the price of tobacco did rise, but Brown's position on tobacco
pricing remained both inexplicable and, from the perspective of Kentucky
tobacco farmers, inexcusable.[18]

The two campaigners each worked hard to secure victory. Neither man
could be faulted for lack of effort. Brown and Johnson traveled to eastern Kentucky, western Kentucky, and central Kentucky. They appeared
in Louisville and Lexington as well as in every town of any appreciable
size throughout the state. On his journey through Kentucky, Johnson
grew more and more encouraged by the reception he received. Central
Kentucky, Happy Chandler's stronghold, seemed in the bag. Louisville
looked good. Eastern Kentucky concerned Johnson because of Lewis's
hold on the coal miners, but some counties in that part of the state leaned
toward the lieutenant governor. Only western Kentucky was a lost cause.
Even in that area, as he passed through Hopkinsville, Mayfield, and other
places on to Owensboro, Johnson discovered a measure of support that
uplifted him. Barkley, Rhea, and Morganfield judge Earle Chester Clements, all western Kentuckians, might have the best of it in these parts,
yet five hundred people greeted Johnson at Scottsville and a thousand in
Elkton. Buoyed by the big crowds, which seemed "sympathetic and atten-
tive," Johnson pronounced himself "pleased with [the] situation generally
down here" and expected to get more votes from western Kentucky than
some prognosticators believed.[19]

From July 1939 on, with only about a month left in the primary campaign, the political rhetoric reached a higher volume. Brown and Johnson
loudly repeated their earlier accusations. Brown complained that every
agency of the Chandler administration "was being used to advertise . . .
the candidacy of . . . Johnson." State jobs went to Johnson supporters, and
then only if they promised to vote the right way. Brown told voters not to
be misled by Chandler–Johnson charges of radicalism against him. Johnson blasted Brown as a man of "plastic convictions" who constantly made
"reckless and extravagant promises." Johnson warned Kentuckians that it
would mean reimposition of the old sales tax to "raise the $15,000,000
required by the lavish promises of my opponent." Johnson continued to
pound Brown for his support of the CIO, "a communistic organization
and the most dictatorial group in existence in the nation today."[20]

On August 5, 1939, election day arrived. Registered Democrats trooped to the polls to choose their nominee for governor of Kentucky. With 118 of Kentucky's 120 counties reporting, Johnson led Brown by 244,084 votes to 214,011. The margin continued to widen. Johnson defeated Brown by over 33,000 votes.[21]

A regional analysis is enlightening. As expected, Brown captured western Kentucky. Rhea's strong political machine delivered his Logan County base by 4,235 votes and a number of nearby counties as well. Eastern Kentucky's Seventh District, which included Floyd County and other coal mining areas, also went heavily to Brown. Johnson overcame his weakness in those places by piling up strong majorities in central Kentucky, where Chandler did not let him down, and in the urban areas of the state. Jefferson County alone, home of Louisville, gave Johnson almost 13,000 more votes than Brown.[22]

Johnson's victory, in a hotly contested race with large voter turnout, came about for many reasons. His emphasis on economy in government resonated with voters, especially when contrasted with Brown's many promises about expanding services. Kentuckians intuitively grasped the notion that substantial increases in education funding and social services probably would translate into an increase in taxes, and they did not want that at all. Brown's association with the CIO gained him some working-class support, especially in eastern Kentucky, but hurt him everywhere else. Given the connection between Brown and Rhea and Laffoon, men whom many among the party faithful saw as betrayers, Johnson also appeared more trustworthy than his opponent, and that may well have been the fulcrum upon which the election turned.

King Swope faced John Sherman Cooper in the 1939 Republican primary for governor. Swope, a state circuit court judge from Lexington, had run for governor against Democrat Happy Chandler four years before and lost. Swope sought redemption this time around. Cooper, a Pulaski County judge making his first run for statewide office, entered the race earlier than his challenger. He campaigned diligently, and for a while it appeared that there would be no serious opposition. Swope's entry into the primary field turned the race topsy-turvy.[23]

Each Republican gubernatorial candidate counted on the support of powerful friends. Northern Kentucky boss Maurice Galvin, Louisville judge Charles I. Dawson, and a group called the "young Republicans" backed Cooper. Congressman John M. Robsion, former governor Flem Sampson, and Louisville's Jouett Ross Todd urged Swope to run for the GOP nomination and supported him when he did. Robsion and Sampson, who represented rural, eastern Kentucky Republicans, were a particularly formidable combination.[24]

Cooper and Swope embraced similar platforms. Both candidates went on record for clean, efficient government. Both urged more funding for education, mental health facilities, prisons, and the elderly. Cooper put a bit more stress on reduction of the state debt than his opponent, while Swope seemed a little more committed to road construction. Neither man attacked the other directly. In effect, the ideas of the two candidates canceled each other out.[25]

The question of electability decided this race. As the Republican-oriented *Mount Sterling Gazette and Kentucky Courier* put it, Cooper was a "brilliant young man" and "very popular," but Swope's reputation made him the better choice. Simply put, Swope gave the Republicans their best chance to defeat the Democrats in the fall. Republican voters throughout Kentucky seemed to accept this conclusion. Name recognition and a stronger organization propelled Swope to a 48,000-vote victory over Cooper.[26]

Fate intervened at this point. On October 3, 1939, Kentucky U.S. senator M. M. Logan died. Chandler responded to Logan's passing by resigning his own position as governor, thereby thrusting Lieutenant Governor Johnson into the governorship. Johnson subsequently appointed Chandler to fill out the unexpired portion of Logan's Senate term. In this manner, Keen Johnson became governor of Kentucky, though it remained to be seen if he would keep the high office for very long. The November 1939 general election for governor thus matched newly minted Democratic governor Keen Johnson against Republican King Swope. Swope blamed Roosevelt administration tax policies for "strangling business" and retarding economic recovery. He contended that the New Deal and the Democrats bore responsibility for the state debt, a bloated payroll, and decaying state institutions. Johnson pointed to an improving state economy and a shrinking debt. He reiterated his promise to use existing resources, not new ones, to fix mental hospitals and prisons. He also contrasted peace in Kentucky with the outbreak of war in Europe. The voters sided overwhelmingly with Johnson, giving him 460,834 votes to 354,704 for Swope. Johnson won because the economy was on the upswing and a temporarily reunified Democratic party capitalized on its heavy voter registration advantage over the Republicans.[27]

Keen Johnson had traveled an unusual path to reach the governorship. Born on January 12, 1896, at Brandon's Chapel in Lyon County, southwestern Kentucky, he grew up in humble circumstances as the son of a Methodist circuit rider. His first home was a small, two-room, wooden-and-brick parsonage—not a log cabin, but not too far removed from that. He received his initial education in Kentucky's public schools. Since his minister father moved around a lot, so did young Keen. Johnson gained familiarity with the Pennyrile and Purchase sections of the state. A bright young man with a flair for words, he started his higher education in 1915 at Central College in Fayette, Missouri. There he published tracts decrying the excessive materialism of American society and calling for the "extermination of alcohol." These things, he believed, stood in the way of a perfectible society. His youthful idealism was soon interrupted by U.S. entry into World War I, in which he served as a first lieutenant in France. Awarded a wound stripe, the predecessor of the Purple Heart, Johnson studied military strategy and tactics at an officer school there. He also exchanged literally dozens of love letters with his new wife, Eunice, at this time, and he returned to her after the war. By 1922, he completed a bachelor's degree in journalism at the University of Kentucky and went from there into the newspaper business. Johnson became editor and copublisher of the *Richmond Daily Register* in 1925. As Eastern Kentucky State Teachers College president Herman L. Donovan put it, the *Register* "soon took on a new life. Editorials worthy of a metropolitan paper began to appear daily." In 1932, Johnson moved into politics when he accepted the position of secretary of the Democratic Party State Central and Executive Committee. As we have seen, he became lieutenant governor in 1935, and Kentuckians elected him governor in 1939. Johnson's rise to the top was extraordinary because he had been a journalist, not a lawyer or judge, and it took him only seven years in politics to claim the governor's mansion as his own.[28]

Johnson's age and lack of wealth also distinguished him from many of Kentucky's earlier governors. At forty-three, he was a relatively young chief executive. Having been a soldier and a newspaperman, he was far from rich. He did have an above average intellect and a solid moral and ethical foundation, and his youthful idealism had been tempered by experience. People who knew him often described him as a fine fellow, perhaps because he exhibited an air of sober rectitude and on occasion a self-deprecating wit. As Johnson prepared himself for a full term as governor of Kentucky he told an audience of well-wishers in Madison County that his election was a "doubtful experiment which may just ruin a pretty fair sort of country newspaper fellow." His wish was that he would grow with the responsibility of being governor and not just "swell up."[29]

Keen Johnson served as governor from 1939 to 1943. Johnson sought a further reduction in the state debt and its eventual elimination. Keeping the budget in mind, his other goals included bolstering old-age pensions, modest aid for education, repair of state mental hospitals and prisons, and road construction. As time wore on and war in Europe and Asia intensified, Johnson made it clear that he supported President Roosevelt's aid-short-of-war program for Britain and that Kentucky, like every other state, must do its part to help fashion FDR's "arsenal of democracy." Preparedness for the possibility of war occupied Governor Johnson, and the grim reality of war itself required even more strenuous efforts.

"Politics as usual" continued in Kentucky despite troubling events overseas. Democrat Johnson got along well with the Democrat-controlled state legislature. This result was not inevitable, as Democrats had sometimes fought with Democrats in the past, but Johnson managed not to alienate the legislature, and it proved compliant. The 1940 legislative session ended with passage of a law that provided $1 million more each year for old-age assistance. Another measure funded the 1938 Teachers' Retirement Act. In the name of better government, Johnson and the legislature established soil conservation districts, a Farm Tenancy Commission, and a Kentucky Aeronautics Commission. A statute against the sale of cannabis appeared.[30]

Details related to several of these enactments are instructive. Many elderly Kentuckians received slightly larger pension checks because of the new old-age assistance law, though nowhere near the increase that certain overzealous politicians had promised them. Johnson, not Brown or Barkley, told the old folks the truth. Legislators allocated $500,000 to the Teachers' Retirement Act, its initial appropriation. Teachers might opt to retire as early as age sixty, with mandatory retirement at age seventy. Upon retirement, a teacher would get an annual pension of between $100 and $1,000, depending upon length of service and other relevant factors. The creation of soil conservation districts allowed for the introduction of the federal program of flood control, reforestation, and replenishment of depleted, nutrient-poor land. Experts estimated that the Soil Conservation Law would bring 2.5 million to 3 million federal dollars into Kentucky annually. The ban on selling cannabis applied only to the recreational use of *Cannabis sativa L.*, which still could be employed for medicinal and scientific purposes under certain conditions. Legislative advance within Kentucky in 1940 can be described as decent, if unspectacular.[31]

Johnson embraced Roosevelt's military buildup in the wake of Germany's blitzkrieg and the fall of France. Speaking before the American Legion in Ashland on July 22, 1940, the governor expressed his sincere desire that American soldiers would not have to fight in Europe again but said that wisdom dictated taking whatever steps were necessary to prepare the United States for that contingency. Johnson underlined the significance of the national government's burgeoning defense program and pledged his cooperation to the emerging defense agencies, the Army, and the Navy. He labeled German dictator Adolf Hitler a "godless creature" who must be stopped.[32]

Industrial mobilization for the possibility of American entry into the war had already begun in Kentucky. As early as autumn 1939, the U.S. War Department mailed sealed envelopes to major businesses in the state, which were not to be opened until further notice. The envelopes contained orders for the manufacture of arms and munitions. If necessary, and only if necessary, word would be given to the businesses and they would unseal the envelopes and find out what kinds of weapons or related items they would have to make for the American military. In June of 1941, Governor Johnson noted that the federal Office of Production Management "has correct information as to the location and equipment of every factory in Kentucky that can be used to advantage." By that time, defense production in the state was well under way. In Ashland, ARMCO had already broken ground for the construction of its giant new blast furnace for the manufacture of steel—that most valuable of all war-related materials. In Henderson a $15 million ammonia plant opened up. Orders for Kentucky firms to make naval buoys, radio parts, rifle stocks, parachutes, and countless other items had gone out, and defense production in the commonwealth gradually ratcheted upward. Defense contracts awarded to Louisville firms alone in the period from July 1, 1940, to June 30, 1941, amounted to $39,174,618. If Fort Knox and Charlestown, Indiana—just outside Louisville—were taken into account, that figure leaped up to about $200 million. Johnson told Kentuckians, "We cannot defend ourselves or aid our allies effectively until the full resources of the nation have been mobilized for the manufacture of airplanes, tanks, munitions, and the auxiliary accoutrements of modern warfare." With the assistance of Senators Alben Barkley and Happy Chandler as well as Kentucky's U.S. representatives, Johnson made sure that Kentucky, though not a state of vast industrial capacity, participated in defense preparedness activities from the earliest days on.[33]

Japan's surprise attack on Pearl Harbor made the United States an official participant in World War II. Governor Johnson said that "Kentuckians died the death of heroes" in the Pacific and that the people at home must exert themselves much more strenuously than before to defeat the "slant-eyed Japanese and high-handed Hitler." A state defense organization was needed, and greatly expanded production of arms and munitions; American soldiers in all theaters of operations required weapons to achieve victory over the Axis. Johnson also pressed legislators to move forward on electrification, redistricting, state institutions, education, and the roads.[34]

The 1942 regular legislative session met many of these needs. A six-member State Defense Council was established, with the governor as ex-officio chairman. The Defense Council provided some overarching direction to wartime activities throughout Kentucky, including, but not limited to, preservation of law and order, prevention of subversive activities, police mobilization, fire protection, and disaster prevention and relief. All agencies of state government were charged to cooperate with the council. In addition, a corps of "Special Police" was formed, designed to keep watch over locations that might be subject to sabotage. Johnson appointed John J. Greenleaf to become Vice Chairman of the State Defense Council and the state's Civil Defense Director. A Tennessee Valley Authority Enabling Act was passed, which permitted Kentucky towns to buy and distribute electrical power from the Tennessee Valley Authority. This law anticipated production of electricity at Gilbertsville Dam, with a resultant decrease in electricity rates for many customers.[35]

Governor Johnson convened a special session shortly after the regular session to take up the issue of legislative reapportionment. A breakthrough was achieved when the first comprehensive legislative redistricting of Kentucky in a half-century passed. Kentucky's thirty-eight Senate districts now contained anywhere from 57,000 to 93,000 people, and its 100 House districts ranged from 15,000 to 48,000 persons. Jefferson County, the most populous county in the state, received five senatorial districts; other counties received fewer. Fairer political representation resulted from these changes, despite the population imbalances and the fact that Jefferson County's large population entitled it to two or three more senatorial districts than legislators saw fit to grant it. The traditional bias in favor of rural areas remained but was smaller than before.[36]

Johnson constantly exhorted Kentucky's people and businesses to do more for the war effort, and he praised their achievements. Johnson wanted every Kentuckian to buy war bonds, conserve electricity, grow their own food if possible, and in general support FDR's war program. He asked workers to stay on the job and denigrated strikes. He celebrated the production accomplishments of Ford Motor Company in Louisville, Ken-Rad in Owensboro, ARMCO, and others. The people and firms of Kentucky, with only a few exceptions, made Johnson proud.[37]

Industrial mobilization for war advanced throughout Johnson's term as governor. As U.S. Senate majority leader and a confidante of President Roosevelt, Senator Alben Barkley was in a better position to help Johnson with war projects and war jobs than anyone else. The "Iron Man" proved tireless in bringing the naval ordnance plant to Viola, Kentucky. After the plan for the Paducah aluminum plant fell through, he continued the fight to see that the commonwealth got a fair share of war work. Not only did Senator Barkley obtain funding for a Paducah airport; he also helped insure additional money for Bowling Green and Lexington airports. Fort Knox, Camp Breckinridge, and Camp Campbell benefited tremendously from his patronage. Though the origins of the Kentucky

Governor Keen Johnson (center) listening to President Franklin D. Roosevelt speak on the occasion of FDR's inspection visit to Fort Knox, April 28, 1943. Lieutenant General Jacob Devers, Commanding Officer, Armored Forces, is also part of the conversation. (Courtesy of Franklin D. Roosevelt Library, Hyde Park, NY.)

Dam project at Gilbertsville preceded the war, construction finished in 1944, and electricity production there was often described as a valuable defense commodity. Local authorities said Barkley was instrumental in the establishment of the TNT plant near Paducah. War plants often came with road construction and railroad expansion as built-in features. "Old Alben" brought home the bacon. By late 1943, when Governor Johnson left office, Kentucky companies were near or at peak production of military hardware. Army jeeps poured off Ford's assembly line; Ken-Rad cranked out a wide variety of radio parts; ARMCO produced incredible amounts of steel; naval shells and explosives flowed out of Viola and Paducah; and it just went on and on. Kentucky was doing its share to supply American troops—including Kentucky troops—with the implements of war. These implements, in turn, helped the Allies turn the corner on the Axis and begin the march to final victory.[38]

Keen Johnson compiled a satisfactory record as governor. During his four years in office, he eliminated the state debt and left behind a $10 million surplus. Old-age pension payments rose from an average of $8.66 per month in 1939 to $10.66 per month in 1943. Teachers now had an operational Retirement Law and a tenure act, and in thirty-three poorer counties received higher pay. Places for the mentally ill, such as Central State Hospital in Lakeland and Eastern State Hospital in Lexington, were renovated, transforming them from run-down, "vermin infested" institutions to quarters that were "clean . . . and attractive." The governor cooperated fully with the federal government's war program and provided wholesome encouragement to Kentucky's citizens and businesses when it came to the war effort. Though he could justly be criticized for failing to hike the pay of all teachers in the state, and for spending too little on education as a whole, he kept his promise to be a "saving, thrifty, frugal governor." On the issue of corruption, which arose periodically during his tenure, much was said but little was substantiated. Johnson believed state employees should make voluntary contributions to the political party of their choice, but denied involvement in mandatory assessments. Charges that the state Purchasing Department spent too much money for soap and other products were refuted or came to nothing. The one truly suspicious act of Johnson's administration involved acceptance of a $22,000 1939 campaign contribution from the State Trucking Association, which was not reported as required by law. Everything considered, Johnson performed the job of governor competently enough, though it must be noted that he did not set truly ambitious goals in the beginning and that war-induced economic recovery and a concomitant growth of state revenue made his job easier than that of his immediate predecessors.[39]

Kentucky politics before, during, and after World War II operated in impure ways. One hand washed the other, and a win-at-all-costs mentality manifested itself too often. The old spoils system could be criticized as unethical or worse, and politicians sometimes played fast and loose with public funds. Practices such as these cannot be excused, yet some Southern states, such as Tennessee, were just as bad, and Louisiana worse.[40]

The 1943 race for governor in Kentucky turned out to be both interesting and unusual. Outgoing Governor Johnson strongly endorsed his highway commissioner, J. Lyter Donaldson, for the Democratic nomination, and Donaldson fended off two challengers for the victory in the primary. Simeon Willis announced for the Republican nomination, and ultimately ran unopposed. Kentucky's 1943 general election for governor therefore matched Donaldson against Willis, and in the end the Republican beat the odds.

Johnson's decision to throw the state administration behind Donaldson surprised few people, but upset the other candidates for the Democratic nomination. Donaldson, after all, had managed Johnson's successful campaign for governor back in 1939. Donaldson also served Johnson loyally for almost four years as head of the Highway Department. Just the same, Johnson's powerful support for Donaldson earned the enmity of Lieutenant Governor Rodes K. Myers and former Farm Bureau chief Ben Kilgore. Myers and Kilgore became Donaldson's chief opponents in the Democratic primary.[41]

Personalities and mud-slinging rather than issues dominated the Democratic primary. Donaldson promised a $3 million increase in the public school fund if elected. He touted farm-to-market roads built under his watch as highway commissioner, saying more would be constructed when he became governor. He supported Johnson's TVA Enabling Act, the Rural Electrification Administration, and Kentucky Public Service Commission supervision of electricity rates. Kilgore and Myers, too, emphasized the importance of education. Kilgore noted specifically that he would raise teacher pay. Myers promoted free toll bridges and repeal of the state income tax, which he said could be done without adding any other taxes due to rising state revenues from a booming economy. Yet campaign rhetoric, which ran the gamut from merely colorful to downright nasty, overwhelmed the issues. After Kilgore and Myers charged that the Johnson-Donaldson administration was giving away highway jobs for votes and stressed repeatedly that the Purchasing Department bought goods for exorbitant prices, an incensed Johnson lashed out. In July 1943, he denounced Kilgore—who had been born in North Carolina and moved to Kentucky at age twenty-seven—as a "carpetbagger" and "phony farmer." The governor branded Myers, a handsome man who had just been married for a third time, the "Casanova from Bowling Green."[42]

Kilgore and Myers did not relent. Both men kept up attacks on Johnson and Donaldson for employing "weedcutters" and "sleepers" who did not do much highway work but could be counted upon to vote the "right way" in August. They continued to vilify the Purchasing Department for corruption and graft. D. C. Moore, an enemy of Johnson within state government, dredged up the old matter of the large campaign contribution from the Trucking Association to the Johnson campaign. Moore even produced canceled checks for the $22,000 and a witness who swore that Johnson lieutenants took the money in return for a pledge to give the Trucking Association legislative preference. In a speech given at Mayfield, Myers cut Donaldson to the quick by characterizing him as "the most colorless . . . most unpopular and the coldest man that has every appeared before the majority party seeking the nomination for the governorship of Kentucky."[43]

Johnson counterattacked, while Donaldson stayed above the fray. Lieutenant Governor Myers, according to Johnson, was pouting because Donaldson, not Myers, received the administration's endorsement. This fact had turned the "glamour-boy" into a crybaby. As for Kilgore, he wanted to claim all credit for administration farm improvements and for rural electrification, but "Baloney Ben" had as much to do with those things as "the abdication of Mussolini." The administration never favored the Trucking Association over other special interests or gave it any undue attention. Character had more to do with being an effective governor than color, and Donaldson had both. Johnson believed that Donaldson's integrity and ideas made him far and away the best choice to be Kentucky's next governor.[44]

Kentucky's Democratic voters concurred. In the August 1943 Democratic primary election Donaldson took 135,576 votes and Kilgore 81,027, with Myers a distant third. Even with all the vitriol, the turnout was light and Donaldson's victory relatively easy. The Kilgore-Myers attacks against the administration may well have backfired, since these stung Governor Keen Johnson, and he worked harder than most previous governors to see his man elected. Johnson's assistance put Donaldson over the top.[45]

Simeon Willis, a former state court of appeals judge, threw his hat into the ring for the Republican gubernatorial nomination. Willis had been out of political office for over a decade by this time but was recognized as one of the best legal minds in northeastern Kentucky, if not the very best. State senator D. C. Jones of Harlan looked like he might challenge Willis, but decided against it. Willis received the backing of Louisville Republican leader Jouett Ross Todd and the mountain coalition of U.S. congressman John Robsion and former governor Flem Sampson. In the end, Jones stepped aside, and Willis took the Republican nomination without any opposition at all.[46]

Senator Alben Barkley could not resist commenting on this result. He said that many people in Kentucky talk on and on about the great strength of the so-called Democratic machine. Then he reminded everyone how the Democratic party had just been through a primary campaign where the three candidates belted each other around pretty good, contrasting that with the Republican experience. Barkley concluded that the Republican party must have an even stronger machine than the Democratic party "to get 'Baby' Jones . . . out of their primary and nominate Willis without opposition."[47]

The Republicans smelled blood. The Johnson administration was under siege for corruption. Democrat Donaldson was not a dynamic candidate. Willis saw a tremendous opportunity, letting his supporters know that if "we don't win in November who can say when we will have a chance like this again." He asked everyone to redouble their efforts on his behalf.[48]

One issue really separated the two candidates. Both men expressed their desire to improve education, construct more roads, and help the elderly. They wanted to ease the transition of servicemen back into civilian life and engage in postwar planning. But Willis championed an end to the state income tax, while Donaldson insisted that the state government could not function without that money.[49]

As usual in Kentucky politics, the two camps traded verbal blows. Donaldson contended that a change from the Democratic party to the Republican party in the midst of war would be harmful to the war effort. "The price and possibilities of an enduring peace are far too great," he said, "far too extensive as affects all humanity, far too sacred to chance such a peace being jeopardized, even in a remote way, by the election of Republican state officials in Kentucky in 1943." Barkley, one writer noted, "declared a Republican victory in Kentucky would be proclaimed a repudiation of the national administration and its conduct of the war." Willis responded that all of this was just nonsense, since Kentuckians of every political party supported the overall war program and the great national goal of victory. A Republican electoral triumph would not imperil the war effort, only the continued existence of the Democratic political machine and the old spoils system.[50]

A confident Simeon Willis expected success. Speaking in his hometown of Ashland just before the November 1943 election, Willis said he trusted that the people would not put crooks and thieves into office. Having earlier reminded Kentuckians of the smelly Johnson-Donaldson Trucking Association money, Willis repeated allegations that the Democratic Purchasing Department had spent way too much on soap, shoes, and tires. He charged that "a two per cent campaign fund tax (had been assessed) against state employes' salaries," which gave the opposition $1.25 million a month. Nevertheless, Willis predicted victory.[51]

Once more, Governor Johnson attempted to save Donaldson. Johnson explained again that his administration was innocent of corruption charges. The Trucking Association received no special treatment. The Purchasing Department performed well; for instance, to describe the soap compound as merely a block of regular soap was disingenuous at best, purposeful lying at worst. Mandatory assessments never occurred. For Johnson, Judge Willis "is just like an owl—the more light I turn on him, the blinder he gets."[52]

Simeon Willis won the 1943 general election for Kentucky governor anyway, taking 279,144 votes to Lyter Donaldson's 270,525. Willis's margin of victory was slim, just over 8,600 votes. He took only four of Kentucky's nine congressional districts, but that was enough. Willis's triumph owed most to Donaldson's lackluster, ineffectual campaigning. As lieutenant governor, Myers pointed out correctly during the Democratic primary, Donaldson lacked charisma. He filled his speeches with platitudes and seldom touched the hearts or souls of voters. Moreover, it too often appeared that Johnson did Donaldson's dirty work, and it may have seemed to some voters that Donaldson was not his own man. The perception, if not the reality, of malfeasance within the Johnson administration also dogged Donaldson. Willis's character, by contrast, proved hard to assail. Some voters were also swayed by Willis's advocacy of tax reduction,

Governor Simeon Willis. (Courtesy of the Public Information Photo Collection, Public Records Division—Kentucky Department for Libraries and Archives.)

and Senator Happy Chandler did not provide much assistance to Donaldson. In addition, Willis won more votes from blacks in Louisville and from labor in the mountains than anticipated. In such a tight race, each of these factors made a difference.[53]

Simeon Willis's experiences prepared him well for the governorship. Born in Lawrence County, Ohio, on December 1, 1879, his family moved across the Ohio River to Greenup County, Kentucky, around 1889. After receiving appropriate training, young "Sim" became a teacher and then principal of an elementary school. Switching to the law, he gained admittance to the bar in 1901 and set up practice in Ashland. Politics called out to him. A Republican in a heavily Democratic state, he tasted defeat before victory. He did win a term as Ashland city solicitor, serving from 1918 to 1922. On the last day of 1927, Governor Flem Sampson named Willis to the state court of appeals. In 1928, Willis retained his seat by winning election in his own right. A dignified, statesmanlike man of high intelligence, he always did his homework and decided cases based upon sound legal principles and prudent judgment. A scholar by nature, he received plaudits for his revision of the six-volume masterwork *Thornton on the Law of Oil and Gas*. One indication of the high esteem in which Willis was held is that during the middle of his term James Garnett of the Kentucky State Bar Association asked President Herbert Hoover to consider Willis for appointment as associate justice of the U.S. Supreme Court. Hoover nominated another man instead, but this episode reveals what many Kentucky lawyers thought about Willis's abilities. After losing his bid for reelection to the Court of Appeals in 1932—a time when voters everywhere blamed the Republican party for economic catastrophe—Willis resumed his Ashland law practice. Despite Willis's spending slightly more than ten years out of politics, the Republican leadership in Kentucky did not forget this talented man. Over the decades, he had performed a number of important jobs well, and he was eminently qualified for the state's highest office. When friends like Sampson and Robsion urged him to run for governor in 1943, Willis listened.[54]

Governor Simeon Willis led Kentucky from December 1943 to late 1947. Willis's objectives included operation of an honest, efficient administration, improvements in education, and establishment of tuberculosis hospitals. He implored Kentucky's people and businesses to do even more to help win the war. Triumph over the Axis powers required additional sacrifice as well as maintenance of high levels of war production.

During the 1943 campaign, Willis had characterized the Democratic administration as corrupt. He promised clean government and the elimination of fat. Once in office, Willis's philosophy was to "cut expenses wherever possible, but not in any way to impair essential services." Toward this end, Willis discharged nine highway advisory commissioners and one rural highway commissioner, deeming them Democratic patronage appointees whose positions were unnecessary. However, he retained the services of many Democrats who were doing a good job even though Republican spoilsmen howled. Willis's campaign for better government resulted in a relatively smooth transition from one administration to the next and a reduction in administrative costs for most departments of state government.[55]

Education emerged as Willis's top priority for the 1944 legislative session. He felt that the schools were badly underfunded and that the issue demanded immediate redress. Unfortunately, the Republican administration clashed with the Democrat-controlled legislature, and the regular session ended without a budget. Unwilling to accept continuation of the old level of education spending, Willis called a special session of the state legislature to deal with the matter of education alone. Disregarding that charge, the legislature put together an entire budget. As it played out, Willis found himself in accord with the new budget. Nevertheless, the legislature had exceeded its constitutional authority by moving beyond Willis's original instructions, and that necessitated additional action. Willis rectified the situation by speedily convening a second special session, whose job it became to ratify the work of the first session (that is, to approve the state budget with the more liberal provisions for education). Through this convoluted process, education made the gains Willis had in mind. In 1942–1943, spending per student for the common schools stood at $12.88. For 1944–1945, it rose to $19.16 and for 1945–1946 reached $19.77. The University of Kentucky, the teachers colleges, and educational institutions for blacks received additional money as well.[56]

A law was passed during the Willis administration that financed construction of five new tuberculosis hospitals. Ashland, London, Paris, Glasgow, and Madisonville were chosen as sites for the new facilities. In August 1946, Governor Willis laid the cornerstone for the Madisonville Sanatorium. In late September 1950, after having left office, he returned for the dedication of the finished hospital. Construction of the other TB hospitals proceeded just as well. All of them aided Kentuckians who suffered from the ill effects of this crippling disease.[57]

Other achievements of the Willis administration during the wartime period deserve mention. During the 1944 legislative sessions, Kentucky's Corrupt Practices Act was bolstered. Passage of the budget insured construction of more farm-to-market roads. Old-age assistance continued to flow from Frankfort to the elderly. Willis appointed a black man, Republican Onis M. Travis of Lexington, to a position of authority within the Education Department—a first. More state money went to fund blacks who attended graduate schools out of state. The Kentucky Senate, regrettably, did block a bill that would have permitted African Americans to enroll at previously all-white professional schools. Governor Willis helped improve public education for blacks, albeit within the overarching framework of segregation.[58]

The terrible struggle against the Axis continued. By the time Willis entered office, the Allies had gained the upper hand over the enemy. Italy, for instance, switched sides in the war and ousted Mussolini. The Germans and the Japanese were giving ground in Europe and Asia. Governor Willis noted that the United States and its partners must keep the pressure on the Axis powers until they submitted. He praised Kentucky's soldiers, who were helping "to carry the banner of freedom triumphantly to every battleground." He swore that the servicemen could count on "the love and loyalty and prayers of the people of Kentucky [which] will follow them and abide with them in all trials and triumphs."[59]

Support for the troops and the pursuit of victory required everyone on the Kentucky home front to give their all. Selfishness and partisanship would not be tolerated. Absolutely nothing, according to Willis, should be allowed to get in the way of the "production of food stuffs, war materials, supplies, and weapons." America's fighting men desperately needed these goods, and the commonwealth would not let them down.[60]

Kentucky's war machine delivered in a big way. Proteins and starch from the commonwealth found their way into the stomachs of American troops stationed at home and abroad. Large quantities of coal, steel, and synthetic rubber poured out of Kentucky mines and factories. Jeeps, cargo planes, naval buoys, radio parts, aviation vests, and parachutes were distributed to soldiers, sailors, and fliers. Many American fighting men used Kentucky rifles, artillery shells, and bombs. Peak production of wartime goods in Kentucky was maintained from 1943 into 1944 and then only gradually reduced as mandated by Allied military successes. Kentuckians at home performed war work well, which buttressed the efforts of Allied soldiers everywhere and contributed significantly to Axis defeat.[61]

Germany surrendered in May 1945 and Japan in September. Governor Willis congratulated Kentuckians—at home and abroad—for all they did to achieve this salutary result. At a time like this, Willis noted, jubilation was natural, and that was fine. Just the same, he asked Kentuckians to remember the men and women who "have made the supreme sacrifice for their country" and requested the assistance of all people in rebuilding "a torn world." Humanity cried out for the reestablishment of peace, security, and liberty throughout the globe.[62]

A state Postwar Planning Commission made its final report public in 1945. Commission recommendations included a new constitution for Kentucky, since the old one was too detailed and some parts of it were obsolete; construction of additional state parks; and establishment of a housing commission. "Just" social legislation and a higher minimum wage received endorsement. Governor Willis and the Postwar Planning Commission stressed that the federal GI Bill of Rights offered valuable educational opportunities for returning Kentucky soldiers, and part of the commission's report dealt with ways to ease the adjustment of these men to civilian life. Many of the report's recommendations would be achieved later, including an enhanced park system, a hike in the minimum wage, and various gains for blacks. The old constitution, however, remains, and is still a problem today.[63]

The 1946 legislative session resulted in a number of gains for Governor Willis and one significant setback. Segregated schools for blacks received a good deal more money. Education as a whole continued to advance as Kentucky's economy moved forward. Spending per student rose to $24.40 in 1946 and $25.56 in 1947. Teacher pay almost doubled during the Willis years. The average old-age pension increased from about $11.00 a month to $17.50. Coal miners benefited from stronger mine safety laws enacted in 1946. A concealed weapons law was improved. After a postponement of two years, Willis revived his effort to gain legislative approval for repeal of the state income tax. His quest fell short, however, and the income tax stayed in place. This rebuff constituted Willis's single biggest disappointment as governor.[64]

In 1947, Governor Willis struggled to find a suitable Republican to replace him in office. With the election for governor upcoming, two prospective candidates for the job turned him down flat. His third choice, Superintendent of Public Instruction John Fred Williams, agreed to run. Williams faced attorney general Eldon S. Dummit in the Republican primary. Despite Willis's support for Williams, Dummit won. The Democrats elected Earle C. Clements, an anti-Chandlerite, in their primary. Clements then vanquished Dummit in the general election. Clements's triumph owed most to the fact that the primary divided the Republican party, which it could ill afford given the bedrock strength of the Democrats. Ironically, Willis had compiled a significant body of achievements as governor only to face rejection by some Republicans and a November return of the Democratic party to power.[65]

Simeon Willis proved to be a good governor. Jumping hurdles set down by a legislature dominated by Democrats, Republican Willis registered gains in many areas. He balanced state budgets, leaving behind the largest surplus ever accumulated in the history of Kentucky up to that time. He nearly doubled spending on Kentucky's schoolchildren and for the public school teachers. The elderly saw their pensions rise dramatically. Tuberculosis sanatoria obtained funding and eventually took shape. Blacks found an ally in Willis. More roads materialized, and the park system improved. Willis implored Kentuckians to do their utmost to win the war. No scandal touched the Willis administration, and it operated relatively efficiently and relatively effectively.

Continuity more than change shaped Kentucky politics from 1939 to 1945. Preexisting patterns of political action and behavior prevailed, even though Kentuckians passed through a gut-wrenching, worldwide conflict. Elections for governor occurred at regularly scheduled times. The lively tussle between the Democratic party and the Republican party continued. Factionalism, which was nearly a constant, plagued both parties, and each employed the use of patronage. The New Deal coalition of the 1930s held together during the 1940s: urbanities from Louisville and Lexington, labor from the Eastern Kentucky mountains, more and more blacks, and some farmers repeatedly gave their votes to the Democratic party. Indeed, the Democratic party bounced back from setbacks in 1943–1944, becoming stronger than before, and would dominate Kentucky politics for decades. Anti-Chandlerites gained temporary ascendancy over the Chandlerities by 1947, though their battle would continue for another fifteen years. Within this political framework, keeping in mind too that the New Deal and the wartime economy gave them more resources to work with than earlier governors, Keen Johnson and Simeon Willis performed their jobs in a respectable manner. Willis, the lone Republican governor over the long stretch from 1931 to 1967, deserves special commendation because he managed to steer many important laws through a largely Democratic general assembly. In the end, Johnson and Willis used Kentucky's traditional political system to fashion their World War II victory programs, and the New Deal tradition strongly influenced Kentucky political outcomes throughout the war and deep into the postwar period.

6

Kentucky on Guard

Axis air strikes against Asian and European nations attracted great attention from the American press during the 1930s and early 1940s. The Japanese air force blew up parts of China. The bombardment of English cities by the German Luftwaffe alarmed Americans even more. Americans worried that their own towns could be devastated by powerful bombs, and they insisted on a prudent institutional response. Voluntary civil defense councils appeared by 1940 and the national Office of Civilian Defense shortly thereafter. After December 7, 1941, federal, state, and local civil defense organizations took additional steps to protect civilians and property from any German or Japanese attack. The old adage "Better safe than sorry" made sense, and a zealous civil defense effort brought people together in common cause. Even after the passage of time convinced most Kentuckians that the Axis would not hit the commonwealth, Kentucky officials urged civil defense workers to maintain all protective functions and perform nonprotective activities related to the overall war effort.

President Franklin D. Roosevelt formed the Office of Civilian Defense (OCD) by executive order on May 21, 1941. New York mayor Fiorello LaGuardia headed the OCD, whose job was to safeguard civilians, erect local defense councils across the country, and boost morale. LaGuardia set up nine regional OCD offices throughout the United States; the Fifth Region included Kentucky, Ohio, Indiana, West Virginia, and Michigan. The regional offices served as conduits between the national OCD and a myriad of state and local defense councils. Altogether, over 10 million people worked for the Office of Civilian Defense in one capacity or another during World War II.[1]

Mayor LaGuardia's interests were obvious for all to see. He worked in his characteristically intense way to construct a vast cadre of air raid

New York mayor Fiorello LaGuardia (left) converses with new WPA Administrator F. C. Harrington in December 1938. LaGuardia took over the Office of Civilian Defense in 1941. (Courtesy of the Library of Congress.)

wardens who would sound the warning should enemy planes appear and would extinguish fires caused by enemy bombs. New York City alone became home to 56,000 air raid wardens. Chicago swore in 23,000 block captains, each of whom had subordinates. LaGuardia also emphasized protection of vital water supplies. Critics charged with some accuracy that he neglected morale, a rather nebulous subject, to concentrate on other matters. LaGuardia's priorities influenced the general approach and direction that the Office of Civilian Defense would take throughout much of the war.[2]

Governor Keen Johnson of Kentucky appointed John J. Greenleaf as state civil defense director. Greenleaf, who also served on the Public Service Commission, had been one of Governor Johnson's campaign managers back in 1939. He had both Johnson's confidence and his ear. The U.S.

Army assigned Major David Williams to help Greenleaf with civil defense matters. The state legislature at Frankfort granted Johnson a defense fund of $200,000 for 1942.[3]

Local civil defense councils sprang up under LaGuardia's Office of Civilian Defense and the state civil defense apparatus. The local defense councils performed the tough day-to-day work. Procurement of civil defense personnel, most of whom were volunteers, fell to the localities. Local councils scrambled to come up with requisite firefighting equipment. While mayors usually provided titular leadership, an appointed coordinator of a local defense council dealt most often with OCD underlings and with town authorities such as fire and police chiefs. Lexington, Louisville, Paducah, Somerset, Ashland, and many other Kentucky cities established civil defense councils, which operated for varying lengths of time. At first, they concentrated on taking precautions against aerial assault and sabotage. Later, the councils helped push forward a host of nonprotective endeavors such as bond sales and blood drives.[4]

Mayor T. Ward Havely of Lexington spearheaded the drive for establishment of a Lexington and Fayette County Civilian Defense Council, and the Lexington Civilian Defense Council appeared in June of 1941, making it one of the first of its kind in Kentucky. Under Havely's direction, Lexington and nearby communities took steps to counteract a variety of potential Axis strikes. Air raid wardens were named and volunteers recruited to assist firemen and police against incendiary bombs. Two weeks after Pearl Harbor, Lexington experienced its first blackout test, complete with air raid sirens. The Lexington Telephone Company planned for the worst, bracing itself for possible sabotage. The Lexington Water Company shut its grounds to public visitation. Lexington officials and companies viewed civil defense as a matter of considerable gravity, refusing to be caught off guard.[5]

President Roosevelt and Governor Johnson insisted that civil defense efforts be taken seriously. FDR noted that, under the right circumstances, the German air force could bomb New York, Detroit, and other American cities. Johnson repeatedly asserted that the presence of war plants in the commonwealth made it "highly probable enemy bombs will fall." The heavy industry of Louisville, as well as Cincinnati, Ohio (a big city located just a few hundred yards away from northern Kentucky towns like

Covington), and Charlestown, Indiana, put these places at risk; facilities such as the Ford plant in the "Falls City," the Cincinnati Milling Machine Company, and the Charlestown smokeless powder plant required protection against potential enemy attack. Everyone knew, too, that German and Japanese submarines prowled the East and West coasts of the United States, making it a distinct possibility that at least a few Axis saboteurs would slip into the country. The obvious point was that cities and towns throughout Kentucky should maintain themselves in a constant state of readiness.[6]

Events indicated that Kentucky was not invulnerable. On September 9, 1942, a Japanese pilot launched from a sub off the Pacific coast flew a single-engine float plane over Oregon, releasing two 168-pound incendiary bombs, which exploded in the forest below. The pilot repeated this exercise two weeks later. Although the four bombs caused no significant damage, they might have started a major forest fire had conditions been drier. As it was, with these two episodes Japan showed it could strike at least a light blow against the U.S. mainland. A German sabotage effort hit closer to Kentucky, raising a more serious alarm. Eight agents trained by the Abwehr—the German counterintelligence agency—slipped into Florida and New York in June 1942. Their papers included drawings of Aluminum Company of America plants in Tennessee, Illinois, and New York, along with sketches of the New York City water supply system and locks on the Ohio River. The saboteurs' mission was to damage the aluminum plants in order to keep vital aluminum away from airplane production, to blow up New York City water supply pipes, and to destroy canal sluices at St. Louis and Cincinnati. Although Operation Pastorius (as it was code-named) failed, it nearly touched Kentucky and heightened apprehensions.[7]

Federal Bureau of Investigation warnings, coupled with these other events, put Kentucky officials on edge. The FBI informed air raid instructors and others that a "branch office" of Abwehr existed in Louisville and that Lexington, Elizabethtown, Frankfort, Owensboro, and several nearby Indiana towns were home to individual spies. Three shortwave radio stations in direct communication with the Third Reich had been uncovered in Louisville since the Pearl Harbor attack. Other shortwave radios in the Falls City and elsewhere continued to transmit vital information back to Germany. Spies captured in the eastern part of the United States possessed a map of Louisville's industrial plants with each one circled in red. Enemy activity in Kentucky, according to the FBI, was both brisk and dangerous and must be counteracted. Although the Federal Bureau of Investigation exaggerated the dangers of German spying in the commonwealth, along with the capacity of the German air force to hit targets so far away, Kentucky authorities and many Kentuckians were convinced that the cost of vigilance was justified.[8]

Given government statements and conditions on the ground, Lexington's commitment to protection of civilians remained steadfast. Indeed, the city expanded its civil defense operations. In August 1942, city and Fayette County protection and health officials decided to add reinforcements to the civil defense organization. Auxiliary fire and police units were created, bolstering manpower by 300 firemen, 600 fire-watchers, and 300 policemen. When the Washington headquarters of the Office of Civilian Defense deemphasized protection, the Lexington Civil Defense Council ratcheted up nonprotective efforts. In April 1943, the Office of Civilian Defense recognized Lexington's accomplishments by naming it as the first defense council in the entire Fifth Region to receive a citation of merit.[9]

Louisville's devotion to civil defense ultimately proved even more powerful than Lexington's. The population and industrial base of the River City dwarfed those of all other towns in Kentucky. Louisville alone produced more than 50 percent of the war-related goods made in the commonwealth. Because of these factors, the War Department designated Louisville a "target city"—one of a couple dozen in the United States that faced the greatest likelihood of Axis attack. Under these circumstances, Louisville's defensive measures acquired special urgency.[10]

Wilson Wyatt's intense involvement with civil defense was what first brought him national attention. Wyatt took office as mayor of Louisville on December 1, 1941. Six days later, the Japanese bombed Pearl Harbor. Wyatt served as chair of the Louisville Metropolitan Area Defense Council and was a guiding force for regional civil defense planning. Young and enthusiastic, he spent much more time and energy on civil defense matters than the average mayor. Wyatt helped to set up the organizational chart for the Louisville Metropolitan Area Defense Council, which included

Louisville and adjacent areas of Kentucky, plus Floyd and Clark counties in Indiana. He proved instrumental in the selection of Neil Dalton as Louisville area civil defense coordinator. Mayor Wyatt helped supervise and improve civil defense activities throughout World War II.[11]

The Louisville Defense Council was made up of five divisions: safety, welfare, health, works, and volunteer service. Personnel for the safety division included air raid wardens, auxiliary firemen, and auxiliary policemen. They shared the responsibility of minimizing the loss of life and property resulting from any kind of German or Japanese incursion against Louisville, especially an aerial assault. The welfare division would call in works division trucks and other forms of transport to evacuate citizens from disaster areas and locate temporary housing for refugees. Doctors, nurses, and nurses' aides filled the ranks of the health division, which existed to provide field and hospital care for any civilians wounded during bombardment or from subversive activity. Aside from its part in evacuation, works supplied the manpower and much of the equipment for the installation of blackout and air raid warning systems. Volunteer service personnel helped recruit volunteers for the other divisions and addressed assorted manpower deficiencies. A bomb-proof communications center, with appropriate telephone and radio equipment, was established in a subbasement of Louisville City Hall. The communications center established links to cities farther east and west, such as Ashland and Bowling Green, so Louisville could receive advance warning of an enemy attack. Mayor Wyatt and Defense Coordinator Dalton stressed that teamwork must prevail over egotism.[12]

Louisville's air raid warden network was extensive. Of the 50,000 or so civil defense workers scattered around the Falls City by 1943, approximately 12,000 belonged to the air raid organization. Walter H. Shackleton served as chief air raid warden. Five division commanders, one for each of the city's police districts, and sixty-six sector wardens were under Shackleton. Ordinary air raid wardens, numbering 834 at the start, and more later, received direction from the sector wardens. Thousands of others assisted the higher-ups. Designation as an air raid warden, or even as a rank-and-file member of the air raid network, came with greater prestige than other civil defense positions, and these jobs were highly coveted. The mere notion of informing one's fellow citizens about an impending attack struck many not only as important but also as altruistic and romantic.[13]

Earl Quinn, a Louisville civil defense officer, in 1942. (Courtesy of Ohio River Portrait Project, Kentucky Historical Society.)

Auxiliary firemen were seen as first responders in the case of any enemy attack that generated a blaze. The auxiliary firemen would race to the scene, find the fires, and stamp them out before they could spread. Sand could be used to extinguish sparks and really small fires, while four-gallon pump-tank fire extinguishers would be employed against bigger fires. Since the Office of Civilian Defense estimated that just one enemy bomber could start 166 fires, the auxiliary firemen would be busy. Later, fire watchers and fire guards were enlisted to assist the auxiliary firemen. Only if a blaze threatened to get out of control would the city firemen be called as a last line of defense. Fewer than six hundred auxiliary firemen and their helpers were expected to put out the vast majority of fires quickly and efficiently, with no aid from the professionals.[14]

One of the best examples of organizational teamwork, designed to achieve a major firefighting goal, transpired in 1942. The Office of Civilian Defense transferred ninety-two 500-gallon water pumpers to the Louisville Defense Council. The Defense Council solicited companies in the Louisville area, asking them to deed over trucks for the duration of the war plus sixty days. The trucks would be fitted with the 500-gallon pumpers, giving the city ninety-two makeshift fire trucks in a short time at very little cost. The corporate response proved excellent, and the Works Progress Administration supplied the tools used to attach the pumpers to the trucks. By November 5, 1943, ninety-two auxiliary fire stations existed around Louisville, and thirty-five of them had the new firefighting trucks. Louisville led the OCD's Fifth Region in this regard; indeed, it set a national standard. Public-private cooperation made this fine result possible.[15]

Civil defense leaders also saw the need for auxiliary policemen. Over 1,100 auxiliary policemen patrolled Louisville's streets, parks, and other places by January 1, 1943, on the lookout for saboteurs and others involved in criminal activity. They also engaged in crowd control. If Axis planes bombed Louisville's buildings and residences, auxiliary police were expected to control loitering and looting. These auxiliary police supplied their own uniforms, badges, guns, and clubs, served without pay, and gave of their time and energy "because it is needed to make up for the manpower shortage in our Police Department and to be ready for emergencies." This job, like others connected with civil defense, permitted citizens to show their support for the war effort and give of themselves in a noble cause.[16]

Health care professionals also helped out. Many doctors volunteered their services; a larger number of nurses joined up. A course on nursing care under wartime conditions held from April to June 1942 at Louisville General Hospital, for instance, attracted more than 200 nurses. There they learned how to treat serious burns, major wounds, and shock, and how to use sulfa drugs. One of the teachers, Dr. Joseph Hamilton, stressed that "everyone concerned with the burned patient should wear a mask," adding that "the close scrutiny of loved ones may be the very thing that will kill the patient." Many other nurses pitched in, as did nurses' aides and concerned citizens who merely had taken a Red Cross first-aid course or two. Nurses' aides took 100 hours of class work, first aid, and supervised practice in the hospital setting; "their job was to relieve graduate nurses of simple chores so they could tend to more serious, complicated matters." Altogether, some 25,000 civil defense workers (most of them beginners and many of them women) were to provide treatment of various sorts for civilians and soldiers injured in a German or Japanese attack on the city.[17]

Ambulance drivers, of course, also participated in civil defense. Patients would have to be transported from the place where they were hurt to hospitals and other treatment centers. The Louisville Women's Ambulance and Defense Training Corps sprang up just before Pearl Harbor to perform this vital function. Four hundred women made up the Corps by December 21, 1941; more joined later. Hundreds of men served as ambulance drivers, too.[18]

With the Louisville civil defense apparatus up and running, practice and more practice seemed to be the best course. Air raid drills began. A simulated disaster, complete with major casualties, played itself out. Ohio River pleasure boat owners formed an Auxiliary Coast Guard, an appendage of the United States Coast Guard. War plants, corporations, and utilities put into place measures designed to insure continuous, uninterrupted operation in an environment that the Federal Bureau of Investigation insisted was crawling with spies. The River City prepared itself for any Axis threat, no matter how likely or unlikely that threat might be.

Louisville's first blackout took place on April 20, 1942. Only part of the city was involved, along with neighboring areas of Indiana. Approximately 100,000 people participated, switching off their lights from 9:10 to 9:30 that night. Army observers, flying in an airplane over the city, peered into the blackness, able to make out "half a dozen minute pinpoints of light at most." They judged the test a stirring success.[19]

Colonel Robert S. Harsh witnessed the whole operation. With so little light available, had this event been real, enemy planes would have had a difficult time hitting their Kentuckiana targets. The damage to war plants, as well as the number of casualties, would have been light. "I think you've done a wonderful job here tonight," Colonel Harsh remarked to Mayor Wyatt.[20]

The April 20 air raid practice had gone off quite well, with just a few small hitches. A church at Fourth Street and Oak in Louisville deemed a meeting more important than the air raid drill, refusing repeated requests to douse its lights. A drunk man threw a punch at an air raid warden who had asked him to go home. A few cars with headlights on rolled through the streets when they should not have. The authorities characterized these violations as minor, however, and the Army suggested more comprehensive events be planned, leading ultimately to a complete blackout of the city and surrounding locations in Kentucky and Indiana.[21]

During the evening of June 8, 1942, downtown Louisville and additional parts of the city were plunged into darkness, as were other parts of Jefferson County and extensive areas in Clark and Floyd counties, Indiana. This drill involved 200,000 residents, twice the number of the previous exercise. Some 15,000 civil defense workers were also involved, including air raid wardens, auxiliary firemen, auxiliary policemen, health care professionals, Works Department personnel, and assorted volunteers. Despite the increase in territory and population, the second blackout went just as smoothly as the first.[22]

A tiny number of people still refused to comply with the blackouts. At the DuPont Paint Service Store on 325 West Jefferson Street, inside and outside lights shone brightly throughout the drill. Spokesmen for several businesses in the First District, when asked by air raid wardens to turn off their lights, replied, "Go to hell." Increasingly perturbed by this kind of behavior, Mayor Wyatt informed the press, "We're really going to work on [violators], probably with prosecutions in some aggravated and willful

cases." Most of the nonconformists got the message and, in the end, violations of air raid rules never amounted to a significant problem.[23]

Buoyed by the positive results from the latest air raid test, the Louisville Defense Council and the Army announced a blackout for the entire
Louisville metropolitan area to be held on the night of Wednesday, June
24. All of Jefferson County, Kentucky (including Louisville), plus Floyd
and Clark counties, Indiana, fell under this mandate. Nearly 1,000 square
miles of land and almost half a million people were affected. The lights
went out at 9:29 p.m. and stayed off for thirty-one minutes. Darkness
again engulfed the area. Civil defense personnel numbering 20,000 scur-
ried about, carrying out their duties. Ten-year-old Barry Hill noticed air
raid wardens and fire watchers rushing past him, brandishing flashlights
and carrying buckets of sand. Barry knew that in the event of a true
emergency these people were there to pour sand and water on fires and to
assist victims. This time around, the only problems were one car accident
and five or six instances of drunkenness. One small part of the unfolding drama involved six Boy Scouts, who were drafted by civil defense to
act like victims of Axis bombardment. Stationed at Bardstown Road and
Douglass Boulevard, the Scouts faked grave injuries, using catsup as a
substitute for blood. Medical help soon arrived, whisking the casualties
away with little difficulty. The blackout as a whole was accomplished both
effectively and efficiently.[24]

Mayor Wilson Wyatt, speaking again in his capacity as chairman of
the Louisville Metropolitan Defense Council, hailed the efforts of everyone involved with the blackouts. The Army praised civil defense workers
and the people of Kentucky and Indiana who participated. The authorities
concluded their commentary by reiterating that the possibility of enemy
attack was still real, so there would be surprise air raid drills in the future.
The people of the Louisville metropolitan area had to stay alert because
the next air raid siren or whistle "may mean enemy planes are in sight."[25]

Several months later, in November 1942, yet another air raid drill
took place, and this one came without any warning whatsoever. Mobilization of the civil defense network and "lights out" occurred without major
incident. Earlier practices led to a good result now, under more stressful
circumstances. Meanwhile, the Works Department had identified seventy
locations which might be used as air raid shelters, and Chief Air Raid

Warden Walter Shackleton ordered that air raid sirens be blown once a week to make sure that they stayed in good order. If an Axis aerial assault ever occurred, the Louisville area was about as ready as it could be without having experienced the shocking reality of actual warfare.[26]

Tests of various types were carried out even after 1942. As late as May 29, 1944, the Louisville Defense Council staged an elaborate simulation designed to keep emergency medical service (EMS) personnel on their toes. A "disaster" occurred at the Beargrass Station of the Louisville Gas and Electric Company, resulting in fifty-five casualties. EMS workers had to apply emergency first aid on the scene, move the wounded to a nearby casualty station, and send the most seriously injured to a hospital in the city. For the purposes of this exercise, members of the EMS carried the victims to an improvised casualty station; the Standard Country Club, located one mile to the east, served as a "hospital." The EMS handled this pretend disaster easily, making sure that the injured received prompt treatment. For its part, the Louisville Defense Council made it clear once again that it saw emergency preparedness as a responsibility that must not be shirked and that positive results were expected.[27]

While authorities stressed over and over again that Germany and Japan possessed the technological capacities to strike Louisville from the air, it was also conceivable that Axis saboteurs might inflict damage on Louisville from the water or ground. With these threats in mind, the Louisville Coast Guard Auxiliary (LCGA) came into being, and Louisville war plants, companies, and utilities stepped up security measures. Vigilance was a must.

The Louisville Coast Guard Auxiliary was established in 1942. Approximately forty pleasure craft, of many sizes and shapes, comprised the fleet. These vessels plied the Ohio River, keeping watch for any suspicious activities on the river itself and along its banks. The LCGA let boat owners know that area war plants, railroad depots, airports, utilities, and other places were vulnerable to Axis saboteurs and that the agents of destruction might well come from boats on the Ohio River. The job at hand was to prevent anything of that sort from happening. The Auxiliary Coast Guard acted as "eyes and ears" on the waterways and operated for a good part of the war.[28]

Weapons plants, companies that manufactured other defense-related items, railroads, utilities, and the like understood that they might be subject to spying and sabotage. New rules were formulated to mitigate against enemy activities. Companies hired more watchmen. The Louisville Water Company, to cite just one example, installed fencing and floodlights in sensitive areas and employed armed guards. The prewar policy of allowing curious visitors to view company facilities, equipment, and procedures was ended. The Crescent Hill Reservoir and the new Cardinal Hill Reservoir received additional scrutiny designed to thwart any plans to mine water mains or contaminate water supplies. The FBI encouraged practices such as these, given its high estimate of the menace.[29]

Lexington and Louisville were not the only cities in Kentucky to establish strong civil defense organizations. Many smaller towns, such as Paducah, Somerset, Maysville, and Franklin, built impressive defense networks of their own. Counties, too, created defense councils and enlisted members of their respective communities to watch out for the enemy. Schools conducted air raid drills.

Paducah's civil defense program grew quickly. The Municipal Defense Council took shape on December 8, 1941, just a day after Pearl Harbor. Somewhere between 600 and 700 persons rushed to apply for defense positions right at the start. As of January 16, 1942, roughly 1,500 people were working in Paducah's burgeoning civil defense effort. Paducahans, like other Kentuckians, wanted revenge against Japan for its dastardly attack, believing that the Japanese had "no thought for ten years but to steal and kill." Vengeance would be sweet, but much work and sacrifice were required first, and the people of Paducah got to it fast.[30]

Charles Sawyer did the heavy lifting for civil defense in Paducah. Sawyer, a district manager for Southern Bell Telephone Company, served as vice-chairman and coordinator for the Paducah Municipal Defense Council. He proclaimed, "There is no reason to believe that we will be immune from bombing and other attacks. It is a certainty we will have to guard against sabotage in plants." Abiding by this sober pronouncement, Sawyer put together an organization that integrated firemen, police, air raid wardens, public works, streets, medical services, water and sewage facilities, utilities, legal services, and public relations.[31]

Fire Chief Ray Wilkins, one of Sawyer's subordinates, reiterated that spies and saboteurs were a concern. Wilkins noted that the "number of

Axis sympathizers in Paducah is surprisingly large and [they] must be kept under surveillance." He said he had received his information about Nazi elements from the FBI, so it was no joke.[32]

Vice-Chairman Sawyer and other officials declared that the presence of gasoline bulk plants and the Illinois Central Railroad shops in the Paducah area made all sorts of precautions necessary. The companies involved had already taken steps toward increased protection, such as requiring employees and visitors to show identification badges and hiring additional watchmen. The Paducah Defense Council supported such practices and called for them to be more extensive. Sawyer summed up the philosophy of civil defense when he announced that "it is better . . . to be prepared for something that may never happen rather than unprepared for something which certainly could happen."[33]

In Somerset, the American Legion assumed the key role in establishing a defense council. The Legion thought first about establishing air raid warning groups in the city and throughout Pulaski County. The original organization called for a Chief Air Raid Observer and two deputy observers. Auxiliary fire and police departments took their initial members from the ranks of the American Legion. Paul Dexheimer was named chair of the Pulaski County defense council, while Dr. Carl Norfleet became coordinator of medical services. Some two hundred World War I veterans, including several African Americans, volunteered for civil defense duties by December 25, 1941; more people joined thereafter.[34]

Maysville put together a civil defense outfit. John Perrine lived in that Mason County town throughout World War II. Perrine was only seven years old when the attack on Pearl Harbor occurred, too young to understand it all. As the war continued and he got older, Perrine began to grasp the seriousness of the conflict, and it disturbed him. He remembers thinking that German and Japanese tanks might show up on his doorstep any day. He also recalls blackouts and air raid wardens going about their business in and about Maysville.[35]

Franklin, Kentucky's population was not as large as that of Paducah or even Maysville. Nevertheless, Mildred Harris remembers a civil defense unit there. Its members kept "a weather eye on transportation and on power lines and things like that." Harris noted that the civil defense volunteers "didn't have any specific information about what might happen

American Rolling Mill Company officials and interested guests from Kentucky, Ohio, and West Virginia meet in an air raid shelter located in Ashland. (Courtesy of the Hagley Museum and Library.)

. . . they were just sort of guarding." A tower appeared by Potts Lumber Company from which men could scan the skies for approaching enemy aircraft. The tower operated twenty-four hours a day for a while.[36]

Various counties, like cities and towns, set up defense councils. The Oldham County Civilian Defense Council provided guidance for about 400 civil defense workers. A blackout took place in that county on August 20, 1942. Residents of Shelby County participated in air raid drills, too. The Paducah civil defense network ultimately expanded, encompassing all of McCracken County. Somewhere between 3,000 and 5,000 people engaged in various tasks related to civil defense there.

Children at public and private schools participated in daytime air raid drills. They sat in hallways with their backs against the walls and their heads down on their knees, or in classrooms under tables or desks. Teachers told them when to take their positions and when to go back to regular activities. Some children took the drills seriously; others clowned around.

Civil defense organizations made their presence felt in Kentucky before Pearl Harbor, and many more popped up in the aftermath of Japanese aggression. Counteracting potential Axis air raids—and sabotage plans—drew the greatest amount of attention and effort in the beginning, if only because the death of Americans at Pearl Harbor had stunned and galvanized the citizenry. A consensus quickly emerged that Americans needed to do everything possible to prevent the enemy from catching them napping again.[37]

The stress on civilian safety diminished with the passage of time, largely because the military equation improved. The Japanese advance that began with Pearl Harbor halted after the battles of the Coral Sea and Midway. The United States managed to establish a defensive perimeter in the central Pacific and southern Pacific areas beyond which Japan could not go. Meanwhile, Germany was preoccupied with Russia. By summer 1942, the chances of either Axis power sending its air force over America were slim to none. Kentucky air raid wardens who spent countless hours and days searching clear skies for enemy planes that never came understood this reality and their ardor decreased, though many of them kept constant watch until the end of the war.[38]

Kentucky took civil defense seriously, especially for a state located within the interior of the United States. Kentucky civil defense officials for the most part proved to be conscientious, carrying out their responsibilities with zealousness or at minimum in a dutiful manner. No town in Kentucky behaved like Newcastle, Wyoming, which flatly ignored a statewide blackout. All the lights in Newcastle, noted one writer, "continued to burn," and if the Japanese had come Newcastle would "have been bombed to hell." Nor did Kentuckians find endless excuses to avoid serving on civil defense bodies. Iowans cited "health concerns, family issues, business pressures, lack of employees, lack of time, involvement with other committees, or commissions in the military" to sidestep positions on civil defense councils. Although a handful of Kentuckians found reasons to excuse themselves from civil defense work, such examples were few and far between. Kentucky carried out the various protective functions of civil defense diligently. The laxity apparent in Wyoming and parts of Iowa and Ohio was not so obvious in Kentucky.[39]

By 1943 even the OCD grasped the fact that aerial assault of the United States was highly unlikely. Civilian protection plans were gradually deemphasized and nonprotective activities encouraged. Nonprotective activities took many forms, including bond sales, scrap drives, blood drives, and other pursuits. Anything that aided the war effort, no matter how indirectly, or that even just fostered fellow feeling, fell into this category.[40]

Defense councils throughout Kentucky experienced this change. While protective functions such as air raid drills and maintenance of air raid equipment continued, albeit with less frequency, nonprotective activities became more common. The Louisville, Lexington, Paducah, Ashland, and Newport defense councils embraced a host of war-related services that had little or nothing to do with the carnage that Axis weaponry might inflict on Kentucky populations.

In Louisville, air raid wardens and other civil defense workers performed many new jobs. They urged the public to buy U.S. government war bonds; indeed, air raid wardens even sold bonds themselves. They promoted the collection of materials such as tin, waste paper, and cooking fats. Jack Marx, manager of the City Hide and Tallow Company, joined with the Louisville Defense Council in 1944 to amass some 40,000 pounds of waste fat per month from stores, restaurants, and other sources. Waste fat went into such war products as synthetic rubber, parachutes, deicing fluids for planes, and explosives. The Nutrition Committee of the Louisville Defense Council extolled the virtues of a healthy diet, which included eating less meat. A blood plasma drive received the help of Falls City civil defense personnel.[41]

One of the most unusual and interesting tasks finished by the Louisville Defense Council dealt with the so-called Rat Menace. Apparently, rats flourished in certain parts of Louisville under the crowded, chaotic circumstances of war. More food and less sanitation pleased the vermin, leading to their proliferation. In October 1944, the Defense Council carried out a rat extermination campaign for East Jacob Avenue, East College Avenue, South Fifth Street, and a few other places. The civil defense exterminators used "red squill," a poison derived from the bulbs of a lilylike subtropical plant, to eradicate the troublesome rodents. When the rat ate food mixed with red squill, it quickly died. Other animals experienced less severe problems with red squill because they could eject the poison by vomiting, whereas the rats could not. Hundreds and hundreds, perhaps thousands, of rats were killed, and the people in the affected neighborhoods pronounced themselves well pleased with the results. The Rat Killing and Cleanup Campaign even came with a movie called *Keep 'em Out.*[42]

Lexington and Paducah furnished other examples of nonprotective work. The Lexington Defense Council urged the people of that city to contribute aluminum scrap to the nation's war machine, and they cooperated. The Paducah Defense Council excelled when it came to the sale of war bonds and stamps and collection of waste materials. The Boy Scouts helped out with nonprotective activities in the Paducah area.[43]

One last civil defense effort bears mention. Although the Axis never dropped bombs on the commonwealth, civil defense workers in Kentucky faced an emergency of a quite different type. When the Ohio River flooded in the first days of January 1943, the Red Cross called on the civil defense apparatus and on civil defense manpower for help. With so many men in the military, and emerging manpower shortages in industry and agriculture, few organizations commanded so many people and resources as the defense network. The civil defense system quickly swung into action, fighting a major flood instead of German and Japanese might. The results were gratifying.

The January 1943 flood turned out to be a nasty one. Though not nearly as deadly or destructive as the 1937 Ohio Valley flood, which produced ninety deaths and $50 million of property damage in the Louisville area alone, the 1943 flood held the potential to generate substantial chaos. December 1942 snows combined with warmer temperatures and a Christmas rain to send vast amounts of water from streams and creeks careening into the Ohio River—which quickly overflowed its banks. When the river exceeded flood stage at Pittsburgh, Pennsylvania, the American Red Cross requested assistance from state defense authorities. Pennsylvania, Ohio, West Virginia, and Kentucky braced for the worst, but the aid of civil defense personnel proved instrumental in minimizing property damage and casualties from the flooding. The January 1943 flood was serious,

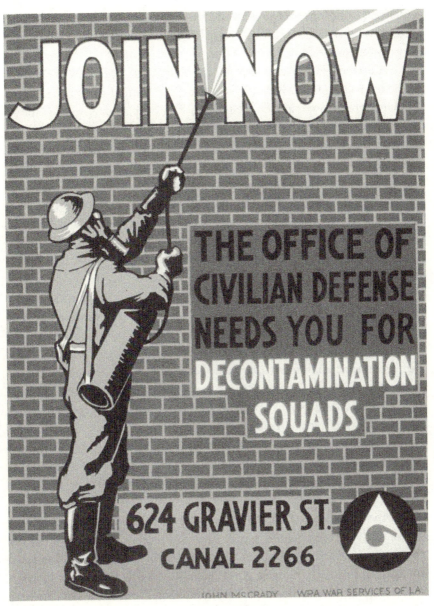

"Join now. The Office of Civilian Defense needs you for decontamination squads." This poster encouraged civilians to join civil defense squads such as the one in Louisville that did away with the "Rat Menace." (Courtesy of the Library of Congress.)

damaging buildings and homes and displacing large numbers of people across several states, but it would have been worse had not the civil defense network intervened.[44]

Catlettsburg and Ashland were the first Kentucky cities in the path of the onrushing Ohio River. Rising waters on January 1 and January 2, 1943, put these towns at risk. Water eight feet deep soon covered Catlettsburg's business district. A total of fifteen blocks were flooded. Civil defense personnel, along with the Red Cross and the American Legion, moved sixty-five people to safe places. Nearby Ashland suffered a similar fate. Parts of this city were under seven feet of water; hundreds of homes and businesses were partially submerged. Fortunately, rescue teams evacuated 250 families "without mishap." The high waters proved bad enough to force a one-day suspension of operations at the Ashland plant of the American Rolling Mill Company, with the subsequent loss of steel for the war effort that that entailed.[45]

Other Kentucky towns also battled the flood. Rushing water swamped a good part of Maysville. More than one hundred families were forced to leave their homes and another hundred found themselves trapped on the higher floors of their houses. A dozen businesses were drenched. Total damage in that small town approached $20,000. Newport, which lay farther west, had more time to prepare and therefore fared better than most places. W. D. Anderson, coordinator of the Campbell County Civilian Defense Council and director of Newport's Department of Municipal Defense, led some 600 civil defense workers in the fight against the torrent. These men and women included air raid wardens, auxiliary police and firemen, fire watchers, and emergency medical services. They used boats to rescue stranded people. Telephone calls were made to warn others on the edge of the flood to relocate. Over 300 people per day found shelter at the Arnold School, where they also received food. Civil defense volunteers guarded warehouses and stores to prevent looting. Newport emerged from the flooding in good shape. Louisville lucked out in 1943. After the devastating flood of 1937, planning for a flood wall to keep water out of the city had begun, but U.S. entry into the war had led to postponement of all construction. The Falls City remained unprotected and vulnerable. Fortunately, the Ohio River at Louisville crested at thirty-four feet; it would have taken thirty-five to forty feet to begin the destruction. It was not until 1957 that the first section of Louisville's flood wall was finished.[46]

The Ohio River flood tested the mettle of Kentucky's civil defense forces, and they performed splendidly. Newport's W. D. Anderson noted that his defense workers "were all at their places, just as promptly as if we had been subjected to a bombing attack," Mayor J. J. Pennington of Catlettsburg declared that less damage took place with the 1943 flood than with "previous floods of the same size." Civil defense personnel made the difference.[47]

Civil defense endeavors in towns and cities across Kentucky generally met with success. If the response to the flood provides any indication, the commonwealth's defenders would have handled an Axis bombing run in a relatively orderly, efficient manner (just as the British dealt calmly and sensibly with the Blitz). This is not to say, however, that defensive efforts never ran into problems. The most important cities in Kentucky created civil defense organizations that functioned smoothly, but not every town had its own defense council. Another concern was that state and local defense councils were dominated by white, middle-class males. Gender and racial norms prevented women and blacks from taking leadership positions, even from procuring some rank-and-file jobs.[48]

Kentucky's women found places in traditional areas. They served as nurses, nurses' aides, and first-aid volunteers. A few became ambulance drivers. Almost none took posts as chairs, coordinators, air raid chiefs, and auxiliary police and firefighters.

African Americans complained about a lack of spots for them. Charles V. Carr, a black lawyer and politician from Cleveland, became Race Relations Adviser for the Fifth Region, OCD—which included Kentucky. Carr, who had worked with Cleveland's Future Outlook League during the Great Depression to help secure jobs for semiskilled and unskilled blacks, worked hard to increase the presence of African Americans in the civil defense organization but achieved only small gains. The Louisville and Somerset defense forces, along with some others, included a smattering of blacks, yet they labored in the least prestigious posts and as a whole were underrepresented. Preexisting racial patterns largely determined the circumscribed role that blacks played in defense of the homeland.[49]

Civil defense activities began to wind down by the latter part of 1943.

On November 1 of that year, the War Department advised defense councils across the United States that they should end air raid drills. War Department officials admitted that "token air raids are always a possibility," but that "the present degree of danger" was extremely small. Many towns and cities, in dozens of states, had abandoned air raid drills and sabotage efforts even before the War Department announcement, and still more quit after it. The Hamilton County National Defense Council (HCNDC), which included Cincinnati, Ohio, provides a good example. The HCNDC shut down its operations in September 1944 but had not done much at all for months before that. Even nonprotective endeavors started to fall by the wayside as it became increasingly clear that America would be on the winning side in the great struggle.[50]

Kentucky bucked the trend. Louisville defense officials, in particular, advocated continued vigilance against even the slightest chance of enemy attack. Walter Shackleton, who moved up from chief air raid warden to coordinator, the job that Neil Dalton once held, stated that the "war is not yet over and while the news to the most part is good, [fighting] can still 'happen here.'"[51]

Civil defense efforts in Louisville remained vigorous throughout the winter of 1944–1945. The auxiliary police and auxiliary firemen kept up their work because the military's almost insatiable demand for manpower meant that nobody else was around to walk an extra beat or rescue treed cats. Air raid wardens sold more and more war bonds, encouraging others to do the same. Defense personnel sponsored blood plasma drives. While Shackleton bowed to complaints about excessive noise from weekly air raid sirens, deciding by July 1944 to stop that practice, he still operated the sirens "at such times as may be necessary to test the equipment." Occasional tests continued until May 1, 1945, at which point they were finally discontinued.[52]

V-E Day accelerated curtailment of defense activities, yet they lingered still. The Jefferson County Fiscal Court responded to Germany's surrender by cutting annual appropriations for the Louisville Defense Council from $5,700 to $3,500. Shackleton now set his sights on an "orderly liquidation of civilian defense." He thought it necessary to collect and return various supplies that had been provided by the federal government. He also expressed a desire to sell excess equipment, including the air raid sirens. Of course Shackleton realized that the sirens would probably not find a buyer because the supply far exceeded any postwar demand. Walter Shackleton's defense service concluded when he accepted a job with the Schuler Koster Motor Company in late October 1945; by that time, the Louisville Defense Council's work was done, as was that of the other defense councils in the state.[53]

Kentucky's civil defense experience was largely positive. Though Axis planes never bombed any part of the state, authorities such as Governor Keen Johnson stressed that it could happen, and tens of thousands of Kentuckians gave willingly of their time and effort to minimize any destruction or loss of life that might have occurred from such a traumatic event. All necessary precautions—such as conducting air raid drills and guarding potential sabotage targets—were taken, an approach that only made sense during a time of total war. As the chance of an enemy strike diminished, nonprotective activities assumed greater importance. The sale of war bonds, collection of scrap metal, and accumulation of blood supplies rose as a result. Efforts to combat the Ohio River flood of New Year 1943, which included the active participation of civil defense workers from Ashland to Newport, proved quite effective and may well have justified all civil defense exertions without taking any other event into account. Both protective and nonprotective functions of Kentucky's civil defense network fostered cooperation and shared sacrifice when it was most needed. The omission of women and blacks from the leadership of civil defense was wrong, but it did not substantially impair unity. Taking everything into account, Louisville's commitment to civil defense clearly exceeded that of Cincinnati's, and the commonwealth as a whole proved steadfast in defending itself from the threat of German and Japanese assault.

7

A Black Man's Place and a New Place for Blacks

Throughout Kentucky history, African Americans have faced inequality. Slavery brought them subordination, the worst kind of poverty, and other types of pain. Blacks rejoiced when the Civil War destroyed slavery, only to confront mob violence and "separate but unequal" treatment. On the eve of World War II, Kentucky's shrinking African American community continued to fight back against the burdens imposed by racism and segregation. The war brought positive economic change and a small increment of political advancement. White society tolerated black gains only because of wartime exigencies. Once the war ended, Kentucky's African Americans again found the way forward more difficult, but this time they responded more assertively than they had before. Having served the United States well, both in the military and on the home front, they deemed a return to the old, unfavorable status quo unacceptable. Black protests against injustice in Kentucky increased after 1945, culminating in the civil rights crusade a decade later.

White planters and farmers came to early Kentucky with their slaves, who provided valuable services. Field hands, who had the most difficult jobs, brought in corn, hemp, and tobacco. Some slaves became household servants. A few in the late eighteenth century, and a growing number later, found themselves employed in salt mines, ironworks, and other manufacturing endeavors. Slaves were routinely whipped when they angered the master. Black flesh was torn apart. Sometimes, African American families were broken up when the owner decided to sell a family member to make money. When Kentucky statehood arrived in 1792, whites "rewarded" blacks for their hard work and suffering by enshrining slavery in the state constitution. The same thing happened again in both the 1799 and 1850 constitutions.[1]

The Civil War brought freedom to Kentucky slaves. Union victory over Confederate forces at the Battle of Antietam led President Abraham Lincoln to issue the Emancipation Proclamation on January 1, 1863. The Emancipation Proclamation did not free Kentucky bondsmen, but it did give them great hope that that monumental day did not lie too far ahead. Later in 1863, the United States offered Kentucky slaves legal freedom if they chose to join the Union Army and fight against the Rebels. Approximately 28,000 Kentucky slaves earned freedom for themselves and their family members this way. The underpinnings of slavery in Kentucky had begun to unravel. Final Union triumph over the Confederacy in April 1865 insured the death of slavery everywhere in the United States. When the Thirteenth Amendment to the U.S. Constitution passed in December 1865, almost 200,000 more Kentucky slaves were officially freed, and blacks everywhere in the commonwealth cheered.[2]

White leaders, backed by large white majorities in Kentucky, reacted to the emancipation of blacks by terrorizing them. White supremacists burned ten Freedmen's Bureau schools within the state and bombed another. Between 1865 and 1880 white mobs in the commonwealth lynched some 140 blacks. Each lynching told blacks to toe the white line or else. The demise of slavery left the dominant race in Kentucky without a stable, socially sanctioned means of racial control, engendering powerful feelings of resentment and apprehension that often found expression through illegal means.[3]

Segregation ultimately replaced slavery as the preferred method for regulating race relations in Kentucky. Whites called the shots, receiving superior public facilities, while blacks got inferior facilities or none at all, and the two races stayed apart. Segregation came to Kentucky in a slow, fitful manner and grew until it was nearly all-encompassing. By the 1880s, public schools for whites and public schools for blacks existed. By the 1890s, Kentucky trains equipped with a white coach and a black coach passed from town to town. The Kentucky Institution for the Education of the Blind, ludicrously, established a "White Department" and a "Colored Department." Separate but unequal accommodations spread into many other areas as well. In almost all cases, black facilities received less money from state government than white facilities. African Americans could vote in Kentucky, which offered them some solace, and rare victories occurred. In the vast majority of cases, however, the white majority simply outvoted the black minority. As the years passed and segregation crystallized, white anxieties about black usurpation eased, and lynchings and other physical attacks against African Americans became less frequent. White opposition to racial equality, however, remained steadfast.[4]

During the first four decades of the twentieth century, Kentucky blacks fought hard against injustice and achieved just enough to think that the future would be better than the past. Litigation became the major avenue for African American advancement. The Louisville branch of the National Association for the Advancement of Colored People (NAACP) devoted three years in a successful legal effort to invalidate a Louisville residential segregation ordinance mandating that neither race could move into a neighborhood predominantly occupied by the other race. Triumph came when the U.S. Supreme Court struck down the ordinance in 1917, declaring it unconstitutional. In 1938, the Supreme Court ruled again. This time it declared that Kentucky blacks must be allowed to sit on juries deciding cases of an interracial nature. They had been barred from cases of this type for thirty years, and this practice had to cease so as to guarantee blacks their Fourteenth Amendment rights. During the same year, in the *Gaines* case, the High Court determined that border and Southern state grants for blacks to attend out-of-state universities for graduate-level study violated the equal protection provisions of the Fourteenth Amendment.

The *Gaines* ruling buoyed black hopes for the desegregation of the University of Kentucky (UK). In 1939, Alfred Carroll, a Louisville African American, applied for admission to the UK Law School rather than take state money to go to a university in the North. UK turned Carroll's application down, citing both state law against blacks attending colleges with whites and the fact that the applicant held a bachelor's degree from an unaccredited institution of higher learning. Top leaders of the NAACP did not want to sue UK on Carroll's behalf because it would be too easy for a court to rule against him on the narrow grounds that he lacked proper academic credentials for admission. No lawsuit materialized from the rejection of Carroll's application, and he could not enter UK. In October of 1941, Charles Eubanks, another young black man from Louisville, filled out an application form requesting entrance into UK's civil engineering program. Like Carroll, Eubanks received an emphatic "no" from the university. This time a legal case did ensue, alleging violation of Eubanks's rights. Eubanks's lawyers argued that the new civil engineering program at traditionally black Kentucky State University (KSU) did not measure up to the civil engineering program at UK in any way. Eubanks encountered trouble because KSU president Rufus Atwood refused to acknowledge the grave weaknesses that were so readily apparent in the KSU program. Atwood's stance made it easier for UK lawyers to pretend that the KSU civil engineering program was on par with its UK counterpart. University of Kentucky lawyers dodged and stalled their way to another legal victory. The court dismissed the Eubanks case in January 1945 on the technical grounds that Eubanks's legal counsel had not acted over the course of two consecutive court terms. The system of segregated education in Kentucky—from elementary schools up through the university level—thus survived World War II, though it was under increasing attack and would not last much longer.

Progress of another sort did occur when the Kentucky state legislature unanimously passed an antilynching law in the wake of a 1920 lynching in Versailles. The key provision of this statute involved automatic removal of any peace officer from his job if a lynching took place under his watch. Enforcement of this part of the new law, along with other factors, helped bring lynching in Kentucky to a belated, merciful halt by 1940. On the political side, blacks won elective offices in Hopkinsville during the late 1890s and at Harrodsburg, Winchester, and Mt. Sterling during the 1910s. These kinds of breakthroughs buoyed blacks, keeping their dream of a better day alive, but they happened only through tremendous effort and with the passage of much time. Whites could never be convinced that blacks ought to be treated as equals, and segregation as an institution withstood these glancing blows easily.[5]

Jim Crow hurt Kentucky blacks in myriad ways. Loraine Mathis, an African American from Paducah who grew to adulthood in the 1930s, recalled that she "could not eat at the counter in Woolworth's nor Kresge's." Mary Northington of Covington remembered that the town had a movie theater and a YMCA, but blacks could not go to either. Little Mary often trudged across the bridge to Cincinnati when she wanted to watch a moving picture or play at the "Y." Ben Montgomery—a light-skinned Negro who passed for white—worked for American Radiator and Standard Sanitary Company in Louisville. When some white workers found out Ben's true color, they made it clear that they wanted him to be discharged. Happily, the company president disagreed and let it be known that Ben was staying in his job and that anyone who did not like it could leave. One imagines that other African Americans in Ben's situation were not quite so fortunate.[6]

When the United States entered World War II, the African American minority in Kentucky represented a distinct underclass, which had suffered greatly from a long period of white supremacy. Family, social clubs, church, schools, and racial uplift organizations offered blacks comfort and assistance as they endured seemingly never-ending prejudice. Circumstances, however, were finally changing in a way that favored them. As 1940 gave way to 1941, the Roosevelt administration took steps to prepare the United States for war should it come, and blacks glimpsed a big opportunity to move ahead. The national preparedness program meant the creation of many new jobs in defense plants and the possibility of better employment for African Americans. U.S. government declarations rebuking Germany, Italy, and Japan for taking away the liberty of millions of people struck blacks as hypocritical given that they faced hurtful restrictions in their own country. Nevertheless, the obvious disparity between government language pertaining to worldwide conflict and government behavior at home gave them a better chance than usual to make the case for more equitable treatment. Jews, Ethiopians, Chinese, and American blacks deserved to be treated equally, not as inferiors. At minimum, Kentucky blacks desired a fair share of war work and desegregation of the U.S. military. These goals animated them throughout the preparedness period and the war.

Statistics reveal a lot about the contours of the commonwealth's black community as World War II broke out. Just over 214,000 blacks lived in Kentucky in 1940, 7.5 percent of the total population. In both absolute and percentage terms, these numbers were declining. Fifty-five percent of the commonwealth's blacks lived in urban areas and 45 percent in rural areas. More blacks left the farm for the city with each passing year. Over one-quarter of all blacks in the state (28 percent, to be exact) inhabited

Louisville and Lexington. Hopkinsville's black population in 1940 stood at 35.4 percent of the whole, higher than any town in Kentucky with a population above 10,000. Census data and other materials make it clear that Kentucky blacks were concentrated in central and far western Kentucky, with relatively few in eastern and northern Kentucky.[7]

Kentucky's African Americans of the World War II era exhibited a surprising degree of diversity. While the majority of them fit snugly into the working class, making on average only a little more than one-half the income of whites, a few had accumulated substantial wealth. A number of blacks had shifted to the Democratic party by January 1, 1940, but many clung to their traditional affiliation with the Republican party. Blacks viewed their culture—which included music, literature, art, and sports—with great pride. Most favored desegregation, while others were leery of it because they suspected that mixing the races might dilute their unique African American heritage.[8]

The family remained the most important African American institution. The Kentucky Department of Health determined that the average number of persons in the black family during the wartime period was 3.3, compared to 4.2 persons for the average white family. Contributing factors for the smaller size of the black family included a higher mortality rate for blacks than whites and a greater number of families headed by a single parent (usually the mother). Lower incomes for African American families than for white families may also have restrained the size of the black family. No matter what causes limited the numbers of the black family, it had gained stability and strength since the end of the Civil War. By the time of World War II, most black family units in Kentucky were of the nuclear variety, meaning that they were composed of a father, mother, and children living under one roof. Fewer black families were led by single parents than was the case earlier, and extended families were not as common. In general, the black family provided its members with love, care, and sympathy in a world dominated by bigoted whites. African Americans Henrietta and Brownie Wallace of Jackson, Kentucky, put it well: "Family meant everything to us."[9]

Social clubs offered blacks additional succor. African American fraternities, the Young Men's Christian Association (YMCA), and the Young Women's Christian Association (YWCA) were among the most impor-

Henrietta
Wilson Wallace
of Jackson,
Kentucky, in
1944. (Courtesy of
Brownie Wallace.)

tant organizations of this type. The fraternities included the Elks, the Masons, the Odd Fellows, and the Pythians. Each of them allowed black men to forge friendships with each other and gave them a sense of belonging. The fraternities also helped families of members who needed financial assistance. During the war, the African American Elks of Louisville raised scholarship funds for deserving youth and underwrote oratorical competitions. In Hopkinsville, the Masonic Lodge promoted a type of brotherhood that led blacks there "to greater self-respect and identification." The YMCA and YWCA brought African American men and women throughout Kentucky together, fostering friendships while its members pursued recreational activities. Although the fraternities and the rest were primarily places of social interaction, supplying companionship, social standing, and relaxation to members, they sometimes became involved with broader political efforts aimed at racial enhancement.[10]

The African American church followed only the family in terms of significance. Free blacks prior to the Civil War had established churches of their own. When slavery was abolished, former slaves who had attended white churches left them, and many more independent African American churches appeared. A black Baptist church and various black Methodist churches took form. In Kentucky, more blacks belonged to the black Baptist church than to all other denominations combined. The African Methodist Episcopal Church (AME), the African Methodist Episcopal Zion Church, and the Colored Methodist Episcopal Church attracted significant, but lesser, memberships. A scant number of blacks chose the Lutheran or Episcopalian faiths, with the Roman Catholic church doing only slightly better. The First African Baptist Church of Lexington, Quinn Chapel AME and Broadway Temple African Methodist Episcopal Zion in Louisville, and the Virginia Street Baptist Church in Hopkinsville were all prominent places of worship throughout the war. Religious services at these churches and literally hundreds of others across the commonwealth stressed themes such as that of "an omnipotent, omniscient, and sometimes capricious but merciful God; the difficulties and sorrows of earthly life; and the desire for security and salvation." Black ministers delivered sermons that combined their formidable knowledge of the Bible and its lessons with an intensity of feeling often missing from white pulpits. African American churches functioned not only as Christian citadels but as meeting places for civic groups, athletic teams, business organizations, literary clubs, and other entities. The Wallaces of southeastern Kentucky summed it up this way: "The church was one of our basic support systems—it was religious and social." They also recalled that some children went to school in churches when school buildings were not available.[11]

School ranked behind only family and church among all African American institutions. During the time of slavery, most Kentucky blacks received little to no education. Only free blacks and a few others with sympathetic masters—a tiny minority—attended school regularly. After the demise of slavery, the Freedmen's Bureau set up forty-six schools throughout Kentucky—in places such as Lexington, Frankfort, and Versailles—open to African Americans, and formal education of the race reached a higher stage. In 1874, the Kentucky General Assembly established a separate system of common schools for blacks. "Separate but equal" education became the norm in Kentucky thereafter, endorsed by the 1891 state constitution and the U.S. Supreme Court in the 1896 case of *Plessy v. Ferguson*. African American education, though clearly inferior to the education whites received, was better than no education at all. Black Kentuckians viewed education as "the key to a better lifestyle."[12]

Additional support for black education in Kentucky came from the Julius Rosenwald Fund. Rosenwald, a white Jew who was majority owner of Sears, Roebuck Company, provided millions of dollars to help build schools for blacks across the American South. Opposed to a "mere dole," he matched money that Kentucky blacks themselves raised toward the construction of one-room and two-room schoolhouses. Indeed, Rosenwald money went into larger school buildings as well. Between 1917 and 1932, collaboration between the Rosenwald Fund, blacks, and public officials in Kentucky resulted in the completion of 158 Rosenwald schools. Julius Rosenwald's assistance was much needed, given the commonwealth's inadequate funding of African American education. Even with Rosenwald funds and Rosenwald schools, Kentucky blacks obtained a second-rate education.[13]

A little over a decade later, when World War II burst upon the scene, the state of African American education was little changed. Separate black schools and white schools still existed. The school year for black children was often shorter than that for white children. The curriculum for black students was not as extensive as that for white students. Equipment for black schools was inadequate or nonexistent, especially in the sciences. Black teachers made less money than their white counterparts, and they were not as well trained. A shrinking number of blacks in rural areas of Kentucky resulted in the closure of many schools. Students from these places were bused long distances or simply dropped out. In 1942, L. N. Taylor, director of the State Division of Negro Education, stressed the large number of county officials throughout Kentucky who saw no option other than shutting black schools in low-population areas and the hardships their actions imposed on black families and students. Taylor described the black teachers of the state as "an earnest group of men and women" doing the best they could to advance "the progress of the colored race of Kentucky" despite a host of impediments.[14]

Because Kentucky's African American community suffered from so many problems, running the gamut from poverty through low social status to an unsatisfactory educational environment, it is not surprising that a multitude of uplift organizations had come into being to serve black needs by the early twentieth century. These organizations included, but were not limited to, the National Association for the Advancement of Colored People, the National Urban League (NUL), the Commission on Interracial Cooperation (CIC), the Kentucky Negro Education Association (KNEA), the YMCA, and the YWCA. NAACP branches were established in Kentucky during the 1910s; the Louisville chapter, for example, opened in 1914 to combat the ordinance there designed to keep blacks out of certain white neighborhoods. The Louisville Urban League (LUL) got its start by 1920 with a mandate to help rural blacks adjust to life in an urban, industrial metropolis. The LUL focused most on the attainment of employment and housing for newcomers, with a long-run goal of community development. The CIC promoted interracial communication and understanding; it was less strident in its denunciation of "separate but equal" than the NAACP or the Urban League. The KNEA labored to improve the system of black education in the commonwealth, advocating such things as longer school terms for black students and higher salaries for black teachers. Ultimately, it encouraged its membership to back the NAACP and participate in CIC, YMCA, and YWCA projects—because this "meant . . . advancement of the race."[15]

Albert Ernest Meyzeek, an African American educator and civil rights advocate, stood in the midst of this ferment. Meyzeek served as principal of many Louisville schools, including Central High School and Jackson Junior High School. He helped establish Louisville's first colored branch of the YMCA, in 1892. He became president of the KNEA in 1927 and was one of the founders of the Louisville Urban League. He chaired the latter organization for nearly thirty years. In these positions and others over the course of an extremely long and productive career, Meyzeek voiced black disapproval for Kentucky's segregated coach law, housing discrimination, police brutality, and all-white public parks and public libraries. Meyzeek's half-century as a school administrator was nearing its conclusion when World War II began, but he found other ways to serve during the conflict, and his protests against racial inequality continued.[16]

From September 1939 to December 1941, the Roosevelt administration geared up the United States for the possibility of war, and African American leaders responded by formulating goals they deemed appropriate under the circumstances. President Roosevelt increased the number of men in the Army and Navy. He initiated a program to mobilize the industrial resources of the nation so that the soldiers and sailors would have enough arms and ammunition. Black leaders, such A. Philip Randolph of the Brotherhood of Sleeping Car Porters (BSCP) and Walter White of the NAACP, made it clear to FDR that African Americans demanded two things from the preparedness program: desegregation of the military and a just proportion of newly created defense jobs. Blacks wanted to serve alongside whites in integrated Army and Navy units, and those who remained stateside wished to go into the factories to aid in the construction of weapons. Either way, blacks thought they had as much to offer the country during the emergency as whites and should not be denied. After the Japanese bombed Pearl Harbor on December 7, 1941, plunging the United States into the worldwide conflict, African Americans' demands remained the same and they pursued American victory resolutely.[17]

Like African Americans in every other state of the Union, the great majority of Kentucky blacks desired American triumph over the Axis. Despite mistreatment by white supremacists, blacks in the commonwealth understood that their situation would be worse under the Germans or Japanese. Rufus B. Atwood, the black president of Kentucky State College, declared that under "a Hitlerized government there would be no hope. The blood purity doctrine alone would exclude us entirely from benefits in his society." An editorial by the *Louisville Leader,* an African American newspaper, declared that "if Hitler wins[,] every single right the Negro enjoys and which he has struggled for in America will be wiped out." Atwood, I. Willis Cole of the *Leader,* and others knew full well that blacks in Kentucky had been "jim-crowed," force-fed an inferior education, ignored by some labor unions, denied the best jobs, and

A. Philip Randolph, head of the Brotherhood of Sleeping Car Porters and driving force behind the March on Washington movement. (Courtesy of the Library of Congress.)

victimized by violent actions on the part of the worst element of white society. Just the same, the Nazi regime offered blacks no chance at all for future advancement and the likelihood of a degree of degradation and misery that would make their present circumstances seem pleasant. While Kentucky blacks viewed Japan less negatively than Germany, most realized that the Japanese were motivated more by hunger for land, natural resources, and imperial status than by a desire to uphold the banner of the world's colored people. In short, Kentucky blacks believed just as strongly in the need for victory over the Axis as Kentucky whites.[18]

At a White House meeting in late September 1940, Roosevelt talked with Randolph and White about ending segregation in the military. The discussion was cordial. It seemed to go well. Randolph and the other representatives of the black community went away with the distinct feeling that they would get what they wanted.

This was not to be. In October, a Roosevelt assistant made a public statement that "the policy of the War Department is not to intermingle colored and white enlisted personnel in the same regimental organizations." The African American leadership thus learned the truth: FDR had told them what they wanted to hear, but nothing was going to change.[19]

A. Philip Randolph was more upset about this turn of events than anyone else. Tough and determined, he would not let FDR get away with it. Randolph decided on a direct challenge to the president, since conferences obviously did not work. He envisioned an unprecedented march of 100,000 blacks on Washington, all of them clamoring for desegregation of the military and defense jobs. While the idea frightened some blacks, who thought it radical, it excited others. The March on Washington movement was born, and it caught on.

Roosevelt tried to stop the proposed march, to no avail. On June 18, 1941, he met again with Randolph, hoping that the black leader would back down. Randolph refused to budge. The march on Washington would take place in a couple of weeks unless the president issued an executive order outlawing discrimination in defense plants. Roosevelt, not Randolph, gave in. In return for Randolph's calling off the march, FDR would do as the black leader directed.[20]

Executive Order 8802 was signed on June 25, 1941. It forbade discrimination based on race (and several other factors) when it came to employment in defense industries. The president also created a Fair Employment Practices Committee (FEPC) to "receive and investigate complaints of discrimination" and take "appropriate steps to redress grievances." Blacks throughout America applauded the measure, though in the first year the victory was more symbolic than substantive. Meanwhile, integration of the military awaited further developments.[21]

FDR's new industrial policy put the federal government behind the employment of blacks in the expanding national defense program. Members of the FEPC rolled up their sleeves and got busy. Blacks looking for work, however, did not see immediate results because many businesses acted as if Executive Order 8802 had never been promulgated. A National Urban League study of March 1942, which examined eighteen industries in Louisville, found that ten of them used blacks only in traditional positions such as janitor and porter and two more refused to employ blacks at all. Eight months had passed since the announcement of Executive Order 8802 and little progress had been made on the job front.[22]

Kentucky blacks would not give up. While reiterating their support for victory over the Axis, they refused to suspend the quest for black advancement. African Americans not only wanted to beat the enemy, a bunch who had no use for democracy or for the liberties of the masses, they also kept up the fight for more and better wartime employment as well as an end to discrimination in housing and public places. Given that this was their position, it is not at all surprising that Kentucky blacks overwhelmingly endorsed the "Double V" campaign.

James G. Thompson, a black man from Wichita, Kansas, touched off the "Double V" campaign. On January 31, 1942, Thompson wrote a letter to the *Pittsburgh Courier,* a leading African American newspaper. In this letter, he expressed deep ambivalence about a nation that would ask him and other blacks to risk their lives in war when they were denied the full benefits of citizenship. Thompson resolved his dilemma by arguing that African Americans should pursue victory over the Axis abroad and victory over racism at home. With that, the "Double V" formulation was born, and the *Pittsburgh Courier* ran with it. The theme of a double victory over totalitarian nations and American racial bigotry appeared many times in the *Pittsburgh Courier* and other African American newspapers from February 1942 through the conclusion of the war.[23]

The *Louisville Defender* and the *Louisville Leader,* Kentucky's major black newspapers, fell into step with the *Pittsburgh Courier.* Indeed, the *Defender* anticipated the coming "Double V" campaign when it published a cartoon about the killing of Cleo Wright in Sikeston, Missouri. Wright, a black ex-convict, allegedly attempted to rape a white woman. In an effort to avoid arrest, he stabbed a policeman, who defended himself by shooting Wright. Wright was subsequently incarcerated, but a mob of approximately 500 people broke into his jail cell and carried him away. Wright was eventually bound tightly to the rear bumper of an automobile, dragged through the streets of a black section of town, doused with gasoline, and burned. It was not clear exactly when he died, since the wounds he received from the police officer were life threatening, and he had been beaten by the mob prior to being attached to the car. The cartoon itself showed Hitler, Mussolini, and Hirohito looking on as the white mob burned the black man. Hitler then spoke to the other two, saying, "Boys! That's Democracy a la USA." The *Leader* noted, "We have had lynching before and since, but none has reminded us so much of the Italians at Ethiopia, the German at Poland and the Japs at Pearl Harbor as the whites at Sikeston." The paper made clear the dual nature of the war for African Americans, who had a "solemn duty to be loyal to their country" during the conflict, yet should fight "against every discriminatory practice."[24]

Roosevelt's good words barring racial discrimination in wartime industry meant less than changing economic conditions. Not long after completion of the National Urban League report stressing the reluctance of Louisville corporations to give blacks decent defense jobs, employers in Kentucky began to experience labor shortages. In effect, the pool of available white workers left over from the Great Depression had dried up, and other sources of help had to be tapped. This development forced Kentucky companies to hire more and more blacks by early 1943, if only to fulfill lucrative War Department contracts and to win more. The exigencies of war, not so much government action, and certainly not reformed white attitudes toward blacks, boosted the economic fortunes of African Americans in Kentucky during the middle and latter years of World War II.

Blacks in the commonwealth registered substantial economic gains. According to the United States Employment Service (USES), more than 75,000 "non-white" workers received job placements in Kentucky from 1940 through 1944. Almost all of these "non-white" workers were African Americans, and most of them—though not all—hailed from inside the Bluegrass State. The 75,000 figure is impressive considering that the entire black labor force of Kentucky amounted to about 94,000 persons in 1940. While the increase in the sheer number of jobs stands out most, many blacks got better jobs. Blacks moved into the war industry in a big way, working as machine operators, buffers, painters, welders, riveters, chemists, and electricians. They took slots in synthetic rubber plants. They secured employment in government, often as clerks and typists but also in some cases as foremen and officials. Civilian jobs opened up, too, since so many whites were away in the military. More blacks became truckers, railroaders, and miners than before the war. The percentage of blacks in semiskilled and skilled positions rose, though most members of the race still held unskilled positions. By 1944, African Americans in Kentucky enjoyed something quite close to full employment, their incomes were up, and so too was the fulfillment they took away from useful jobs performed well.[25]

Employment statistics and job categories are useful, but they reveal only so much. Some Kentucky blacks achieved career and financial success before Pearl Harbor, adding to it afterward. Others, a much larger number, took advantage of wartime conditions to propel themselves forward. Of the latter group, many found opportunity in Kentucky and a smaller number by going elsewhere. The experiences of individuals who prospered during the war, when examined collectively, permit a greater understanding of the nature of African American economic progress in the commonwealth during these years than would be possible otherwise.

Albert Meyzeek's long career as a public school administrator reached its end in 1943, when he retired from Jackson Junior High School. Still vigorous at age eighty, Meyzeek wished to contribute to the war effort. He did so by securing a position with the Office of Price Administration (OPA), the federal agency charged with restraining price increases during the war. Meyzeek acted as a liaison officer between the OPA and African American businessmen, helping to make sure that they understood the rules and regulations of the anti-inflation program and that misunderstandings were minimized. Meyzeek's high status within the African American community made him particularly well suited for this type of work.[26]

Like Meyzeek, Samuel Plato of Louisville built a considerable reputation for himself before the war. An African American architect and contractor, Plato's work had received critical acclaim for its originality, versatility, and beauty. In 1915, he designed the Classical Revival–style Broadway Temple AME Zion Church at Thirteenth and Broadway in Louisville. In 1926, he planned and constructed the Pythian Temple in Columbus, Ohio—now the Martin Luther King Jr. Performing and Cultural Arts Complex. The U.S. government awarded Plato's firm a contract to build a post office in Decatur, Alabama, in 1918, making Samuel Plato the first African American in the history of the nation to direct the construction of a post office. Plato did his job so well (despite dumbfounding Decatur officials when they met him) that he went on to build thirty-eight more post offices, in the states of Ohio, New York, New Jersey, and Pennsylvania. When World War II arrived, he was involved in a long-run project to develop the Westover subdivision in Louisville's West End. By then, Plato was one of the best-known black contractors in the United States.[27]

War brought Plato as much work as he could handle. A man already well connected to the federal government, he became one of just a few blacks nationwide who got in on the construction of defense housing. Plato secured almost $3 million of this kind of work; his fee alone came to

$109,600. He completed an 88-unit civilian housing project at Camp Taylor on the outskirts of Louisville, near the Curtiss Wright defense plant; a 304-unit complex at Sparrows Point, Maryland, near the war industry of Baltimore; and two dormitories totaling 829 rooms with infirmary and recreational attachments in Washington, DC. The Sparrows Point complex, ironically, was intended for whites only, since black migrants to Baltimore were crammed into the city's preexisting ghettos. The dorms were for young black women. Plato's efforts contributed significantly to the overall war effort.[28]

African American educator and businessman Rufus S. Stout also made a difference. Born in Little Rock, Arkansas, Stout arrived in Louisville as a child. He turned out to be a fine student, graduating from Central High School and matriculating at Indiana University. After receiving his bachelor's degree from IU, Stout returned to the Falls City, finding work as a teacher at Jackson Junior High School in the 1920s and 1930s. During World War II, he left education for a position at Louisville's National Carbide Company. While at this concern, he played a small but constructive role in the production of synthetic rubber for the American war machine.[29]

Stout served as an assistant personnel manager at National Carbide from 1942 through the rest of the war. Among other duties, he gave out paychecks to all employees and got to know many quite well. Management and outside agencies credited him with the promotion of a harmonious relationship between whites and blacks at the firm. The workers got along well there, which helped keep the output of calcium carbide (a mixture of refined coal and lime) up. National Carbide subsequently shipped its calcium carbide to DuPont, which combined the calcium carbide with other substances to make neoprene—a type of synthetic rubber. Neoprene was then used to make gas masks, pontoon boats, and many other types of war-related goods. Without Stout, the smooth functioning of this system might well have been interrupted. Certainly, he was one of many people who helped keep the production chain operating without a hitch.[30]

Other black Louisvillians who got ahead at least partly as a result of war-induced economic activity include Robert F. White, J. E. Givens, and J. Adolphus. Robert White established the White Printing Company during the early part of the war. Lacking capital, a common problem for black entrepreneurs, White built his business on a shoestring. He bought a large, well-used table from a junk shop, hauling it to his small Walnut Street office in a wheelbarrow. A three-by-five-foot hand press went on top of the table. White offered customers letterpress printing, offset printing, and various types of engraving. He made White Printing Company into a profitable enterprise, which lasted long after the war concluded. J. E. Givens began by selling sandwiches in baskets, taking advantage of the large number of people walking city streets during the war. He parlayed those profits into a successful restaurant and bakery. By 1948, Givens was supplying sandwiches for the concessions at Churchill Downs, and convention planners ordered food from him as well. J. Adolphus opened up a clothes cleaning business toward the end of the war, which thrived. By the late 1940s, he owned a modern cleaning plant and a chain of four cleaning stores. These black businessmen and others like them used the wartime economy as a springboard to bigger and better things.[31]

Blacks from all over Kentucky vaulted ahead. Louisville, of course, provided the most examples of this sort due to the fact that it contained far more people and industry than any other place in the commonwealth. Just the same, blacks in every region of the state exploited wartime conditions to advance their economic fortunes. Major improvements transpired for these men and women and their families.

Jackson's African American population benefited financially from the war. So many whites went off to fight that companies hired more blacks than ever before. Alec Lewis and Warnie Collins got jobs as truck drivers with Powell-Hackney Company. Lewis and Collins loaded their trucks with wholesale supplies such as flour, coffee, and sugar, drove many miles to little country stores in places like Irvine and Hazard, and unloaded the goods. The work was not easy, since there were no power lifts or even dollies. Muscle power was all they had. Powell-Hackney was not unionized, so the pay was not the best either. Nevertheless, Lewis and Collins were glad to have the jobs, which represented a step up from their previous employment, and they stayed with Powell-Hackney for over thirty years.[32]

Robert Ballard's story was similar. Ballard, an African American from Irvine, was hired by the Louisville & Nashville Railroad during the war. He worked as a porter on the L&N route from Cincinnati to Louisville, retiring decades later.[33]

Alexander "Alec" Lewis in 1974, after his long service with Powell-Hackney. Alec is pictured with his wife, Measie Spicer Lewis, at their residence on Hurst Lane in Jackson, Kentucky. (Courtesy of Brownie Wallace.)

A significant number of blacks from Kentucky traveled to other states to secure employment. Hopkinsville's Francis E. Whitney took a position at Wright Patterson Field, outside of Dayton, Ohio, in the midst of the conflict. Whitney, a mechanic, serviced B-24 bombers and other planes, taking "care of the engines and the fuselage." Lexington's Amanda Cooper Elliott also worked at Wright Field. Elliott became a clerk-typist, keeping records on the servicemen who passed through the base. She typed thousands of forms, which included information on where the men were ultimately stationed and a general description of their assignments. Interestingly enough, a Major Robinson, a white, male officer from Texas, shielded Elliott from the racism of her immediate supervisor, a white woman from Colorado. The white lady made snide racial comments from time to time but could not do greater damage because Robinson out-ranked her. Charles Jewell Francis, who lived in the eastern Kentucky hamlet of Salt Lick at the beginning of the war, found himself trans-ferred from Lexington to Philadelphia, Pennsylvania, in 1942. In 1943, he, wife Lelia, and their children ended up in Dayton, Ohio. Charles had been trained in electronics, and he did this type of defense work in both places.[34]

World War II brought Kentucky's blacks a massive amount of new employment. As the examples above indicate, jobs became available both inside and outside the state, and African Americans hungrily gobbled them up. The sheer variety of jobs also bears emphasizing; they ranged from government officials through defense workers to truckers, porters, and electricians. The diversity of employment opportunities amazed some blacks, since there was no real precedent in Kentucky history for it.

Blacks in wartime Kentucky made notable political progress, too, though it did not stand out as sharply as on the economic side. A. Philip Randolph of the Brotherhood of Sleeping Car Porters, Walter White of the NAACP, and other African American leaders continued to apply political pressure for desegregation of the military. The Kentucky branches of the NAACP followed White's lead. Mixing of blacks and whites in the Army and Navy began during the latter part of the war. By 1945, Jim Crow in the military was on shaky ground, and it would not last much longer. The visibility of black politicians in the commonwealth rose; more of them won elective office. Some were appointed to important positions. The political winds, which had long blown against Kentucky blacks, shifted in a way that clearly benefited them.

Civilian leaders of the U.S. Armed Forces and the brass opposed desegregation of the military. Secretary of War Henry Stimson and Army Chief of Staff George C. Marshall made it clear at various points that they did not have time for social experimentation when there was a war to win. Anything that might cause bad feelings in the ranks or bring about insta-bility was not welcome.[35]

In the pages of the *Louisville Courier-Journal*, Rufus B. Atwood stressed the unfairness of the Stimson-Marshall policy and its counterpro-ductive nature. Atwood, president of Kentucky State College for Negroes, opined that blacks had served the United States well in previous wars but "they always have had to plead that their services be used, and it has been plain that efforts have been made to assign them to stevedore regiments or to the labor battalions." Not only did they get menial jobs, they also were rarely admitted to the front lines to fight for their country. They wanted to do more to help win future wars, and they wanted better treatment. Blacks should be used with whites to best maximize military results. "A man's color," Atwood declared, "does not determine his efficiency."[36]

Just the same, the Army and Navy clung to the status quo through 1942 and 1943. The Army assigned black soldiers to the Quartermaster Corps, where they worked as common laborers. The Navy directed black sailors to load and unload arms and munitions or gave them mess duties. Very few blacks at all saw combat.

The black leadership and black press demanded that black soldiers be allowed to do more. They argued that blacks and whites could fight together and be an effective team. This kind of pressure on President Roosevelt and his underlings, coupled with immediate military needs on the ground, led to a few cases of de facto desegregation.

Black servicemen were sometimes thrown together with white servicemen during battle, and the results were mostly positive. The best-known example of this type occurred at the Battle of the Bulge in December 1944–January 1945. Due to a critical manpower shortage at the time of the last-gasp German counteroffensive, approximately 2,000 black riflemen who volunteered for reassignment to combat fought with whites in the forests of Belgium and Luxembourg. The African American troops did well, helping to thwart the German surge while simultaneously earning the respect of whites alongside them. Even the War Department, no friend of integration, concluded that the black infantrymen had "established themselves as fighting men no less courageous or aggressive than their white comrades."[37]

Lyman Johnson, a black Kentuckian who served in the Navy during the war, witnessed more evidence that segregation was cracking. In the summer of 1945, Johnson was at the Great Lakes Naval Station in Illinois. One day, black and white sailors were at their separate camps, the next day they were mixed together. Barbers of both races, who had been kept apart, were now grouped together and cut the hair of both whites and blacks. By

December 1945, the Navy halted segregation completely. After the war, Lyman Johnson returned to Kentucky, where he played a leading role in desegregating the University of Kentucky.[38]

Segregation in other parts of the military lingered only a little longer. In 1948, President Harry S. Truman decreed by executive order that segregation in all branches of the Armed Forces end, and it was done. Truman took this step partly because he thought it right and just, and partly to repay blacks who had voted for him in his successful 1948 presidential race. African Americans in Kentucky and the nation finally were able to make some headway in the political realm as a result of good conduct during the war and growing support from New Deal–Fair Deal forces.[39]

A historic electoral breakthrough for Kentucky blacks transpired just before World War II—and that was only the beginning. The fact that Kentucky blacks possessed the vote while blacks in a number of other states did not contributed to new successes. In November 1935, Charles W. Anderson of Louisville, an African American lawyer, won election to the Kentucky state legislature. Anderson therefore became the first black man ever to sit in the general assembly and the first black legislator in any Southern state since 1901. African Americans J. Daniel Massie and Eugene S. Clayton captured elective offices not too long after Anderson. A few high-ranking white officials named blacks—such as Rufus Stout and Robert Black—to advisory and regulatory bodies. Blacks in Kentucky not only witnessed the establishment of an integrated American military, they also celebrated political victories unlike any they had experienced before.

Charles W. Anderson, a Republican, led the way. Anderson took a law degree from Howard University and gained admittance to the Kentucky bar in 1933. He soon proved himself to be a fine lawyer. He also understood the importance of personal connections for someone entertaining the idea of a political career, and he made these connections through a host of leading organizations. Anderson joined the Quinn Chapel AME Church in Louisville. He became a member of the Elks, the Masons, and the Women's Progressive League. He also rose to a leadership position in the Louisville NAACP. When he ran for the state legislature late in 1935, he had already made a name for himself in the Louisville African American community despite his youth. Once Anderson received the nod from the Republican party hierarchy, his chances for victory were excellent.[40]

Black Republicans from Louisville's 58th District had appealed time and again to leaders of the Republican party to run a black man for high office there. Time and again, they were ignored. White Republican nominees ran and won in an overwhelmingly black district. As the *Louisville Leader* noted, it seemed to African Americans that "blind and narrow Republican leaders . . . had no use for the intelligent, upstanding type of Negro, other than to use his vote to their own advantage."[41]

The New Deal changed the local political landscape in a surprising way. Once the Democratic party selected its own black candidate from the 58th District for the state legislature, it forced the hand of the Republican party. If the Democrats ran a black candidate and the Republicans a white one, the Republicans might well lose. Better to counter the Democrats with a black GOP candidate and increase the odds of holding a traditionally Republican seat. The result was that both major parties fielded black candidates in 1935. In a decidedly lopsided contest, Republican Anderson captured 2,337 votes to 956 for Democrat C. Eubank Tucker.[42]

Charles Anderson served Kentucky as a state representative from 1936 to 1946. Sometimes he challenged segregation, while at other times he acted in a manner that seemed to imply acceptance of it. He cosponsored a law granting blacks a stipend to attend out-of-state graduate schools because the University of Kentucky graduate school did not accept blacks. Some blacks, at least, thought Anderson might have gone further, perhaps speaking out forcefully against UK's "whites only" policy. That issue aside, Anderson contributed significantly to passage of legislation that improved working conditions for domestic servants throughout Kentucky and was a proponent of minimum wages. These things helped blacks and whites alike, but especially blacks. Anderson also spearheaded a drive that ended in the defeat of a bill to force blacks to ride behind glass partitions in buses. Toward the end of his tenure as a state representative, he attacked segregation more often than he had before. All in all, Anderson represented black interests effectively during a period of limited options.[43]

Dan Massie and Eugene Clayton captured local offices. Massie, a Democrat, won a 1940 election to become magistrate for the 1st District in Hopkinsville. His victory resulted from the presence of a large black majority in that district, which fell in the northeast part of the town. Hopkinsville had been divided for political purposes earlier, leaving two of its twelve districts in black hands. This arrangement, unlike that anywhere else in Kentucky, explains why blacks in Hopkinsville gained so many elective positions from the 1880s on. Massie's true distinction was not that he was voted into office in the first place, but that he kept his magisterial post through seven full terms and part of an eighth, making him the longest-serving black elected official in Kentucky at the time of his death in 1977. Clayton, a Republican like Charles Anderson, was foreman of the Brass Department at American Radiator & Standard Sanitary Corporation. He emerged triumphant in a 1945 race for 10th Ward alderman in Louisville, becoming the Falls City's first African American member of the Board of Aldermen.[44]

White politicians in Kentucky, be they Democrat or Republican, usually stood in the way of black political advancement. Whites deemed blacks unfit to govern, and they were determined to maintain their hold on power. With the advent of the New Deal, certain Democratic white politicians and policy makers proved more receptive to the concerns of blacks, and the Republican party adjusted its political calculus in certain unusual cases, such as the 1935 race for state legislator in Louisville's 58th District. Even so, the average white politician behaved in a manner that worked against black interests or that at least did them little good. Only a few white politicians proved sympathetic to blacks during the World War II period—or did much that benefited them.

Governor Simeon Willis and Mayor Wilson Wyatt of Louisville were two white politicians who did take blacks into account. Willis, a Republican, established the Kentucky Commission on Negro Affairs in 1944. Wyatt, a Democrat, put blacks on various policy-making committees during the war. Black leaders used these positions to publicize their views on many important subjects, while they acquired political experience and contacts that served them well later. While this type of political interaction was no panacea for the problems of the black community, it was not just window dressing either.

The Kentucky Commission on Negro Affairs operated from September 1944 into 1945. The commission included white and black members. It compiled a report describing the problems that plagued blacks in industry, education, health care, and other areas. Representative Anderson's committee on civil affairs called for repeal or modification of the Day

Law, which prohibited blacks from attending college or university with whites throughout the commonwealth. Anderson wanted to push beyond graduate education of Kentucky blacks in northern states to enable blacks to attend an in-state graduate school. Other parts of the report recommended steps that could be taken to improve the employment outlook for blacks and to insure they received better medical treatment.[45]

Release of the Kentucky Commission on Negro Affairs report in late 1945 did not bring immediate results. The great majority of whites in the state still embraced the view that blacks were inferior beings. Whites certainly disliked the idea that they should pay for institutional improvements designed to aid blacks. Nevertheless, decisions in a number of important court cases coupled with steadfast African American opposition to the Day Law forced its revision and then repeal during the late 1940s and early 1950s. Hospital additions, new hospitals, and tuberculosis sanatoriums funded under governors Keen Johnson and Willis were eventually opened to blacks. Progress of various sorts came in a sluggish, almost leisurely manner, but over time it began to add up to something substantial.[46]

Mayor Wyatt, a liberal, devoted considerable attention to the black community of Louisville. He gave them a real presence in city government, which was augmented by Eugene Clayton's ascendancy to alderman. Wyatt named blacks to positions on the Louisville Municipal Housing Commission, the Mayor's Legislative Committee, the Library Board, the Family Service Organization, and the Board of Equalization. By the time Wyatt's term as mayor ended in 1945, blacks had a greater say in city politics than ever before.[47]

Some blacks emerged from World War II better known than they had been before, and they played significant roles later. Charles Anderson and Rufus Stout were among them. Anderson stepped down from his position as state representative in May 1946, accepting a job as assistant commonwealth attorney for Jefferson County. No black man had ever held this kind of post in any county throughout the American South. Anderson capped his career in 1959, when he was selected by President Dwight D. Eisenhower to be an alternate U.S. delegate to the United Nations. In this capacity, he worked to eliminate various sorts of discrimination based on race and other factors in a number of countries. Anderson might have done even more, but he died prematurely in a tragic 1960 collision between his car and an oncoming Chesapeake & Ohio passenger train in Shelby County. Stout, who served with Anderson, Robert Black, and others on the Kentucky Commission on Negro Affairs, continued with National Carbide Company for many years after the war. In 1962, he became the first black person chosen for the board of directors of the Louisville Community Chest, an organization that solicited businesses for charitable contributions to be designated for worthwhile community projects. In 1966, Stout began a term on the State Personnel Board—another first for Kentucky African Americans.[48]

World War II and the immediate postwar period brought certain political gains for black Kentuckians. Desegregation of the military, a much-cherished goal sought for a good many years, finally occurred. State government became a bit more receptive to black aspirations. The African American constituency in Hopkinsville spoke its mind, as had been the case for decades, discovering in Daniel Massie a strong, young leader who would be around for a long while. Blacks in Louisville also made headway, especially with the election of Eugene Clayton. In every region of the commonwealth, a substantial number of blacks switched their political affiliation from Republican to Democrat, responding to the help they received from the Franklin D. Roosevelt and Harry Truman administrations. The process of political reidentification, however, was not instantaneous or uniform, as the elections of Louisville Republicans Anderson and Clayton remind us. A sizable percentage of blacks remained loyal to the GOP even after many years passed. Moreover, most places in Kentucky had never elected a single black man or woman to public office by the time the war ended in September 1945.

The "Double V" campaign produced mixed results. Supporters applauded the demise of the Axis. Racism at home, however, remained a potent force, which stood in the way of the African American quest for justice and equality. While Kentucky blacks had more, and some better, jobs than before the war, as well as a greater say in the political arena, whites in the state still looked down on them and rejected any notion of social parity.

Whites and blacks in the commonwealth just did not see eye to eye on racial matters. With victory over Germany and Japan, whites wanted to go back to the way things were before the war. Specifically, the vast majority believed that returning servicemen should get back their old jobs or equivalent ones, and they saw little or nothing wrong with the maintenance of segregation. Blacks opposed this kind of thinking, which would quickly erode their wartime economic gains and reinforce inequality.

An enduring, powerful, and profound disconnect prevented the races from truly coming together. Blacks saw themselves through the prism of oppression. Past and present exploitation by whites, more than any other single factor, accounted for the lowly status of African Americans in Kentucky. Whites dismissed this view, refusing to accept blame for the benighted, impoverished circumstances of many blacks. Whites, falling back on stereotypes, attributed the condition of blacks to their own shortcomings. They saw blacks as dull, shiftless, or inclined toward criminality. The ideological divide between whites and blacks passed through the war easily, proving exceedingly difficult to bridge.

Injustices against blacks and their wartime sacrifices demanded that the racial status quo be changed. John Wesley Hatch, an African American youth, watched with considerable dismay as German prisoners of war in western Kentucky ate at a restaurant that barred black GIs. Segregation survived the conflict—the "separate but equal" fallacy remained very much in place. The Day Law, for instance, still lingered, keeping blacks and whites from attending Kentucky colleges together. A 1946 bill before the state legislature, which would have allowed black women to try on clothes in white department store changing rooms rather than purchase the clothes and take their chances that they would fit, died. About 20,000 Kentucky blacks served in the U.S. military during World War II, giving up a precious part of their lives and often performing hard labor. At least a few died, including Scott Countian Robert Brooks. Private Brooks posed as a white man to enter the service, so anxious was he to help defend his country. A member of the U.S. Armored Forces, he fell in the Philippines during 1942. Little wonder that Kentucky blacks found the glacial pace of racial change unacceptable.[49]

Racial discord in Kentucky increased after 1945. White and black attitudes clashed, and tension rose. White respondents to a questionnaire put out by the Louisville Urban League in 1948 overwhelmingly rejected social equality between the races; one made the comment that Kentucky blacks "have no contribution to make" in any area. Blacks repudiated the antebellum status quo. Jackson's Alec Lewis, Louisville's Rufus Stout, and many others hung on to their wartime jobs into peacetime, indeed for as long as they wanted them. Having tasted a bit of the good life, they did not want to give it up. African American veterans and their allies struck back against "Jim Crow" in education and other areas, bound and determined to destroy segregation wherever it existed. These vets deserved a reward for their military service, not a return to second-class citizenship. World War II generated a new militancy among Kentucky blacks, which fueled the Kentucky civil rights crusade of the 1950s and 1960s.[50]

African Americans in Kentucky have experienced vast hardship. From the late eighteenth century until the Civil War, almost all blacks in the commonwealth lived lives defined by the restrictions and cruelties imposed by the slave regime. After slavery was abolished, the white majority, taken aback by freedom for blacks and frightened by it, clamped down on the freedmen. Beatings and lynchings followed. Eventually the violence subsided, and white politicians found an adequate replacement for slavery: segregation. The "separate but equal" doctrine left blacks with subpar schools, shabby railroad coaches, inferior recreational facilities, and back-of-restaurant pickup places. When World War II burst upon the scene, segregation, with all its inequities and quirks, still held fast. Family and church, along with other social organizations, helped blacks endure both old burdens and the new ones associated with the conflict. Wartime conditions, of course, shook Kentucky up and redounded to the benefit of African Americans. A severe labor shortage forced the white employers of Kentucky to hire black workers by the tens of thousands. Blacks made substantial economic progress as a result. Political advancement, which became noticeable during the middle 1930s, accelerated during the conflict, although the transition from the party of Abe Lincoln to the party of Franklin D. Roosevelt took longer for some Kentucky blacks than others. Blacks welcomed victory over the Axis, made possible in part by the contributions of Samuel Plato, Rufus Stout, Robert Brooks, and others, though racism proved a more intractable foe. Kentucky's white establishment expected blacks to stay in their place after the war; they would not comply. More assertive now than previously, the African Americans of Kentucky merited a better shake and, when it was not forthcoming, acted. Lawsuits, protest marches, and sit-ins occupied them in the late 1940s, 1950s, and 1960s. Progress came, most notably the long overdue death of "Jim Crow"; yet bigotry remained. Discrimination in areas such as housing and the higher professions, coupled with low incomes and broken families, still block the way forward for many Kentucky blacks. True racial equality is an ever-elusive goal, and not even the election of an African American president has changed that fact.

8

Choosing to Go

Migration, Identity, and Social Change

For whites and blacks alike, migration was an important phenomenon of the World War II Kentucky home front. Tens of thousands, then hundreds of thousands of Kentuckians left their homes in search of economic gain. They moved from one place in Kentucky to another place in Kentucky or left the state entirely. While the vast majority of migrants found material advancement, many missed the land of their origins and family and friends who were left behind. Once the war ended, some migrants remained where they were; others returned home. Whatever choice the individual citizens made, it affected their identity to one extent or another. Movement to places of wartime industry also contributed to overcrowded cities, insufficient housing, and other worrisome social problems.

Without question, Kentucky sustained constant, heavy migration throughout the war. Taking into consideration movement within the state and outside of it, approximately 350,000 Kentuckians (excluding military personnel) became migrants from 1940 to 1945. Since the United States census records a total population figure for Kentucky of 2,845,627 in 1940, this means that one out of every eight Kentucky civilians migrated over those five years. One authority notes that this voluntary migration rivals the forced movements of Europeans and Asians over roughly the same time period.[1]

More details may be gleaned from the data. Out of the 350,000 Kentucky migrants, roughly 140,000 hailed from poverty-stricken eastern Kentucky, with the rest coming from other parts of the state. Eastern Kentucky's population in 1940 stood at 820,115, or 29 percent of the total population, yet it provided 40 percent of the total migrants over the five-year span in question. Western Kentucky also yielded many migrants, perhaps more than has been previously suspected, as its population decrease from 563,848 in 1940 to 538,402 in 1950 seems to indicate. The fewest migrants in percentage terms—though still a significant number—came from the wealthier parts of Kentucky, namely central Kentucky and northern Kentucky.[2]

A steep increase in migration, which traced its roots back to the American defense buildup of 1939–1940, also affected Kentucky's counties and towns. Knox County, located in southeastern Kentucky, lost 30 percent of its people from 1941 to 1945 as they relocated from farms and very small towns to manufacturing areas such as Cincinnati, Ohio; Hamilton, Ohio; and Detroit, Michigan. Wolfe County, Magoffin County, Lawrence County, and other eastern Kentucky counties suffered similar losses. Casey County in south-central Kentucky and Trigg and Lyon counties in western Kentucky are examples of other counties where substantial population declines are attributable in large part to out-of-state migration. Towns hit hard by wartime out-migration included Barbourville, Campton, Beattyville, Liberty, and Cadiz. Conversely, a handful of exceptional towns attracted migrants. Louisville provides far and away the best example of this type. Drawn to the Falls City by wartime industry, such as the synthetic rubber plants on Bells Lane and the nearby Charlestown, Indiana, smokeless powder plant, 15,000 newcomers arrived by 1941 and 70,000 overall. Other Ohio River cities, such as Owensboro and Henderson, made smaller gains. Nevertheless, out-migration still overwhelmed in-migration for the state as a whole.[3]

A comparison of all states illustrates the magnitude of migration from Kentucky. Only sixteen of the forty-eight states experienced net out-migration from 1940 to 1943 and again from 1943 to 1950; Kentucky was one of them. Just seven states had migratory losses of 10 percent to 15 percent from 1940 to 1950; Kentucky was one of them. Only Oklahoma and North Carolina lost more people to interstate migration during the interval from April 1940 to November 1943. Taking into account Appalachian areas from West Virginia southward to northern Alabama during the 1940s, Eastern Kentucky had the greatest number of migrants. Had it not been for Kentucky's high rate of natural increase (births exceeding deaths), the state population would have fallen dramatically from 1940 to 1950 due to out-migration. As it was, out-of-state migration restrained Kentucky population growth for this decade, limiting it to just 3.5 percent, placing Kentucky forty-second out of the forty-eight states. By almost any measure, Kentucky ranked near the top for total out-migration during and just after World War II.[4]

Kentucky migrants included whites and blacks, men and women. Eastern Kentucky contributed mainly young, white, unmarried males to the migratory stream, but as the draft continued the proportion of women from there slowly rose. Central Kentucky and western Kentucky gave many whites and a smaller number of blacks, along with a higher percentage of women, than the mountainous portion of the state. Overall, female migrants may well have exceeded male migrants by the end of the war because so many men had entered into military service.[5]

Many factors explain why Kentuckians changed their places of residence. The lure of economic advancement proved by far the strongest consideration. Patriotism, a desire to establish a home near family members who had moved earlier, the spirit of adventure—or a mixture of these—also drove them forward.

Migrants desperately wanted a higher standard of living. They abandoned farms, villages, and small towns hardly deserving of the name, in search of jobs in bigger towns or cities where war industries existed. Knox County men, when asked about their employment situation at home, responded that they were "farming, doing odd jobs, or did not have any work." African Americans needed jobs just as badly as Appalachian Kentuckians. Not surprisingly, people like these, plagued by underemployment and unemployment, wished to find work that would increase their income. War jobs drew them away from impoverished circumstances, generated by an overemphasis on agriculture and coal mining, to a new reality. Huge numbers of Kentucky migrants took jobs elsewhere that paid a higher hourly wage or worked far more than eight hours a day to maximize their return. They made more money than ever before.[6]

Love of country influenced Kentucky migrants. They denounced Hitler, Mussolini, and Tojo, doing everything they could to achieve victory over the Axis. Right after the surprise attack on Pearl Harbor, of course, Kentuckians saved their most venomous comments for the Japanese, whom they labeled "buck-toothed Japs," the "yellow menace," "stinkin' Nips," and worse. A war job furthered the cause of victory. Of course, individuals might well improve themselves economically while aiding the Allied cause.

Kentuckians, particularly eastern Kentuckians, who are often noted for their intense devotion to family, followed loved ones to locations in the state and out of state. When a father or brother departed, setting himself up in Louisville or Cincinnati, this provided an incentive for other relatives to move to these places. In this manner, they could reestablish valuable family connections and the old culture. As historian Alan Clive put it, extended family networks, "originating in the hills and hollows of Kentucky[,] . . . had long before stretched to Detroit, Flint, Monroe, and other [Michigan] production centers, and now guided newcomers to housing, jobs, and friends, and gave the migrants some sense of continuity with their former life."[7] This statement applies not only to Michigan but to many other places as well.

Kentucky migrants settled in a variety of new areas. Over half of them relocated to another place within Kentucky or chose a Midwestern state such as Ohio, Indiana, Illinois, or Michigan. A minority ended up elsewhere: some in the Northeast, some others in Southern states like Tennessee and Virginia, a few in the West.[8]

Movement from one place in Kentucky to another place in Kentucky became commonplace. Louisville attracted far more Kentuckians than any other in-state destination because so many war-related jobs opened up there. Indeed, Louisville metro area industries employed more war workers than all the other towns of Kentucky put together. If the availability of jobs themselves were not enough, Louisville firms such as Reynolds Metal Company used newspaper advertising effectively. Reynolds took out ads in the *Jackson Times* and other local newspapers to entice Breathitt County readers and others to become workers in the River City, and people of both sexes and all races accepted the invitation. Owensboro, Ashland, Paducah, and parts of Hardin County, Christian County, and

Union County, received Kentucky migrants as well, either because large corporations with defense contracts operated in their vicinity or because of the presence of military bases that needed civilian help. Owensboro, for instance, benefited from the presence of Ken-Rad Company, which made radio tubes for the military, and from other corporations there. The population of Hardin County, to cite another example, increased faster than that of any other county in the commonwealth from 1940 to 1950 because of its proximity to Louisville industry and Fort Knox.[9]

Agriculture, while not nearly so heralded as wartime industry, got its fair share of Kentucky migrants. Taken together, the military draft and the arms industry soaked up available labor like a sponge. A farm labor shortage developed by 1943–1944. Yet the state and the people still needed food, and many continued to depend upon the old cash crops for a livelihood. Thus, the call went out for any available hands to do the tobacco harvesting and similar jobs. "It used to be possible for us to go down on Vine Street and pick up as many workers as were needed during the busy farm seasons," Bruce Poundstone of the College of Agriculture at the University of Kentucky said, "but that time is rapidly getting away from us." Eastern Kentucky male migrants above draft age, 4-Fs, black and white women from various central Kentucky locales, and others answered the cries for help, and the tobacco went into the barns. Other crops might have rotted but for migrant labor. The University of Kentucky College of Agriculture and Home Economics, working in conjunction with local extension agents, recruited men from Johnson, Floyd, and Pike counties to work on farms in Mason, Bourbon, and Fayette counties. Strawberries and other fruits and vegetables were picked. Agricultural jobs did not pay like war production jobs and lacked glamour, but they certainly beat having no job at all.[10]

Out-migration from Kentucky flowed mainly to Midwestern cities, where many plants ultimately operated twenty-four hours per day to meet war production targets established under federal contracts. Detroit, Michigan, stood out prominently for Kentuckians because it was not too far away and it did more war work than any other American city. The home of the automobile industry reconfigured plants and equipment in such a way as to make tanks and airplanes. Kentuckians rushed to satisfy Detroit's enormous appetite for labor, improving their material lifestyle in the process. Cincinnati, Ohio; Evansville, Indiana; Chicago, Illinois; and a few other cities appealed almost as much to the hillbillies and flatlanders of the Bluegrass State.

Thinner streams of migrants journeyed to the Northeast and the South. Even before Pearl Harbor, the National Youth Administration (NYA) began training Kentuckians for defense-related jobs in Massachusetts and Connecticut. NYA workshops located at Ashland, Bowling Green, Covington, Hazard, Louisville, Paducah, and Richmond taught students welding, machine-tool, sheet-metal, and radio work. By December 18, 1941, 200 NYA youths from Kentucky had already been dispatched to Northeastern defense plants to help install defense machinery, build airplane motors, and construct submarines. Kentuckians continued to arrive at New England war plants thereafter at a rate of fifteen to twenty-five per week. Knoxville's population tripled during the war, partly due to the new arrivals from Kentucky. Only sheer distance kept significant numbers of Kentuckians away from the rapidly expanding West Coast states of California, Oregon, and Washington.[11]

The experiences of James Wright, Jim Hammittee, Rose Will Monroe, Thelma Jo Noble, Mildred Harris, and several other Kentuckians help personalize the migration story, underlining earlier themes while adding nuance to them. These individuals' stories also tell us much about the meeting of cultures that occurred when the migrant fashioned a new existence in an unfamiliar land.

James Wright, an African American from the southwestern Kentucky town of Russellville, traveled 140 miles, reaching Louisville on September 1, 1941. Wright wanted a decent job but found it hard to get one. For a time, he lugged cross ties for a railroad. After that, he performed menial labor for a moving company. A DuPont construction firm gave him his third job. Wright finally moved on to the Vultee Aircraft factory near Louisville, a bona fide defense position. Though it had taken effort and perseverance, along with the absence of many white, male workers who served in the armed forces, Wright succeeded in his quest to find meaningful, higher-paying employment.[12]

The U.S. military intervened at this point. Wright was drafted and entered the service himself. After a stint in Burma, he returned to Louisville in 1946. His decision to go back owed to his previous positive experiences there and to a conviction that he could repeat them. International Harvester took him on, confirming the confidence he had in himself and his adopted town. Wright followed the path of internal migration to better himself.[13]

Other blacks (as well as a greater number of whites) took a similar road. James Glass, another African American migrant, hailed from the southeastern Kentucky town of Jenkins. A coal miner there, he moved to Louisville in 1942, only to find the city inhospitable. He took a series of lowly jobs that paid only one-half to one-third what he had made in the mines. Frustrated, Glass gave up and returned to eastern Kentucky. He tried Louisville again in 1944, mainly because his father lived there and James wanted to be with him. This time, he got a job he liked at Louisville Gas & Electric Company, and he established permanent residence by purchasing a house on South Forty-Second Street. In Glass's case, the familial bond induced him to come back to Louisville, and the job not only insured that he would stay but also allowed him to achieve the American dream. Mildred Bradley and Rebecca Smith were black women who benefited from wartime opportunities, helping themselves—as had Wright and Glass—to a piece of the economic pie. Upton, Kentucky's Bradley and Cumberland County's Smith secured defense-related work with the Louisville & Nashville Railroad. Their incomes rose. Between 1940 and 1946, due largely to wartime circumstances, Louisville gained almost 9,000 black inhabitants, and many of them experienced small triumphs like the ones just described.[14]

Kentucky migrants who left the state outnumbered Kentucky migrants who remained within its borders. Thriving as it was, Louisville really could not compete with the larger industrial cities of Ohio, Michigan, and Illinois. These cities received a greater number of defense contracts than Louisville and needed vastly more workers. Like giant magnets, they pulled Kentuckians seeking a better life to them. Conversely, Kentucky suffered from the loss of so many enterprising and talented folk to the North. The brain drain was greater in the Bluegrass State than almost anywhere else. Jim Hammittee, Rose Will Monroe, Polly Ashley, and others felt the tug of opportunity and left for Northern cities.

Jim Hammittee can be described as a rather typical Kentucky outmigrant. A white male born in Bell County, in eastern Kentucky, Hammittee answered Detroit's call for workers. At age twenty-five, in 1942 he arrived in the Motor City, securing a job on the east side at a roller bearing plant. Happy enough there, he earned promotions and increased pay. By the time World War II ended, Hammittee had become a supervisor at the plant with a couple hundred people under his authority. He had certainly proven himself a valuable employee. His company benefited and so did he.[15]

Hammittee did indeed earn a great deal more money in Detroit than he had back in Bell County's coal mines. Though his beginning wage at the roller bearing plant was 76 cents an hour compared to $1.02 an hour in the coal mines, the long hours he worked in war industry allowed him to surpass his previous earnings by a large amount. Hammittee remembered making $35 or so a week digging coal but took home $57.60 from his first war job. By 1945, his hourly wage reached $1.76 and his weekly pay topped out at approximately $135. Even taking into consideration the rate of inflation from 1942 to 1945, Hammittee's real income tripled.

Jim Hammittee needed the money. His father had been killed in a coal mine accident, forcing twenty-one-year-old Jim to assume responsibility for his younger siblings. Hammittee kept watch over his big family from afar and used part of his savings to bring his brothers up to Detroit. He'd see to transportation and "help them get started in the plants" or find some other job. Hammittee family ties remained strong despite the war and separation.[16]

It will be recalled that Rose Will Monroe of Pulaski County, Kentucky, reached Ypsilanti, Michigan, just southwest of Detroit, after Pearl Harbor. Rose took a job as a riveter at Henry Ford's famous Willow Run plant, helping to assemble B-24 and B-29 bombers. A mother of two children, whose husband had been killed earlier in a car accident, she appreciated the job because it allowed her to put food on the table for her kids and a roof over their heads.

Actor Walter Pidgeon discovered Rose Monroe at the Ford plant and asked her to appear with him in a film promoting the sale of war bonds. Rose, of course, would portray the cultural icon "Rosie the Riveter"—a strong, capable woman wearing a bandanna and overalls pictured in a host of wartime posters. Rose Monroe agreed to participate in Pidgeon's project. The moviemakers simply could not resist the temptation of hiring a woman named Rose, who actually worked as a riveter in a bomber factory, for the part. Monroe starred as "Rosie the Riveter" in films while lending her name and energy to a poster campaign. Both Rosie the woman and Rosie the image worked hard, providing substantial support to the war effort.[17]

Like Jim Hammittee, Polly Ashley journeyed to Detroit and found success there. A native of Knott County, Kentucky, not too far from either Bell County or Pulaski County, Ashley made Detroit her new home in 1943. A white woman, age fifty-three at the time, she described her work as "making planes and sorting things to make planes. You know, bolts and things. They'd get them messed up and we'd have to pick them out, washers, too." The job had its perks as well, such as being able to get into a finished plane and "go try it out." Ashley's pay impressed her greatly, something that almost every migrant recalled. She earned $53 to $56 a week, less than her fellow male workers on the Detroit assembly line, but more than she could ever have made at home.[18]

Thelma Jo Noble traveled a more circuitous route than Hammittee, Monroe, or Ashley—literally. Noble lived in Lawson, Kentucky, for a time. She attended Lees College in Jackson, the seat of Breathitt County. A self-reliant and ambitious young woman, she decided that war work was for her and knew enough to see that it required special training. Noble therefore departed eastern Kentucky for Iowa State University. Once there, she enrolled in a ten-month Aeronautical Engineering Cadette training course. Upon passing the course, Curtiss Wright Corporation, maker of many different types of military planes, extended her a job offer at their Columbus, Ohio, plant. Noble accepted, joining the engineering section there, where she had a hand in the manufacture of SB2C Helldiver dive bombers and the Curtiss Seagull, a naval scout observation plane.[19]

While Hammittee, Ashley, and Noble were from the mountainous east, Mildred Harris and Emma Martin called western Kentucky home. Harris and Martin joined many others from their part of the state who entered war factories. Unlike Monroe, neither woman became a riveter, but both did their share to help achieve victory and aided themselves in the process.

Mildred F. Harris watched her husband, Pascal, go off to war. An intelligent woman who had once been a schoolteacher, Mildred applied for a war job and got a position in 1943 as a civilian inspector for the U.S. Army Air Corps. Like so many married women at this time, she worked in a key wartime industry, hoping that her efforts might help bring victory sooner rather than later. Throughout her wartime experiences, she prayed that no mishaps would befall Pascal.[20]

Harris worked at Republic Aviation's airplane plant in Evansville, Indiana. She took a car pool from her house in Providence, Kentucky, to the plant and back six days a week. The round trip came to 110 miles a day at a time when authorities had imposed a 35-mile-per-hour speed limit to conserve rubber.[21] After getting to the factory, Harris put in eight hours or more a day. Republic Aviation made the famous P-47 Thunderbolt, a tough, adaptable single-pilot fighter plane that performed well in both the European and Asian theaters as a bomber escort, interceptor, and ground-attack aircraft. As a civilian inspector, Mildred roamed around the factory, checking to see that the work was being done on schedule, that the men did not loaf, and that the P-47 airplane parts were not defective. Harris remembered that most of the workers did a good job and the parts almost always fit together properly. On rare occasions, however, she did have to reprimand workers and return parts. She and the other inspectors helped smooth out the production of P-47s.[22]

The men under Harris at the Evansville plant did not cause her much trouble. They understood she was in charge and that inspections were necessary and valuable. This does not mean that Harris was never tested. Mildred recalled one occasion when a male subordinate who operated a forklift drove his gigantic machine directly at her "as if he intended to . . . dump the box right on top of me. I just stood there. He stopped and backed off. He said, 'You don't scare easy, do you?' I said [in schoolteacher tones], 'No sir, I don't.' See, what he expected me to do, and what would have tickled him if I had done it, was scream-squeal, hoot, and holler." Harris was not about to give this man satisfaction, nor did she ever shirk her war-related duties. Happily, Mildred and Pascal Harris were reunited after the war and spent many good years together.[23]

Emma Martin of Butler County became engaged to Jesse Martin in 1941. After Jesse left for the military, Emma decided to go south to Nashville, Tennessee. "It was a matter of survival," she recalled. "You didn't have any money on the farm, so I went there."[24] Emma performed a variety of jobs in Nashville. She began as a maid and did household chores, making just $1.50 a week. After that, she took care of six children while their parents worked. Finally, in early January 1943, a DuPont rayon plant near Nashville hired her, and her wages improved dramatically, to fifty cents an hour. Whereas she made $1.50 a week as a domestic servant, she now made $4 to $5 a day![25]

Emma did a "man's job" for DuPont. She proved herself strong enough to "lift like fifty pounds at a time all day long." Speaking with understandable pride, she noted that some men could not handle all the toting and "passed out right on the job. I didn't think anything because I was just trying to get along—trying to live!"[26]

Like so many other Kentucky female migrants, Emma Martin worked hard during the war, gained confidence, and moved ahead financially. When Jesse returned on May 16, 1945, after an absence of close to four years, Emma married him. She continued at DuPont for some time thereafter, suffered a cut in pay related to a shift in position, and eventually left. Jesse yearned for a return to Butler County, so he and Emma moved back there in 1950.[27]

Newcomers from Kentucky to the Midwest, South, and other places achieved a higher standard of living for themselves during the war, but it came at a cost. Jim Hammittee, Polly Ashley, Thelma Jo Noble, Emma Martin, and the others brought home more money than ever before and could afford nicer things. They sampled America's consumer culture, buying radios, refrigerators, used cars, even cottages. Some, like Hammittee, broke away from the working class entirely, finding a permanent place in America's growing middle class. Just the same, material gain is not everything, and the migrants felt both the sting of Northern bigotry and that special melancholy that derived from being so far away from their "old Kentucky home."[28]

Many Northerners, though by no means all of them, disliked the outsiders. Old, negative stereotypes flourished during the war. Once again, "hillbillies" were denigrated and run down for their supposed shortcomings. The Office of War Information reported that Detroit natives believed the Southerner to be "clannish, dirty, careless, gregarious in his living habits. He lives on biscuits and beans, never buys more than the most basic necessities of life, saves his money, is illiterate and yokelish."

This caricature contained only a grain of truth, ignoring the fact that many Kentuckians and other Southerners were clean, friendly, literate, and as smart as any Northerners. Most important, Kentucky labor helped produce the Midwestern weapons that played such a big part in winning the war.[29]

Bell County's Jim Hammittee experienced Northern intolerance first-hand, while he struggled to adjust to his new life in Detroit. Although Hammittee received promotions and enjoyed his pay, he felt certain indignities rather deeply. Some Northerners seized on his Kentucky accent, making fun of him for it. The kidding, it seemed to Hammittee, ran toward the nasty side, and it bothered him. He also sensed that Northern people thought Southern whites to be inferior—"only just one step ahead of the blacks." Getting used to Detroit challenged him, too. He hated being "cooped up" in a small apartment, in a giant city; he was used to the great outdoors of eastern Kentucky. The impersonal nature of human relations in the city grated on him. You walked past people on the street and "they don't talk to you—you don't talk to them. If you tried to smile and talk to somebody, why they thought you's up to something, gonna rob them or something." Jim's wife could not get comfortable with a Northern hospital, so she returned to eastern Kentucky to have their third baby. Hammittee did not talk politics or religion for fear of upsetting his coworkers. Neither he nor his wife took well to Northern food and the cold weather. By dint of considerable effort and self-discipline, the Hammittees overcame a myriad of challenges from the Michigan environment, prospered in an economic sense, and made a permanent, warm home in a new part of the country.[30]

Interaction between Kentuckians and Northerners proved to be something of a two-way street. Kentuckians perceived the people of Detroit, Chicago, and Gary to be "cool," "reserved," even unfriendly. The impersonal nature of Northern culture disturbed Kentucky folks, who knew everybody back home and would never dream of passing them by without a "How do you do." As outsiders who came to the North in large numbers, however, Kentuckians faced a harsher brand of discrimination than the comparatively few Northerners who migrated southward. Friction between migrants and natives resulted most often because Kentucky culture and Northern culture differed so markedly.[31]

Kentuckians in the Midwest and other parts of the country certainly missed the Bluegrass State, probably all the more so if they had been irritated or even alienated by Northern ways. Kentucky migrants longed to see family members, friends, and the land itself. Loving relationships and attachments to the mountains, meadows, hills, and river areas of Kentucky called out to the people who left. They never forgot these things, and almost every migrant felt their pull to one degree or another.

As sociologist Loyal Jones has stressed about Appalachian Kentuckians, "Family loyalty runs deep and wide." Mountain Kentuckians remember their "homeplace," and many "go back as often as possible." Little wonder that many migrants in Detroit paid the $15 to $20 during the war for a weekend round-trip bus ticket to eastern Kentucky and back. Little wonder that Jim Hammittee's wife went home to have her baby rather than do it in a Motor City hospital; she was just more comfortable in the mountains and wanted to return during a time of high stress. Migrants possessed a strong desire to visit mothers, fathers, and other members of the family, friends from old school days, and familiar haunts.[32]

Even the names of places caused Kentucky migrants to wax nostalgic: Quicksand, Pilot Knob, Hindman, Keeneland, Perryville, Dale Hollow, Walnut Grove, Paducah. Each of them held a special place in the hearts and minds of migrants, reminding them of a languid, supremely relaxing summer day somewhere in the past or of a secret adventure. These places meant something and brought a smile to the migrant's face or a bittersweet tinge of homesickness.

White and black Kentuckians working in other states had a powerful attraction to their homes. They cherished loved ones they left behind and wished to reunite with old friends. Being away from their churches and other supportive institutions hurt them. Ironically, blacks who migrated to Northern states recalled that the South was "safe." Perhaps they meant that their Kentucky home had been cozy and familiar, without the robust challenges posed by the Northern environment and Northern racism.[33]

Kentuckians revere the land. Many share an almost mythic bond with the very soil and water of their origins. Eastern Kentuckians in particular are said to be this way. Not surprisingly, then, migrants lamented the loss of "space," the cramped surroundings, the lack of outdoor activities, and the weather up north. Hammittee found Detroit to be crowded, his first apartment claustrophobic, and the winter weather almost unbearable. He was not alone.[34]

Other migrants emphasized that the urban environment outside Kentucky was just plain ugly or that it ruled out hunting, fishing, "sangin'," and other pursuits. These Kentuckians contrasted the beauty of Kentucky mountains clad with mist, or the translucent green of bluegrass meadows, to the drab, gray buildings of Northern cities and found them badly wanting. They missed the Kentucky ground under their feet and the pleasant, sometimes profitable diversions brought by stalking deer, hooking bass, and searching for ginseng. Nor did Northerners talk about "redbud winter" or the "moonbow" over Cumberland Falls. The disconnect between Kentucky ideas about nature and those of Northerners was just as profound as the differences over the proper way to treat people.

In the end, the individual migrant made the decision about whether to stay or go. A small number of Kentuckians traveled to another place, did not like it, and returned home during the war. Most of the migrants lasted for the duration, buoyed by improving finances, the urge to assist the war effort, or by a combination of factors. They coped with Northern culture and Northern bias as best they could, though some prejudice always remained. As one Kentucky migrant noted wryly after the Japanese surrendered and a push began by some in Michigan to rid the place of Southerners, "I don't know if we can adjust our appetites back to cornpone bread after eating all the beefsteak and pork loins we have had here." The truth is that some Kentuckians, like the Martins, went home after the war, while others, like the Hammittees, chose to stay in the North. It should not be forgotten that Kentuckians who remained in the North did not simply abandon their old identities. They built Southern Baptist churches in Detroit, Akron, Gary, and other places; sang bluegrass music; tilled gardens to remain close to the land; and hung out together in urban restaurants and bars. Efforts to replicate their Southern lifestyle and culture were at least partially successful and brought Kentuckians considerable solace.[35]

Massive migration strained Kentucky's infrastructure and its society. Louisville, northern Kentucky towns south of Cincinnati, and a few other wartime production centers received so many migrants that basic services in these places could not always keep up. Housing shortages developed by 1942 and grew worse thereafter. Utilities struggled to meet public demand. With one or both parents working long hours to further the war effort, the number of cases of juvenile delinquency rose steadily. Prostitution became more deeply entrenched than ever as the streets of Louisville (and some other places) teemed with migrants, servicemen, delinquent girls, and others. These problems reached their wartime peak in 1944–1945 and did not automatically go away with the celebration of V-J Day.

The lack of housing in Louisville became a serious issue. As migrants moved into the city beginning in 1940–1941, taking defense jobs, they needed to find someplace to live. Louisville landlords responded by subdividing houses and adding more apartment units. Public housing for whites and blacks was also available. Not too long after Pearl Harbor, however, migrants and others occupied the available dwellings, and a shortage materialized. The housing market simply could not keep pace with wartime demand.

War Production Board (WPB) orders in 1942 made it even more difficult to deal with the situation. Desirous of conserving important raw materials such as steel for war production, WPB cut back sharply on new private home construction and it stopped the building of new public housing projects entirely. Under these circumstances, the pressure in Louisville, indeed throughout urban Kentucky, to further subdivide existing houses and apartments mounted terrifically.[36]

Statistics reveal the size of the effort to deal with migrant war workers. In 1942 alone, 550 homeowners in Louisville converted their homes to multiple living units in order to rent them out. In Kentucky as a whole that year, landlords improved, remodeled or converted almost 12,000 properties into living quarters for war workers, at a cost of $4.3 million. Most of this construction took place in Louisville, Henderson, Hopkinsville, Morganfield, Covington, Newport, Lexington, Richmond, Elizabethtown, Fort Knox, and Ashland.[37]

Even with the hue and cry from landlords and migrants for assistance, zoning authorities sometimes resisted their pleas. In parts of Louisville, subdivision of residences was allowed, but not in other areas. In mid-April 1943, the City-County Board of Zoning Adjustments and Appeals refused requests to remove zoning restrictions that barred multiple dwellings in certain places. The board had also turned down numerous earlier

Kentucky migrants lived in war housing located near the Willow Run bomber plant in Michigan. This picture shows a mix of dwellings; some of the houses are decent and others just shacks. (Courtesy of the Library of Congress.)

requests. "There are some 28,000 dwelling units that can be converted into multiple units in Louisville without violating zoning regulations," Chairman Arthur G. Tafel explained. "With this situation I don't feel that we should let down the bars in other areas even though a shortage of housing does exist for the present."[38]

Nicholas Dosker, chairman of the Louisville War Housing Center Committee, agreed with Tafel about the housing shortfall, though probably not about the Zoning Board decision. Aware that the War Housing Center Committee could not find housing for over 400 persons in the month of January 1943 alone, and that many landlords who did have rooms available did not want to lease them out to adults with children, Dosker described the overall Louisville housing situation as "most acute right now" and that it was likely to "get worse" before it got better.

Chairman Dosker's prediction about the future panned out. The Louisville housing shortage intensified month by month through 1943 into midyear 1944. The prohibition against new public housing projects, the curtailment of new private housing, and the reluctance to ease zoning impediments all played their part. Perhaps of greatest significance, wartime production peaked in 1944, as did wartime labor demands. The influx of newcomers to Louisville and other towns reached its zenith at this time, and the housing pinch worsened. The crunch let up slightly in the winter of 1944–1945, though it was still problematic. The housing situation deteriorated once again by May 1945, when discharged servicemen returned home to Louisville from Europe, claiming their old houses and apartments. Evicted tenants needed places of their own, adding to the critical nature of the problem. Work on the new rocket propellant plant in Charlestown also brought in additional workers, who quickly encountered the nasty shortage of living spaces. The Louisville housing market eased up only gradually after the Japanese surrender.[39]

Utilities, like the housing market, experienced stress. Given higher usage of water, sewers, and electricity, the war years proved to be a challenging time. Instances of impure water, bad sanitation, and electrical outages cannot be denied, yet the Louisville Water Company (LWC) and the Louisville Gas & Electric Company discharged their responsibilities better than many such corporations across the country. The LWC even managed to recharge the Louisville Aquifer in 1944 with water from the Ohio River, thus getting three distilleries—which had temporarily suspended pumping—back into full operation.[40]

Juvenile delinquency touched Kentucky, though not to the extent that it affected Los Angeles, Detroit, or New York. Migrant parents who lived in Louisville or Newport traveled to those places to locate jobs and increase their economic standing. Of necessity, they worked ten or twelve hours a day, six or even seven days a week. Unfortunately, this did not leave much time or energy for their children. Parental neglect became the number-one cause of rising juvenile delinquency in Kentucky, though the issue was a complex one involving many other factors. In at least one case, autocratic local officials triggered an uprising of adults and minors alike.

Latchkey children attracted great attention across the United States by 1942–1943. Parents heading off to the war plants often left their kids in the house or apartment to fend for themselves. Understandably, the children grew lonely or bored, and sometimes wandered away. The lack of adult supervision put children in danger from car accidents or gave them the leeway to get caught up with gangs and gambling. If the youngsters were adolescents, sex might become a problem. Indeed, the most common form of delinquency for Kentucky girls was sex offenses. Crimes such as truancy, vandalism, and assault also became commonplace under these conditions. Venereal disease and unwanted pregnancies occurred.[41]

Washington Post journalist Agnes E. Meyer described the plight of the latchkey children well. "From Buffalo to Wichita," she noted, "it is the children who are suffering most from mass migration, easy money, unaccustomed hours of work, and the fact that mama has become a welder on the graveyard shift." Her observation applied just as well to the wayward boys and girls of Louisville, Newport, and Covington, who entertained themselves by drinking bourbon, playing cards for money, ogling nude girls in red-light districts, and handing out sexual favors. Though the Lanham Act of 1940 provided some federal money for child-care facilities, it was never enough for all the latchkey kids; and some parents would not have availed themselves of these services anyway because they did not want strangers taking care of their children or because they resented the inference that they could not handle child rearing themselves.[42]

A lack of adult supervision contributed mightily to juvenile delinquency in Kentucky, and some teenagers were just plain ornery, meriting the odious term "incorrigible"; yet neither of these factors adequately explains what happened at Olive Hill, Kentucky, during the late evening and early morning of July 11–12, 1943. Something more than inadequate parental oversight and wild kids was at work in this small town in eastern Kentucky—something that had been brewing for a long while, and it stunk.

At around 10:00 on the night of July 11, the trouble began. Olive Hill Police Chief Luther LeMaster and another officer approached a group of men and boys who were discharging loud, powerful firecrackers. Chief LeMaster demanded that they stop, but the group refused. Some of the perpetrators were apparently in the Olive Hill theater, owned by L. H. Mills. When LeMaster approached the theater, Mills and Raymond Waggoner blocked the door, denying entrance. The crowd grew larger, ultimately metamorphisizing into a mob. Some 100 people at minimum, perhaps as many as 400, moved across the town, setting off more firecrackers. Described in one account as dynamite, the blasts could be heard in rural houses as far as six miles away. Gunshots were fired here and there. A fraction of the mob made it to the Olive Hill Municipal Building around 1:30 a.m. "After that there was no holding them," said Corporal James Scott of the Kentucky Highway Patrol. The rioters broke out windows, overturned desks and chairs, and smashed telephones. They turned telephone books, police records, and mattresses into a huge bonfire outside the City Building. Roads into and out of town were apparently barricaded. The Olive Hill riot lasted at least four hours, completely overwhelmed the small Olive Hill police force and civil authorities, and ended with significant property damage.[43]

Police from Ashland, Morehead, Mt. Sterling, and other towns, along with the Kentucky Highway Patrol, were called to Olive Hill to deal with the disturbance. They converged on the place, some from thirty miles or more away. The riot had subsided by the time they got there and calm was restored. Twenty-two people were ultimately arrested and charged with "confederating and banding." Among them were Mills and Waggoner. All charges were eventually dropped.[44]

Olive Hill and Kentucky state officials blamed the upheaval on a reaction against a curfew order by Police Judge James Carpenter. Judge Carpenter had ordered all minors to be indoors by 8:00 p.m. The teenagers, whom the authorities claimed made up the vast majority of the mob, disliked the regulation and responded to it in an inappropriate, violent manner. Only a few adults were involved; one was known to hold a grievance against Carpenter over being arrested on the judge's order years before.[45]

The official story just does not jive with the facts. L. H. Mills and Raymond Waggoner, both leading businessmen of Olive Hill, were adults and orchestrated a good part of the demonstration. Other persons over eighteen joined the crowd; they were not juveniles. A number of unruly teenagers undoubtedly got in on what they perceived as "fun," and some parents should have exerted more control over their kids, but the wrecking of the Municipal Building and the firecrackering of the town had more to do with other developments. A clash of personalities and the despotism of certain Olive Hill politicians and policemen, more than simple meanness by adolescents, spawned this riot.

A similar, though smaller, firecrackering had occurred at Olive Hill in 1937. It resulted in the resignations of several city officials and police-men. That episode served as a precedent for what happened in 1943. The "mob" wanted heavy-handed officials to give up their offices and wished to establish fairer rule. Democracy was at the heart of it.[46]

Mills and Waggoner figured heavily in the proceedings. Mills's the-ater had thrived, and some officials and jealous businessmen in town did not like it. Waggoner, a garage operator, sided with Mills. Their businesses also depended heavily upon the support of young people in Olive Hill. A natural alliance formed. When queried, the two businessmen said that the riot had to do with city leaders who didn't like the success of Mills's movie business and the "high-handed manner in which our city and police offi-cials enforce the law."[47]

Jim Short, a former mayor of Olive Hill who has researched this epi-sode extensively, adds another element to the story. Short believes that the police, with cooperation from Judge Carpenter and Magistrate J. E. Ray-burn, made it their practice to arrest servicemen on leave from the mili-tary for drunkenness. As soon as a serviceman got off the train at Olive Hill, the police would take him aside to see if he had been drinking. If so, the serviceman was arrested, fined, and then sent back to the war, where he might be killed. This practice struck people in the know as despicable and one that demanded redress. The upshot is that the whole Olive Hill episode is best seen as an outgrowth of local government abuse and an attempt to recapture democracy rather than as a case of juvenile delin-quents out of control.[48]

Kentucky government made some effort during the early and mid-1940s to help juvenile delinquents. Ormsby Village in Anchorage, near Louisville, took in children who suffered from neglect as well as those who had committed minor crimes. A progressive institution, Ormsby allowed adolescent boys and girls to eat together and socialize. Dances were held. The adolescents wore no prescribed uniform; they could and did choose their own styles of dress. Corporal punishment for rules infractions was abolished, and offenders received detention or individual counseling.[49]

Over sixty years later, residents of Ormsby Village and others recall it fondly. The consensus is that this institution was an excellent one. At nearly eighty years old, Gloria Blakely recalled that Ormsby Village was "a very nice facility, clean and well-maintained." Gus Wheatley remembers that he arrived there at age eight in 1939 and stayed until 1948. Gus thought that the administration was fair and the teachers were great. He joined the Boy Scouts at the facility and almost made it to Eagle Scout. When asked if Ormsby Village was a good place, Wheatley replied, "Hell, yeah, it was the best thing that could happen to a kid."[50]

Several former residents mentioned "lockup." Kids who misbehaved were not paddled or spanked, but went into a form of detention where they were put in a room for several hours and told to remain there. Orville Morris, who arrived at Ormsby Village in 1945, once snuck into a girl's cottage to get a peek at the girls undressing. He went to lockup.[51]

Boys and girls at Ormsby Village who proved too tough to handle were sent to the Kentucky Houses of Reform at Greendale, just outside Lexington in Fayette County. Albert Kraus went to Greendale after refusing to conform at Ormsby Village. The final straw was when Kraus got into yet another fight and stole money.[52]

By virtually every measure Ormsby rated as one of the best schools for troubled children in the United States. Unfortunately, its space and enrollment were limited, and other schools of its type in Kentucky made for a poor comparison. The Osborne Association, evaluator of training schools across America, after extolling the virtues of Ormsby Village, stated that the other Kentucky schools for juvenile delinquents shaped up badly because of insufficient funding, dilapidated physical plant, untrained workers, "and, most important of all, political interference." Not surprisingly, juvenile delinquency remained a concern for many Kentuckians throughout World War II and in the 1950s garnered greater attention than before.[53]

World War II exacerbated the problem of prostitution in Kentucky. While prostitution had always existed in the state, it expanded considerably after Pearl Harbor. Lexington and the northern Kentucky outskirts of Cincinnati had more than their share of "working girls," attracted to the growing population centers by the abundance of "johns." Near Fort Knox, in Hardin County, a trailer camp featured a number of surprisingly old parents with large families of "dubious daughters available for hire by the hour." In early April 1942, police shut down ten houses of prostitution in Paducah after passage of a new, tougher antiprostitution ordnance. The U.S. Army encouraged passage of this law to cut down on the number of troops who engaged the services of the women. Venereal diseases were becoming a real problem among the soldiers and the general public. Louisville, naturally enough, witnessed far more prostitution than any other place in Kentucky and had few peers in the nation.[54]

Soldiers, migrants, and native Louisvillians kept Louisville's brothels hopping. During the war, more than a dozen brothels operated on South Seventh Street between Market Street and Broadway, an area known simply as "the line." Army and Navy personnel and war workers could frequently be seen entering and leaving these establishments, testimony to their lure and profitability. Since the number of prostitutes in the red-light district by 1938 was already about 500, one can imagine a much larger number by 1943–1944. Taking into account the true pros and the numerous amateurs who had arrived from rural areas, perhaps 750 to 1,000 hookers could be found in Louisville at the wartime peak. The commerce in human flesh clearly thrived in Kentucky's largest city during the hustle and bustle of the worldwide conflict.[55]

While Louisville certainly contained the greatest number of prostitutes in all of Kentucky, Bowling Green was home to the oldest and most famous brothel in the commonwealth. Madam Pauline Tabor ran this establishment on Clay Street from the 1930s to the 1960s. Its fame, or infamy, depending upon your perspective, spread far and wide. Up to eight ladies serviced GIs from Fort Knox, Camp Campbell, and other places during World War II. Efforts by the Army and a state legislator to shut the brothel down failed, and the soldiers just kept coming.[56]

Authorities recognized that prostitution had gotten out of hand. The official U.S. Army position declared prostitution a menace, mandating "rigorous repression." The May Act of 1941 gave localities significant authority to close down brothels near military bases. Louisville police launched periodic raids of whorehouses and cracked down on "street-walkers." Prostitutes taken into police custody ended up at nearby hospitals to be tested for venereal diseases before they went to jail. Gonorrhea and syphilis, it became only too obvious, ran rampant among the prostitutes and their customers. Yet many Army officers chose to "wink at prostitution," and police efforts—for whatever reason or reasons—did not shut down the brothels or stop the independents. "Victory girls," who gave their bodies away for free to needy servicemen, broke the Kentucky statute against fornication but were even more difficult to stop. An inordinate number of sex crimes, and vast sexual licentiousness, continued in Louisville, Bowling Green, Newport, and other places through 1945 and for decades thereafter.[57]

For numerous Kentuckians of the World War II era, migration shaped their lives more than any other factor. Just as military service became the central experience for hundreds of thousands of Kentucky men and women of this time, migration helped define the lives of hundreds of thousands more. The migrants left their homes primarily to advance themselves economically, and most met with success. They gave their labor to the war effort, contributing in this way to Allied victory over the Axis. The migrants understood that any move represented a significant trade-off: material gain had to be measured against such important abstractions as living without loved ones and being away from the land of their origins. One's very identity hung in the balance. Recognizing this truth, transplanted Kentuckians reconstituted parts of their old culture in the North, and that helped them overcome a variety of challenges. War-induced migration also contributed to congestion and housing shortages in Kentucky's largest cities, a jump in juvenile delinquency, and the proliferation of prostitution. When World War II ended, many of these social ills remained.

9

Loved Ones

No study of the World War II home front would be complete without a consideration of human emotions. War is an intense, often emotional undertaking, and Kentuckians with loved ones in the U.S. military experienced a wide array of feelings as time passed. Happiness accompanied the safe return of a son or daughter from the military. Anxiety plagued relatives of Kentucky soldiers whose status was unknown or who were seriously wounded or taken prisoner of war. Grief overwhelmed parents who learned of the death of their child in action. The Second World War not only involved the manufacture of machines and weapons, massive economic change, and new opportunities for women and blacks; it also included an undeniable human dimension.

Statistics tell part of the story. Over 16 million men and women served in the U.S. armed forces during the Second World War. Of that number, approximately 307,000 hailed from Kentucky. The vast majority of Kentuckians in the service escaped the conflict without genuine harm, but not all. About 14,000 were wounded, 2,000 became prisoners of war, and just under 8,000 died. States with populations similar to that of Kentucky suffered a similar number of battle-related deaths. Virginia, Tennessee, and Minnesota fit into this category. Virginia, for example, experienced just over 7,000 killed compared to just under 8,000 for Kentucky. Though Kentucky's casualties were not disproportionately high, the chances that a loved one in the Army, Navy, or Marines might be hurt, captured, or killed were real enough, and the actual event brought varying degrees of pain. The home-front experience thus included a great deal of worry about the fate of relatives and friends fighting abroad and a lesser amount of trauma. Almost everyone in the commonwealth shouldered these kinds of burdens for extended periods.[1]

The devastating nature of the war, by far the most destructive in all of human history, only exacerbated matters. Even though the U.S. government went to great lengths to shield the American public from the most horrific aspects of the fight, the truth got out. Bullets from so-called "small arms" ripped deep, gaping holes in the human body, leading to terrible infections, lost limbs, and in some cases death. Artillery, tank fire, and bombs dropped from airplanes tore men into hundreds of pieces. Most soldiers labeled missing in action had literally "been blown to vapor."[2] Many Kentuckians caught on to this terrible reality, though perhaps not to the full horror of what hurtling metal and high explosives could do to flesh and bone, and that made waiting for loved ones to come back even more difficult to endure. The imagination proved harder to restrain for some people than for others.

Most of the apprehensions, fortunately, turned out to be unfounded or exaggerated. Roughly 285,000 of the 307,000 Kentuckians in the armed forces returned home without any physical injury serious enough to bear recording. Of the ones who were wounded, most did not suffer permanent impairment, although they might well have hair-raising stories to tell. Howard Coffman, William R. Buster, Harry L. Jackson, and El Hannen Stacy experienced these kinds of results.

Howard Coffman of Hopkinsville, Kentucky, and William R. Buster of Harrodsburg were in the sizable majority who made it through the war unscathed. Coffman graduated from the U.S. Military Academy at West Point in 1943, entering the Army as a second lieutenant. He led a company of combat engineers in the European theater. Periodically he wrote home to his mom, dad, and younger brother Edward to reassure them that he was "alive and well." The Coffmans knew people from around Hopkinsville who had been killed, wounded, and captured in the war, but their family did not experience these types of pain. Edward did note that "we were probably more conscious of the basics of existence—life and death—than those who have been fortunate enough never to have known what wartime is like." Also a West Point graduate, William Buster fought in France, Belgium, and Germany. An operations officer for the 92nd Armored Field Artillery Battalion, 2nd Armored Division, he periodically gave orders to his men to open fire on various German tank units with their 105-mm howitzers. Though Buster was never wounded, he recalled that during the Battle of the Bulge he and his men spent much time huddled in their tents, "trying to keep from freezing to death." When his battalion entered Berlin in July 1945 the nauseating smell of death "hung over [the city] like a cloud."[3]

Harry L. Jackson corresponded with family members in Bowling Green. A man of cultural refinement, Jackson had worked for *Vogue* magazine and as supervisor of Works Progress Administration art projects for the Kentucky Department of Education. After a short stint with the National Guard, he became a second lieutenant in the U.S. Army and rose to the rank of captain. Jackson's letters home from various parts of Europe contained information that he thought would interest family members and reduce their anxieties about his well-being.[4]

Jackson spent time in France and Germany, among other places. He served as Special Services Officer for the 120th Regiment of the 30th Division. In this capacity, he witnessed various aspects of the fight for France, the Battle of the Bulge, and the drive into Germany. Though not assigned to direct combat, Jackson and his subordinates operated just behind the front lines and sometimes found themselves in dangerous situations.

As Special Services Officer, Captain Jackson directed the activities of a group of men who carried out a myriad of activities. His men wrote press releases about the regiment's activities and authored a history of the regiment. They filled out paperwork necessary for the award of decorations and metals. Other duties occupied them from time to time as the brass saw fit.

Jackson put his family's welfare first. When his mother mailed him homemade candy, marshmallows, and canned chicken, which took up part of the family food ration, he begged her not to do it. He sent the family souvenirs from the front, giving his parents and sisters advice on how German money and Nazi flags might be used in Bowling Green bond drives and window displays. Jackson did everything he could to aid and comfort his family from afar.

Inevitably, Jackson's letters revealed the rigors of his wartime experience. He detested the destruction of beautiful old chateaus and monasteries. He told his mom and sister Beatrice that after three months in wet, chilly France he felt like a "frog" (the amphibian, not a Frenchman) and had named Normandy the "mud hole of Hell." Assigned to burial detail on one occasion, Jackson and his men came across the corpse of a German soldier "so ripe we dared not move it." Jackson reported back to his Bowling Green loved ones that he witnessed men coming out of battle with "torment" in their eyes. Worse still, many soldiers returning from battle had become mere automatons, the "living dead without fear, evil, or comfort." Jackson and many other soldiers lived for months or years with discomfort, morbid sights that one could hardly forget, fear, and fatalism.[5]

European landscapes, architecture, and art could be magnificent. Jackson certainly thought so. He preferred to think about these things rather than the destruction and death all around him, carefully nurturing what enriched the soul rather than what deadened it. A decent, kind man, he nonetheless wished the "groveling submission" of "every square headed German bastard" and the extermination of "all Nazi fanatics" after witnessing the death of his longtime comrade, Sergeant Clifford Greenwood. Jackson never forgot the beauty and culture of Europe, nor the multiple horrors of war. Lucky enough to dodge physical injury and death, he traveled back to Kentucky with a much better understanding of the cruelty man can so easily inflict upon his fellow man.[6]

Unlike Howard Coffman, William Buster, and Harry Jackson, who were all officers, El Hannen Stacy served the U.S. military during World War II as an enlisted man. Born near Jackson, Kentucky, in the Appalachian mountains, Stacy joined the Army on July 16, 1940—long before Pearl Harbor—and remained with it until June 18, 1945. During this eventful five-year stretch, he was promoted from private to sergeant; left base without permission; participated in combat, receiving a serious wound; witnessed the punishment of a young French woman who collaborated with the Germans; and killed a number of enemy soldiers.[7]

Patriotism and a sense of adventure motivated twenty-year-old Stacy to volunteer for service with the Army. A historical plaque at the site of the Breathitt County Courthouse reminded him that during World War I no man from the county had been drafted because volunteers filled the entire quota. He thought this to be a grand tradition and that it would be shameful for a man to delay so long that he had to be compelled to serve. He would not let that happen to him. The world outside his rural home also held some appeal; he wished to see it, and the Army would certainly let him do that. Consequently, El Hannen joined the Army of his own free will and proved to be a good enough soldier that he advanced to company clerk and then supply sergeant.

Stacy did run into a spot of trouble with military rules. Still stateside in the summer of 1943, he received word from the Red Cross that his mother, Louanna, had fallen gravely ill from pneumonia. The family doctor did not think she would live. El Hannen immediately requested a leave of absence to be at his mom's bedside, but was turned down by the last officer in the chain of command. Not to be denied, he simply snuck away from his base at Fort Ethan Allen in Vermont and hitchhiked all the way back to Kentucky. There he comforted Louanna and stayed just long enough to see her condition begin to improve. After returning to Fort Allen, Stacy was charged with being absent without leave (AWOL), and eventually a military court cut his rank back to private and docked him $8 a month in pay for one year. He thought this punishment a small price to pay given the circumstances.[8]

Shortly after this episode, the Army sent Stacy overseas. He fought in the Italian campaign as part of General Mark W. Clark's Fifth Army. Clark's job was to take Italy from the Germans; and, though it was a tough slog, he succeeded. Stacy got in on part of the Italian fighting, where he experienced combat for the first time. Later, he trod the soil of France, Belgium, and Germany, participating in the Battle of the Bulge and the Allied surge across the Rhine River into the Fatherland itself.

Stacy won a number of medals. He earned his first Purple Heart in January of 1944, while participating in the Italian campaign. The Fifth Army had moved slowly up the peninsula from Naples, taking one mountain at a time. Stacy occupied a small outpost on Mt. Majo when he felt "a thud to my left thigh, and it almost turned me over." He believed at first that the thud was a grenade, which might explode at any second. Fortunately, the impact came from a 9-millimeter bullet rather than a grenade. The bullet lodged in his left thigh, about halfway up, the tip of the metal actually grating against his femur. A doctor eventually removed the bullet, and Stacy rejoined his outfit after six weeks.[9]

Transferred from Italy to France, Stacy witnessed the humiliation of a young French woman in Biot who had earlier traded sexual favors for preferential treatment from German soldiers. She was not alone in her activities. A French court convicted these women of prostitution and collaboration with the enemy. Their sentence involved having a barber shave off all their hair. "One of the young women," according to Stacy, "became hysterical when her beautiful golden locks were dropped to the floor of the council chambers, and when she was released . . . began tearing her clothes off and by the time she reached the front door she was completely naked and she ran right down the middle of the street crying her eyes out."[10]

The war, of course, included moments infinitely more brutal than what befell the French women, and a soldier's job is sometimes to kill. Stacy remembered just how tough it got at the Anzio beachhead. A fierce German counterattack threatened some American troops, including El Hannen himself, with annihilation. U.S. artillery fire, mortar fire, and machine gun fire stopped the German assault from succeeding. Stacy recalled his own part in the battle, where he fired a 60-millimeter mortar shell into the open turret of an advancing German Mark IV tank. The resulting explosion killed the entire tank crew. Stacy could not be certain of just how many German soldiers died at his hands during the war, but the number was more than a few.[11]

El Hannen Stacy left the U.S. Army shortly after V-E Day, making his way back to Jackson, Kentucky. Stacy's time in the Army had been interesting, occasionally grisly, and honorable. Louanna was overjoyed to have El Hannen back, and they enjoyed almost six more years together before she passed away in 1951. Stacy became a successful building contractor in eastern Kentucky, a student at Lees College while in his seventies, and a writer.

El Hannen Stacy, Harry Jackson, William Buster, and Howard Coffman, like nine out of every ten Kentucky soldiers in World War II, emerged from the conflict in relatively good shape. They maintained loving relationships with family members. They functioned well within Kentucky society. They led productive, successful lives. The ravages of war might well have damaged their psyches to some extent, but not greatly.

Another group of soldiers, much smaller in number, were not so fortunate. These individuals did not come through the war whole. They were maimed, either physically or mentally. Dee Carl Perguson Jr., Edwin Rue, and Paul Witt symbolize this bitter aspect of the Kentucky wartime experience.

Dee Carl Ferguson Jr. left the war after being severely wounded, since he could no longer aim a rifle properly or carry heavy equipment. Ferguson had grown up in Horse Branch, a rural town in Ohio County, Kentucky, and enlisted with the Army at age twenty-one in late 1942. After a period of time in North Africa, he was reassigned to Italy. On January 21, 1944, while fighting during the Cassino campaign, a machine-gun bullet tore through his left forearm, broke the large bone in his upper arm into pieces, and finally passed through his shoulder. A great deal of muscle, tendon, and bone damage resulted, relegating Ferguson to the sidelines for the duration.

Ferguson's recuperation proved difficult. He spent almost a month in a Naples, Italy, hospital. Transported back to the United States after that, he went through surgery and painful physical therapy at Kennedy Military Hospital in Memphis, Tennessee. Despite treatment, the nerve damage from the bullet wound was too great, and he lost the use of his arm forever. An optimist, or perhaps just making the best of a bad situation, Ferguson described his Army career as being "wonderful," while battling the handicap for the rest of his life.[12]

Edwin Rue and Paul Witt experienced mental problems rather than physical ones. Their emotional wounds derived from terrible sights, sounds, and events that left them devastated. As in the case of Ferguson, Rue and Witt never made a complete recovery.

Edwin Rue, an Army tank officer from Harrodsburg, Kentucky, carried a heavy psychological burden out of the war. Captured by the Japanese in the Philippines during the spring of 1942, Rue spent over three years as a prisoner. He trudged along with tens of thousands of others on the infamous Bataan Death March, where over 5,000 American soldiers died. Some of these men were shot; others were bayoneted, buried alive, and beheaded. He faced hellish conditions at Japanese POW camps, where overcrowding, rampant diseases such as malaria, and the brutality of guards claimed many more American lives. The worldwide conflict led to the death of his brother, Arch B. Rue, who perished when the *Oryoku Maru,* a Japanese ship carrying a large number of American POWs, was bombed by U.S. Navy fighter planes. Edwin learned that Arch was among the many POWs who either suffocated, drowned, or were shot while in the water. Little wonder, then, that Edwin Rue never got over the war. He once remarked, "I've tried to put it behind me. . . . But there are things you can't forget, things I sometimes can't get off my mind. It bothers me to bring it up."[13]

Paul Witt of Levee, Kentucky, in Montgomery County, endured similar hardships. Witt served as a military ambulance driver in Europe, arriving there just after the D-Day invasion. Hand-to-hand fighting between American and German troops had left many dead. Witt recalled hauling two dead soldiers to a French cemetery, which he found by following a stream of blood into the graveyard itself. Later, Witt toured concentration camps at Godgan and Nordhausen. "You see piles and piles of people starving to death and crawling around the ground getting ahold of your britches leg," he said, "it doesn't take much to do you." Perhaps the worst of it all (or maybe not) came when Witt watched a fellow ambulance driver run over a land mine. The driver's vehicle burst into flames, the driver jumped to the ground to stamp them out, stepped on another mine, and was blown apart.

Paul Witt could not escape the war even after it ended. Witt confessed that he drank too much for many years afterwards, "to calm his nerves." After realizing he had a serious problem, he gave up the booze, "but still [got] the jitters when he [thought] about the war much." "How we made it I'll never know," Witt reflected.[14]

Edwin Rue and Paul Witt became long-term victims of a terribly destructive war. Their nightmarish memories never deserted them. Whether or not they were casualties of post-traumatic stress disorder does not really matter; what does matter is that their lives were marred by the wartime experiences; their injuries were at least as bad as those of men who forfeited an arm or a leg.

Kentucky relatives of Perguson, Rue, Witt, and others like them encountered difficulty, too. Wartime events changed these men, either physically or emotionally. Perguson lost the use of a limb. Rue and Witt came home depressed, shaky, and brittle. They were not really the same people as they were before the war, and loved ones had to adjust to that fact. Some managed to do so; some could not. Rue did not like to dwell on the war nor on his postwar relationships. Witt's dependence on alcohol adversely affected those closest to him. Veterans of the war often retreated from family members, and family members from the veterans.

Home-front Kentuckians gave thanks when loved ones emerged from the war unscathed; exhibited sadness when a son, brother, or uncle returned with a permanent impairment; and worried themselves sick when a relative in the service fell under Axis incarceration. Next to the death of a loved one in the service, imprisonment may well have caused Kentuckians back home the greatest angst. Everyone understood that grave uncertainty accompanied prisoner-of-war status and that your loved one might die in captivity. An unfair social stigma also attached to the person who became a prisoner: Why did not he fight to the bitter end or at least escape the clutches of the enemy? Perhaps allowing oneself to become a prisoner reflected a certain flaw in an individual's character.

Whatever Kentuckians lucky enough to be at home thought, the Axis powers took a fair number of Kentucky servicemen prisoners of war. Of the couple thousand or so Kentuckians rounded up by the Axis from 1942 to 1945, the Germans held roughly 80 percent of them and the Japanese the other 20 percent. This ratio turned out to be a good thing, because Germany treated its American prisoners far better than Japan did.[15]

German soldiers seized airman David Gaitskill on August 18, 1944. A native of Mt. Sterling, Kentucky, Gaitskill had entered the American air force after being drafted two years before. He manned a turret gun on a B-17 bomber, going on numerous missions over Germany. On his twenty-fourth sortie, German antiaircraft fire—probably from a flak tower—struck his bomber, which caught fire and went down. Gaitskill parachuted away from the doomed craft at 28,000 feet, soon passed out from lack of oxygen, and came to at less than 10,000 feet. He did not recall ever pulling the rip cord, but does remember German troops yelling at him as he floated down to them. Apprehended in a Berlin yard, Gaitskill's stint as a prisoner of war lasted until May 3, 1945.[16]

David Gaitskill spent time in two places. Just after his capture, the Germans transported him to a nearby Hitler Youth Camp. After that, he stayed for a much longer time at Stalag Luft XVII B, located at Krems, Austria, not far from Vienna. This facility held 400 prisoners in David's barracks alone, and there were many barracks and other buildings. Gaitskill made do with his new surroundings for eight months, managing to get by without too much difficulty. He was freed just before V-E Day, with German forces in full collapse.

Barracks 36, Stalag Luft XVII B, where Mt. Sterling native David Gaitskill spent time as a prisoner of war. (Courtesy of Bill Doubledee.)

Frances Jones of North Middletown, Kentucky, David's girlfriend back home, learned from the U.S. War Department that David had been taken prisoner. She received a telegram saying that he was "missing" after his bomber had crashed. Later she was informed that he had become a POW. Frances recalls that the War Department notifications seemed to be "very, very slow" and that she felt "worried, scared, concerned—all of the above."[17]

Frances—whom friends and loved ones called Fan—had met David just after Christmas 1941. She was on a blind date with a fellow that David chauffeured. The guy she dated did not catch her fancy, but David did. They went out together a few times before David went off to war, then wrote each other. Their relationship deepened over time, surviving both the distance between them and the prisoner experience. Fan and David wed on August 11, 1945, soon after he returned home.

Frances and David Gaitskill talked a lot about the war. Frances says that David's teeth were "just chattering" when he landed amidst the German troops in Berlin, he was so scared. Referring to David's treatment

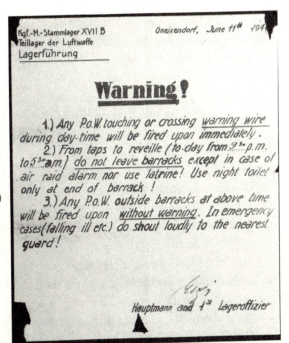

Warning notice posted for all
prisoners by Commandant,
Stalag Luft XVII B.
(Courtesy of Bill Doubledee.)

by German guards, Frances notes that he "wasn't beaten; boredom was the biggest problem." Another annoyance for David and the other men was that the Germans permitted the POWs almost no showers—David thinks he had only two showers over many months' time. Although the food was not good, David managed to keep his weight up. Perhaps the "beetle soup" he ate provided essential protein (this thin broth consisted of water, dehydrated vegetables, and beetles that somehow got into the vegetable cans before they were opened).[18]

Fan was tough. She kept her head up while David remained under German custody, hoping for the best. She remarked, "I had faith—hopefully." When David was released and made it safely home, she was "overjoyed." The couple were married almost immediately and remained together for over sixty years.[19]

David Gaitskill's days as an American prisoner of war under German authority proved fairly typical. He was not assaulted. The Germans gave him and the other prisoners at Krems enough food to get by, even as German resources shrank by war's end. There was no obvious mistreatment here, maybe no real mistreatment at all. David did his time and returned home little worse for the wear.

Kentucky soldiers captured by the Japanese in the Pacific theater could not say the same thing. These soldier-POWs passed through a hellish world of stabbings, shootings, overcrowding, epidemic disease, overwork, malnutrition, and "friendly fire." Dozens, perhaps as many as a couple hundred, Kentuckians perished in the desperate struggle to survive this hideous ordeal.

Sixty-six Harrodsburg, Kentucky, men best typify this experience. Twenty-nine ultimately lost their lives, including the aforementioned Arch Rue. Thirty-seven survived, though many (such as Edwin Rue) were disfigured in one way or another. The conflict ate these men up, swallowing some whole and spitting out others.[20]

The Harrodsburg soldiers began their military careers in the Kentucky National Guard, where they received the training necessary to operate tanks. In 1940, the U.S. Army took over the National Guard tank unit, and the men received additional training at Fort Knox as Company D, 192d Tank Battalion. Dispatched to the Philippines, the Harrodsburg tankers saw action against Japanese forces there. With the Japanese triumph, the sixty-six tank men were scooped up by enemy forces at places like Corregidor and made to go through a wicked trial that none of them could have imagined.

William Lee Peavler was one of the Harrodsburg tankers. While he and the others were on the Bataan Death March a Japanese soldier suddenly thrust his bayonet into Peavler's leg. There seemed to be no provocation at all; it just happened. Peavler screamed but kept marching, because the alternative was certain death.[21]

Driven by terrible thirst, some POWs bolted from the line of ragged marchers, making a beeline for nearby wells. Lawrence Martin of Harrodsburg succeeded in getting a few precious swallows of water this way. Other Harrodsburg men watched in horror as Japanese guards gunned down American prisoners who attempted the same thing.

Survivors of the death march ended up at Camp O'Donnell, a former Philippine army training site that the Japanese had designated a prisoner of war camp. Unfortunately, O'Donnell quickly became overcrowded, holding almost twice as many POWs as the Japanese originally intended for it. With the prisoners packed together so tightly, poor sanitation resulted and mosquitoes, dysentery, and malaria thrived. Tankers Wesley Hungate, Willard Foster, and Herbert Steel died here.

Kentuckian Alvin Powleit, a doctor, described conditions at a Camp O'Donnell hospital. Powleit noted that the area was "filled with prisoners milling around, defecating anywhere. . . . Men were lying, sleeping, and dying in their own waste."

Many of O'Donnell's prisoners were later shipped to Camp Cabanatuan also in the Philippines. Torrential rains caused latrines to overflow, and flies carried feces everywhere; minute particles stuck on food the POWs ate, and dysentery struck hard again. Mosquitoes bred in puddles and flew away, biting prisoners and spreading malaria. Thousands died. Ten more Harrodsburg prisoners succumbed at Cabanatuan.

Lack of food and malnutrition plagued the Kentuckians. Too often, they lacked protein or such nutrients as vitamin C. Beriberi, pellagra, and scurvy became common. Harrodsburg's Cecil Sims suffered not only from malaria, but from beriberi as well. The death knell often sounded when a prisoner who suffered from physical problems lost the will to fight.

Overwork threatened the POWs, especially given their poor diet. Harrodsburg's Earl Fowler lifted railroad ties and unloaded heavy railroad cars at a Japanese camp in Manchuria. Fowler witnessed the beatings of tired prisoners who tried to take unauthorized breaks. Cold weather proved crippling. Dead POWs were stacked in warehouses until spring, when the ground would soften up enough to allow for burial. Fowler managed to survive and tell his story.

American air raids also claimed Kentucky lives. Sometimes U.S. planes unwittingly dropped bombs on Japanese ships and camps that held prisoners. Arch Rue died from such friendly fire, as did a few other Harrodsburg men. The Americans also bombed Camp Hoten in Manchuria, Earle Fowler's temporary home, resulting in nineteen more American prisoners dead. Harrodsburg prisoners Morgan French and John Sadler, who were both in Japan by August 1945, found themselves uncomfortably close to the two atomic bomb blasts. Near Nagasaki Sadler listened to a "roar" and watched an "awful toadstool across the bay."[22]

Clearly, POWs from Kentucky fared much worse under the Japanese than under the Germans. The Germans had ratified the Geneva Convention of 1929, which offered protection to prisoners of war, whereas the Japanese had not. Germany made an effort to adhere to the Convention, mostly because its government understood that the Americans treated German POWs in the United States quite well. The Third Reich did not wish to invite retaliation against its own soldiers by abusing American captives. The numbers also made a difference: the United States held roughly 375,000 German prisoners of war on American soil, whereas Germany held only 95,000 American POWs in the Fatherland and occupied parts of Europe. Japanese mistreatment of American prisoners owed most to lack of preparation and to cultural orientation. The Japanese simply were not ready to house and care for the sheer number of American and Philippine prisoners who were taken after the seizure of the Philippine Islands. Facility size, food sanitation, medical supplies, leadership, and other resources proved woefully inadequate, and the resulting disorganization only invited additional abuse and tragedy. The Japanese cultural emphasis on obedience, duty, and responsibility often outweighed reverence for life. If a Japanese soldier could be shot by a superior for breaking a rule or neglecting his duty, what response might result from a transgression by an American prisoner of war? In addition, the Japanese considered it a disgrace to surrender and thus treated Americans who did so badly. A simple statistic reveals the awful truth: 40 percent of all U.S. Army and Army Air Force (AAF) prisoners of war held by the Japanese died compared to just 1 percent of Army and AAF prisoners held by the Germans and Italians.[23]

Harrodsburg survivors traveled back to the United States after Japan's surrender. Victory had been achieved. Hometown friends met again aboard ships and reacquainted themselves. They talked easily enough, having the war and the horrendous prisoner of war experience in common.[24]

Back in the United States, the former captives struggled. After exchanging declarations of love and other pleasantries with family members, adjustment proved difficult. Wartime events, including numerous atrocities, had changed the Harrodsburg survivors. Relatives could not quite understand what they had been through, and the ex-prisoners found it hard to get back to a normal existence. Meaningful reconnections too often eluded both parties. Second Lieutenant William H. Gentry—one of the few ex-POWs willing to talk at all about close relationships after the

war—could say just this: "The ones who died while I was gone are missing, and the ones that are still here are still here." Cecil Sims was not as
damaged as Edwin Rue or William Gentry, but he grappled with bouts of
depression. Sims began to hoard food like blackberry cobbler, taking away
whatever dessert was left from dinner and eating it all by himself. A lack
of joy in life, full-fledged depression, fatalism, and even nihilism gripped
more than a few Kentuckians who had been under Japanese control during the war, and they did not let go of these feelings easily.[25]

Family members, of course, worried most of all that a loved one would
die in combat, and the "unthinkable" cast a dark shadow over thousands
of Kentucky families. Though the death of a Kentucky serviceman went
against the odds, it happened with numbing regularity from 1942 to 1945.
Newspapers from hamlets, towns, and cities across the commonwealth
carried stories of boys who paid the ultimate price to help the Allies defeat
the Axis, and mothers, fathers, and others bowed their heads in grief and
wept. The Otters, Larkins, Wheelers, Maddoxes, Sousleys, Buckners, and
Wellses—just to name a few of many Kentucky families—fell victim to
war's most feared and costly harvest.

Bethel V. Otter of Speed Avenue in Louisville pursued a military
career. A smart boy, he made it into the U.S. Naval Academy, graduating
in 1937. Otter had red hair, enjoyed sports and girls, and was a high-spir-
ited young man. In 1940, the Navy assigned him to the Philippines, and
it was there he met his end.[26]

The Japanese invasion of the Philippine Islands, which began just
after Pearl Harbor, pushed American forces onto the Bataan peninsula
and from there back to the small, fortified island of Corregidor. Lieutenant Otter was one of approximately 11,500 defenders, trying with all their
might to hold the place. The Japanese managed to put troops on Corregidor on the night of May 5, 1942, but American and Filipino forces
refused to give up. At this point, many soldiers had only small arms to
use against the invaders. On the morning of May 6, the Japanese landed
tanks and artillery on the island. Lieutenant General Jonathan Wainright,
who had taken over for the evacuated General Douglas MacArthur, fear-
ing the annihilation of most if not all his men, sorrowfully gave the surrender order.

Bethel Otter may or may not have been dead by the time of the official surrender, but whatever the case he decided not to become a prisoner of war. On that fateful May 6, Bethel's unit was fighting outside the strategic Malinta Tunnel, which contained Wainright's command headquarters and communications. This area could not be forfeited without defeat. All alone, Otter charged toward a Japanese machine gun nest, throwing grenades and firing a Colt-45 revolver. Machine gun fire ripped through his body, killing him instantly.[27]

Bethel Otter was not forgotten. A fellow soldier dug a shallow grave on Corregidor, pushing the body into it and covering it up. In 1949, his remains were removed from the Philippines and reinterred at Cave Hill Cemetery in Louisville. The Navy had posthumously bestowed upon him the Navy Cross, the second highest honor possible, behind only the Congressional Medal of Honor. The Otter family held a private ceremony for Bethel upon his return, deeming the funeral too personal for public involvement. Even after the passage of nearly seven years, the Otters' pain and melancholy were self-evident.

Sergeant George E. Larkin Jr., like Otter, died relatively early in the war. Larkin, from Colesburg in Hardin County, participated in Lieutenant Colonel Jimmy Doolittle's celebrated raid of April 18, 1942, on the Japanese mainland. Doolittle's bombers struck Tokyo, boosting American morale just a little over four months after Pearl Harbor. Larkin therefore became the first Kentuckian to bomb an enemy capital, winning a Distinguished Flying Cross in the process. Tragically, Sergeant Larkin was killed in Asia before 1942 ended. He was just twenty-three years old.[28]

Alma Wheeler learned that her husband, Gene, died during the D-Day invasion. Since the body lacked "dog tags," a scintilla of uncertainty surrounded the identification. Alma could not bring herself to believe that Gene was really gone, agonizing over his fate for a year or so before convincing herself it had indeed happened. She passed through the whole gamut of emotions associated with the loss of a dear one: uncertainty, apprehension, denial, anger, and ultimately acceptance.[29]

Alma Blancett and Gene Wheeler of Calhoun, Kentucky, were a storybook couple. They dated in high school, eventually falling in love. Gene was dark-haired, handsome, and athletic. Alma was slim, attractive, and "the life of the party." The two married in 1943. Before Gene left for the service, Alma was pregnant, and son James—soon called "Jimbo"—was born in January 1944.

Gene Wheeler became an Army Air Force pilot. On June 6, 1944, when General Dwight D. Eisenhower gave the go-ahead for the cross-channel assault against German-occupied France, Wheeler flew his C-47 Skytrain into enemy air space. German fire struck the plane, and it plummeted toward the ground. Wheeler ordered the crew to parachute away, as he struggled to maintain control of the floundering craft. Tragically, he did not have time to escape, and the C-47 crashed near St. Pellerin, France. As fate would have it, a picture of the crash scene, which came to light later, revealed Gene's handsome face, which was almost unmarked, and part of his ruined body.

A War Department telegram provided Alma her first notice that something had gone badly awry. The June 22, 1944, telegram classified Gene as "missing in action." In reality, only the separation of the dog tags from the body prevented the military from labeling him "killed in action." Alma knew all this information, and it scared her badly. Yet she clung to the bare hope that somehow a mistake had been made and that Gene was still alive.

Halfway believing Gene Wheeler would return, Alma started a diary, documenting Jimbo's development and her own efforts to cope with a cruel fate. Alma did not want her husband to miss out on the infant's early experiences, and she needed some outlet for her own feelings. At a subconscious level, Alma understood that Gene would almost certainly not come back even as she tried to squelch that knowledge. Anxiety and disaffirmation mixed together.

Various entries in the diary offer a glimpse of Alma's ordeal. On January 1, 1945, almost six months after D-Day, she noted, "It's another year [and I hope] this one won't be as awful as the last one." She remarked that the baby "has grown to be a healthy, strong boy and I know [Gene] would be proud as punch with him." On April 6, Alma recorded, "I still believe [Gene is] safe somewhere." By May 30, after passage of almost a full year, she conceded that there "is really no reason for me to keep hoping. The war has been over and I know you could have got me some word by now." A July 3, 1945, entry shows receipt of a letter from Lieutenant Howard L. Huggett, who had been aboard Wheeler's C-47 just before it went down.

Huggett had parachuted to safety but reported that Gene Wheeler did not make it. Alma now knew the horrible truth with certainty; further denial was impossible.[30]

A final burst of anger and resentment remained. Gene himself bore the brunt of it. Alma wrote, "Darling, why didn't you bail as soon as the plane was hit? I wonder if you completely forgot about Jimbo and me."

As the rest of 1945 played itself out, Alma Wheeler battled depression and loneliness. Acceptance and time brought some measure of relief. She abandoned her diary on December 31, 1945. The last entry contains a prayer for God's blessing on Jimbo and a declaration that Alma could remember Gene "just as plain as . . . day," though the two had not seen each other in almost two years. In an excerpt from a poem published in the *McLean County News* on June 6, 1946—exactly two years after Gene's death—Alma expresses her love for Gene one last time in print:

He's flying now. He has his wings
And they are perfect, God made things.
His soul's been growing them since youth.
Not feathered like the cherubim
But, oh, so much a part of him!
Not life nor death can stop his flight.
His soul has wings into the night.
Through dark-to-dawn-He shall fly on!
Sorely missed by wife and son.[31]

The war ended just as sadly for George and Oma Mae Maddox. The Maddoxes made their home at 809 South Thirty-Fourth Street in Louisville. They raised their son, Kenny, there. Kenneth Maddox was mortally wounded during the Battle of the Bulge.[32]

Kenny was a good boy who grew into a thoughtful, considerate young man. He loved the Boy Scouts, rising to be a troop leader and ultimately skipper of Ship 41, Sea Scouts. Perhaps his years with the Scouts kindled his interest in the military. In 1941, he entered the 138th Field Artillery, 38th Division, U.S. Army. Superiors offered him a chance to go to officer training school, which he accepted. After graduating, he became a second lieutenant of artillery. Reassigned to the 28th Division, Maddox was promoted to first lieutenant. While in the Army he wrote numerous letters to his parents and other relatives. He let them know many times that he was fine but desired a quick end to the war so he could get back to Louisville.

Lieutenant Maddox took a ship to Europe in October 1943. He stayed in England for a while, then went to France and Luxembourg. While in England, he took in a show at Piccadilly Circus, wandered around during a blackout, witnessed the changing of the guard at Buckingham Palace, and enjoyed other magnificent places and sights. As he traveled across the French countryside, he exchanged greetings with French children. He knew enough French to say "Good morning," "Good afternoon," and "How are you today?" He reassured George, Oma Mae, Doris, and Hunt Maddox that all was well.

By late 1944, however, Kenneth Maddox's mood had become somber. The fighting just got tougher and tougher. More men died. He wrote his mom and dad that God must be watching over him because it seems "absolutely impossible for me to come through a day without being injured or killed." He noted, "Now that we have Jerry on his own land he is getting very stubborn. Maybe now he will realize just what total war means if we flatten out more of his cities. I certainly hope he discovers in a hurry. I am ready to come home any time."[33]

By November 23, 1944, part of the American Army was in Luxembourg, including Kenny. Lieutenant Maddox wrote George and Oma Mae that his Christian upbringing was really paying dividends, helping him to hold on in a time of great danger and bloodletting. Then Hitler launched a last-ditch counteroffensive against the weakest part of the Allied lines in the Ardennes Forest of France. Fourteen German infantry divisions, reinforced by five Panzer divisions, spearheaded a drive into France, Belgium, and Luxembourg on December 16. Maddox found himself in the wrong place at the wrong time.

On December 17, the second day of the Battle of the Bulge, Lieutenant Maddox's antitank crew found themselves occupying a thoroughly untenable position. Armed with a single 57-millimeter antitank gun, Maddox and his men comprised the lone American force holding a bridge into the ancient town of Clervaux, Luxembourg. Elements of the German Second Panzer Division moved toward the bridge, as Maddox's repeated radio calls for help went unanswered. Eyes riveted on the approaching Panzers, nobody saw a single German grenadier slip in until it was too late. Maddox himself spotted the German at the last instant and yelled to warn his men, but the din of battle proved too loud for anyone to hear him. Maddox did the only thing he could, jumping in front of his men and firing at the German grenadier. The German soldier discharged his machine pistol at Maddox, who took the full burst squarely in his chest. By his action, Maddox saved at least three of his men's lives, if not more. Unfortunately, nobody could survive the blast he himself received. Remarkably, Maddox would linger for another eight days, and his single pistol shot had killed the grenadier. As for the antitank unit, the Panzer division ripped through it and Clervaux fell. Yet Maddox's sacrifice was not in vain: it and others like it helped to slow the German advance, and the Allies ultimately regrouped, winning the Battle of the Bulge.

Lieutenant Kenneth Maddox was subsequently captured by German soldiers, who found him lying unconscious on the ground, bleeding profusely. The Germans moved Maddox to a German military hospital, where he was classified as a prisoner of war. Hanging on to life by the barest of margins, Maddox expired on Christmas Day 1944. It was almost as if this devoted Christian made a special effort to make it to the day Jesus Christ was born, then relaxed and surrendered himself to the Savior.

The War Department officially informed the Maddoxes of their son's death seven months later, during July 1945. Months after that, with World War II over and servicemen returning to the United States, George and Oma Mae received a visit from Kenny's gunner, Bob. He told them how much Kenny meant to the antitank crew and explained what happened to Kenny on the day he was shot. He tried his best to comfort George and especially Oma Mae.

Bob said Lieutenant Maddox was a fine man, a good officer, and a hero. Maddox had been "firm and stern . . . but . . . had no enemies and all liked him." When George asked if Kenny had ever been angry, Bob said, "No," then added, "and if he ever had been he didn't take it out on his men." Bob told them how Kenny died while intercepting bullets that would otherwise probably have struck Bob and two more men. Oma Mae listened to all this and tried to be courageous. As Bob and his friend began to leave, she finally broke down, because "it felt like they were taking Kenny with them." She cried and cried, but they "told me it was all right" and that they "thought I had been mighty brave about the whole thing."[34]

Children, like adults, suffered from the worst that World War II dished up. Little John D. Perrine of Maysville worshipped the ground teenager Doug Newell walked on, following Dougie around the farm constantly. Dougie ended up in the U.S. military; he was shot in the neck and paralyzed in Italy. Perrine remembers reading the War Department telegram along with Mrs. Newell. Both of them "just bawled." They thought Dougie might die. Fortunately, Doug Newell not only lived but eventually walked again. Mary Ellen Perrine, first cousin to John Perrine, was not so lucky. Sam Perrine, Mary Ellen's father, served as an officer in an engineering division. Periodically he sent Hershey chocolates home to his daughter from Europe because they were hard to get at home. Young

U.S. Army officer Sam Perrine with his daughter Mary Ellen at Camp Robinson, Arkansas, in 1941. (Courtesy of Mary Ellen Perrine Massenburg.)

Major Perrine was killed at the Battle of the Bulge in December 1944. This photo shows him a year or two before his death. (Courtesy of Mary Ellen Perrine Massenburg.)

Mary Ellen squealed with delight each time the sweets came. Sam died at the Bulge after a land mine exploded near him. When word of her daddy's death reached the family, Mary Ellen recalled years later, she was "terribly sad once she processed what happened." Because her childhood up to that point had been filled with love and happiness she was able to overcome this tragedy and now says she's led a good life. Just the same, kids such as John Perrine and, to a greater extent, Mary Ellen Perrine were innocent victims of this awful war. Children certainly knew that a war was on, and for some it brought great personal pain.[35]

Alma Blancett Wheeler, Oma Mae Maddox, Mary Ellen Perrine Massenburg, and others who lost loved ones had no other choice but to go on with their lives. They were poorer for the war, which left them bereft and desolate, at least for a time. Their own words testify eloquently to the awful wastefulness of war and to the folly of power-hungry, greedy, violent leaders such as Hitler and Tojo.

Even as the Allies gained tremendous ground in Europe and Asia in 1944–1945, moving inexorably toward final triumph, more Kentucky soldiers perished. The Pacific war claimed both Franklin R. Sousley and Simon B. Buckner Jr. In Germany, Millard C. Wells died, though his fate remained a mystery for more than sixty years. The battlefields of World War II continue to disgorge its dead, so it is likely that more Kentucky victims of that long-ago conflict will be discovered in the future.

Franklin Sousley hailed from Hilltop, Kentucky, a small town in the northeastern part of the state. After being drafted, he joined the U.S. Marines and achieved a measure of fame: he was one of the six men in the famous photograph of Marines raising the flag on Mt. Suribachi, Iwo Jima. Sousley is the tallish man, second from the left in the photo, helping to put the flag into place.[36]

Iwo Jima's capture by American forces, of course, had great significance. Two airfields there allowed B-29 bombers, accompanied by fighter escort, to reach Japan and target its great cities. Seizure of the island also permitted B-29s to make emergency landings, saving lives. Sousley played a part in taking the island, and Joe Rosenthal's celebrated picture of the flag raising itself perfectly expressed American patriotism and wartime progress toward retribution for Pearl Harbor. A decisive victory over Japan was not far away.

The end of Franklin Sousley's story was not nearly as uplifting as its beginning. Shot in the back by a Japanese sniper while walking down a road on the nearly secured island, Sousley fell to the ground and had time enough only to say, when asked about how badly he was hurt, "Not bad, I can't feel a thing." He passed away seconds later, on March 21, 1945. The thin, baby-faced Sousley was but nineteen years old; his Fleming County family soon mourned him, and his simple desire to marry a girl back home and raise a family was dashed.[37]

Simon B. Buckner Jr. came from one of Kentucky's most illustrious families. Buckner's father was a late-nineteenth-century Kentucky governor. Buckner himself was a West Point–trained career Army officer, who rose to the august rank of lieutenant general. Yet Simon Buckner Jr. expe-

Brigadier General Simon B. Buckner Jr. (left), head of the Alaska Defense Force, pins the Distinguished Service Medal on Colonel Benjamin Talley. Circa 1942. (Courtesy of the Library of Congress.)

rienced exactly the same fate as Private Sousley; both gave their lives for their country.

Simon Buckner Jr. was born in Hart County, Kentucky, on July 19, 1886, less than a year before his father took over the governorship. Raised in elite surroundings, Buckner Jr. became a member of the West Point class of 1908. He then advanced quickly through the ranks, earning promotion after promotion. Returning to West Point, he taught military tactics and eventually ascended to commandant of cadets. While at the U.S. Military Academy he stressed duty, discipline, and drill.[38]

During World War I Buckner missed out on combat. He served in the Washington, DC, offices of the air service. It must have rankled him that he was out of the action.[39]

When World War II arrived, Buckner was named commander of the Alaska Defense Force and eventually promoted to brigadier general. In this capacity, he led the successful effort to block the Japanese advance through the Aleutian Islands and then to cast out Japanese forces. For his strenuous efforts here, Buckner received the Distinguished Service Medal.[40]

By 1945, Buckner ran the American Tenth Army and was given the toughest assignment of his military career. He was to take the island of Okinawa from the Japanese. Okinawa was just south of Japan itself, and once secured would be used as a staging area for a massive conventional assault against the Japanese mainland. Japan could not afford to let Okinawa go and battled tremendously hard to keep it.

Lieutenant General Buckner launched the Okinawa assault on April

1, 1945. Advancing American forces encountered little resistance on the beaches but ran into strongly defended positions in the interior. The Japanese also struck back with kamikaze raids. For an instant, the attack stalled, and Buckner received press criticism for supposed "conservatism" and "timidity." Then, on May 14, U.S. forces severed the main Japanese line, moving steadily forward from there. Okinawa would eventually fall, though Buckner did not live quite long enough to see the final result.[41]

On June 18, 1945, General Buckner decided to go to a forward area for a good look at the fighting around the little town of Nagusuku, Okinawa. Through field glasses, he watched the 8th Marine Regiment engage a pocket of Japanese forces. One of the few remaining Japanese artillery pieces happened to lob a shell toward Buckner's entourage. The shell struck nearby, propelling a piece of rock into Buckner's chest cavity. He bled out in barely ten minutes' time, an unexpected casualty of a war almost over. Buckner became the highest-ranking American officer killed in action during World War II.[42]

Buckner's remains traveled the long route home, like those of some other Kentucky dead. Originally buried on Okinawa, Buckner's body was moved back to Kentucky in 1949. He was reburied at the Frankfort Cemetery beside Governor Buckner and not far from Daniel Boone.

The reinterment ceremony proved to be quite a spectacle. Governor Earle C. Clements attended. Also there was soon-to-be five-star general Omar Bradley. The West Point class of 1908 was represented by Major General Hartwell Bonesteel, a longtime friend of Buckner's. Many other officers and politicians paid their final respects. Adele Buckner, General Buckner's wife, and their children were also present. Adele, a native of Louisville, had gone into seclusion three and a half years earlier, upon receiving the tragic news of her husband's death. On February 5, 1949, she stood slightly apart from everyone else, a reporter wrote—"a dignified, somber figure at the side of the General's casket." Taps played; sadness and regret suffused the air. Had Lieutenant General Buckner survived, he and Adele had planned to take up residence in Alaska, but that was not to be. The war took away men both great and small.[43]

In 2007, sixty-two years after World War II ended, the riddle of yet another Kentuckian was solved. Nobody knew what had happened to Second Lieutenant Millard C. Wells of Paris, Kentucky, for all those many years. His remains were finally unearthed on a German farm. It is certain now that Lieutenant Wells was killed during the summer of 1944, going down with his B-24 bomber on the return trip from bombing an aircraft factory at Bernberg, Germany. Wells's son, Wayne, remarked when his father's remains were found that his dad "was only 21 years old when he died. It's hard to think of your father as a kid, but he never got beyond that."[44]

On Mother's Day 1943, Mrs. W. C. Bragg of Irvine, Kentucky, wrote a poem that accurately reflected the feelings of home-front Kentuckians about an increasingly costly war and what they could do to help win it. Mrs. Bragg's husband was stationed at Pearl Harbor, and she had one son in the Air Force and another in the Navy. She knew full well the danger that all the men in the military faced, not just her family members, and stressed in verse that they were all "in service for you and me." She also made it clear in the poem that she, and others like her at home, must carry on as the servicemen would have them do. It is no stretch to suggest that implicit within her words was the conviction that love and duty required all people on the home front to do everything possible to bring home military fathers and sons as quickly as possible—and that included working as hard as possible in Kentucky's war plants.[45]

Victory and the concomitant release from wartime tensions was finally achieved. As Hopkinsville's Edward Coffman recalls, Germany's surrender in May 1945 brought "a feeling of relief but no celebration as all of us were too well aware of the heavy tolls taken at Iwo Jima and Okinawa and understood that the Japanese were still very much in the war." Months later, when Japan surrendered, the mood was different. Coffman noted that there was great rejoicing in his hometown. His older brother, Howard, was fine and would return home soon enough. Most Kentucky servicemen were, like Howard Coffman, both safe and sound when the noise from the final shots faded away. John Perrine remembers the end of the war in Maysville—"horns were blaring everywhere." Joyous reunions took place, and peace returned. Henrietta Wallace, an African American woman from Jackson, says that she was "very happy" when the Japanese surrendered and the war was over. That was wonderful, but even better was getting back her nephew Brown Wilson unharmed.[46]

Mothers, fathers, wives, and others with loved ones in the U.S.

U.S. Army Quartermaster Corps trainer Brown Wilson of Jackson, Kentucky, in 1944, while he was stationed at Fort Thomas. Wilson, the nephew of Henrietta Wilson Wallace, was later transferred to the Philippines. After the war, Brown Wilson worked for the Wallace Barbershop in Jackson. (Courtesy of Brownie Wallace.)

armed forces experienced substantial strain throughout World War II. The chance of a son or husband dying or being crippled in combat was real. Oma Mae Maddox and Alma Wheeler, for instance, were branded by the war and bore those scars with them to the grave. Yet the great majority of Kentucky soldiers and sailors made it back home relatively unscathed. Joy therefore outweighed grief when the end of the war came. The people in Kentucky did manage to carry out their war-related responsibilities even as they struggled with anxieties related to the well-being of loved ones abroad. A powerful material and emotional bond connected the home front and the battle front. Given the burdens of work and worry that home-front Kentuckians shouldered from Pearl Harbor to Japanese capitulation at Tokyo Bay, it was little wonder that they required periodic breaks and that entertainment was so important during the conflict. Sports, music, the theater, and movies provided a respite, however brief, from a variety of hardships.

10

Rupp on the Rise and Rubinstein's Wine

Entertainment in a Barbaric Age

War is a grim undertaking. As the largest, most devastating conflict in human history, World War II spawned unprecedented suffering, bearing down on the human spirit with a grinding, unrelenting pressure. Thousands of Kentucky soldiers died and others received wounds of various types. Those who lived in Kentucky worked long and hard and worried about their relatives and friends in uniform. Under these often depressing circumstances, entertainment assumed greater importance during World War II than in the peacetime years that preceded it. Football, basketball, baseball, high school sports, horse racing and horse sales, singing, and the cinema took the minds of Kentuckians away from the fight in Europe and Asia to a better place—if only briefly.[1]

In September 1939, when Germany's invasion of Poland triggered the European phase of World War II, more Kentuckians followed college football than college basketball. Even at the University of Kentucky (UK), fan interest in the football team exceeded that for the basketball squad. Throughout the commonwealth, football drew larger crowds than basketball, brought in more money, and commanded greater institutional resources. The South, which included Kentucky, cared deeply about the gridiron game, and like other sports it provided a break from the war.

Football's popularity and importance in Kentucky before and during World War II can be measured in many ways. Twenty thousand fans might show up for a University of Kentucky Wildcats football contest, while the basketball facility, Alumni Gym, held just 3,500 spectators. Basketball coach Adolph Rupp took his job in 1930 on condition that he would also serve as an assistant football coach, and he struggled for years to get his salary up to that of the head football coach. In 1931, football produced 64 percent of all UK athletic department earnings, basketball only 6 percent. On an average fall weekend during the war, bettors at Ed Curd's gambling establishment in Lexington wagered over $500,000 on college football games. Many people in Kentucky displayed an avid interest in the university's football program and its year-to-year performance, and that did not change when the war came.[2]

Albert Kirwan served as UK's head football coach during most of World War II. Born in Louisville in 1904, Kirwan liked both school and sports. He excelled at football, starring at Louisville's Male High School and then at the University of Kentucky. At Kentucky, he played both halfback and end. A true scholar-athlete, he earned his bachelor's degree from UK in 1926 and later obtained a master's degree from Louisville and a PhD from Duke. Intelligent and enthusiastic, the "big Irishman," with blunt features and steadfast principles, went on to become a top-notch history professor at UK, dean of the graduate school, and finally its seventh president. Of the many challenging jobs Kirwan held over a long and distinguished career, being football coach at his alma mater was undoubtedly the most thankless.[3]

Kirwan's 1938 squad, his first at the University of Kentucky, struggled mightily, but the 1939 Wildcats executed a nifty turnabout, posting the best record of the Kirwan era. The second game proved pivotal. Kentucky beat Vanderbilt 21–13 in Nashville, its first victory over the Commodores after sixteen defeats and one tie. The key play occurred when Joe Shepherd raced in front of a Vandy pass in the third quarter, picked it off, and scooted 70 yards for the go-ahead touchdown. With momentum on its side, the Cats never looked back. Two weeks later, Kentucky bested Georgia 13–6. A 7–7 tie against Alabama followed, bringing Kentucky's record to 5–0–1. Joe Creason of the *Kernel*, UK's student newspaper, labeled the Wildcats' undefeated record the "most unexpected thing to hit football since the flu epidemic of 1918." Unfortunately, Kentucky gradually returned to form, dropping hard-fought battles to Georgia Tech and Tennessee. Despite losing two of the last three, a fine 6–2–1 record was the end result.[4]

From the 1940 season through 1944, Kentucky's football fortunes declined markedly. Kirwan managed a record of only 16–19–3. More telling still, UK won just two games against Southeastern Conference (SEC) competition during this entire span. One SEC victory came in 1940, when UK whipped Georgia Tech 26–7; the other in 1944, when Kentucky pounded Mississippi 27–7.[5]

After the 1942 campaign, which ended at 3–6–1, denunciations of Kirwan's performance reached a new height. A few important people, perhaps more, wanted a better coach. In a UK athletic council meeting, someone broached the subject of "retiring" Kirwan. University of Kentucky president Herman Lee Donovan rejected this idea, asserting that "Kirwan is the equal of any coach in the Southeastern Conference." Donovan then explained that Tennessee, Alabama, and Georgia Tech "have more manpower than we possess. We can't cut them down to our size, so that leaves one alternative—we must build the University of Kentucky up to their size." Donovan retained the services of Coach Kirwan.[6]

A shortage of male students due to the draft and voluntary enlistments led UK to cancel the 1943 football season. "We feel it will be impossible to get enough 17-year-olds to field a team," Athletic Director Bernie Shively announced. Another factor in the decision was the difficulty UK would have faced putting together a schedule. By this time, Florida, Vanderbilt, Mississippi, and Mississippi State had already suspended football for the upcoming season. Kirwan and his assistants learned that they would be reassigned to other duties at UK. The next year, however, football returned.[7]

As fate would have it, the 1944 football campaign turned out to be Kirwan's last. The Wildcats gave their coach that last SEC win in the opener against "Ole Miss," then proceeded to crumble. Close, heartbreaking losses in the third and fourth games to Michigan State and Georgia ended any chance for an upbeat season. Alabama, as usual, thumped Kentucky. Tennessee beat Kentucky twice that season, adding insult to injury. The Wildcats finished with a 3–6 record, and Kirwan had had enough.[8]

Several factors convinced Kirwan to resign his position as head football coach at UK. Losing had become harder and harder to accept. Competition between the football program and the basketball program did not sit well with him. Basketball coach Adolph Rupp pursued supremacy for basketball over all other sports at UK with unrelenting fervor, and football, of course, was his great target. Kirwan had never liked the friction that Rupp's quest brought. Most importantly, Kirwan wished to change careers. He gave up football coaching for graduate study in history and the life of a professor and administrator.

University of Kentucky football floundered during the war years. The poor results can be explained easily enough. Kentucky devoted fewer financial resources to football than some other SEC schools and played in a smallish stadium. The SEC competed at a high level, which made it hard for Kentucky to win on a consistent basis. Kirwan himself disliked out-of-state recruiting, and Kentucky high school football alone did not produce enough quality players to meet Georgia, Alabama, and Tennessee on a level playing field. These other teams had much greater depth: their second- and third-string players were almost as good as their starters, but at Kentucky that was seldom the case. Kirwan was also scrupulously honest, turning down all illegitimate offers to make life in Lexington sweet for recruits; other coaches in the SEC may not have been so pure. Kirwan once wrote to President Donovan about the situation, noting, "It is a terrific problem to build up winning football in a place where losing has become a tradition." This fact serves well as the epitaph for Ab Kirwan and all his football coaching successors at UK—with the exception of Paul "Bear" Bryant.[9]

Other state universities and colleges fielded football teams during the war. Western Kentucky State Teachers College, Eastern Kentucky State Teachers College, Morehead State Teachers College, and Murray State Teachers College, predecessors of today's regional universities, played the game with varying degrees of success. Kentucky State College for Negroes (KSCN) remained a powerhouse in the early years of the conflict. Georgetown College and Transylvania College liked football and wanted to keep it. Despite a declaration by the nation's colleges just after Pearl Harbor that they intended to maintain a full schedule of sports, the worldwide conflict made that impossible, and each of these Kentucky schools suspended football at some point before the war ended.[10]

Western Kentucky posted victories over two of its biggest rivals before discontinuing football for the rest of the war in 1943. In a game played at Bowling Green, where both teams were "out for blood," the Hilltoppers came from far behind to defeat Eastern Kentucky 27–20 in 1941. Western also used a staunch defense to shut out the Morehead State Eagles in 1942.[11]

Morehead State registered a notable victory of its own. The Eagles ended years of futility by vanquishing Murray State for the first time ever in 1942. The final score of 13–0 sent shivers of delight through Morehead fans.

Kentucky State experienced almost as much football success from 1940 to 1942 as it had earlier. Champions of Negro collegiate football in 1934 and 1937, the Thorobreds pursued a third national championship with gusto. Guided by coach Henry Arthur Kean, a brilliant proponent of the forward pass, KSCN fell just short of its goal while amassing a three-year record of 17–5–1. Quarterback "Bullet Bill" Bass and left guard Herb Trawick, a three-time Negro College All-American, led the charge. A January 1, 1942, victory in the Oil Classic over Prairie View ended the 1941 season on a high note. The 1942 football campaign witnessed Thorobred victories over Alabama Normal School, Benedict, and Lincoln University. After four games, Kentucky State had outscored its opponents 113–0. Heading into the final contest of the season the Thorobred record stood at 6–0 with another national championship within grasp. In that game, Kentucky State led West Virginia State 15–6 with four minutes left only to see its dream slip away: after engineering one quick score, quarterback Jack Housen of West Virginia State tossed a short pass to receiver Guyton, who turned it into a 78-yard bolt for an 18–15 lead and the win. A brilliant season concluded with Kentucky State ranked third in the nation among all African American football schools.[12]

Eastern Kentucky, Morehead, and Kentucky State, like Western, suspended football in 1943. Of all the war years, this one proved to be toughest on college sports. Athletic department after athletic department canceled football because of a shortage of players. Too many players had been drafted, and it no longer seemed feasible to straggle by using seventeen-year-olds and 4-Fs.

Small colleges struggled more than the bigger schools. Georgetown discontinued football because of the war but resuscitated it later. In February 1942, the Transylvania Board of Trustees canceled the upcoming football season, hoping to reinstate football sometime down the line; but it never returned. Throughout the United States, 190 small colleges suspended football at some point during the war, and some programs were never seen again.[13]

Football's popularity in Kentucky remained strong throughout World War II. Suspensions only whetted the appetites of fans for more, and the demise of the Transylvania program proved to be an aberration. The University of Kentucky football team reappeared after a brief absence, and Southeastern Conference football only got bigger and better after the war. Eastern Kentucky, Western Kentucky, and Morehead State entered the new Ohio Valley Conference in 1948. Kentucky State resumed its winning ways by the late 1940s. Signs of football's vitality were not hard to find and, like other amusements, let Kentuckians get away from "thinking up hates against the Hitlerites."[14]

College basketball rivaled college football in Kentucky during World War II, coming in second among all intercollegiate sports in terms of fan interest. The University of Kentucky basketball team attracted the most attention, followed by Western Kentucky. Louisville came from almost nowhere to prominence just as the war ended. Eastern Kentucky and Morehead State had their moments along the way. College basketball advanced during the war years, cutting into football's lead.

The University of Kentucky started playing basketball in the early twentieth century. UK won the first Southern Intercollegiate Athletic Association tournament championship in 1921, defeating Georgia. By 1927, however, the Wildcats had fallen on hard times, and Coach Basil Hayden was replaced by John Mauer. Mauer led UK back to respectability, leaving a solid team for his successor—Adolph Rupp. Rupp made Kentucky into the best basketball program in the nation, though the progression to the top was not yet finished by World War II.

Adolph Frederick Rupp was born near Halstead, Kansas, in 1901, and grew up on a farm. He started playing basketball in the second grade, practicing shooting for hours at a time at school and home. Rupp developed into a pretty good player, averaging 19 points a game in his senior year at Halstead High School. Jeptha Carl Stone, his coach, noticed that Rupp "seemed interested in what few plays [the team] ran."[15]

After receiving his diploma, Rupp enrolled at the University of Kansas. He went out for the basketball squad and made the cut. Though Rupp did not start for the Jayhawks, he did earn some minutes as a backup on Coach Forrest "Phog" Allen's 1923 national championship team. Rupp graduated from Kansas with a degree in business administration.

While at Kansas, Adolph Rupp learned a great deal more about basketball. Phog Allen, already one of the game's great coaches, taught Rupp the value of fast-break offense, precision passing, and tenacious defense. Allen, according to Rupp, instilled in him the overriding need for hustle, "which is the secret of any defense." Rupp also met James Naismith, basketball's founder, at Kansas. Naismith served as head of the University of Kansas physical education department and assistant basketball coach. Rupp picked Naismith's brain for nuggets of basketball history and lore. Rupp's encounters with Allen and Naismith helped shape his later coaching philosophy and fed his love of the game.[16]

After college, Rupp turned his attention to career opportunities. He took a job as a teacher and coach at Burr Oak High School in Kansas. From there, he moved to another, similar position at the Marshalltown, Iowa, high school. In the fall of 1926, he changed jobs again. Freeport High School in northern Illinois hired him. Rupp's Freeport team compiled a record of 59–21 over a four-year period. His demanding style of coaching, even during practices, was already evident. "Rupp wouldn't let you waste time," former Freeport player George Schmelzle recalled. "You automatically played to win basketball games."[17]

Hearing that the University of Kentucky had a basketball coaching vacancy in 1930, Rupp applied for the job. He was one of seventy applicants. During his interview at UK, Rupp made the audacious claim that he was "the best damned basketball coach in the United States." The search committee probably did not believe Rupp, but it did select him for the job.[18]

When Rupp took over the basketball program at UK he was just twenty-nine years old. A relatively big man, at 6'1" and 200 pounds, his head was large and roundish. He wore his dark hair short, cropped close to the skull. His prominent nose was long and broad. His lips were thin, his eyes intense. A no-nonsense sort, Rupp pursued his goal of winning basketball games with single-minded determination. Often he came across to his players, the media, and the fans as curt or abrasive. Unlike Phog Allen or James Naismith, who wanted to earn the affection of their players, Rupp did not seem to care. He demanded only strict discipline and unswerving obedience. One of his favorite sayings applied to basketball practice: "Don't speak unless you can improve upon the silence." On another occasion, he declared, "I don't care if your girlfriend leaves you or if your pet rabbit dies. I just care if you produce for me on the basketball court." In his family life, by contrast, the evidence points to Rupp's being a caring and loving person. He could also be generous, as his service on the board of directors of Shriners Hospital indicates. Nevertheless, Rupp's public behavior on many occasions can fairly be described as abrupt, sarcastic, or arrogant.[19]

Whatever one might think of Adolph Rupp's personality, he possessed a thorough knowledge of basketball. "The Baron" preferred fast-break offense over the slow, methodical style that was fashionable when he first arrived at Kentucky. He thought the fast break created opportunities to get ahead of the defense for layups and other easy baskets. When the fast break was not available, he stressed to players that they should set screens to open up their teammates for high-percentage shots. Rupp loved stingy man-to-man defense, which required the kind of hustle he so favored. Defenders needed to run around screens or through them and get in the face of the opposing player before he could shoot. A sticky, rugged, man-to-man defense became his trademark.[20]

From the 1930–1931 season through the 1940–1941 season, Rupp's University of Kentucky basketball squad experienced considerable success. Building from the base provided by former coach John Mauer, Rupp compiled a sterling record of 179–45 during this interval. His teams won Southeastern Conference tournament championships in 1933, 1937, 1939, and 1940. The 1933 team captured a mythical national championship. Seven UK players during this time made All-American, including two National Players of the Year: Aggie Sale and Leroy "Cowboy" Edwards. Just the same, Kentucky had to work hard to establish a national reputation, and it was not quite so powerful as some other teams.

University of Kentucky basketball
coach Adolph Rupp in 1939,
just before the outbreak of the
European war. (Courtesy of the
University of Kentucky.)

During the 1930s, basketball teams from the Northeast and the Midwest were deemed superior to teams from the South. Moreover, the University of Kentucky switched from the Southern Conference to the new Southeastern Conference in 1932. This move took Kentucky away from strong teams like Maryland and North Carolina, which had defeated the Wildcats in previous years, to a weaker league. Part of Rupp's success in the beginning can be attributed to this change. Even UK's 1933 national championship looks questionable, given the team's 46–30 drubbing at the hands of Ohio State on January 2 in Lexington. Throughout the 1930s, Kentucky never managed to defeat Notre Dame or New York University, and it was probably not the equal of Ohio State or Indiana either. Kentucky was good, and it was rising, but better days lay ahead.

America's entry into World War II came one day after the opening game of the 1941–1942 Wildcats basketball season. The war changed the landscape of college basketball. Players soon became subject to the draft, and coaches scrambled to find replacements and field respectable teams. Everyone knew, too, that victory over the Axis took precedence over everything else. When Rupp referred to the "big game" now, he meant winning the war. Basketball, even for the Baron and the Cats, took second place.[21]

The 1941–1942 UK basketball season did prove memorable, despite the worldwide conflict. In 1941, UK awarded basketball scholarships for the first time—football scholarships had been handed out for years by this juncture. UK also won its sixth Southeastern Conference basketball tournament championship, defeating Alabama 36–34 in the final tournament game. Guard Kenny England led the way to victory with 13 points, including two clutch free throws near the end of the contest. The Cats were rewarded for their SEC tournament title with their first ever bid to the National Collegiate Athletic Association (NCAA) tournament. In the 1942 NCAA tourney, they upset the Illinois Whizz Kids 46–44 before bowing to Dartmouth in one NCAA semifinal game. The Wildcats basketball program continued its march forward.[22]

The exploits of the Kentucky basketball team could not obscure the fact that a war was on. Several Kentucky players had left for the military during the 1941–1942 campaign. Rupp promoted the sale of war bonds. Kentucky also agreed to take on the ultra-powerful Great Lakes Navy basketball team in a benefit game. This contest occurred between Kentucky's SEC tournament championship and the NCAA tournament. The Great Lakes Navy squad featured numerous former college All-Americans who had been inducted into the Navy. Great Lakes steamrolled the Cats, running off to a 21–4 lead before coasting to a 58–47 victory. This game raised $5,800 for Navy Relief.[23]

The Cats stumbled just a bit during the 1942–1943 season. Many teams would have been thrilled by a 17–6 record, but not Kentucky. The Cats did not make the National Invitational Tournament (NIT) or NCAA tournament, nor did they win the SEC tournament. Rupp's first victory over Notre Dame marked the high point of the season, coming after seven consecutive defeats at the hands of the Fighting Irish. Two factors accounted for Kentucky's subpar performance. The loss of Kenny England and Lloyd Ramsey to the military hurt. A tough schedule made it even more difficult on the Cats. Losses to such strong teams as Indiana, Ohio State, and a George Mikan–led DePaul team put a damper on things.[24]

Coach Rupp continued his work on behalf of the war effort. A second benefit game against Great Lakes took place. The Baron let it be known in a series of speeches in the Lexington area that college basketball produced young men who would become excellent soldiers. After all, boys who played basketball learned the importance of physical fitness, poise under trying circumstances when a game might be on the line, and teamwork. These qualities would stand them in good stead when they entered the military and served their country. Informed on one occasion that former UK players Jim King and Ermal Allen served in the Army Air Corps and that one-time Tennessee player Frank Thomas was there as well, Rupp responded that they are "three of the toughest competitors I've ever seen. . . . Put King and that Thomas at the controls and Allen dropping the bombs, and the Japs would fall like flies." Rupp went so far as to say, "Nobody's going to enslave us—there's too many athletes fighting on the various fronts in this war."[25]

Talk about suspending UK basketball for the 1943–1944 season proved premature. Though the university canceled football that year, it retained basketball. Rupp insisted that he could find enough players, despite the draft and the need for labor in war plants, to put forward a decent team. Since basketball required only eight or ten players, many fewer than football, the university administration relented.

Nobody expected much of the 1943–1944 Wildcat squad. Rupp described the UK players that year as a "bunch of kids who showed up for basketball practice . . . when we decided for sure to have a team." An unimposing lot, composed of freshmen and 4-Fs, this group of Wildcats surprised everyone by their excellence. The "Beardless Wonders" finished 1943–1944 with a 19–2 record, including an SEC championship and a third-place finish in the prestigious National Invitational Tournament.[26]

Kentucky's fine performance owed to the acquisition of one stellar player, team cohesiveness, and a light schedule. Bob Brannum, a freshman from Kansas, made All-American that year. Brannum, nicknamed "Tank" for his rugged style, provided the best pivot play since the time of "Cowboy" Edwards. This squad also passed well, sharing the ball rather than hogging it. Kentucky's opponents, including such teams as Fort Knox, Carnegie Tech, and Wright Field, were not as strong as usual either. (Tennessee did not appear on the Kentucky schedule due to war-related disturbances.) The result was an unanticipated banner year.

Kentucky did defeat some good teams. Ohio State fell to the Cats 40–28, victimized by sterling play from Brannum and a sizable early deficit. Wins over St. John's, at Madison Square Garden, and over Notre Dame were satisfying; two straight over the Irish certainly went down well. A loss to Illinois away was avenged by a home victory over the Illini. Triumphs over Georgia, Louisiana State, and Tulane gave the Cats yet another SEC tournament crown.

Kentucky captured the SEC title in 1944 despite bringing a depleted squad to the tournament. Don Whitehead, Walter Johnson, Bill Cravens, and Glen Parker had left the Wildcats during the season for the armed services. The loss of Whitehead and Johnson really hurt, but the team persevered and triumphed. Jack Parkinson poured in 27 points, mostly from long range, in a 62–46 championship game rout over Tulane. "Tank" Brannum added fifteen more points, despite being constantly double teamed.

The "Beardless Wonders" then moved on to the NIT tournament. An opening win over Utah put the Cats into the semifinal against St. John's. In a terrific struggle, which witnessed many lead changes and ties, Kentucky suffered its second and final defeat. Since Kentucky blew an 8-point lead (and had beaten St. John's during the regular season), this loss proved particularly hard to take. Kentucky did go on to whip Oklahoma A&M in the third-place game, but Rupp could only mutter to himself that he "got little consolation from winning a consolation game." Even so, the 1943–1944 team made its mark as the youngest UK squad ever, and as one of the most pleasant surprises.[27]

Another youthful but talented Kentucky team took to the hardwood in 1944–1945. As it turned out, this team was to be the last one during the war. Bob Brannum left for the military, but UK picked up the services of freshman Alex Groza and hardly missed a beat. Groza proved to be a spectacular addition, leading UK to an 11–0 start, which included nice victories over teams such as Indiana, Temple, Long Island, and Ohio State. Groza then received his draft notice and departed. A tough 35–34 setback to Tennessee in Knoxville ended the Cats' winning streak. UK bounced back after that, concluding the regular season at 17–3. The postseason saw UK garner its eighth SEC tournament crown and entry into the National Collegiate Athletic Association tournament field. In a rematch, Ohio State defeated the Wildcats in the NCAA opening round

45–37. The Cats had defeated OSU with Groza, but fell without him. A consolation game triumph over Tufts completed the year. The loss to the Buckeyes meant a disappointing end to an otherwise fine season.[28]

Victory over the Axis by August 1945 brought celebration and reflection. Freedom had triumphed over totalitarianism, but at a terrible cost. Five former Kentucky basketball players perished during the war: Mel Brewer, Kenny England, Jim Goforth, Jim King, and Walter Johnson. Brewer was killed during the successful effort to establish a second major front against Germany in France. England, whom Rupp had once described as "a great little athlete," died in Italy while traversing a minefield. Machine-gun fire claimed the life of Goforth during the Battle of Saipan. King's B-24 was shot down on a mission over Germany. Johnson's ship sank after being hit by a Japanese torpedo; he had been part of a crew dropping off atomic bomb supplies to American forces in Guam. Joy commingled with grief, and the Wildcat faithful were not immune.[29]

University of Kentucky basketball registered substantial gains during the war years. From 1941 to 1945, Rupp's teams compiled a 77–18 record. The Cats took three SEC tournament titles, advanced to one NCAA tournament semifinal, and placed third in the NIT. Kentucky's 1944 and 1945 recruiting classes proved instrumental in its late wartime basketball success, and players like Groza would return from the service to lead Kentucky basketball to its greatest heights in the postwar period.

Not coincidentally, UK basketball advanced as UK football experienced continuing travail. As Rupp looked back, he recalled that "when I came here to Kentucky they were all football minded." This was much less the case at war's end than at the war's beginning. Rupp's campaign to "put football in its place" had progressed and would continue. If he could not make basketball number one throughout the South, he seemed more and more likely to get that job done at the University of Kentucky.[30]

Western Kentucky, like UK, played terrific basketball in the early 1940s. Under Coach Edgar A. Diddle, the Hilltoppers dominated the other teachers colleges. Indeed, Western may have been as good or even better than UK at that time. Of course, nobody will ever know for sure how Western Kentucky would have fared against UK because it was Rupp's policy not to play in-state schools. Regrettably, Kentucky and Western Kentucky never tangled on the basketball court during the war.

Ed Diddle, the man who led Western Kentucky basketball to national prominence, was born in 1895 near Gradyville, Kentucky. Diddle grew up on his parents' farm, where he learned the value of hard work and built up his muscles. At Centre College, he led the 1919 basketball team that many thought was the South's best in scoring. After leaving Centre, Diddle took a job as head basketball coach at Greenville High School in Muhlenburg County. From there, he moved to Western Kentucky State Teachers College in Bowling Green. Originally, Diddle served Western as athletic director and coach of all sports. He became best known as the longtime coach of the Hilltoppers' basketball team.[31]

Diddle possessed several attributes that helped him become a successful coach. He cared deeply about the welfare of his players, wanting them to succeed on the court and in life. He understood the value of showmanship, often waving a red towel during games to express his emotions. He slapped the court when he was angry, twirled the towel overhead to convey happiness, wrung it repeatedly when the game was tight. He also fought "like a bobcat" to win games.[32]

Diddle certainly knew the game of basketball inside and out. Arriving at Western Kentucky in 1922, eight years before Rupp started at UK, Diddle installed the fast-break style immediately. Though schools like Rhode Island and Purdue pioneered the up tempo, Diddle used it early on. He believed that intense practices best prepared his players for games. He would not allow his players to relax or socialize in practice. While he was not known for defense, he understood its value for a team that desired championships.

Western Kentucky State Teachers College did win championships under Diddle's tutelage. Indeed, Western captured a large number of championships. Diddle's team won nine consecutive Kentucky Intercollegiate Athletic Conference (KIAC) tournaments through 1940. Western Kentucky dominated in-state competition from 1934 to 1943, going 11–1 against Morehead State, 23–9 against Murray State, and 20–2 against Eastern Kentucky. Diddle's overall record during this decade was 250 wins to just 41 losses. Western Kentucky produced its best wartime teams in 1941–1942 and 1942–1943. After that, the draft took its toll, and Diddle suffered through two subpar seasons. Western's wartime record of 83–27 still sparkled.[33]

Diddle's first wartime team, the 1941–1942 aggregation, may well have been his best; it was certainly the most successful. After the regular season, Western captured both the KIAC tournament and the Southern Intercollegiate Athletic Association tournament. The Hilltoppers' record at this point stood at a gaudy 27–4, with the team riding a thirteen-game win streak. The National Invitational Tournament Committee then rewarded Western for its great season, extending the Hilltoppers a bid to play in their first ever NIT.

Seeded seventh in an eight-team field, Western Kentucky surprised the basketball world by posting a runner-up finish. The Hilltoppers upset the City College of New York team 49–46 in the opening round. Substitute Ray Blevins poured in 22 points to lead the Diddlemen; he was almost unstoppable. Buck Sydnor scored two late buckets to bring Western from behind, and his steal in the final moments sealed the victory. The Hilltoppers bested the Creighton Bluejays 49–36 in the second round. The NIT championship game featured Western against a tough West Virginia University squad. After moving out to an 8-point lead, Western Kentucky bowed to the Mountaineers in a heart-breaker, 47–45. Nevertheless, a second-place finish in the most prestigious college basketball tournament in all the land was spectacular.[34]

The World War II years also proved eventful for the Louisville basketball program. After years of losing seasons, Louisville hired Bernard "Peck" Hickman as basketball coach in 1944, and he turned around Louisville's basketball fortunes. Hickman played his college basketball under Ed Diddle at Western Kentucky. Hickman had been a good player and later decided to become a coach. He described the Louisville basketball position as "the worst job in America," accepting it because he was ambitious and Louisville had nowhere to go but up. The fine Cardinal basketball tradition, which today brings to mind such names as Denny Crum and Rick Pitino, goes back to Peck Hickman.[35]

Coach Hickman's first year with the Louisville Sea Cards (as they were known back then) was 1944–1945. Using players he borrowed from the Navy's V-12 program, Hickman recalled that U of L "knocked off some teams we probably shouldn't have." The Sea Cards, for instance, walloped the Hilltoppers 66–41 after losing the first of two games between the teams that year. Hickman bested Diddle, his old coach, and at the tail end of World War II Louisville and Western Kentucky carried on a keen rivalry.[36]

Morehead State, Eastern Kentucky, and Murray State, while not at the level of Kentucky or Western Kentucky, also experienced flashes of basketball brilliance during World War II. Morehead State beat Kentucky Wesleyan and Eastern Kentucky in the 1943 KIAC tournament before bowing to perennial favorite Western Kentucky in the championship game. In 1944, Morehead took advantage of Western's temporary decline to claim the KIAC regular season title. The Eagles continued their winning ways in 1944–1945. Led by All-American center Warren Cooper, Morehead finished at 16–6. A lack of depth, due to players being away with the military, did not hamper the team much. Cooper's brilliant play made up for many deficiencies. After the suspension of basketball for one season, the 1944–1945 Eastern Kentucky Maroons posted a 20–5 record and earned a third-place finish in the National Intercollegiate Basketball tournament held in Kansas City. Sadly, Bert Smith, a former multisport star at Eastern, perished in the Pacific. Meanwhile, Murray State benefited from the electric play of "Jumping Joe" Fulks—a slender 6'5" small forward who averaged 13.2 points per game during the 1941–1942 and 1942–1943 campaigns. Fulks helped make the modern jump shot popular and later starred in the National Basketball Association. On February 10, 1949, he scored 63 points in a single NBA game—a record that stood until it was eclipsed by Elgin Baylor a decade later. In 1949, Joe Fulks, from tiny Birmingham, Kentucky, was undoubtedly one of the five best basketball players in the world.[37]

College basketball in Kentucky gained strength during World War II. Adolph Rupp's success at the helm of the University of Kentucky basketball program accounted for the greatest part of this progress. Rupp recruited several truly great players from 1943 to 1945 who would lead the Wildcats to Southeastern Conference championships before the fighting stopped, and to national championships later. Ed Diddle of Western Kentucky also pushed college basketball forward in the commonwealth, and in the early war years the Hilltoppers were on a par with mighty Kentucky. The quality of college basketball in the Bluegrass State as a whole proved high, and the round-ball game provided yet another way to escape from the horrors of war.

Kentuckians liked baseball, too. Fans of the national pastime in the Bluegrass State could choose from a range of options. They might cross the Ohio River to see the Major League Cincinnati Reds play. They could travel to Louisville, home of the minor league Louisville Colonels and the Negro League Louisville Black Colonels. High-school baseball and small-town amateur leagues offered good viewing. With the notable exception of the Majors, baseball thrived in Kentucky during the war years.

By some criteria, certainly, Major League baseball did least well among the various levels of baseball during World War II. Some of the best major leaguers were drafted or volunteered for military service, which decreased the quality of play and acted as a drag on attendance. Ted Williams of the Boston Red Sox, Joe DiMaggio of the New York Yankees, and Stan Musial of the St. Louis Cardinals all went into the armed services. Teams made do with veteran players too old to be called up and with youngsters. Growth in attendance stalled during the conflict, and interest in big-league ball flattened out.[38]

The performance of the Cincinnati Reds seemed to parallel the condition of Major League baseball. Just before American entry into World War II, the Reds reached the pinnacle of success. During the conflict, they declined. Aging players and the loss of personnel to the military draft explain the Reds' fall.

In 1940, the Cincinnati Reds won the World Series. The Reds defeated the Hank Greenberg–led Detroit Tigers four games to three to become the kings of baseball. In the seventh and deciding game, which was just as tightly contested as the rest of the series, the Reds nipped the Tigers 2–1. Doubles by National League Most Valuable Player Frank McCormick and by Jimmy Ripple, plus a long sacrifice fly by Billy Myers, made the difference. This was the first world championship for Cincinnati in twenty-one years.[39]

The next few seasons were not so good for the Reds. Cincinnati slipped to third place in the National League in 1941, and fourth place in 1942, then rebounded to second in 1943 before plunging to seventh in 1945. Throughout the rest of the 1940s and early 1950s, Cincinnati resided mostly in the second division.[40]

Minor league baseball suffered less from wartime circumstances than Major League baseball. By its very nature, the players in the minor leagues were young, and many were not yet subject to the draft. Fans did not expect minor leaguers to be as good as major leaguers. The minor leagues held their own during World War II, though some teams suspended play.

The Louisville Colonels, a minor league farm club of the Boston Red Sox, proved themselves a powerhouse during the latter part of World War II. Playing at Parkway Field in the Falls City, the Colonels captured American Association League pennants in 1944 and 1945. In both seasons they advanced to the Little World Series, losing to the Baltimore Orioles in 1944 and besting the Newark Bears in 1945. In the fourth game of the Orioles series, played in Baltimore's spacious new stadium, the two teams drew a then record minor league attendance of 52,833 people—over 16,000 more than any single World Series game that year. The Colonels actually beat the Orioles in that game, but dropped the next two to lose the series. In 1945, Louisville redeemed itself by closing out Newark four games to two. The Colonels were minor league champions.[41]

Negro League baseball attracted crowds of both black and white Kentuckians during the war. Segregated baseball was still a fact of life, with no black players in the Major Leagues yet. Also, the Negro League lacked strong organization. Black baseball teams played fewer games than the Major League or minor league teams, and contests were often scheduled in a rather haphazard way by promoters. Throughout the war, the Metropolitan Sportsman's Club booked various teams to play in Louisville, while the Louisville Black Colonels carried on as well.

Black and white people attended Negro League baseball in large numbers. The play was often top notch. On not a few occasions, the best Negro League teams had beaten teams filled with white major and minor league players. The Metropolitan Sportsman's Club brought great black baseball to Parkway Field, the same venue where the Louisville (White) Colonels played. In late June 1943, to cite just one example, the Kansas City Monarchs—black baseball world champions—came to play the Nashville Crawfords. The Monarchs, who pitched the legendary Satchel Paige in game one of a doubleheader, took both contests easily.[42]

The Louisville Black Colonels played from time to time throughout the 1940s. They were not one of the better teams in the Negro League, nor did they have players of the caliber of Paige, Josh Gibson, or "Cool Papa" Bell. "Junior" Miller of Lebanon Junction, Kentucky, did start a fine career with the Black Colonels, making his Negro League debut in 1942 and appearing sporadically with the Colonels and the Indianapolis Zulu Cannibal Giants through 1945. A powerfully built, though short, man, Miller batted around .300 lifetime and hit many home runs. Sellout crowds were not unheard of for the Colonels, Monarchs, Zulu Giants, and other black teams that appeared in Louisville.[43]

Like college football, college basketball, and the various levels of baseball, Kentucky high school sports claimed its share of supporters. Kentucky high school sports during the 1940s included basketball, football, baseball, tennis, and track and field. Though basketball reigned supreme, the other sports had their devotees.

High school basketball in Kentucky began before World War I. Henderson captured the first state tournament in 1916. The game soon caught fire. By the World War II years, high school basketball ranked above all other high school sports in Kentucky when it came to fan allegiance and passion. Whole towns in the mountains, meadow lands, and flats of the commonwealth exulted and despaired with each victory and defeat experienced by their team. The names became legendary, in many cases all out of proportion to the size of the community: Carr Creek, Ashland, St. Xavier, Inez, and many more.

From 1941 to 1945, Harlan, Hindman, St. Xavier, and Male were certainly among the best high school basketball teams in the state. Led by Wallace "Wah-Wah" Jones, the Harlan High Green Dragons finished as state runner-up in 1942 and state champion in 1944. Along the way, Jones accumulated 2,398 career points—then a national record. He made first team all-state three times, going on to star at the University of Kentucky. Hindman took the state title in 1943, defeating St. Xavier 29–26. St. Xavier also bowed to Inez in the 1941 state championship game. Male High School of Louisville took the state basketball title in 1945. Ralph Beard, a multisport star, pushed the Bulldogs to the championship. Beard joined Jones at UK in the late 1940s as part of the "Fabulous Five."[44]

Notable developments occurred in other high school sports during World War II. Ty Holland of Murray High School was in the middle of a long and distinguished career, which ended with his 1973 retirement. Before he went out, Holland was the winningest high school football coach in Kentucky, with a grand total of 249 victories. In the midst of the

European war, Tom Ellis guided his 1941 Bardstown High football team to an undefeated season. Most remarkable of all, Bardstown did not yield a single point the entire year. The same Ralph Beard mentioned above as a leader of the Male basketball squad also helped the Bulldogs to a 1943 state baseball championship and a 1945 state track championship. Beard took first place in the 880-yard run in the 1945 state track meet. Hopkinsville High School athlete Jerry Claiborne, a star in football, managed to get to the 1945 state semifinals in tennis before he bowed out. Claiborne later excelled as a defensive back under Coach Bear Bryant at UK and became a Hall of Fame college football coach himself.[45]

High school sports exerted a large degree of influence on Kentucky communities and Kentucky youth. High school basketball, in particular, shaped the identity of many small towns in the commonwealth. A winning team bolstered community pride and gave places like Carr Creek, Brooksville, and Inez celebrity. Even big towns and cities in Kentucky prized highly their successful high school teams. High school sports also helped keep teenagers out of trouble and instilled within them the value of hard work, subordination of the self when necessary for the good of the collectivity, and respect for authority. The young men were better off because of high school sports, and so was Kentucky society.

Kentuckians embraced the horse industry long before the advent of football, basketball, and baseball. By the early nineteenth century the Bluegrass State was renowned for its fine horses, and by 1840 it led the nation in horse breeding. Horse racing provided a way to assess the results of equine breeding efforts, and it became a leading form of entertainment. In 1875, when Churchill Downs race course opened in Louisville, the quest to produce the fastest horses possible and test them against each other was already well under way. Horse racing provided many Kentuckians with recreation, and horse selling became a big business.[46]

Thoroughbred horse racing grew stronger during World War II. Kentuckians needed to put the war out of their minds on occasion, and going to the track let them blow off some steam. Great horses such as Whirlaway and Count Fleet excited racegoers. Colonel Matt J. Winn of Churchill Downs kept Kentucky horse racing going in tough times, and his promotion efforts bore tremendous fruit. Many speed and purse records were set.

The 1941 horse racing season belonged to Whirlaway, a big, chestnut-colored horse with a tail that hung almost to the ground. Whirly started that year erratically, but then came on like gangbusters. In early May, Whirlaway won the Kentucky Derby. In eighth place after a half mile, he closed to sixth at three-quarters, then fourth. Unleashing his characteristic burst of speed toward the end of the race, he rushed past Dispose and reached the finish line a full eight lengths ahead of his nearest rival. Whirlaway set a record time of 2:01 2/5, which lasted two decades before it was eclipsed. Whirlaway went on from there to take the Preakness and Belmont, becoming Calumet Farm's first Triple Crown winner.[47]

"Mr. Long Tail's" racing career lasted a bit longer. In 1942, Whirlaway performed almost as well as in the previous year. After a loss in the Phoenix Handicap at Keeneland, he rebounded by capturing the Massachusetts Handicap, the Trenton Handicap, and the Narragansett Special. By this time, he had surpassed Seabiscuit's record for career earnings. Despite losing to Alsab in two out of their three confrontations, Whirlaway had been more consistent and took away Horse of the Year honors for the second time. In 1943, Whirlaway retired from racing as the biggest moneymaker to that time, and he still ranks as one of the fastest closers ever. Of equal importance, many Kentuckians had grown to love Whirly, thrilling to his gallant, last-second charges.[48]

Racing in Kentucky flourished. Churchill Downs attracted over 90,000 fans to the Kentucky Derby in 1941 and 1942. Crowds almost as big attended some lesser races. In 1941, Calumet Farm sent thirty-five different horses to the post, and collectively they earned $475,091—a new record. Keeneland, too, held successful meets. Shut Out's victory in the Blue Grass Stakes was a highlight, as was Devil Diver's victory in the Phoenix Handicap. On April 14, 1942, long-shot Savage Sailor raced home first in the fourth race, paying $212.20, a Keeneland record. Despite losing general manager W. T. Bishop to the military, Keeneland maintained a first-class operation. Betting on horses in the United States—and Kentucky—reached a new high.[49]

In 1943, war impacted the American horse industry more than ever before. National leaders implored citizens to make greater sacrifices for the sake of victory over the Axis, and horse racing clearly was not essential. Indeed, patrons of horse racing who drove automobiles to the track could be accused of squandering rubber, an important resource for the war effort. The need for shared sacrifice and the scarcity of transportation facilities and materials threatened the continued existence of all horse racing and changed the established system for horse sales.

Federal government pressure led to significant modifications in the Kentucky horse industry. From 1943 through 1945, Keeneland held its races at Churchill Downs in Louisville. Colonel Matt Winn kept Churchill Downs open by transforming the place into a center of patriotic activity. Yearling sales shifted from New York to Kentucky because freight space on Eastern railroads simply was not available.

Located just outside Lexington, Kentucky, on a gently rolling piece of land near Calumet Farm, Keeneland race course fielded its first race card in 1936. Keeneland quickly grew in stature over the next several years, owing to its outstanding location, beauty, and commitment to high-quality horse racing. Owners and managers cared as much about tradition and atmosphere as maximizing profits. Purists and casual racegoers alike came to revere Keeneland.

After war broke out, Keeneland continued normal operations until authorities in Washington, DC, insisted that they end. After the fall 1942 meet, the government designated Keeneland as a suburban war plant, shutting down racing there. Santa Anita race course in California and many others across the nation met the same fate, so Keeneland was not alone.

Rather than see racing end completely, Keeneland officials leased Churchill Downs facilities to hold the spring meeting of 1943. A ten-day session followed, which proved successful. All stakes races—including the Blue Grass Stakes, the Phoenix Handicap, and the Ben Ali Handicap—went off without a hitch. The leasing arrangement between Keeneland and Churchill Downs continued through the end of the war. In 1946, the Keeneland track in Lexington reopened and has operated continuously since then.[50]

The 1943 racing season was truly memorable. Not only did Keeneland shift its races to Louisville, but the first "Streetcar Derby" was held, and Count Fleet launched a three-year-old campaign that cannot be topped because he beat every horse he faced.

Churchill Downs did not suffer the fate of Keeneland, Santa Anita,

Hialeah, and many other racetracks. The Downs maintained its meetings and race cards throughout the Second World War. This result was not inevitable; Churchill Downs might have been closed for a time if not for the shrewd, calculating efforts of Colonel Winn.

Matt J. Winn lived in Louisville his entire life. As a youngster, he attended the first Kentucky Derby in 1875. A bookkeeper, salesman, and tailor by trade, he loved horse racing and made it to the Derby every year. In 1902, Winn was asked if he would like to buy Churchill Downs. By this juncture, the racetrack was losing money, and Winn learned that if he did not purchase it the place would close. After much consideration, Winn agreed to the deal because Churchill Downs had been too important a part of his life to give up. Winn and a group of his associates bought Churchill Downs for $40,000. Winn himself became the chief promoter of Downs racing and of the Kentucky Derby. He succeeded marvelously well, making Churchill Downs profitable and raising its profile to the point where it became the mecca of American thoroughbred racing.[51]

After Pearl Harbor, Winn understood that Churchill Downs might be targeted by the federal government, and he did everything in his power to prevent suspension of racing. When the Office of Defense Transportation (ODT), under Joseph Eastman, issued a February 1943 statement saying that it did not approve of the running of the Sixty-Ninth Kentucky Derby, Winn swung into action. He wrote the ODT chief that everything possible would be done to minimize the use of scarce resources. Winn stated that the 1943 Derby would involve only Louisvillians, not out-of-towners. City residents would not drive to the Derby; instead, they would take streetcars or walk. No trains would be used at all. In a master stroke, he explained that out-of-towners would be asked to buy Kentucky Derby tickets and then turn them over to GIs quartered in and about Louisville. The Derby, this year, would be about the local people and the troops from Fort Knox and Bowman Field. Eastman relented, allowing the Derby to go on.[52]

"Streetcar Derbys" transpired in 1943 and 1944. Louisvillians attended and outsiders stayed away, including the millionaire set. Soldiers took the seats of out-of-towners. Green tents appeared in the Downs infield, and Sherman tanks were tested there before being shipped out to North Africa and Europe. Despite the transportation situation and other impediments,

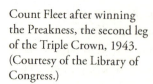

Count Fleet after winning
the Preakness, the second leg
of the Triple Crown, 1943.
(Courtesy of the Library of
Congress.)

a crowd of 62,000 watched the 1943 Derby. Though this crowd was one-third less than the previous year, it was sizable. Winn said, "I believed we could have a good Derby this year. . . . Here it is—a good crowd and a good Derby."[53]

The horses did not disappoint. Count Fleet alone made 1943 a bright, shining year in the annals of thoroughbred racing. The Count won every race he entered. During the running of the Wood Memorial, he hurt his left hind foot but emerged victorious anyway. Concern mounted; everyone wondered how he would run in the Kentucky Derby given his injury. It did not really matter. Count Fleet raced out of the gate to the front, bested his nine rivals easily, and coasted to the finish line a victor by three lengths. He took the Preakness by eight lengths and the Belmont Stakes by a whopping twenty-five lengths. Despite having no challenger, he ran a record time for the Belmont.[54]

Count Fleet's true brilliance can never be measured. The disparity between him and the other thoroughbreds born in 1940 was huge. Other horses since then have run faster, but perhaps only the immortal Secretariat dominated those of the same age as much. Count Fleet became the second Triple Crown winner of the war years and the one who most overpowered his competition. Though Whirlaway was a great horse, Count Fleet did not have an Alsab. Count Fleet, in a word, was a colossus.

Wartime circumstances also led to a change of location for the sale of thoroughbreds. Before World War II, Saratoga, New York, hosted the great, combined sale of the best American yearlings. Kentucky horsemen and others traveled there to sell young horses and socialize. After the 1942 Saratoga sale, given the shortage of railroad cars and the necessity of utilizing existing space to ship war-related goods, the Office of Defense Transportation issued a directive stating that railroad facilities for moving yearlings east for sale would no longer be available. After a quarter-century, the ODT declaration ended the Saratoga horse sales. As an alternative to no horse sales at all, Kentucky horsemen such as Walter J. Salmon of Mereworth Farm and Thomas Piatt of Brookdale Farm opted to hold the 1943 yearling sale at Keeneland.[55]

The first Keeneland horse sale proved highly successful. Most of the big Saratoga sellers and buyers showed up, and a new contingent of Southern, Midwestern, and Western horsemen attended as well. Kentucky buyers and sellers saved money, since they did not have to travel such a great distance or pay the usual horse shipping charges. At the auction, buyers purchased 312 yearlings for $929,850, an average of $2,980 a horse. By comparison, the 1942 Saratoga sales resulted in the sale of 485 yearlings, but the average price was only $994. Gross sales were nearly twice as high at Keeneland than at Saratoga. Of course, the quality of horses does vary from year to year, and other factors enter into the equation. Still, the inaugural Keeneland horse sale must be seen in a positive light.[56]

The year 1944 witnessed some interesting changes. Fasig-Tipton Sales Company decided not to carry on with the Keeneland horse sales. Kentucky breeders took it upon themselves to perpetuate the sales, given the excellent results of the year before. The new Breeders' Sales Company formed to conduct the auctions at Keeneland. The 1944 auction, carried out over a four-day period, led to the sale of 437 yearlings for an average price of $5,231. This average smashed the 1925 Saratoga record. Not surprisingly, the yearling sale remained in Lexington after the war and has continued on to this day.[57]

Horse racing continued to climb in popularity in 1944 and 1945. National records for fan attendance, purses, and betting were recorded.

In Kentucky, Calumet Farm won $601,660 during 1944, a new record. Calumet owner Warren Wright bred winners that earned almost a million dollars, also a record. Pensive, a melancholy-looking colt, captured the 1944 Kentucky Derby, and Hoop Jr. took the 1945 Kentucky Derby. As World War II ended, Kentucky horse racing displayed immense vitality, and fan enthusiasm was sky high. The Kentucky horse industry, which now included sales as well as breeding and racing, comprised a more important part of Kentucky's economy than before.[58]

Music occupied a prominent place within the complex of wartime entertainment in Kentucky. Popular music and classical music coexisted. The war provided material for new songs, and the old masters retained an audience. Music was available to suit virtually every taste, and it offered another means to find relief from the challenges and strains of war.

Big bands thrived during World War II, as did jazz music. Swing, a type of jazz characterized by a strong rhythm section and by a medium to fast tempo, was popular. Radio stations throughout Kentucky, such as WAVE and WHAS in Louisville, played hits by orchestras led by Tommy Dorsey, Sammy Kaye, Glenn Miller, and others. A sixteen-year-old girl from Maysville named Rosemary Clooney earned her first paycheck for singing just before Germany surrendered, though she achieved true stardom after the war.[59]

Many songs that emerged out of the war inspired Kentuckians. "Remember Pearl Harbor" cries out, "Let's Remember Pearl Harbor as we go to meet the foe. Let's Remember Pearl Harbor as we did the Alamo." Another song tells the story of a chaplain who got caught up in the fighting at Pearl Harbor. He exhorted his comrades to "Praise the Lord and Pass the Ammunition." Kentuckians especially liked the latter melody because it was based on a real-life incident involving Murray minister Howell M. Forgy. Aboard the heavy cruiser *New Orleans* as the Japanese attacked, Forgy encouraged a line of tired seamen to keep on passing shells to the gunner by shouting the now-famous remonstrance.[60]

Other war songs contained different messages. Soldiers and civilians from Kentucky could easily relate to "Don't Sit under the Apple Tree with Anyone Else but Me" or "Somebody Else Is Taking My Place." Spike Jones made fun of Hitler with his little ditty "Der Fuhrer's Face." "There'll be Bluebirds over the White Cliffs of Dover," by Jimmy Dorsey and His Orchestra, reflected the hope for a better day when peace returned.[61]

A 1940 Glenn Miller swing hit, "In the Mood," resonated even more deeply during the conflict than before it. A young lady sees a handsome guy and is immediately attracted to him. Some flirting and dancing ensues. Romance—or at least lust—seems to be in the air. She says, "Hey, baby, it's a quarter to three. There's a mess of moonlight, won't-cha share it with me." He answers, "Well . . . baby, don't-cha know that it's rude . . . to keep my two lips waitin' when they're in the mood." This song and others by Miller expressed a yearning to escape the war, and what better way to do it than in the arms of another.[62]

Patrons of classical music throughout Kentucky also found ways to indulge themselves. The Louisville Philharmonic Orchestra moved forward under the direction of Maestro Robert S. Whitney. Whitney had put together a full-sized ensemble by the time war broke out, and it played with many of the greatest concert soloists of the day. He worked hard to spread classical music throughout the commonwealth through the medium of radio. Great singers, such as Marian Anderson, also appeared in Louisville at this time. Aficionados of fine music were not left bereft by the war.[63]

Perhaps the most celebrated musician to play with the Louisville Orchestra during the conflict was pianist Artur Rubinstein. On April 4, 1944, he performed Beethoven's Third Piano Concerto and Chopin's Waltz in A-flat Major with his usual brilliance. The Beethoven concerto thrilled the audience with what one reviewer characterized as its "delicacy," "lightness," and "power." The other piano solos on the program were just as good. Rubinstein showed once again why many deemed him "the most exciting pianist of our time."[64]

Rubinstein's trip to the United States had become a rather prolonged one. He left his Paris home in early 1939 for his annual American tour and had not yet returned after the passage of some five years. "A German general occupies my place now," Rubinstein said. "I hear he likes it. But I really should have left some strychnine in the wine."[65]

Marian Anderson, the great African American contralto, visited Louisville on November 10, 1942. Before a large assemblage at Memorial Auditorium, she displayed the one-of-a-kind voice that had made her so

Marian Anderson sings "The Star-Spangled Banner" inside the Department of the Interior Auditorium on January 6, 1943. (Courtesy of the Library of Congress.)

rightfully famous. Anderson's "Ave Maria," a famous Schubert composition, was a joy, complete with the most sublime legato and, a reviewer noted, "the perfect attack" on the words "Ave Maria." Her aria "Pleurez mes yeux," from Massanet's opera *Le Cid,* pulsed "with frantic fervor and warmth of expression." Her spirituals enthralled the audience. Once again, Anderson showed why she was one of the greatest singers in the world.[66]

Music of all types, be it pop or highbrow, provided a "heartening light against the shadows" of war. President Roosevelt had underlined this point on many occasions, as did others in authority. Glenn Miller, Artur Rubinstein, and Marian Anderson made life in Kentucky during a worldwide catastrophe a bit easier to take. The gift of entertainment is always valuable, all the more so during war, and should not be underestimated.[67]

Hollywood movies touched Kentuckians in many ways, bringing them together against a common foe, making them think, laugh, and cry. In the early 1940s, movies might be about propaganda or not. They might be about a serious subject or escapist in nature. War movies abounded during the conflict, but most studio fare had to do with non–war-related subjects. GI Joe was big, but so too were Abbott and Costello.

Kentuckians loved the movies. Louisville theaters included Loew's, the Rialto, the Strand, the Kentucky, and the Uptown. Lexington, Ashland, Covington, Somerset, Owensboro, Hopkinsville, and Paducah all had their motion picture houses. Two theaters operated in the small southeastern Kentucky town of Jackson; there are none there today.[68]

Just after Pearl Harbor, Hollywood put out a large number of war movies, which portrayed the Japanese and the Americans in predictable ways. "Buck-toothed, runty Japs" engaged in treachery and villainy; they were shown as a cruel, despicable bunch with no human sensibilities or redeeming value. By way of contrast, Americans embodied righteousness and justice. Freedom and democracy depended upon an American victory over the Japanese empire. While this view contained some truth, it was crude and permitted no room for historical complexities, individual differences, or the moral and ethical ambiguities of war.[69]

Guadalcanal Diary, Air Force, and *Remember Pearl Harbor* depict the Japanese in the conventional manner. The "Japs" are characterized as "apes and monkeys" who kill without conscience. In *Guadalcanal Diary,* Lloyd Nolan plays a gritty, determined sergeant who knows a great deal about enemy methods. His take on killing the Japanese is simple: "Well, it's kill or be killed—besides, they ain't people." One scene from *Air Force* shows an American flyer whose plane has been hit floating slowly down toward the ground in a parachute. Suddenly, a Japanese fighter plane swoops down on the vulnerable American, striking him with a bullet as he nears the ground. The wounded man lands hard, crawls slowly toward safety, sees the Japanese plane making another pass, and holds up his hands piteously toward the aircraft as if begging for mercy, but is strafed and dies. In the same film, a crew member aboard the B-19 bomber *Mary Ann* shoots down a Japanese fighter pilot, who is immediately engulfed by flames. The American screams out gleefully, "Fried Jap going down!" A significant part of the American viewing public ate up this simplistic fare, buying into the notion put forward in *Remember Pearl Harbor* that the Japanese were a barbaric group "nurtured at the breasts of hate and destruction."[70]

Such language as "Fried Jap going down!" is appalling but understandable in the aftermath of the surprise attack at Pearl Harbor. *Guadalcanal Diary, Air Force,* and similar films reflect Americans' hostility toward an enemy that feigned peace negotiations as it plotted to attack the United States. There is no mention made by Hollywood, however, of the 1940 American oil embargo, which induced the Japanese to take military action against America; nor is there any acknowledgment that some "Japs" may have been barbarians but others were not. War is endlessly complicated, presenting human beings with terrible moral dilemmas, and Hollywood gave that no play either, at least in the early years of the conflict.

Later movies did exhibit more nuance. One of the best, *They Were Expendable,* appeared in 1945, starring John Wayne and Donna Reed. This film tells the story of PT boat commanders (Wayne is one) who strove mightily to prove the worth of their little boats in combat. PT boats eventually end up in the fight and acquit themselves well. Wayne, as PT boat commander Ryan, began dating nurse Sandy Davyss (Reed) in the midst of fighting, but their relationship ends when Ryan is reassigned stateside to train more men for PT boat service. Unfortunately, even as the PT boats display their effectiveness, some were sunk and crew members died. Moreover, U.S. forces as a whole proved too weak to hold the Philippines, and the Japanese took the islands. Davyss and others were left behind to suffer a horrible fate. *They Were Expendable* is about defeat rather than victory. It shows that while the United States won many battles, it also lost a few. The defenders of the Philippines bought valuable time, which aided the U.S. effort to rebuild its Pacific fleet and establish a defensive perimeter in the Central and South Pacific, but this was not a glorious mission—it was necessary, painful, and thankless.[71]

Newsreels covering the war often accompanied feature films. Adults watched them with interest, since they revealed the course the conflict took and eventually American progress against the Axis. Their impact on children, however, was greater. Meleta Crim Hill, who lived near Louisville and was ten years old during World War II, said the war reels "scared kids to death. Guns going off—planes crashing. That sort of thing." Maysvillian John Perrine, who was roughly the same age as Meleta Crim at that time, recalls that the reels depicted "Tojo as a kind of demon, as was—of course—Hitler." Being more impressionable than adults, kids sometimes were truly shaken by the newsreels and needed comforting. The war became a living, breathing, frightening event for these children.[72]

Hollywood studios began to change the subject matter of their films beginning in 1943. Fewer war films were made and the level of violence in the ones that did come out diminished. Movies with themes unrelated to war appeared more often, including comedies, romances, thrillers, and westerns. Paramount's executive producer B. G. De Sylva put it this way: "Patrons are keen for escapist movies, and they obviously believe that, after an arduous day working in munitions plants and other defense industries, they deserve a few hours of surcease from the war."[73]

According to one estimate, 70 percent of the movie plots from 1941 to 1945 dealt with topics other than the worldwide conflict. Abbott and Costello and the team of Bob Hope and Bing Crosby turned out comedies that drew large audiences. Romances, westerns, and horror movies attracted their fair share of supporters. Box-office receipts proved that war movies were not as popular or profitable as movies that made their viewers laugh or feel happy.[74]

Bud Abbott and Lou Costello experienced tremendous success during World War II. In 1942, Abbott and Costello took the top spot as a box office attraction, ahead of such stalwarts as Clark Gable and Gary Cooper; in 1941 and 1943, Abbott and Costello placed third. *Ride 'em Cowboy,* a typical Abbott and Costello wartime hit, finds the duo hiding out at the "Lazy S" ranch after Lou accidentally proposes to a homely Indian girl named Moonbeam. He does not want to get married, but she does. Indians chase after Abbott and Costello, who try to dodge them. The comedians get laughs by sidestepping bulls, riding a wild horse, dressing up in outlandish cowboy garb, and outracing mounted Indians in a rickety jalopy. Everything turns out well in the end: Lou avoids marriage, and the pair's friends, Bronco Bob and Anne, win a rodeo and launch a romance. This type of comedic fluff went over quite well as Americans sought relaxation in the midst of a world at war.[75]

Hope and Crosby rivaled Abbott and Costello from 1941 to 1945. Bob Hope made the top ten box office list every year, including a number two finish in 1943. Bing Crosby ended up number one in 1944 and 1945, beating out Gary Cooper and Van Johnson. Audiences thoroughly enjoyed the witty banter between Bing and Bob and their constant efforts at one-upmanship.[76]

The Road to Morocco, which debuted in 1942, is a good example of the two at work. It begins with Jeff (Crosby) and Orville (Hope) aboard an ocean liner, which sinks. They get washed ashore and begin an odyssey which leads them to exotic Morocco. Jeff puts Orville in quite a fix by selling him for jellied turtle eggs (the two had been starving). Orville is now a slave, whose original owner passes him on to Princess Shalmar. Shalmar, who has never married, wants to wed Orville, but only because her first husband is fated to die horribly within a week: with Orville dead and gone, she can marry her true love—Mullay Kassim—and the two can live happily ever after. Orville learns about this arrangement and tries like the dickens to avoid it. You can also be certain that he is going to get back at Jeff. After various twists and turns, Shalmar falls in love with Jeff, rejecting Kassim. Kassim captures Jeff, Orville, Shalmar, and a harem girl who has fallen for Orville. All of them manage to escape from Kassim's clutches and make it to America, where both couples are to be married, thus bringing the movie to a blissful ending.[77]

Romances, westerns, and horror movies fared almost as well in wartime Kentucky as comedy. The Jaxon Theatre, in Jackson, showed *Talk of the Town* in early 1943. Cary Grant plays Leopold Dilg, a factory worker who is falsely accused of arson and murder. Dilg's defense lawyer is Professor Michael Lightcap (Ronald Colman), who eventually clears Dilg of all charges. Along the way, Dilg and Lightcap compete for the affection of Nora Shelley (Jean Arthur). In the end, Dilg gets the lady while Lightcap receives an appointment as associate justice of the U.S. Supreme Court. In February 1944, the Virginia Theatre of Somerset featured *Black Market Rustlers* and *Calling Dr. Death. Black Market Rustlers,* with Ray Corrigan, is a prototypical western about a group of cowboys called the Range Busters who break up a cattle rustling ring. *Calling Dr. Death,* a horror film starring Lon Chaney Jr., focuses on a neurologist who is plagued by the distinct possibility that he may have killed his unfaithful wife in a moment of mad delirium. Dr. Mark Steele (Chaney) is ultimately exonerated, though it looks bad for a while. *Talk of the Town* is a great film, whereas the others mentioned here are more pedestrian; together with the war movies, they typify the taste of moviegoers in the Bluegrass State during the Second World War. The growing popularity of movies in Kentucky, fueled by the efforts of the government and Hollywood to promote national unity, by an increase in individual income, and by a need to escape the war, was obvious.[78]

Entertainment as a whole gave Kentuckians and other Americans a break from the hardships of war. College football and basketball, baseball and high school sports, horse racing, music, and the movies furnished people with a welcome diversion. The University of Kentucky football squad could not escape the doldrums from 1941 to 1945. Adolph Rupp's basketball program continued its ascent to greatness. Major League baseball stagnated, though minor league and Negro baseball prospered. High school sports remained a source of community pride. Horse racing enjoyed a resurgence during the war, and big bands dominated music. War movies, which underscored Axis wrongdoing, reinforced the commitment of Kentuckians to victory, while other kinds of films amused, enthralled, or scared the citizenry. All in all, the Kentucky entertainment scene proved to be surprisingly rich and diverse despite the draft and transportation difficulties. Popular entertainment in the state progressed even further after the war, as Kentuckians devoted more time and money to it than ever before.

Conclusion

The months from December 1944 through September 1945 saw World War II come to an end. The last battles were fought. Germany and Japan surrendered. Efforts to reconstruct the defeated nations were begun. Kentuckians ceased war production and resumed peacetime activities, trying to find their bearings again. The people of the commonwealth looked to the future with a combination of optimism, hope, and trepidation; they also understood that they inhabited a far different world than the one that existed before the war.

On December 16, 1944, German dictator Adolf Hitler launched a last-gasp, massive counteroffensive against the Allies at their weakest point, in the Ardennes Forest of Belgium. The fighting spread to Luxembourg as well, claiming the life of Louisvillian Kenny Maddox. German forces made significant headway, putting a fifty-mile-wide bulge in the American line. After weeks of intense struggle, the Allies managed to check the Germans and reformed their line. By mid-January 1945 the Battle of the Bulge was over and Nazi Germany nearly finished.

American and British armies continued their push to the German border and beyond. The VII Corps of the First U.S. Army forded the Rhine River in large numbers on March 15, 1945. Now exhausted, the Wehrmacht began to disintegrate. Russian forces moved into Germany from the East. With no way out, Hitler committed suicide in his Berlin bunker on the last day of April. V-E Day came on May 7, 1945, when Germany capitulated.

Events unfolded a bit more slowly in the Far East. The Americans' island-hopping strategy continued to bear fruit. The Americans needed Iwo Jima, a speck of volcanic rock in the Bonin group, so that they could send B-29 bombers with fighter escort over Japanese cities like Tokyo. The Marines took Iwo Jima after a bloody contest with Japanese soldiers that lasted from February to March 1945. Here Frank Sousley of Fleming County helped hoist the American flag only to suffer a fatal gunshot

"United we are strong, united we will win." America and its allies will finish off the Axis through cooperation, including joint use of military resources. (Courtesy of the Library of Congress.)

wound from a Japanese sniper later. The U.S. Tenth Army, originally commanded by a Kentuckian, General Simon B. Buckner, secured Okinawa
by late June. Okinawa, which lay just south of the Japanese home islands,
had been projected as the staging area for a U.S. invasion of Japan itself.
The conventional assault never materialized because President Harry Truman ordered atomic bombs to be dropped on Hiroshima and Nagasaki in
early August. Not even Japanese fanaticism proved sufficient to withstand
those titanic blasts. General Douglas MacArthur took the official Japanese surrender on September 2, 1945, while aboard the battleship USS
Missouri in Tokyo Bay. The war was over.

The Second World War generated an unprecedented amount of death
and destruction, as well as an enduring measure of good. Fifty million
people perished during the conflict, and the world sustained approximately $2 trillion of property damage. The mushroom clouds over Hiro-
shima and Nagasaki and the firebombing of Dresden, Germany, made
the horrific scenes at Pearl Harbor look like child's play. Kentuckians who
wanted retribution against the Japanese and Germans certainly got it.
Almost 8,000 Kentuckians died in the war, a tiny number compared to
overall worldwide losses, but a tough pill for Kentuckians to swallow just
the same. Yet the ugly ends that Hitler and Tojo met eliminated mon-
strous evil from the world while sending a message to future dictators that
they might ignore only at their own peril. Though under siege for a time,
freedom and individualism—certainly among the best values of Western
civilization—survived World War II to inspire future generations.

Given the sting from the war, which it did not want to repeat, and
the desire for a better future, the United States attempted to remake Germany and Japan in its own image. After Germany was divided between
the United States and the Soviet Union, a "denazification" campaign
removed Nazi officials from West German offices and did away with the
old Nazi symbols, such as the swastika. An initial American plan to strip
away German industry so as to diminish its future war-making capacity
was abandoned in favor of efforts to build an economically diverse, democratic West Germany. Under Chancellor Konrad Adenauer, who assumed
power in 1949, West Germany achieved these goals. Meanwhile, in the
immediate postwar period, Japan fell under American occupation. General MacArthur became the real leader there. MacArthur completed the

destruction of Japanese militarism, gave Japan a constitution that included rights for women, and presided over the transfer of a large amount of land from big landholders to peasants. He left the island-nation a stable place, with elections, potential for economic growth, and a much closer relationship with the United States than it had experienced in the tumultuous decade before World War II. American reconstruction of West Germany and Japan turned them into U.S. trade partners and allies in the Cold War.

Announcement of the end of World War II brought great celebration to Kentucky. In Mt. Sterling, the Baptist Church and other churches held special meetings to give thanks to Almighty God for triumph over the enemy. Citizens of Bourbon County "went wild," honking car horns, shouting at each other gleefully, and shooting pistols in the air. In Harlan, the victory crowd was large and boisterous, breaking up only late in the evening. Parades were held in many Kentucky places, replete with American flags, streamers, and confetti. Politicians and other VIPs accompanied brave and valorous soldiers in many of these celebrations. The forfeiture of American lives in the war cast a bittersweet pall over some of the displays, and the unlucky souls who had lost a loved one were never too far away. At least a few church congregations voiced the magnanimous sentiment that in "our rejoicing we [should] not forget to pray for our foes."[1]

The restoration of peace led to a period of readjustment that carried on from mid-1945 to 1947. Demobilization of industry occurred. The American state shed wartime agencies and programs rendered superfluous by victory. Servicemen from Kentucky returned home from Europe and Asia. People inside the commonwealth wanted things to get back to normal as soon as possible, so they reemphasized the importance of religious faith, planned family reunions, and eagerly awaited the end of restrictions such as rationing. Economic aftershocks from the war caused some discomfort in Kentucky, but not nearly as much as many experts had feared. Kentuckians experienced some bumpiness during the transition from war to peace, but nothing worse.

Businesses throughout Kentucky received communications from the U.S. War Department terminating war production contracts. The Kentucky Shell Manufacturing Company of Campbell County in northern Kentucky found out that the government expected it to wrap up manufacture of 8-inch shells, with the concomitant release of all employees, by June 1, 1945. Ford Motor Company assembled its last jeep at the Louisville plant in August 1945, resuming production of passenger trucks without missing a beat. DuPont and Goodrich opted to buy the Rubbertown plants that the government had financed and that they had run during the war, anticipating a quick return to peacetime operations and profits. The Kentucky Ordnance Works near Paducah processed its last TNT in 1946, then the land was turned over to the Federal Farm Mortgage Corporation. The Charlestown, Indiana, munitions complex stopped making powder bags and rocket propellant just after World War II, but the facility was reactivated later as a smokeless powder maker during the Korean and Vietnam wars. Various outcomes resulted from the reconversion decisions of federal authorities and individual firms.[2]

In the grand scheme of things the exact date of contract cancellation made little difference. Kentucky industries and workers had performed their part of the gigantic American war production job successfully, and victory testified more eloquently to that fact than anything else. DuPont, National Carbide Company, B. F. Goodrich, and other concerns that established a base of operations in Kentucky exploited Bluegrass distilleries to generate industrial alcohol, which in turn went into the production of synthetic rubber and smokeless powder. Kentucky led the United States in production of synthetic rubber during the war, while it contributed an indispensable ingredient in the manufacture of smokeless powder. In these instances, companies turned Kentucky's comparative advantage in the production of potable liquor to the express benefit of the American war production effort. Unlike Michigan, California, and New York, Kentucky's share of total U.S. war production was never large, but it possessed a few substances and finished goods that the federal government and military would have been hard pressed to amass from other states. Ralph the Riveter, with the able assistance of Rosie the Riveter, merits commendation as well. Bluegrass workers turned out items as diverse as jeeps, butadiene, TNT, x-ray equipment, and atomic bomb parts.

War production in Kentucky took place almost exclusively in cities and towns. Louisville alone accounted for more than half of all the war goods made in the state. Ashland, Covington, Richmond, and Paducah also gained appreciably from wartime industry. Without a doubt, World

War II pushed urbanization and industrialization ahead in the common-wealth. A rural state before the conflict, it was less so after it.

A tussle broke out in 1945–1946 between zealous New Dealers, orga-nized labor, and consumers on the one side and big business and the armed services on the other. At issue was the length and intensity of regulatory reconversion. The New Dealers and their allies favored a long reconver-sion period with significant federal regulation of food prices and rents. This approach offered consumers in Kentucky and other states low prices and affordable housing while it promoted the welfare of all the people. Big business, aided by the military, desired a shorter period of reconversion, rapid elimination of wartime mobilization agencies, and a quick end to a host of wartime regulations they deemed counterproductive. Whereas the New Deal camp advocated a greater degree of governmental activism to protect buyers and workers from harm, big business demanded a return to market conditions less fettered by governmental intervention. In the end, big business won and the military-industrial alliance advanced.[3]

The War Production Board, the War Food Administration, and the Office of Price Administration, along with a number of lesser agencies, did not long survive the war. Following the ouster of WPB chief Don-ald Nelson, industry influence in the WPB prevailed, and the agency liq-uidated itself. WPB controls on allocation, priorities, and nonessential civilian goods were removed; any supervision of contract termination was abandoned; and operations ceased entirely by November 1945. The War Food Administration died even earlier, in June 1945. The Office of Price Administration, long a New Deal–dominated entity, lasted longer than the WPB and the WFA and fought harder for social justice, only to meet its downfall anyway.[4]

After the war, the dreams of New Dealers, consumers, and trade unionists for some degree of equity in the relationship between giant cor-porations on the one side and workers and customers on the other rested with the Office of Price Administration. The OPA responded to victory over the Axis by ending many types of rationing, including gas ration-ing, before 1945 was out. Rationing of meat, however, continued well into the postwar period, as did OPA direction of rent controls. The OPA positioned itself as a champion of the consumer and the renter, arguing that it retained certain regulations to prevent these individuals from being gouged by business and landlords. The public welfare also demanded a continuation of the wartime anti-inflation program into peacetime, as this would prevent a rapid loss of purchasing power. The OPA lost its fight when meat packers and farmers refused to send their steak, hamburger, and other products to the marketplace until price controls were lifted. When it came down to little or no meat, or meat at a higher price, consumers chose the latter course. Under terrific pressure from industry and housewives, the OPA reluctantly jettisoned meat rationing in October 1946. Over the next year, the OPA watched silently as retail meat prices rose by a whopping 61 percent and then the agency itself perished. Rent controls persisted under the Office of the Housing Expediter a while longer, but then they vanished. Antistatists—that is, the proponents of reduced regulation—emerged victorious, and the federal government found it harder to uphold fair play between big business and weaker special interests.[5]

After Axis surrender, the U.S. military moved as fast as it could to discharge enlisted men. The Army and Navy shrank from a total of 11.8 million men during the wartime peak to 2.9 million by mid-1946 and 1.5 million by 1947. Although it was a much smaller, more streamlined force by then, the military—in particular the Army—never returned to the puny specimen it had been in the late 1930s. Thousands of Kentucky troops, now veterans, joined the exodus home. They streamed back to the state to pick up their old lives. Among them were Hollis Gibson, Von Watts, El Hannen Stacy, and David Gaitskill. Thirty-seven Harrodsburg tank men returned as well.[6]

Some of the soldiers who made it home were just fine; others were most emphatically not. Hollis Gibson was one of the lucky ones. Having failed to induce American draft dodgers living in Mexico to come back to the United States, Gibson received an honorable discharge from the Army in September 1945. He soon got back his old job as an Alcohol, Tobacco, and Firearms agent and began chasing moonshiners through the Cumberland Mountains once more. Von Watts, the anti-aircraft artillery man, survived the fray and returned home in November 1945. Lizzie, his wife, was overjoyed to see him, and Von met his baby daughter Vona for the first time. The birth of a second daughter, whom they named Joyce, soon followed. Watts became principal of a number of public schools after the conflict and died in 1992 as a much-respected educator. El Hannen Stacy, who went AWOL to see his sick mother and later earned multiple Purple Hearts, regretted the arthritis that pained him in later years but other than that was of sound mind and body. David Gaitskill, who weathered his incarceration in a German prisoner-of-war camp surprisingly well, made a relatively easy readjustment to civilian life with his wife, Frances. The Harrodsburg tankers were a different story, having experienced some of the worst horrors that modern, total war can inflict. This group went through abominable circumstances and bore severe physical and psychological scars from the ordeal.[7]

Sixty-six tankers left Harrodsburg, Kentucky, in 1941 for the Philippine Islands. They fought at Bataan and Corregidor, where the Japanese captured them en masse. Years of captivity in various places under the most dreadful conditions, subject to torture by Japanese guards, disease, starvation, and friendly fire, cost twenty-nine of these men their lives. The ones who survived saw comrades die, experienced disease, and suffered from terrible hunger. When the surviving tankers arrived back in Harrodsburg at the war's end, many of the individuals just could not cope with the torrent of painful, even debilitating, memories. Sheltered by a caring community that was only too aware of their plight, a significant percentage of the ex-tankers struggled for years with alcoholism, an inability to hold jobs, and broken marriages. They were victims of posttraumatic stress disorder. The Harrodsburg tankers, of course, were not the only returning GIs with this malady, but their concentration in one small central Kentucky town made them unique.[8]

Economic dislocation from the war proved serious, though it lasted just a little over two years. The end of the conflict meant that labor's no-strike pledge was no longer in effect. A nationwide soft coal strike ordered by unrepentant United Mine Workers president John L. Lewis ensued. Kentucky miners refused once more to work, and uncertainty pervaded their homes. All sorts of industries that depended upon coal were threatened with curtailed production. The UMW bested the government again, procuring a wage increase, improved safety and sanitary conditions for miners, and a union health and welfare fund financed by a royalty on coal. The removal of price controls and various wage increases unleashed inflation, forcing Kentucky consumers to pay almost 20 percent more for

their commodities in 1946. Kentucky buyers had their steak, veal, butter, and sugar back by 1947, but many held their noses at store checkout
counters. Unemployment edged up after the reestablishment of peace, but
remained low for years. The vast majority of veterans located jobs in the
midst of this instability. By late 1947, the Kentucky economy had settled
down.[9]

After the immediate turbulence from reconversion subsided, World
War II continued to shape Kentucky's future. Economic improvement
was the feature that stood out most in the beginning, but shifting social
currents wrought by the dynamics of the war were also obvious. Changes
related to Kentucky politics were more subtle, but discernible nonetheless. A greater number of Kentuckians believed that the federal government had some constructive role to play in their lives after the conflict
than before it, and foreign affairs attracted more attention. Entertainment remained an indispensable component of a healthy lifestyle. Taking
everything into account, especially the return of prosperity and the growing awareness among women and blacks of inequality, Kentucky was a
profoundly different place in 1945 than it had been in 1939.

The war killed the Great Depression, restoring economic health to
Kentucky. Young men got jobs in the military, and older men secured
work in war plants alongside increasing numbers of women. Regular and
overtime pay coupled with rationing of certain goods resulted in a vast
accumulation of individual savings. When price controls were removed,
Kentuckians had lots of money and bought houses, automobiles, steak,
butter, and sugar in record or near-record amounts. The unemployment
rate of just over 1 percent in 1944 inched up to 3.6 percent in 1950—still
quite reasonable. Per capita personal income increased from $320 in 1940
to $803 in 1945 to $990 in 1950. With the sale of lots in Helm Meadows,
Elizabethtown's newest subdivision, the number of house deeds recorded
in Hardin County reached an all-time high in early June of 1946. The
release of pent-up demand fueled postwar prosperity, which deepened for
a time before leveling off in the late 1950s. After that the figures were still
not bad until the late 1970s and early 1980s. In absolute terms, Kentucky
made large gains as a result of wartime stimuli and the postwar boom.[10]

In a comparative sense, the scorecard was not so good. Kentucky
ranked forty-fourth out of the forty-eight states in per capita personal

income in 1940, and that number stayed exactly the same for 1945. Other states, too, had reaped the benefits of the expanding wartime economy, and Kentucky's place among them hardly changed. Kentucky tried hard but only managed to tread water. By 1960, Kentucky stood at forty-third out of the existing fifty states. Having passed Tennessee, West Virginia, and North Carolina, albeit by tiny amounts, the commonwealth trailed the new states of Alaska and Hawaii plus forty older states. Perhaps the most telling statistic, however, was not related to a single state at all but to a nationwide average. Here Kentucky steadily closed the gap, making 53.8 percent of U.S. per capita personal income in 1940, 64.9 percent at war's end, 71.7 percent in 1960, and 83.8 percent in 2003. Kentuckians have improved their position with regard to per capita income, but the progress has been frustratingly slow.[11]

The war reinforced tobacco's place as the foremost farm commodity of Kentucky and therefore retarded long-run efforts at economic diversification. In county after county in the Bluegrass and Pennyrile regions high wartime prices and high revenues succeeded marvelously at renewing the traditional love affair between Kentucky farmers and tobacco. By 1944, over 38 percent of all the cash that farmers received from their labors came from tobacco alone. This kind of return, along with the pull of tradition, kept the farmers' focus on burley most of all; they could not bring themselves to try other crops or to put their money into other areas. The war offered a real opportunity to branch out, but the results were inconsequential. Hemp, sweet potatoes, and especially soybeans might have been cultivated in the postwar period in significantly larger amounts, yet it did not happen. Overreliance on tobacco (along with coal and a few other goods) held back the Kentucky economy, making it more difficult to get ahead than it would have been otherwise.[12]

The average Kentuckian, of course, still made over twice as much income in 1945 as in 1939. Many of these people waited anxiously for Ford, General Motors, Chrysler, Packard, and other companies to speed up production so that they could buy an automobile. New car sales soared in 1946 and 1947. Von Watts of Leatherwood learned to drive in the Army and bought a black pickup truck after he got back home. Hollis Gibson of Hindman purchased a Ford. Dan Razor Sr. of Mt. Sterling gave his son a little yellow Chevrolet coupe.

An interesting side effect of this consumer spending spree was that the mobility of Kentuckians increased and isolation diminished. This was especially true for those individuals located in the mountainous east. The construction of roads during the war and just after it aided this development. Von Watts, for example, often drove his truck from Leatherwood down a river bed to the mouth of Lost Creek. At this point, he connected with old Kentucky Route 15 (now Kentucky Road 1812) to go into Jackson. This mode of travel beat taking the old horse every time. Indiana state routes 62 and 3 were expanded to better connect Louisville and Charlestown, Indiana. More roads appeared around Fort Knox and the Blue Grass Ordnance Depot. In the late 1940s, construction began on Louisville's Watterson and North-South expressways—ideas that had gained momentum during World War II. Farm-to-market roads were first built during the conflict, and more appeared later. The combination of new roads and much larger numbers of vehicles made it possible for rural and urban Kentuckians to travel longer distances than before in relative comfort.[13]

For Kentucky, the maintenance and growth of the military-industrial complex translated into a myriad of economic benefits. Fort Knox; Camp Campbell; the Blue Grass Ordnance Depot; the Charlestown, Indiana, smokeless powder plant; and numerous other facilities attracted massive amounts of federal money, and the communities around them reaped a considerable reward. The Fort Knox Armored School, to cite just one example, included 5,500 instructors and 16,000 students in October 1946. At the same time, the demand for housing from Fort Knox military personnel increased by 25 percent, and the Elizabethtown United Service Organization had a hard time finding living quarters for all these men. Some found quarters in Hardin County and others in adjoining counties. The soldiers paid rent to landlords, bought food in local grocery stores, purchased gasoline from service stations, and spent their extra money in bars and on sporting events. Elizabethtown, Louisville, Hopkinsville, Lexington, Richmond, and many other towns in the commonwealth became accustomed to this type of enrichment. The Korean War only led to more gains of this kind. The American military-industrial complex helped sustain the newfound economic vitality of Kentucky.[14]

The social consequences of World War II for Kentucky were immense.

Women took advantage of wartime circumstances, improving their economic status; a better lifestyle resulted for them during the postwar period. Black men returned from military service, some of them having risked their lives to vanquish the enemies of human dignity, only to encounter continuing discrimination at home. They took steps to diminish racial inequality. Out-migration from all parts of Kentucky had occurred. Another offshoot of the war with long-term implications was the baby boom. Various groups tested the limits of Kentucky society after the war and it proved flexible enough to accommodate diverse needs, though the process generated a considerable measure of frustration and pain.

Kentucky women secured jobs during the war that they would not have gotten otherwise, working as riveters, welders, shell makers, taxi cab drivers, and security guards. They invaded male-dominated occupations in impressive numbers. More females were hired for traditional jobs as well, such as clerical workers. Women benefited handsomely from the receipt of good wages as well as from the fulfillment that came with a job well done. Having had a taste of a new lifestyle, which many found enjoyable, some fought hard to keep their gains. These women often managed to retain their jobs into the postwar period. For them, and ultimately for Kentucky society, things would never quite be the same.

The war years changed the participation rate and occupational distribution of females in the Kentucky labor force. From 1900 to 1930, women and girls made up just over 15 percent of the Kentucky workforce. Given the immediate economic stimulus from the American defense preparedness program, the number of females as a percentage of the overall labor pool reached 17.9 percent in 1940. With outright war, and the huge industrial buildup accompanying it, that figure rose rapidly to approximately 33 percent at the height of the production effort in 1943–1944. With Axis defeat, the return of the servicemen, and a vigorous postwar federal government publicity drive urging American women to give up their wartime jobs and return to home and hearth, that number declined to 21.1 percent in 1950, but rose to 27.1 percent in 1960 and 35.8 percent in 1970. Wartime economic and industrial exigencies, along with the rise of feminism, broke through the old 15 percent ceiling of females in the Kentucky workforce. Furthermore, the number of Kentucky women classified as professional workers and proprietor-managers increased over time. In 1940, 18,885 women in the commonwealth were listed as professionals and 6,733 as proprietor-managers. In 1950, despite the government effort to revivify the "cult of domesticity," 25,575 women fell under the professional category and 9,764 under the proprietor-manager heading. World War II clearly separated one era in the history of Kentucky female labor from a later one, which was characterized by increased numbers of jobs and higher-quality positions.[15]

African American servicemen reentering Kentucky after the war quickly learned that white racial attitudes had not changed. White Kentuckians, by and large, still believed in the old racial status quo. Support for segregation and notions of black inferiority remained strong. Caucasians expected to have their way in all types of situations, and even the idea that blacks should inconvenience whites or make them feel uncomfortable was virtually unthinkable.

Private first class Gerald Dean, a black soldier, became reacquainted with these truths in short order. On December 10, 1945, Dean presented a ticket to an attendant and gained admission to Memorial Auditorium in Louisville to see the Cincinnati Symphony Orchestra perform. Apparently his seat was taken, and he did not want to precipitate a disturbance. Seeking help, Dean found another employee who walked him from balcony to balcony trying to find someplace for him to sit. In the end, no spot could be located that was not in the middle of a sea of white people, so Dean was taken to the box office and was issued a refund. As Dean left, the auditorium official informed him the concert was for "white people only" and added his prediction of any change in seating policy: "Maybe in 100 years, but not now."[16]

Black veterans who had helped defeat Hitler and Tojo fully expected some greater consideration for their deeds and proved unwilling to accept these kinds of insults any longer. Having become more militant as a result of their wartime experiences, they were not about to take injustices lying down. Some of them determined that they would fight back against rampant employment, housing, educational, and recreational discrimination.

Lyman Johnson, for instance, a Navy veteran, filed suit against the University of Kentucky in 1948, claiming that it had denied him admission to graduate school simply on the basis of skin color and that that was unconstitutional. A U.S. District Court judge sided with Johnson, in large part because Kentucky "failed to provide graduate and professional schools for blacks that in any respect equaled the university for whites." Separate but inferior facilities for blacks were increasingly coming under adverse scrutiny. Following the court's ruling, Johnson and a number of other blacks enrolled in graduate classes at UK during the summer session of 1949 and took up their studies.[17]

After the *Brown* decision by the U.S. Supreme Court in 1954, which declared "separate but equal" educational facilities inherently unequal and unconstitutional, progress for Kentucky blacks came more quickly. Marches, sit-ins, and additional legal victories transpired. "Jim Crow" died and inequality diminished. By imbuing black veterans with a greater confidence in themselves, an increased measure of assertiveness, and the newfound feeling that their country owed them something, World War II helped give birth to the Kentucky civil rights crusade of the 1950s and 1960s.[18]

Out-migration and the baby boom affected Kentucky during the war and after it, shaping the state's population in important ways. Higher-paying jobs in war plants in Michigan, Ohio, Virginia, Tennessee, and other states lured huge numbers of Kentuckians away from 1940 to 1945. During the late 1940s and 1950s, this exodus continued. Hundreds of thousands of people from the commonwealth left for greener pastures elsewhere, depriving Kentucky of a goodly share of its brightest, most ambitious citizens. Randy veterans and their wives and girlfriends helped make up for the losses from out-migration. Beginning as early as 1943, intensifying in 1946, and carrying on through the 1950s, a baby boom of unprecedented size struck Kentucky. New births in Kentucky slightly more than counterbalanced out-migration, leaving a net gain of approximately 100,000 persons from 1950 to 1960. Even so, Kentucky's population grew by only a little more than 3 percent in the fifteen years after World War II. Only a handful of states in the United States had a slower rate of population increase than Kentucky experienced, and few if any suffered from such a large brain drain.[19]

The war influenced Kentucky politics to a smaller extent than it did the state's economy and society. Continuity more than change characterized Bluegrass State politics from the late 1930s into the 1950s. The Democratic party dominated Kentucky throughout this interval, as it had before the war. All of the governors were Democrats, with the single exception of Simeon Willis. As noted previously, Willis won an extremely tight race, which might well have gone the other way if only one of many variables had been different. The Democrats, without exception, controlled the state House and Senate during these years. Even with Willis's victory, the Democrats still held 23 of 38 Senate seats in 1944 and 21 of 38 in 1946. Kentuckians also voted for the Democratic candidate for president of the United States in every race from 1932 to 1952, even going so far as to back erudite liberal Adlai E. Stevenson over war hero Dwight D. Eisenhower in the latter year. As in the past, Kentucky politics revolved around Democratic party factionalism and the use of patronage by both Democrats and Republicans to buy support. The Happy Chandler faction still faced opposition within Democratic party ranks after the war, though it emanated from the Earle Chester Clements camp rather than from the older duo of Ruby Laffoon and Thomas Rhea. Successful state politicians rewarded their supporters with jobs in the Kentucky Highway Department and with the Parks. Cheating was still a part of the political culture, as the Edward Prichard ballot-stuffing incident in Bourbon County just after the war so graphically revealed.[20]

Changes of degree, though not kind, did occur. The Democratic party reached its nadir in 1944, then bounced back in short order. By 1948, the Democrats were as strong as ever, and they became even more powerful after that. Whereas the Kentucky Republican party won almost half the gubernatorial contests from 1895 to 1927, the effects of the Great Depression, the New Deal, and World War II set the GOP back. Every Kentucky governor from 1947 to 1967 came from the Democratic party. Black Kentuckians had begun their shift from the Republican party to the Democratic party during the New Deal, and in the postwar period moved squarely into the Democratic column. Whereas Charles Anderson was a Republican, Mae Street Kidd, Georgia Davis Powers, and Gerald A. Neal aligned themselves with the Democrats. The fundamentals of Kentucky politics came through World War II intact; even the movement of Kentucky African Americans to the Democratic party started before the conflict, continued with it, and accelerated thereafter.[21]

Public and private organizations played a larger role in the lives of Kentuckians after the war. Given the demise of the Great Depression and the eventual triumph over America's enemies in the war, the government in Washington, DC, gained great credibility. Federal provision of agricultural subsidies, labor protections, and welfare helped Kentuckians tremendously. Under these circumstances, Kentuckians gradually relinquished their attachment to local control in favor of big government. Meanwhile, private organizations such as Ford Motor Company, DuPont, Goodyear, the United Automobile Workers, the United Mine Workers, and many others affected the daily existence of many Kentuckians. Company and union decisions determined whether a person had a job or not and whether or not he or she could purchase essential goods. The interaction between the federal government, big business, organized labor, the farm block, consumers, and other special interests—whether competitive or collaborative in nature—assumed greater significance over time, while rugged individualism seemed almost anachronistic. Bureaucracies of all types expanded, and concepts such as order, rationality, expertise, and efficiency meant more by 1945 than they did in 1939—and mean much more today than they did then.[22]

A growing number of Kentuckians embraced internationalism as a result of Axis aggression and World War II. After all, the brand of isolationism the U.S. government pursued in the 1920s and 1930s had failed miserably: America was "rewarded" for that policy when bombs rained down on Pearl Harbor. There seemed little choice but to take up a more proactive stance when it came to dealing with world problems likely to have national security implications for the United States. Internationalism, even interventionism, became the order of the day.

National leaders made it clear that the United States intended to involve itself in a continuous, sustained fashion with other nations, and Kentuckians followed along. In a speech on March 12, 1947, President Harry Truman said the United States must be "willing to help free people to maintain their free institutions and their national integrity against aggressive movements that seek to impose upon them totalitarian regimes." An implicit reference to the communist Soviet Union, Truman put the world's other superpower on notice that its expansionist tendencies were unacceptable and that America would take steps to stop them. Truman's foreign policy adviser, Dean Acheson, later Secretary of State, noted that the United States was prepared to shoulder "a novel burden far from our shores." The *Hardin County Enterprise,* a Kentucky newspaper, editorialized that the United States must abandon "isolation and exhibit a willingness to cooperate in the development of the resources of mankind." The *Enterprise* noted that contacts with the outside world, whether they be trade-oriented or otherwise, required a strong military. Peace and prosperity could not be "sustained by resolutions, impotent treaties and well-wishes." Kentucky's political luminaries, such as Democrat Alben Barkley and Republican John Sherman Cooper, espoused internationalism, whether they sat on the National Security Council, dealt with the United Nations, or negotiated with foreign leaders. Many Kentuckians believed that the mistakes of the interwar period should never be repeated and that the Cold War was worth fighting.[23]

Entertainment remained an important feature in Kentuckians' lives after the war. University of Kentucky basketball coach Adolph Rupp reaped the benefits of his hard work during the conflict, directing his Wildcats to national championships in 1948, 1949, and 1951. Returning World War II veterans, including Alex Groza, led Kentucky to the top of the basketball world. By contrast, as described earlier, the football Wildcats struggled to win games in the Southeastern Conference throughout the war years. Fate intervened in 1946, bringing the football team a new coach named Paul Bryant. Under "Bear" Bryant's leadership, Kentucky engineered a quick turnaround and fielded the best teams in the history of the school. In 1950, his Kentucky squad won the SEC football title. The Blue and White then secured a victory over number-one ranked Oklahoma in the Sugar Bowl. After Bryant left UK for Texas A&M, the football program declined, and it has never scaled those heights again. Rosemary Clooney, who began her singing career late in the war, reached true stardom after it. Clooney gained celebrity in 1951 when she performed "Come On-a My House," which became the first of her many singles to hit the charts. She also sang with Bing Crosby in the 1954 movie *White Christmas.* Assault and Citation, Triple Crown winners of 1946 and 1948 respectively, proved worthy successors to Whirlaway and Count Fleet. Athletics, music, horse racing, and movies thrilled Kentucky audiences as much or more in the postwar period as they did during the war.[24]

World War II was a seminal event in Kentucky history. The conflict left Kentucky's economy much better off than before while it challenged

Kentucky society to extend a greater measure of equity to the working class, women, and blacks. Kentuckians wanted more from their politicians during the war and after it, but were too often disappointed; the state's political system has proved resistant to reform. Organizational-institutional complexity increased as the middle of the twentieth century made way to its end. For a dwindling number of men and women, now old, memories of the battles of yesteryear still evoke nostalgia and, in a smaller number, real pain. Yet even the greatest, most momentous events dim with the passage of time, and World War II is no exception. While its influence is still noticeable, Kentucky has moved on, and the impact of the war is less now than it once was. The Kentucky landscape shifted in a fundamental way during the 1980s and 1990s with the coming of the Reagan Revolution, victory in the Cold War, the establishment of free trade, and increasing competition from low-wage nations in Latin America and the Far East. As Kentucky forges further ahead in the early twenty-first century, the Bluegrass State finds itself confronting a notably different set of parameters, imperatives, challenges, and opportunities from those that prevailed during World War II.

Acknowledgments

Producing this book has been a long and arduous undertaking, though worthwhile in the end. Many people helped out along the way, and I am indebted to them.

Lois Puffer has done more work on this book than anyone except for me. Lois served as a sounding board, and typed the manuscript which went to the University Press of Kentucky. Her willingness to do whatever work was needed and her constant encouragement have been greatly appreciated.

Keith Harper is a wonderful friend and an excellent historian. Having blamed Keith for any remaining faults in a previous monograph, I hereby announce that he read this one and gave me a host of valuable suggestions. This time, Keith, any errors of commission or omission that may linger in the text are my responsibility alone. The Lees College campus of Hazard Community and Technical College remains a wonderful place to work. My bosses are friends. My colleagues go the extra mile. There are always good students around, and I have the freedom to teach what I want. Don Barnes, Amanda Spencer-Barnes, Cathy Branson, Leila Smith, Kathy Smoot, and Tom Neace deserve special recognition.

The folks at the University Press of Kentucky have been quite helpful. Ashley Runyon, my acquisitions editor, kept me well informed about the progress of my manuscript toward publication and answered questions of many types. Two anonymous readers for UPK critiqued the entire manuscript, providing input that enhanced the quality of the prose and analysis. Donna Bouvier read and copyedited the entire manuscript; I could not have asked for anyone better. Kudos to all of them.

Along the way, I interviewed approximately thirty people who contributed their knowledge and thoughts about World War II Kentucky. Most lived through the conflict. All of them shared their insights with me in a manner that was both gracious and constructive. Sadly, at least ten of the thirty have passed away between the time I interviewed them and now. I only wish that those men and women had lived long enough to read the book they helped shape.

My family deserves mention here, too—really most of all. Mom continues to offer love and guidance to her eldest son. Dad passed away during the writing of this book, and I miss him. My eight-year-old daughter, Haylie, makes me laugh more than anybody else. Last, but most of all, I want to thank my wife, Jody, for her support, tolerance, and loyalty. The dedication to this book says it all.

Notes

Introduction

1. Lowell H. Harrison and James C. Klotter, *A New History of Kentucky* (Lexington: University Press of Kentucky, 1997), 494. Useful books about more than a half-dozen wartime states already exist. Alan Clive emphasized the economic and social developments that transported 1939 Michigan from "a world now vanished" to one "more nearly recognizable" by 1945. Clive's account of Detroit's conversion from automobile production to bomber and tank production stands out, as does his analysis of the massive adjustments forced on Michigan communities by the presence of so much war work in their vicinities. Whereas Michigan manufactured more combat equipment than any state in the Union, Wyoming fell near the bottom; yet even this amount aided the economy and people there significantly, according to T. A. Larson. Jerry Purvis Sanson's monograph on Louisiana during the conflict, while long on politics, contains a fine account of the war production empire of Andrew Jackson Higgins and insightful comments about African Americans. Higgins's operations in New Orleans cranked out landing craft, PT boats, and other useful military goods. Sanson notes that while blacks in Louisiana "experienced some measure of improvement in their social and economic condition" as a result of the war, the more important consequence was that the conflict "awakened the modern resurgence of the quest for black equality." In his account of wartime Arkansas, C. Calvin Smith is less optimistic. Smith finds that blacks in the Razorback State made little progress from 1941 to 1945 and were "forced . . . to enter the postwar era facing the same formidable obstacles they had confronted when the war began." Lisa L. Ossian's examination of the Iowa home front contains good material on farms. Iowa alone produced 20 percent of all the corn grown in the United States by 1944 and a year before led the nation in chicken and egg output. Ossian notes that food "is a weapon" and that Iowa excelled in this area. Each of these studies is valuable in its own right, and the time is past due for one on Kentucky. See Alan Clive, *State of War: Michigan in World War II* (Ann Arbor: University of Michigan Press, 1979), 242, 21–29, 90–129; T. A. Larson, *Wyoming's War Years, 1941–1945* (Laramie: University of Wyoming Press, 1954), 244–269; Jerry Purvis Sanson, *Louisiana during World War II: Politics and Society, 1939–1945* (Baton Rouge: Louisiana State University Press, 1999), 218–220, 269–270; C. Calvin Smith, *War and Wartime Changes: The Transformation of Arkansas, 1940–1945* (Fayetteville: University

of Arkansas Press, 1986), 130; Lisa L. Ossian, *The Home Fronts of Iowa, 1939–1945* (Columbia: University of Missouri Press, 2009), 21, 42–43.

2. See, for instance, *Henry County Local,* January 6, 1939, p. 1; March 10, 1939, p. 1; *Princeton Leader,* July 4, 1940, p. 4.

3. *Jackson Times,* January 5, 1939, p. 4.

4. Harrison and Klotter, *New History,* 365. See also appropriate parts of George T. Blakey, *Hard Times and New Deal in Kentucky, 1929–1939* (Lexington: University Press of Kentucky, 1986).

5. James C. Klotter, *Kentucky: Portrait in Paradox, 1900–1950* (Frankfort: Kentucky Historical Society, 1996), 307–315; Tracy Campbell, *Short of the Glory: The Fall and Redemption of Edward F. Prichard Jr.* (Lexington: University Press of Kentucky, 1998), 9–19.

6. Klotter, *Kentucky: Portrait in Paradox,* 105–109.

7. John E. Kleber, ed., *The Kentucky Encyclopedia* (Lexington: University Press of Kentucky, 1992), 5; George C. Wright, *A History of Blacks in Kentucky, Vol. 2: In Pursuit of Equality, 1890–1980* (Frankfort: Kentucky Historical Society, 1992), 42–45, 149–151.

8. Klotter, *Kentucky: Portrait in Paradox,* 255; *Park City Daily News,* February 8, 1939, p. 4.

9. John Keegan, *The Second World War* (New York: Penguin Books, 1990), 44; *Jackson Times,* September 7, 1939, p. 2.

10. Richard E. Holl, *From the Boardroom to the War Room: America's Corporate Liberals and FDR's Preparedness Program* (Rochester, NY: University of Rochester Press, 2005), 82–85.

11. George C. Herring, *From Colony to Superpower: U.S. Foreign Relations since 1776* (New York: Oxford University Press, 2008), 534–536.

12. Norman Polmar and Thomas B. Allen, *World War II: America at War, 1941–1945* (New York: Random House, 1991), 465, 863; Keegan, *Second World War,* 255; Herring, *From Colony to Superpower,* 535.

13. *Jackson Times,* December 11, 1941, p. 2; Lizzie B. Watts interview, Jackson, KY, January 29, 1999; *Hodgenville (Ky.) Herald News,* December 11, 1941, p. 2.

14. For a comparison of war goods produced by the states, see *County Data Book, A Supplement to the Statistical Abstract of the United States,* U.S. Department of Commerce and U.S. Bureau of the Census (Washington, DC: U.S. Government Printing Office, 1947), 7.

15. Ibid.; Charles F. Schwartz and Robert E. Graham Jr., *Personal Income by States since 1929* (Washington, DC: Department of Commerce, 1956), 34, 38.

1. Kentucky War Plants and Weapons

1. *Jackson Times,* March 30, 1939, p. 2; *Richmond Daily Register,* March 18, 1939, p. 2; *Madisonville Messenger,* September 12, 1939, p. 4.

2. *Madisonville Messenger,* September 12, 1939, p. 4; *Richmond Daily Register,* November 1, 1939, p. 2.

3. Richard E. Holl, *From the Boardroom to the War Room: America's Corporate Liberals and FDR's Preparedness Program* (Rochester, NY: University of Rochester Press, 2005), 60–65.

4. Ibid., 78–79.

5. Ibid., 78; Richard Polenberg, *War and Society: The United States, 1941–1945* (New York: J. B. Lippincott Co., 1972), 6–7.

6. Holl, *From the Boardroom to the War Room,* 80–81; Paul A. C. Koistinen, *The Military-Industrial Complex: A Historical Perspective* (New York: Praeger, 1980), 88–91; John W. Jeffries, *Wartime America: The World War II Home Front* (Chicago: Ivan R. Dee, 1986), 19–23.

7. *Courier-Journal,* September 3, 1939, p. 4.

8. Ibid.; William Elsey Connelley and E. M. Coulter, *History of Kentucky,* vol. 4 (Chicago: American Historical Society, 1922), 102; John E. Kleber, ed., *The Kentucky Encyclopedia* (Lexington: University Press of Kentucky, 1992), 487.

9. *Courier-Journal,* October 1, 1939, Section 1, p. 6; September 17, 1939, Section 4, p. 3; September 16, 1939, Section 2, p. 6; September 26, 1939, Section 2, p. 6; September 18, 1939, p. 1.

10. Maury Klein, *History of the Louisville & Nashville Railroad* (Lexington: University Press of Kentucky, 2003), 455–456; Kincaid A. Herr, *The Louisville & Nashville Railroad, 1850–1963* (Lexington: University Press of Kentucky, 2000), 274–277; http://Kgs.uky.edu/kgsweb/DataSearching/Coal/Production/prodresults.asp?arentype;all.prod&placeAmt=multiple&country-list=total&year-county=year&yearlmt=between&year2=1935&year3=1950; *Courier-Journal,* September 9, 1939, Section 1, p. 3; *Ashland Daily Independent,* ARMCO Expansion Edition, March 11, 1941, pp. 1, 2.

11. James C. Klotter, *Kentucky: Portrait in Paradox, 1900–1950* (Frankfort: Kentucky Historical Society, 1996), p. 259; John E. Kleber ed., *The Encyclopedia of Louisville* (Lexington: University Press of Kentucky, 2001), 311, 955; Paul A. Tenkotte and James C. Claypool, eds., *The Encyclopedia of Northern Kentucky* (Lexington: University Press of Kentucky, 2009), 363.

12. Holl, *From the Boardroom to the War Room,* 82–83.

13. Ibid., 84–85, 89, 118–119.

14. James W. Fesler et al., *Industrial Mobilization for War: History of the War Production Board and Predecessor Agencies, 1940–1945* (Washington, DC: U.S. Government Printing Office, 1947), 24, 161; Paul A. C. Koistinen, *Arsenal of World War II: The Political Economy of American Warfare, 1940–1945* (Lawrence: University Press of Kansas, 2004), 20–21, 27.

15. *Courier-Journal,* June 5, 1940, Section 2, p. 1; July 2, 1940, p. 5; August 11, 1940, Section 3, p. 1.

16. Ibid., June 2, 1940, Section 3, p. 2; Kleber, *Encyclopedia of Louisville,* 954.

17. *Courier-Journal*, July 28, 1940; George H. Yater, *Two Hundred Years at the Falls of the Ohio: A History of Louisville and Jefferson County* (Louisville: Heritage Corp., 1979), 206.

18. "The DuPont Company's Part in the National Security Program, 1940–1945," 51, Hagley Museum and Library, Wilmington, DE; *Courier-Journal*, June 7, 1940, p. 1; Koistinen, *Arsenal of World War II*, 49.

19. See http://www.abandonedonline.net/2009/08/18/indiana-army-ammunition-plant-and-world-war-ii/.

20. *Courier-Journal*, August 1, 1941, p. 14; April 2, 1941, p. 2; January 5, 1941, p. 3.

21. Ibid., January 5, 1941, p. 3.

22. "The DuPont Company's Part in the National Security Program, 1949–1945," 51; http://www.abandonedonline.net/2009/08/18/indiana-army-ammunition-plant-and-world-war-ii/.

23. *Courier-Journal*, November 30, 1940, p. 4; January 4, 1941, Section 3, p. 8.

24. Ibid., November 30, 1940, p. 4; March 6, 1941, p. 1; Kleber, *Encyclopedia of Louisville*, 648; Yater, *Two Hundred Years at the Falls of the Ohio*, 207.

25. Kleber, *Encyclopedia of Louisville*, 64, 955; *Courier-Journal*, March 6, 1941, p. 1; January 5, 1941, Section 3, p. 8; May 4, 1942, Section 3, p. 8; September 10, 1942, Section 2, p. 1; Norman Polmar and Thomas Allen, *World War II: America at War, 1941–1945* (New York: Random House, 1991), 182–183.

26. *Henderson County Gleaner*, March 19, 1941, pp. 1, 8; *Courier-Journal*, Magazine, September 18, 1949, pp. 40, 43; *Henderson Morning Gleaner*, June 18, 1955.

27. *Paducah Sun-Democrat*, April 22, 1942, p. 1; *Mayfield Messenger*, May 4, 1942, p. 1; September 24, 1942, p. 1; November 3, 1942, p. 1; Studs Terkel, *"The Good War": An Oral History of World War II* (New York: Pantheon Books, 1984), 108–109.

28. *Courier-Journal*, January 26, 1941, p. 3; February 2, 1941, Section 3, p. 9.

29. Frederic D. Ogden, ed., *The Public Papers of Governor Keen Johnson, 1939–1943* (Lexington: University Press of Kentucky, 1982), 274–275.

30. *McCracken County, Kentucky, History* (New York: Turner Publishing Co., 1989), 26; *Paducah Sun-Democrat*, March 4, 1942, p. 1; www.specproenv.com/KOW/FINAL%20SIGNED%20DECISION%20DOCUMENT.pdf.

31. I. C. B. Dear and M. R. D. Foot, eds., *The Oxford Companion to World War II* (New York: Oxford University Press, 2001), 269.

32. David M. Kennedy, *Freedom from Fear: The American People in Depression and War, 1929–1945* (New York: Oxford University Press, 1999), 468–469; Irwin Unger, *These United States: The Questions of Our Past*, combined concise ed. (Upper Saddle River, NJ: Prentice Hall, 1999), 647.

33. Koistinen, *Arsenal of World War II*, 189; Holl, *From the Boardroom to the War Room*, 103–104.

34. Holl, *From the Boardroom to the War Room*, 112–114, 118, 121; Wayne S. Cole, *An Interpretive History of American Foreign Relations*, rev. ed. (Homewood, IL: Dorsey Press, 1974), 368; Koistinen, *Arsenal of World War II*, 189.

35. *New York Times,* December 9, 1941, pp. 1, 6.

36. Holl, *From the Boardroom to the War Room,* 131.

37. Koistinen, *Arsenal of World War II,* 500, 503–504.

38. *Courier-Journal,* February 23, 1941, Section 3, p. 9.

39. Ibid., March 16, 1941, Section 3, p. 10; *Ashland Daily Independent,* ARMCO Expansion Edition, March 11, 1941, pp. 1–2.

40. Jeffries, *Wartime America,* 54–55.

41. Kleber, *Encyclopedia of Louisville,* 955.

42. Ibid.; "The DuPont Company's Part in the National Security Program, 1940–1945," 41; Yater, *Two Hundred Years at the Falls of the Ohio,* 207–208.

43. "The DuPont Company's Part in the National Security Program 1940–1945," 41.

44. Ibid., 41–42.

45. Kleber, *Encyclopedia of Louisville,* 955; Frank A. Howard, *Buna Rubber: The Birth of an Industry* (New York: D. Van Nostrand Co., 1947), 246; Polenberg, *War and Society,* 14–18.

46. Kleber, *Encyclopedia of Louisville,* 955; Jeffries, *Wartime America,* 55; Lowell H. Harrison and James C. Klotter, *A New History of Kentucky* (Lexington: University Press of Kentucky, 1997), 371.

47. *Courier-Journal,* August 28, 1942, Section 2, p. 1.

48. Jerry Purvis Sanson, *Louisiana during World War II: Politics and Society, 1939–1945* (Baton Rouge: Louisiana State University Press, 1999), 247; *Courier-Journal,* July 29, 1941, p. 3; July 13, 1941, p. 2; July 13, 1941, Section 3, p. 8; James D. Cockrum, "Owensboro Goes to War," *Daviess County Historical Quarterly* 2, no. 1 (January 1984): 5; Thomas D. Clark, *Clark County, Kentucky: A History* (Winchester, KY: Clark County Heritage Commission and the Clark County Historical Society, 1995), 339–340.

49. *Courier-Journal,* June 25, 1942, p. 13; August 16, 1942, Section 1, p. 10; July 30, 1942, p. 12.

50. Ogden, *Public Papers of Governor Keen Johnson,* 347–350; *Mayfield Messenger,* October 24, 1942, p. 1; *Courier-Journal,* September 18, 1942, Section 1, p. 10; February 1, 1942, Section 3, p. 8; October 22, 1942, Section 2, p. 1; November 1, 1942, Section 1, p. 14; November 5, 1942, Section 1, p. 4.

51. Ogden, *Public Papers of Governor Keen Johnson,* 353–355; Adron and Mignon Doran interview, Lexington, KY, July 20, 1999; *Courier-Journal,* February 28, 1942, Section 2, p. 5.

52. *Courier-Journal,* June 14, 1942, p. 6; August 16, 1942, Section 1, p. 10; *Ashland Daily Independent,* August 23, 1943, Section 4, p. 9.

53. Jeffries, *Wartime America,* 29–39; Ogden, *Public Papers of Governor Keen Johnson,* 336–337; *Courier-Journal,* August 16, 1942, Sunday Magazine, p. 18; February 27, 1942, Section 3, p. 5; September 27, 1942, Section 1, p. 13.

54. Hoffman quoted in *Kentucky at War* (video), Kentucky Educational Television (KET); Kleber, *Kentucky Encyclopedia,* 157.

55. Kleber, *Kentucky Encyclopedia,* 343; http://www.campbell.army.mil/campbell/Pages/History.aspx.

56. http://kynghistory,ky.gov/places/blugrassstn.htm; John D. Wright Jr., *Lexington: Heart of the Bluegrass* (Lexington: Lexington–Fayette County Historic Commission, 1982), 189.

57. William E. Ellis, H. E. Everman, and Richard D. Sears, *Madison County: 200 Years in Retrospect* (Richmond, KY: Madison County Historical Society, 1985), 329–332; http://www.globalsecurity.org/wmd/facility/blue_grass.htm.

58. *Nation's Business,* January 1942, 30.

59. Hillerich quoted in *Kentucky at War* (video; *Courier-Journal,* January 1, 1942, Section 2, p. 5.

60. Kennedy, *Freedom from Fear,* 622; *Kentucky at War* (video).

61. Kleber, *Encyclopedia of Louisville,* 309; Harry C. Thomson and Lida Mayo, *The Ordnance Department: Procurement and Supply* (Washington, DC: Office of the Chief of Military History, Department of the Army, 1960), 276–279; Mary Jean Kinsman, "The Kentucky Home Front: World War II," *Filson Club History Quarterly* 68, no. 3 (July 1994): 375; Polmar and Allen, *World War II,* 442.

62. Kleber, *Encyclopedia of Louisville,* 381, 388; *Kentucky at War* (video); *Courier-Journal,* February 14, 1942, Section 2, p. 5; February 24, 1943, Section 1, p. 11; December 2, 1942, Section 1, p. 4; April 30, 1941, p. 8.

63. Aaron D. Purcell, "Bourbon to Bullets: Louisville's Distilling Industry during World War II, 1941–1945," *Register of the Kentucky Historical Society* 96, no. 1 (Winter 1998): 61–62, 66–67.

64. Ibid., 78–87.

65. Ibid., 73–75.

66. Carl E. Kramer, *Capital on the Kentucky: A Two-Hundred-Year History of Frankfort and Franklin County* (Frankfort, KY: Historic Frankfort, 1986), 348.

67. J. D. Wright, *Lexington,* 191; *Mt. Sterling Advocate,* January 11, 1945, p. 1.

68. Tenkotte and Claypool, *Encyclopedia of Northern Kentucky,* 922–923, 977–978; *Kentucky Business* (March 1950).

69. See www.monarchcoin.com/about-us; www.projo.com/home/content/kovels06-01-06-08-548FEDF_v19.46c966.html; Tankotte and Claypool, *Encyclopedia of Northern Kentucky,* 28, 663, 977–978.

70. Cockrum, "Owensboro Goes to War," 6; *Courier-Journal,* January 21, 1943, Section 2, p. 1; September 30, 1941, Section 2, p. 1; *Paducah Sun-Democrat,* March 2, 1942, p. 1; June 6, 1943, p. 1.

71. Otto J. Scott, *The Exception: The Story of Ashland Oil & Refining Company* (New York: McGraw-Hill, 1968), 174–175, 179, 193; *Courier-Journal,* October 19, 1941, Sunday Magazine.

72. *Courier-Journal,* February 23, 1941, Sunday Picture Magazine; July 28, 1940; March 16, 1941, Sunday Magazine; December 19, 1940, Section 2, p. 1; October 14, 1941, Section 2, p. 1; February 14, 1942, p. 8; Alan Clive, *State of*

War: Michigan in World War II (Ann Arbor: University of Michigan Press, 1979), 90–129.

73. *Courier-Journal*, February 14, 1942, p. 8; January 1, 1942, Section 2, p. 1; Jeffries, *Wartime America*, 85–86.

74. *Courier-Journal*, October 14, 1941, Section 2, p. 1.

75. Ibid., March 22, 1942, Section 3, p. 8.

76. Clark, *Clark County, Kentucky*, 340.

77. *Courier-Journal*, October 14, 1941, Section 2, p. 1; January 11, 1944, p. 5.

78. Jeffries, *Wartime America*, 101; Polmar and Allen, *World War II*, 844.

79. *Courier-Journal*, May 16, 1941, p. 4; February 1, 1942, p. 6; *Paducah Sun-Democrat*, July 25, 1943, pp. 1, 17; e-mail from historian Nancy Baird to author, June 9, 2011.

80. See www.osha.gov/SLTC/butadiene/index.html#healtheffects; www.epa.gov/ttnatw01/hlthef/butadien.html; E. Delzell, N. Sathia Kumar, M. Hovinga, et al., "A Follow-Up Study of Synthetic Rubber Workers," *Toxicology* 113 (1996): 182–189; *Chicago Tribune*, January 21, 1990; *USA Today*, December 8, 2008; Philip Shabecoff and Alice Shabecoff, *Poisoned for Profit: How Toxins Are Making Our Children Chronically Ill* (White River Junction, VT: Chelsea Green Publishing, 2010), 23.

81. Blue Grass Army Depot (BGAD), Army Defense Environmental Restoration Program, Installation Action Plan, FY 2008, December 2, 2008, pp. 5 and 20, BGA, Environmental Division, 431 Battlefield Memorial Highway, Building S-14, Richmond, KY; *Courier-Journal*, June 26, 2000, p. A5.

82. Terry quoted in Terkel, *"The Good War,"* 108–109.

83. *Courier-Journal*, November 21, 1941, Section 2, p. 4; February 1, 1942, Section 2, p. 9; *Paducah Sun-Democrat*, January 7, 1944, p. 7; *Mt. Sterling Advocate*, January 4, 1945, p. 2; *County Data Book: A Supplement to the Statistical Abstract of the United States* (Washington, DC: U.S. Department of Commerce and U.S. Bureau of the Census, U.S. Government Printing Office, 1947), 7; Klotter, *Kentucky: Portrait in Paradox*, 259–260.

84. Kinsman, "The Kentucky Home Front," 375; Thomson and Mayo, *The Ordnance Department*, 296; Purcell, "Bourbon to Bullets," 85; *Kentucky at War* (video); Kleber, *Encyclopedia of Louisville*, 955; http://kgs.uky.edu/kgsweb/DataSearching/Coal/Production/prodresults.asp?areatype=all_prod&placeAmt=multiple&county_list=total&year_county=year&yearlmt=between&year2=1935&year3=1950; *Courier-Journal*, March 16, 1941, Section 3, p. 10; "The DuPont Company's Part in the National Security Program, 1940–1945," 51; *County Data Book*, 7.

2. Ralph, Rosie, and Labor-Management Relations

1. David M. Kennedy, *Freedom from Fear: The American People in Depression and War, 1929–1945* (New York: Oxford University Press, 1999), 252; *Courier-Journal*, August 4, 1942, p. 3.

2. *Courier-Journal,* August 4, 1942, p. 3.

3. Ibid., June 25, 1941, Section 2, p. 2.

4. Paul A. C. Koistinen, *Arsenal of World War II: The Political Economy of American Warfare, 1940–1945* (Lawrence: University Press of Kansas, 2004), 372–373, 382–383; *Jackson Times,* July 16, 1942, p. 4; *Courier-Journal,* January 1, 1943, Section 2, pp. 3–4.

5. John Morton Blum, *V Was for Victory: Politics and American Culture during World War II* (New York: Harcourt Brace Jovanovich, 1976), 91; *Courier-Journal,* January 2, 1944, p. 10.

6. U.S. Census of 1940, Population, Volume 2: Characteristics of the Population, Part 3, Kentucky (Washington, DC: U.S. Government Printing Office, 1942), 198.

7. Ibid., 198–199.

8. John W. McTighe, *The Barefoot Boy on the Parkway: A History of UAW Local 862* (Louisville: UAW Local 862, 1988), 57–58, 66.

9. Mary Jean Kinsman, "The Kentucky Home Front: World War II," *Filson Club History Quarterly* 68, no. 3 (July 1994): 375.

10. McTighe, *Barefoot Boy,* 57–59.

11. Edward Burns interview, Georgetown, IN, July 31, 2011.

12. Ibid.

13. Ibid.

14. Norman Polmar and Thomas B. Allen, *World War II: America at War, 1941–1945* (New York: Random House, 1991), 126–127.

15. Patricia Porter Newton interview, Louisville, KY, August 1, 2011; James W. Settle memoir, "The Beanery," 120–130, University Archives and Records Center, University of Louisville; *L&N Employes' Magazine,* April 1943: 38; January 1945: 6, 32, University Archives and Records Center, University of Louisville.

16. Burns interview, July 31, 2011.

17. U.S. Census of 1940, Vol. 2, Part 3, pp. 174, 199; Richard Polenberg, *War and Society: The United States, 1941–1945* (New York: J. B. Lippincott Co., 1972), 113–116.

18. U.S. Census of 1940, Vol. 2, Part 3, p. 199; Blum, *V Was for Victory,* 183–184, 189.

19. *Courier-Journal,* October 20, 1970, p. B3; J. Harvey Kerns, *A Survey of the Economic and Cultural Condition of the Negro Population of Louisville, Kentucky, and a Review of the Programs and Activities of the Louisville Urban League* (New York: National Urban League, 1948), 31; Burns interview, July 31, 2011; Thomas E. Wagner and Phillip J. Obermiller, *African American Miners and Migrants: The Eastern Kentucky Social Club* (Urbana: University of Illinois Press, 2004), 76–77; *L&N Employes' Magazine,* February 1945: 8–9.

20. *Kentucky at War* (video), Kentucky Educational Television (KET).

21. U.S. Census of 1940, Vol. 2, Part 3, p. 198.

22. John W. Jeffries, *Wartime America: The World War II Home Front* (Chicago: Ivan R. Dee, 1996), 94.

23. Emily Yellin, *Our Mothers' War: American Women at Home and at the Front during World War II* (New York: Free Press, 2004), 43–44.

24. *New York Times*, June 2, 1997; *Lexington Herald-Leader*, March 31, 2007, Section B, pp. 1, 5; American National Biography online, http://www.anb.org/articles/20/20-01920-article.html.

25. *Kentucky at War* (video); Brenda Baker interview, Louisville, KY, August 11, 2011.

26. *Kentucky at War* (video); Baker interview, August 11, 2011.

27. James Russell Harris, ed., "Rolling Bandages and Building Thunderbolts: A Woman's Memories of the Kentucky Home Front, 1941–1945," *Register of the Kentucky Historical Society* 100, no. 2 (Spring 2002): 168–169, 178–180.

28. Ibid., 180–181.

29. *Courier-Journal*, September 18, 1942, Section 2, p. 7; Studs Terkel, *"The Good War": An Oral History of World War II* (New York: Pantheon Books, 1984), 108–109; Burns interview, July 13, 2011.

30. Teresa Cecilia Sharkey, "The Home Front: The Women of Lexington, Kentucky, during World War II," *Filson Club Historical Quarterly* 68, no. 4 (October 1994): 474–476; *Kentucky at War* (video); *Courier-Journal*, May 3, 1942, Section 2, p. 8; Newton interview, August 1, 2011.

31. U.S. Census of 1940, Vol. 2, Part 3, p. 199.

32. Shirley Mae Harmon, "A Comparison Study of Black and White Women War Workers in Louisville, Kentucky during World War II," MA thesis, University of Louisville, 1999, p. 18.

33. Margaret Peyton Lutes Hayden interview, July 22, 1998, p. 34, World War II Working Women, University Archives and Records Center (UARC), University of Louisville (UL).

34. Nova Hays Downs Rhodes interview, June 30, 1998, pp. 2, 7–8, 17, World War II Working Women, UARC, UL.

35. Everylee Ashby interview, November 24, 1998, pp. 7–8, 24, 35, World War II Working Women, UARC, UL; Harmon, "Comparison Study," 21, 58; Elizabeth Lawson interview, Lexington, KY, March 20, 1999.

36. U.S. Census of 1940, Vol. 2, Part 3, pp. 198–199; U.S. Census of 1950, Vol. 2, Part 17, pp. 36, 38.

37. William H. Chafe, *The American Woman: Her Changing Social, Economic, and Political Roles, 1920–1970* (New York: Oxford University Press, 1972), 158; Sharkey, "Home Front," 474–475; Newton interview, August 1, 2011; Harris, "Rolling Bandages," 181; Rhodes interview, pp. 9–10; Alan Clive, *State of War: Michigan in World War II* (Ann Arbor: University of Michigan Press, 1979), 200.

38. John H. Ohly, *Industrialists in Olive Drab: The Emergency Operation of Private Industries during World War II* (Washington, DC: Center of Military History,

United States Army, 2000), 149–150; McTighe, *Barefoot Boy*, 50–51; *Kentucky Post*, August 20, 1942, p. 1; *Courier-Journal*, August 16, 1942, Section 1, p. 10; Carol Crowe-Carraco, *The Big Sandy* (Lexington: University Press of Kentucky, 1979), 109.

39. Melvyn Dubofsky and Foster Rhea Dulles, *Labor in America: A History*, 8th ed. (Wheeling, IL: Harlan Davidson, 2010), pp. 305, 315; Jeffries, *Wartime America*, 23–24, 56; Kennedy, *Freedom from Fear*, 641–642.

40. *Courier-Journal*, January 1, 1943, Section 2, p. 3; John E. Kleber, ed., *The Encyclopedia of Louisville* (Lexington: University Press of Kentucky, 2001), 495; "The Du Pont Company's Part in the National Security Program, 1940–1945," p. 21, Hagley Museum and Library, Wilmington, DE.

41. Frederic Ogden, ed., *The Public Papers of Governor Keen Johnson, 1939–1943* (Lexington: University Press of Kentucky, 1982), 358.

42. *Courier-Journal*, October 28, 1941, Section 2, p. 1; August 4, 1942, p. 3; Ogden, *Public Papers of Governor Keen Johnson*, 341–342; *Kentucky Post*, August 20, 1942, p. 1; William E. Ellis, H. E. Everman, and Richard D. Sears, *Madison County: 200 Years in Retrospect* (Richmond, KY: Madison County Historical Society, 1985), 332.

43. Ohly, *Industrialists in Olive Drab*, 149–150; John E. Kleber, ed., *The Kentucky Encyclopedia* (Lexington: University Press of Kentucky, 1992), 487.

44. Ohly, *Industrialists in Olive Drab*, 150, 153–154.

45. Ibid., 155–158.

46. Ibid., 163–165.

47. *The New Encyclopaedia Britannica*, Vol. 7, Micropaedia, Ready Reference (Chicago: Encyclopaedia Britannica, 2005), 313.

48. Robert H. Zieger, *John L. Lewis: Labor Leader* (Boston: Twayne Publishers, 1998), 132–137; Dubofsky and Dulles, *Labor in America*, 309.

49. Kennedy, *Freedom from Fear*, 640–643.

50. Crowe-Carraco, *The Big Sandy*, 108–109; Ogden, *Public Papers of Governor Keen Johnson*, 361; Kennedy, *Freedom from Fear*, 643.

51. Melvyn Dubofsky and Warren Van Tine, *John L. Lewis: A Biography* (New York: Quadrangle, 1977), 427–428; Ogden, *Public Papers of Governor Keen Johnson*, 359–361.

52. *Courier-Journal*, November 5, 1943, p. 6; *Paducah Sun-Democrat*, November 7, 1943, p. 4; *Lexington Leader*, November 8, 1943, p. 4; *Harlan Daily Enterprise*, December 15, 1943, p. 4; Zieger, *John L. Lewis*, 145; Dubofsky and Dulles, *Labor in America*, 310.

53. Zieger, *John L. Lewis*, 142–143; Kennedy, *Freedom from Fear*, 643; *Paducah Sun-Democrat*, November 7, 1943, p. 4.

54. Kennedy, *Freedom from Fear*, 643–644; Crowe-Carraco, *The Big Sandy*, 109; *Whitesburg Mountain Eagle*, June 19, 1969, p. 2; Jeffries, *Wartime America*, 25–26; Dubofsky and Dulles, *Labor in America*, 311–312.

55. Zieger, *John L. Lewis*, 148, 163–164; Nelson Lichtenstein, *State of the Union: A Century of American Labor* (Princeton, NJ: Princeton University Press, 2002), 114–125.

56. Dubofsky and Dulles, *Labor in America*, 318–319, 331–332; Richard E. Holl, *From the Boardroom to the War Room: America's Corporate Liberals and FDR's Preparedness Program* (Rochester, NY: University of Rochester Press, 2005), 135–136; Felix Gilbert, *The End of the European Era, 1890 to the Present*, 4th ed. (New York: W. W. Norton & Co., 1991), 438–440.

3. Food for Freedom

1. Lowell H. Harrison and James C. Klotter, *A New History of Kentucky* (Lexington: University Press of Kentucky, 1997), 295; James C. Klotter, *Kentucky: Portrait in Paradox, 1900–1950* (Frankfort: Kentucky Historical Society, 1996), 246.

2. Harrison and Klotter, *New History*, 297; Klotter, *Kentucky: Portrait in Paradox*, 250; *Courier-Journal*, December 8, 1940, Section 3, p. 1.

3. Gilbert C. Fite, *American Agriculture and Farm Policy since 1900* (New York: Macmillan Co. for Service Center for Teachers of History, 1964), 21.

4. Paul A. C. Koistinen, *Arsenal of World War II: The Political Economy of American Warfare, 1940–1945* (Lawrence: University Press of Kansas, 2004), 247–248.

5. Richard E. Holl, *From the Boardroom to the War Room: America's Corporate Liberals and FDR's Preparedness Program* (Rochester, NY: University of Rochester Press, 2005), 83–86.

6. Warren W. Wilcox, *The Farmer in the Second World War* (Ames: Iowa State College Press, 1947), 36–37.

7. *Courier-Journal*, February 23, 1941, Section 3, p. 9; November 13, 1941, Section 2, p. 1; Holl, *From the Boardroom to the War Room*, 118.

8. *Courier-Journal*, November 13, 1941, Section 2, p. 1; John Keegan, *The Second World War* (New York: Penguin Books, 1989), 218.

9. Wilcox, *The Farmer in the Second World War*, 36–41.

10. Ibid., 164–166; Koistinen, *Arsenal of World War II*, 248–249.

11. *Courier-Journal*, October 19, 1941, Section 3, p. 10.

12. Wilcox, *The Farmer in the Second World War*, 4; *Lexington Herald-Leader*, February 28, 1999, Special Section on the Millennium, p. 13.

13. David M. Kennedy, *Freedom from Fear: The American People in Depression and War, 1929–1945* (New York: Oxford University Press, 1999), 640–641; Wilcox, *The Farmer in the Second World War*, 33–34; U.S. Department of Agriculture, Census of Agriculture Historical Archive, 1945 Census Publications, Vol. 1, *State Reports and County Statistics with a U.S. Summary*, Parts 11, 16, 26, 27, 29, 30, 31, 32, 35, 37, 48 (Washington, DC: U.S. Government Printing Office, 1946).

14. David L. MacFarlane and Max M. Tharp, "Trends in Kentucky Agricul-

ture, 1929–1940," Bulletin 429 of the Kentucky Agricultural Experiment Station, University of Kentucky, Lexington (June 1942), p. 12.

15. E. R. Murphy, *A Survey of Agriculture in Muhlenberg County* (Lexington: Kentucky Utilities Co., n.d.), 27–29.

16. MacFarlane and Tharp, "Trends in Kentucky Agriculture," 10–11.

17. John A. Perkins, *A Survey of Agriculture in Boyle County* (Lexington: Kentucky Utilities Co., 1954), 15–17; W. M. Johnson Jr., *A Survey of Agriculture in Fleming County* (Lexington: Kentucky Utilities Co., 1953), 23–25.

18. MacFarlane and Tharp, "Trends in Kentucky Agriculture," 12–13.

19. E. R. Murphy, *A Survey of Agriculture in Grayson County* (Lexington: Kentucky Utilities Co., 1952), 3, 25–26.

20. MacFarlane and Tharp, "Trends in Kentucky Agriculture," p. 14.

21. Hiram A. Morgan, *A Survey of Agriculture in Fulton County* (Lexington: Kentucky Utilities Co., 1953), 3, 14, 18–19.

22. MacFarlane and Tharp, "Trends in Kentucky Agriculture," 9.

23. Woodrow McIntosh, *A Survey of Agriculture in Bell County* (Lexington: Kentucky Utilities Co., 1953), 15; McIntosh, *A Survey of Agriculture in Knox County* (Lexington: Kentucky Utilities Co., 1954), 15, 18–21.

24. U.S. Census of 1950, Census of Agriculture, Vol. 1, Part 19, Kentucky (Washington, DC: U.S. Government Printing Office, 1952), p. 6; A. L. Mehring, Hilda M. Wallace, and Mildred Drain, "Nitrogen, Phosphoric Acid, and Potash Consumption in the United States by Years and by States with Preliminary Figures for 1944," *Journal of the American Society of Agronomy* 37, no. 8 (August 1945): 604.

25. Jeffery A. Duvall, "Knowing about the Tobacco: Women, Burley, and Farming in the Central Ohio River Valley," *Register of the Kentucky Historical Society* 108, no. 4 (Autumn 2010): 318; USDA, Census of Agriculture Historical Archive, 1945 Census Publications, Vol. 1, Parts 26 and 30.

26. Harrison and Klotter, *New History*, 297–298; W. F. Axton, *Tobacco and Kentucky* (Lexington: University Press of Kentucky, 1975), 140; U.S. Census of 1950, Census of Agriculture, Vol. 1, Part 19, Kentucky, p. 15; Duvall, "Knowing about the Tobacco," 319–320.

27. Axton, *Tobacco and Kentucky*, 116; Norman Polmar and Thomas B. Allen, *World War II: America at War, 1941–1945* (New York: Random House, 1991), 679–680; Wilcox, *The Farmer in the Second World War*, 237–242. In addition, see http://www.tobacco.org/resources/history/Tobacco_History20-1.html; Franz A. Koehler, *Special Rations for the Armed Forces: Army Operational Rations; A Historical Background* (Washington, DC: QMC Historical Studies, Historical Branch, Office of the Quartermaster General, 1958); http://www.bgdailynews.com/bicentennial/ax-handles-to-hot-rods/article.

28. *Courier-Journal*, March 11, 1942, Section 1, p. 12.

29. James F. Hopkins, *A History of the Hemp Industry in Kentucky* (Lexington: University of Kentucky Press, 1951), 94; Harrison and Klotter, *New History*, 135.

30. Hopkins, *History of the Hemp Industry,* 203, 217; Erin Michelle Young, "Revival of Industrial Hemp: A Systematic Analysis of the Current Global Industry to Determine Limitations and Identify Future Potentials within the Concept of Sustainability," master's thesis, Lund University (Sweden), 2005, 5.

31. Hopkins, *History of the Hemp Industry,* 211.

32. Ibid., 212; *Courier-Journal,* April 12, 1945, Section 2, p. 9; April 21, 1942, p. 14.

33. *Courier-Journal,* April 21, 1942, p. 14; September 27, 1942, Section 3, p. 7; August 16, 1942, Section 3, p. 8.

34. *Courier-Journal,* September 27, 1942, Section 3, p. 7; Hopkins, *History of the Hemp Industry,* 212–213.

35. John van Willigen and Anne van Willigen, *Food and Everyday Life on Kentucky Farms, 1920–1950* (Lexington: University Press of Kentucky, 2006), 147; *Courier-Journal,* April 12, 1945, Section 2, p. 9; Maralea Arnett, *The Annals and Scandals of Henderson County, Kentucky, 1775–1975* (Corydon, KY: Fremar Publishing Co., 1976), 266; *Jackson Times,* December 2, 1943, p. 4; Annual Cash Receipts, 1924–2010, Kentucky, 1940–1944, Table 5 (revised) (Washington, DC: Economic Research Service, U.S. Department of Agriculture, 2001).

36. Harrison and Klotter, *New History,* 293.

37. Hopkins, *History of the Hemp Industry,* 213.

38. Murphy, *Survey of Agriculture in Muhlenberg County,* 27–28; Murphy, *Survey of Agriculture in Grayson County,* 25; Arnett, *Annals and Scandals,* 266.

39. H. W. Hochbaum, "The 1943 Victory Garden Program" (Washington, DC: U.S. Department of Agriculture and U.S. Department of Civilian Defense,1943).

40. Ibid.; "Guide for Planning the Local Victory Garden Program" (Washington, DC: Office of Civilian Defense, 1942); Polmar and Allen, *World War II,* 867.

41. Wilcox, *The Farmer in the Second World War,* 48–50; Koistinen, *Arsenal of World War II,* 247–250.

42. *Courier-Journal,* March 2, 1942, Section 2, p. 1.

43. Ibid., June 2, 1942, p. 1; *Harrison Heritage News* 6, no. 9 (September 2005): 3.

44. Polmar and Allen, *World War II,* 867; *Jackson Times,* December 16, 1943, p. 7.

45. Harrison and Klotter, *New History,* 297.

46. E. R. Murphy and W. M. Johnson, *A Survey of Agriculture in Bracken County* (Lexington: Kentucky Utilities Co., 1952), 26; Murphy, *Survey of Agriculture in Muhlenberg County,* 28; McIntosh, *Survey of Agriculture in Bell County,* 15, 20.

47. *Hardin County (KY) News-Enterprise,* January 27, 2012 (article online).

48. Morgan, *Survey of Agriculture in Fulton County,* 19; Perkins, *Survey of Agriculture in Boyle County,* 16; McIntosh, *Survey of Agriculture in Knox County,* 20; *Courier-Journal,* May 27, 1942, p. 3; July 5, 1942, p. 13; Harrison and Klotter, *New History,* 296.

49. Hochbaum, "The 1943 Victory Garden Program," 1.

50. *Jackson Times,* February 17, 1944, p. 3.

51. Peter Lewis, review of Lizzie Collingham, *The Taste of War* (London: Allen Lane, 2011), *The Mail Online,* January 27, 2011; *Jackson Times,* February 17, 1944, p. 3.

52. *Courier-Journal,* January 21, 1943, Section 2, p. 1.

53. Frederic D. Ogden, ed., *The Public Papers of Governor Keen Johnson, 1939–1943* (Lexington: University Press of Kentucky, 1982), 299–300; *Courier-Journal,* March 7, 1943, Section 1, p. 1.

54. *Henry County Local,* September 1, 1944, p. 4.

55. Ibid.

56. *Paducah Sun-Democrat,* May 14, 1943, p. 1; H. E. Everman, *Bourbon County since 1865* (Richmond, KY: Book Crafters, 1999), 160–161; *Grant County News,* June 25, 1943, p. 3; *Courier-Journal,* March 30, 1942, Section 2, p. 1; May 16, 1942, p. 8.

57. Richard E. Holl, "Swastikas in the Bluegrass State: Axis Prisoners of War in Kentucky, 1942–1946," *Register of the Kentucky Historical Society* 100, no. 2 (Spring 2002): 139–147.

58. Ibid.; Richard E. Holl, "German Prisoners of War Visit Henry County, Kentucky, September–October 1944," *Quarterly Review* (Henry County) 22, no. 3 (September 1999): 1–6.

59. Antonio S. Thompson, *German Jackboots on Kentucky Bluegrass: Housing German Prisoners of War in Kentucky, 1942–1946* (Clarksville, TN: Diversion Press, 2008), 75.

60. Holl, "German Prisoners of War," 5; Thompson, *German Jackboots,* 55 and 58.

61. Holl, "Swastikas in the Bluegrass State," 147, 154–160; Matthias Reiss, "Bronzed Bodies behind Barbed Wire: Masculinity and the Treatment of German Prisoners of War in the United States during World War II," *Journal of Military History* 69 (April 2005): 476–477, 481–485.

62. Axton, *Tobacco and Kentucky,* 135; U.S. Census of 1950, Vol. 1, Part 19, Section 1, pp. 10–15; *Sources of Personal Income by Major Industry Groups for Kentucky, 1930–2003* (Washington, DC: U.S. Bureau of Economic Analysis, Department of Commerce). Also see *Census of Agriculture* (1945) (Washington, DC: U.S. Government Printing Office, 1946), Vol. 1, Part 30, Kentucky, Table 2, p. 5.

63. Axton, *Tobacco and Kentucky,* 140 (the rise from 16 cents per pound of burley tobacco to 45 cents is a 181 percent increase); John W. Jeffries, *Wartime America: The World War II Home Front* (Chicago: Ivan R. Dee, 1996), 28–29; Koistinen, *Arsenal of World War II,* 249–250.

4. Rationing, Price Controls, and the Black Market

1. James C. Klotter, *Kentucky: Portrait in Paradox, 1900–1950* (Frankfort: Kentucky Historical Society, 1996), 190; Maury Klein, *History of the Louisville & Nashville Railroad* (Lexington: University Press of Kentucky, 2003), 352–358, 363–364.

2. Stephen Skowronek, *Building a New American State: The Expansion of National Administrative Capacities, 1879–1920* (Cambridge, UK: Cambridge University Press, 1982), 289; Jason Scott Smith, *Building New Deal Liberalism: The Political Economy of Public Works, 1933–1956* (New York: Cambridge University Press, 2006), 113–115.

3. Lowell H. Harrison and James C. Klotter, *A New History of Kentucky* (Lexington: University Press of Kentucky, 1997), 365.

4. Skowronek, *Building a New American State*, 289–290. Although I am influenced significantly by Skowronek's interpretation, it is a bit too harsh at times. The "hapless administrative giant," as Skowronek calls the federal government, did reduce the suffering of the American people during the Great Depression and helped vanquish the Axis during World War II.

5. George T. Blakey, *Hard Times and New Deal in Kentucky, 1929–1939* (Lexington: University Press of Kentucky, 1986), 166–167; George Brown Tindall, *America: A Narrative History* (New York: W. W. Norton & Co., 1988), 1199, 1260–1261. See Alonzo Hamby, *Beyond the New Deal: Harry S Truman and American Liberalism* (New York: Columbia University Press, 1973), for more on the New Deal–Fair Deal tradition.

6. Norman Polmar and Thomas B. Allen, *World War II: America at War, 1941–1945* (New York: Random House, 1991), 879, 848–849, 852.

7. Richard E. Holl, *From the Boardroom to the War Room: America's Corporate Liberals and FDR's Preparedness Program* (Rochester, NY: University of Rochester Press, 2005), 5–8; Paul A. C. Koistinen, *Arsenal of World War II: The Political Economy of American Warfare, 1940–1945* (Lawrence: University Press of Kansas, 2004), 8–11.

8. El Hannen Stacy, *A Boy from Appalachia Goes to War* (Lost Creek, KY: Stacy Publications, 1999), 4–9, 164, 234–235; Philip Ardery, *Bomber Pilot: A Memoir of World War II* (Lexington: University Press of Kentucky, 1978), 4–7, 167–174, 221–226; Richard G. Stone Jr., *Kentucky Fighting Men, 1861–1945* (Lexington: University Press of Kentucky, 1982), 63–65; Frank F. Mathias, "A Memoir Is as a Memoirist Does: A Kentucky Bandsman in World War II," *Register of the Kentucky Historical Society* 92, no. 3 (Summer 1994): 294–296, 302–303; Harrison and Klotter, *New History*, 372.

9. Klotter, *Kentucky: Portrait in Paradox*, 259; John E. Kleber, ed., *The Kentucky Encyclopedia* (Lexington: University Press of Kentucky, 1992), 157, 343, 968–969; William E. Ellis, H. E. Everman, and Richard D. Sears, *Madison County: 200 Years in Retrospect* (Richmond, KY: Madison County Historical Society, 1985), 329–332; John D. Wright Jr., *Lexington: Heart of the Bluegrass* (Lexington, KY: Lexington-Fayette County Historic Commission, 1982), pp. 189–190; John E. Kleber, ed., *The Encyclopedia of Louisville* (Lexington: University Press of Kentucky, 2001), 107–108, 955.

10. Holl, *From the Boardroom to the War Room*, 131–132; Richard Polenberg, *War and Society: The United States, 1941–1945* (New York: Lippincott, 1972), 11–14; Polmar and Allen, *World War II*, 880–882.

11. John W. Jeffries, *Wartime America: The World War II Home Front* (Chicago: Ivan R. Dee, 1996), 27–29; Klotter, *Kentucky: Portrait in Paradox*, 262.

12. Anthony S. Campagna, *U.S. National Economic Policy, 1917–1985* (New York: Praeger, 1987), 166; Jeffries, *Wartime America*, 31.

13. Harold G. Vatter, *The U.S. Economy in World War II* (New York: Columbia University Press, 1985), 89; *Courier-Journal*, November 28, 1942, Section 2, p. 1; Jeffries, *Wartime America*, 30–31; Polenberg, *War and Society*, 33–34.

14. Jeffries, *Wartime America*, 28; Polenberg, *War and Society*, 31.

15. Koistinen, *Arsenal of World War II*, 422–423; Jeffries, *Wartime America*, 29.

16. Polmar and Allen, *World War II*, 598; *Courier-Journal*, November 28, 1942, Section 2, p. 1; August 4, 1942, p. 3.

17. Jeffries, *Wartime America*, 31; Marshall B. Clinard, *The Black Market: A Study of White Collar Crime* (New York: Rinehart & Co., 1952), 94–95.

18. Campagna, *U.S. National Economic Policy*, 165.

19. *Owensboro Messenger*, March 30, 1943, p. 3; *Courier-Journal*, October 22, 1942, Section 2, p. 1.

20. *Lexington Herald*, December 29, 1944, p. 12; November 23, 1944, p. 12; August 15, 1944, p. 7; August 8, 1944, pp. 1, 8; Eileen Wooton Sandlin Ingram interview, Jackson, KY, May 16, 2014.

21. Clinard, *Black Market*, 16–20.

22. *Lexington Herald*, December 29, 1944, p. 12; June 1, 1944, p. 10; November 16, 1944, p. 1; August 3, 1944, p. 1; November 22, 1944, p. 12; *Courier-Journal*, December 16, 1942, Section 1, p. 12.

23. *Courier-Journal*, December 16, 1942, Section 1, p. 12.

24. Clinard, *Black Market*, 163–164, 185.

25. *Newsweek*, March 27, 1944, 46; Clinard, *Black Market*, 24, 160–163.

26. *Newsweek*, March 27, 1944, 46; Clinard, *Black Market*, 170–171.

27. *Courier-Journal*, November 17, 1942, Section 2, p. 1; *Lexington Herald*, December 7, 1944, p. 1.

28. *Atlantic Monthly*, July 1946, 49.

29. *Lexington Herald*, December 29, 1944, p. 12; November 23, 1944, p. 12; Daniel Boone Razor Jr. interview, Mt. Sterling, KY, July 18, 2009; Clinard, *Black Market*, 303–304.

30. Richard R. Lingeman, *Don't You Know There's a War On? The American Home Front, 1941–1945* (New York: G. P. Putnam's Sons, 1970), 253.

31. *Owensboro Messenger*, April 28, 1943, p. 1 and 6; *Lexington Herald*, August 3, 1944, p. 1; August 8, 1944, p. 1; Clinard, *Black Market*, 42.

32. Hollis B. Gibson interview, Jackson, KY, February 18, 1999; Betty Boles Ellison, *Illegal Odyssey: 200 Years of Kentucky Moonshine* (Lexington, KY: First Books, 2003), iii, 123–124; Elilzabeth Lawson interview, Lexington, KY, March 20, 1999. Though national prohibition ended in 1933, the making of moonshine was still illegal during World War II because moonshiners did not pay required

federal fees and taxes nor did they engage in any required registration or licensing activities. Moonshiners also used scarce sugar, which they obtained through legal or illegal means.

33. Clinard, *Black Market,* 63; Jeffries, *Wartime America,* 31; T. A. Larson, *Wyoming's War Years, 1941–1945* (Laramie: University of Wyoming Press, 1954), 133.

34. Jeffries, *Wartime America,* 32.

35. Koistinen, *Arsenal of World War II,* 430–431.

36. Jeffries, *Wartime America,* 31–34; Kleber, *Kentucky Encyclopedia,* 266.

37. John Morton Blum, *V Was for Victory: Politics and American Culture during World War II* (New York: Harcourt Brace Jovanovich, 1976), 16–21; Koistinen, *Arsenal of World War II,* 431; Polmar and Allen, *World War II,* 875–876; Sylvia Clark Puckett interview, Murray, KY, May 11, 2014.

38. *Courier-Journal,* April 30, 1942, p. 8; Frederic D. Ogden, ed., *The Public Papers of Governor Keen Johnson, 1939–1943* (Lexington: University Press of Kentucky, 1982), 303–304.

39. Blum, *V Was for Victory,* 19; *Statistical Abstract of the United States,* 68th ed. (Washington, DC: Department of Commerce and Bureau of the Census, U.S. Government Printing Office, 1947), 363.

40. Robert Skidelsky, *John Maynard Keynes: Vol. 2, The Economist as Saviour, 1920–1937* (New York: Penguin Books, 1992), 545; Jeffries, *Wartime America,* 35–36; *Fortune,* March 1939, 124; Robert M. Collins, *The Business Response to Keynes, 1929–1964* (New York: Columbia University Press, 1981), 52.

41. Department of Commerce, Bureau of the Census, Sixteenth Census (1940), Population, Volume 2, p. 130; *Statistical Abstract of the United States: 2003,* U.S. Census Bureau, no. HS-29 (Employment Status of the Civilian Population, 1929–2002), p. 50; Seventeenth Census (1950), Table 66, p. 186. The 1940 U.S. Census reveals that the national unemployment rate stood at approximately 14.4 percent. That figure is determined by adding the percent of the labor force seeking work (9.6 percent) and the percent of the labor force on public emergency work (4.8 percent). For Kentucky, the overall unemployment rate for 1940 was 15.1 percent (9.6 percent seeking work and 5.5 percent on emergency public work). In later years, the U.S. unemployment rate fell to 9.9 percent (1941), 4.7 percent (1942), 1.9 percent (1943), and 1.2 percent (1944). In 1945, the U.S. unemployment rate edged up to 1.9 percent. Since Kentucky unemployment rates were just above the national rates in 1940 and 1950 (according to U.S. Census data), it seems fair enough to peg the Kentucky rate for the years in between at slightly higher than the national average. At worse, estimates of this sort would be off by only a small amount.

42. *Paducah Sun-Democrat,* March 30, 1943, p. 12.

43. Klein, *History of the Louisville & Nashville Railroad,* 457; Kleber, *Kentucky Encyclopedia,* 210.

44. *Lexington Herald,* November 28, 1944, p. 1.

45. *Historical Statistics of the United States, Colonial Times to 1970*, Part 1 (Washington, DC: U.S. Department of Commerce and U.S. Bureau of the Census, 1975), 244; Klotter, *Kentucky: Portrait in Paradox*, 259–260.

46. George H. Yater, *Two Hundred Years at the Falls of the Ohio: A History of Louisville and Jefferson County* (Louisville: Heritage Corporation of Louisville and Jefferson County, 1979), 216.

47. Lizzie B. Watts interview, Jackson, KY, January 20, 1999.

48. Gibson interview, February 18, 1999.

49. Razor interviews, June 27, 2009, and July 18, 2009.

5. Politics as Usual

1. In Wyoming, an interesting proposal to retain all incumbents (Republicans and Democrats alike) through 1942 without elections received a hearing but was discarded. See T. A. Larson, *Wyoming's War Years, 1941–1945* (Laramie: University of Wyoming Press, 1954), 178.

2. George T. Blakey, *Hard Times and New Deal in Kentucky, 1929–1939* (Lexington: University Press of Kentucky, 1986), 175–177.

3. Ibid., 177–178.

4. Lowell H. Harrison and James C. Klotter, *A New History of Kentucky* (Lexington: University Press of Kentucky, 1997), 368.

5. Ibid., 369–370. For a recent discussion of the use of patronage in the 1938 Barkley-Chandler race, see Jason Scott Smith, *Building New Deal Liberalism: The Political Economy of Public Works, 1933–1956* (New York: Cambridge University Press, 2006), 160–175.

6. James C. Klotter, *Kentucky: Portrait in Paradox, 1900–1950* (Frankfort: Kentucky Historical Society, 1996), 317–318.

7. Keen Johnson Papers, Box 8, Correspondence Series, August 1–7, 1939, File Folder, Keen Johnson Campaign Pamphlet, University Archives, Thomas and Hazel Little Building, Eastern Kentucky University, Richmond; Klotter, *Kentucky: Portrait in Paradox*, 317.

8. *Somerset Journal*, July 27, 1939, p. 1.

9. *Russellville News-Democrat*, April 13, 1939, p. 1.

10. *Paducah Sun-Democrat*, July 3, 1939, p. 9; *Russellville News-Democrat*, May 18, 1939, p. 1; June 8, 1939, p. 1.

11. Johnson Papers, Box 8, Correspondence Series, January–July 1939 File Folder, "Digest of the Views on Education of the Candidates for the Democratic Nomination for Governor, as Compared to the Kentucky Education Association Program"; *Courier-Journal*, June 29, 1939.

12. *Russellville News-Democrat*, April 13, 1939, p. 1; August 3, 1939, p. 1.

13. Johnson Papers, Box 8, Correspondence Series, August 1–7, 1939, File Folder, Johnson Campaign Pamphlet.

14. *Russellville News-Democrat,* May 18, 1939, p. 1; June 22, 1939, p. 1.

15. Johnson Papers, Box 8, Correspondence Series, January–July 1939 File Folder, letter from Tyler Munford to Mrs. Keen Johnson, July 15, 1939.

16. *Kentucky Post* (Covington), July 13, 1939, pp. 1–2; Johnson Papers, Box 8, Correspondence Series, August 1–7, 1939, File Folder, Johnson Campaign Pamphlet; Frederic D. Ogden, ed., *The Public Papers of Governor Keen Johnson, 1939–1943* (Lexington: University Press of Kentucky, 1982), 521; *Russellville News-Democrat,* April 13, 1939, p. 1.

17. *Paducah Sun-Democrat,* July 3, 1939, p. 1.

18. Johnson Papers, Box 8, Correspondence Series, August 1–7, 1939, File Folder, "Farmers are for Keen Johnson" (pamphlet).

19. Johnson Papers, Box 8, Correspondence Series, January–July 1939, letter from Keen Johnson to Eunice and Judy Johnson, July 1, 1939.

20. *Kentucky Post,* July 1, 1939, p. 4; *Russellville News-Democrat,* June 29, 1939, p. 1; Ogden, *Public Papers of Governor Keen Johnson,* 524; *Somerset Journal,* July 27, 1939, p. 1.

21. Johnson Papers, Box 8, Correspondence Series, August 1–7, 1939, File Folder, "Nearly Complete Vote Returns in the Democratic Primary for Governor," August 1939; Klotter, *Kentucky: Portrait in Paradox,* 317.

22. Ibid.

23. Richard Clayton Smoot, "John Sherman Cooper: The Paradox of a Liberal Republican in Kentucky Politics" (Ph.D. diss., University of Kentucky, 1988), 62–68.

24. Ibid., 62; Klotter, *Kentucky: Portrait in Paradox,* 318.

25. Smoot, "John Sherman Cooper," 70–71, 73.

26. Ibid., 67, 76.

27. Ibid., 71, 78; John E. Kleber, ed., *The Kentucky Encyclopedia* (Lexington: University Press of Kentucky, 1992), 864; Klotter, *Kentucky: Portrait in Paradox,* 318.

28. Ogden, *Public Papers of Governor Keen Johnson,* 1–2; Johnson Papers, Box 48, Pamphlets File Folder, "The Spirit of the Age," 3, and "The Greater Manumission," 5; Boxes 3 and 4; Kleber, *Kentucky Encyclopedia,* 474; Klotter, *Kentucky: Portrait in Paradox,* 317.

29. Ogden, *Public Papers of Governor Keen Johnson,* 482.

30. See John W. Jeffries, *Wartime America: The World War II Home Front* (Chicago: Ivan R. Dee, 1996), 145–146, 168–169; and William L. O'Neill, *A Democracy at War: America's Fight at Home and Abroad in World War II* (New York: Free Press, 1993), 9, 430. Jeffries and O'Neill point to the centrality of the New Deal experience even as World War II raged. They argue that the war did not alter the basic contours of American politics; instead, "politics as usual" prevailed. In Kentucky, this was the case as well. Kentuckians embraced the New Deal because it offered them critical economic assistance during the Great Depression, and they supported the Democratic party through the peacetime period, into the war, and beyond. The

Democratic party of Kentucky emerged from the war even stronger than before. Klotter, *Kentucky: Portrait in Paradox,* 318–319, deals with the fundamentals of the 1940 legislative session.

31. *Courier-Journal,* March 15, 1940, Section 1, p. 1 and p. 14; Kentucky Acts (1940), 524–528.

32. Ogden, *Public Papers of Governor Keen Johnson,* 370, 440.

33. Ibid., 378, 328–330.

34. Ibid., 41–42.

35. Kentucky Acts (1942), 62–65; Klotter, *Kentucky: Portrait in Paradox,* 320; *Courier-Journal,* August 18, 1940, p. 3; Johnson Papers, Box 58, Speech Series—"Espouses Donaldson" File Folder, Johnson typescript (undated), 9.

36. Malcolm E. Jewell, ed., *The Politics of Reapportionment* (New York: Atherton Press, 1962), 112.

37. Ogden, *Public Papers of Governor Keen Johnson,* 376–377, 492–493.

38. Berry Craig, *Hidden History of Kentucky Soldiers* (Charleston, SC: History Press, 2011), 99; Ogden, *Public Papers of Governor Keen Johnson,* 275; *Paducah Sun-Democrat,* February 27, 1942, p. 1; March 4, 1942, p. 1.

39. Johnson Papers, Box 58, Speech Series—"Espouses Donaldson" File Folder, Johnson typescript (undated), 1, 6A–9A, 7, 10, 15, 20–21; Kleber, *Kentucky Encyclopedia,* 474; Ogden, *Public Papers of Governor Keen Johnson,* 103; Box 58, Speech Series—"Johnson Denies Charges of Dishonesty," October 30, 1943; *Park City Daily News* (Bowling Green), July 15, 1943, pp. 1, 3.

40. See Jerry Purvis Sanson, *Louisiana during World War II: Politics and Society, 1939–1945* (Baton Rouge: Louisiana State University Press, 1999), 8–9, 19.

41. Kleber, *Kentucky Encyclopedia,* 268–269.

42. Johnson Papers, Box 58, Speech Series—"Espouses Donaldson" File Folder, Johnson typescript (undated), 12–16; Ogden, *Public Papers of Governor Keen Johnson,* 510; *Courier-Journal,* May 11, 1943, Section 2, p. 1; *Park City Daily News,* July 11, 1943, p. 1; Harrison and Klotter, *New History,* 373.

43. Johnson Papers, Box 58, Speech Series—"Espouses Donaldson" File Folder, newspaper clippings, July 28, 1943; *Park City Daily News,* July 15, 1943, pp. 1, 3; July 11, 1943, p. 1.

44. Johnson Papers, Box 58, Speech Series—"Espouses Donaldson" File Folder, Johnson typescript (undated), 22, 26; Ogden, *Public Papers of Governor Keen Johnson,* 507–510.

45. Johnson Papers, Box 58, Speech Series—Campaign Speech for Democrats (Lyter Donaldson) File Folder, newspaper clipping entitled "Official Governor Returns"; Klotter, *Kentucky: Portrait in Paradox,* 322.

46. *Courier-Journal,* February 9, 1943, Section 2, p. 1.

47. Johnson Papers, Box 58, Speech Series—Campaign Speech for Democrats, newspaper clipping entitled "Democrats Say Nation Waits on Kentucky Votes to Back Administration."

48. *Ashland Daily Independent,* August 14, 1943, p. 1.

49. Klotter, *Kentucky: Portrait in Paradox,* 323.

50. Johnson Papers, Box 58, Speech Series, newspaper clipping entitled "Donaldson Opens Party's Crusade; Stresses War and Postwar Plans," September 25, 1943; "Democrats Say Nation Waits on Kentucky Voters to Back Administration"; James C. Klotter, ed., *The Public Papers of Simeon Willis, 1943–1947* (Lexington: University Press of Kentucky, 1988), 8.

51. *Ashland Daily Independent,* November 2, 1943, p. 1.

52. Johnson Papers, Box 58, Speech Series—"Johnson Denies Charges of Dishonesty," October 30, 1943, Winchester, KY.

53. Klotter, *Kentucky: Portrait in Paradox,* 323.

54. Kleber, *Kentucky Encyclopedia,* 958; Klotter, *Public Papers of Governor Simeon Willis,* 1–2; Simeon Willis Papers, Box 1, Correspondence—1930 File Folder, letter from Lawrence Richey to James Garnett, March 22, 1930, Special Collections, Margaret I. King Library, University of Kentucky, Lexington.

55. Klotter, *Public Papers of Governor Simeon Willis,* 31, 76, 92; Klotter, *Kentucky: Portrait in Paradox,* 324.

56. Klotter, *Kentucky: Portrait in Paradox,* 324–325; Willis Papers, Box 13, Speeches—Louisville, Kentucky File Folder, typescript of Willis's address over WHAS Radio, July 31, 1947, 1–2.

57. *Madisonville Messenger,* September 18, 1950, p. 1; September 19, 1950, p. 6; September 30, 1950, pp. 1, 6.

58. Klotter, *Kentucky: Portrait in Paradox,* 324; Kleber, *Kentucky Encyclopedia,* 958; Willis Papers, Box 13, Speeches—Louisville, Kentucky—Campaign Address File Folder, Campaign Address over WHAS, October 14, 1947, p. 4; John A. Hardin, *Fifty Years of Segregation: Black Higher Education in Kentucky, 1904–1954* (Lexington: University Press of Kentucky, 1997), 80, 82.

59. Klotter, *Public Papers of Governor Simeon Willis,* 240.

60. Willis Papers, Box 16, Kentucky Executive Budget—1944–1946, vii.

61. Mary Jean Kinsman, "The Kentucky Home Front: World War II," *Filson Club History Quarterly* 68, no. 3 (July 1994): 365–378; *Courier-Journal,* October 26, 2003, History of Rubbertown, p. 1; Kleber, *Kentucky Encyclopedia,* 968–969.

62. Klotter, *Public Papers of Governor Simeon Willis,* 253, 256.

63. Ibid., 257–258, 260.

64. Klotter, *Kentucky: Portrait in Paradox,* 326–327; Willis Papers, Box 13, Speeches—Louisville, Kentucky File Folder, typescript of Willis address over WHAS Radio, July 31, 1947, 2.

65. Klotter, *Kentucky: Portrait in Paradox,* 329–331.

6. Kentucky on Guard

1. Robert Earnest Miller, "The War That Never Came: Civilian Defense in Cincinnati, Ohio, during World War II," *Queen City Heritage* 49, no. 4 (Winter

1991): 3–5; August Heckscher, *When LaGuardia Was Mayor: New York's Legendary Years* (New York: W. W. Norton & Co., 1978), 299.

2. Heckscher, *When LaGuardia Was Mayor,* 301, 324–325; William L. O'Neill, *A Democracy at War: America's Fight at Home and Abroad in World War II* (New York: Free Press, 1993), 130.

3. Frederic D. Ogden, ed., *The Public Papers of Governor Keen Johnson, 1939– 1943* (Lexington: University Press of Kentucky, 1982), 101, 380; *Paducah Sun- Democrat,* February 18, 1942, p. 1.

4. John W. Jeffries, *Wartime America: The World War II Home Front* (Chicago: Ivan R. Dee, 1996), 187; Miller, "The War That Never Came," 14.

5. Randolph Hollingsworth, *Lexington: Queen of the Bluegrass* (Charleston, SC: Arcadia Publishing, 2004), 165; John D. Wright Jr., *Lexington: Heart of the Bluegrass* (Lexington, KY: Lexington-Fayette County Historic Commission, 1982), 189–190; Ogden, *Public Papers of Governor Keen Johnson,* 253.

6. Allan M. Winkler, *Home Front U.S.A.: America during World War II,* 2nd ed. (Wheeling, IL: Harlan Davidson, 2000), 34–35; *Courier-Journal,* August 16, 1942, Section 3, p. 8; http://www.ohiohistorycentral.org/w/Cincinnati _Milling_ Machine. Cincinnati Milling Machine Company was one of the world's largest suppliers of machine tools. Machine tools cut and shape the weapons of war; thus Cincinnati might have been bombed, and nearby northern Kentucky would be vul- nerable to damage from intentional and misdirected bombings.

7. David M. Kennedy, *Freedom from Fear: The American People in Depression and War, 1929–1945* (New York: Oxford University Press, 1999), 568, 746–747; Ladislas Farago, *The Game of the Foxes: The Untold Story of German Espionage in the United States and Great Britain during World War II* (New York: David McKay Co., 1971), 433; Joseph E. Persico, *Roosevelt's Secret War: FDR and World War II Espio- nage* (New York: Random House, 2001), 199–205.

8. Louisville Civilian Defense Papers (hereafter LCDP), Box 1, File Folder 7, Official Training Course for Air Raid Wardens, Lesson No. 7, July 1943, 5–6; File Folder 4 (Office of Civilian Defense, Louisville and Jefferson Co., KY, 1942–1947), WAVE interview of Walter H. Shackleton, December 21, 1943, 2. Special Collec- tions, Kentucky Historical Society, Frankfort.

9. *Courier-Journal,* August 16, 1942, Section 3, p. 8; April 15, 1943, Section 1, p. 3; Ogden, *Public Papers of Governor Keen Johnson,* 253.

10. LCDP, Box 1, File Folder 4, WAVE interview of Shackleton, December 21, 1943, 2.

11. John E. Kleber, ed., *The Encyclopedia of Louisville* (Lexington: University Press of Kentucky, 2001), 956–958; *Courier-Journal,* January 1, 1943, Section 2, p. 5.

12. *Courier-Journal,* December 21, 1941, Section 1, p. 6; Section 3, p. 3; Janu- ary 11, 1942, Sunday Magazine.

13. LCDP, Box 1, File Folder 4, WAVE interview of Shackleton, December 21,

1943, p. 3; *Courier-Journal,* January 1, 1943, Section 2, p. 5; December 21, 1941, Section 1, p.6.

14. Ibid.; LCDP, Box 1, File Folder 1 (OCD, Louisville and Jefferson County, KY, 1942–1947), memo from Keith Wilson, Executive Officer, Civilian Protection, to Commanders, Local Property Officers, Mayors and Executive Officers, on Distribution of Pump Tank Extinguishers.

15. *Courier-Journal,* January 1, 1943, Section 2, p. 5; LCDP, Box 1, File Folder 1, letter from Neil Dalton to Mr. McDowell, April 23, 1943; Dalton to Colonel L. R. Boals, May 27, 1943; File Folder 7, Official Training Course for Air Raid Wardens, Lesson No. 10, September 1943; letter from Colonel J. Kenfield Morley to Shackleton, August 3, 1943.

16. *Courier-Journal,* January 1, 1943, Section 2, p. 5; LCDP, Box 1, File Folder 7, letter from Morley to Retail Merchants Association, August 5, 1943.

17. *Courier-Journal,* April 30, 1942, Section 2, p. 1; January 1, 1943, Section 2, p. 5; LCDP, Box 1, Office of Civil Defense, Louisville and Jefferson Co. 1942–1947, American Red Cross File Folder, Volunteer Nurse's Aides Brochure.

18. *Courier-Journal,* December 21, 1941, Sunday Magazine.

19. Ibid., April 21, 1942, p. 1.

20. Ibid.

21. Ibid., pp. 1, 13.

22. Ibid., June 8, 1942, p. 1; June 9, 1942, p. 1.

23. Ibid., June 9, 1942, p. 1.

24. Ibid., June 25, 1942, Section 2, p. 1; Barry Hill interview, Lexington, KY, March 7, 1999.

25. *Courier-Journal,* June 8, 1942, p. 1; June 25, 1942, Section 2, p. 1.

26. Ibid., September 18, 1942, p. 4; LCDP, Box 1, File Folder 5, letter from A. A. Sharp to Shackleton, July 6, 1944.

27. LCDP, Box 4, Incidents File Folder, Louisville Gas & Electric Company Demonstration, May 29, 1944, Colgan Norman memo.

28. *Courier-Journal,* June 2, 1942, p. 5; June 9, 1942, p. 8.

29. George H. Yater, *Waterworks: A History of the Louisville Water Company* (Louisville: Louisville Water Co., 1996), 26–27; Kleber, *Encyclopedia of Louisville,* 576.

30. *Paducah Sun-Democrat,* December 9, 1941, p. 1; January 1, 1942, p. 1; January 16, 1942, p. 1; *Courier-Journal,* January 4, 1942, Sunday Magazine.

31. *Paducah Sun-Democrat,* December 10, 1941, p. 1.

32. Ibid., p. 11.

33. Ibid.; January 16, 1942, p. 1.

34. *Somerset Journal,* December 18, 1941, p. 1; December 25, 1941, p. 1.

35. John D. Perrine interview, Lexington, KY, March 9, 1999.

36. James Russell Harris, "Rolling Bandages and Building Thunderbolts: A Woman's Memories of the Kentucky Home Front, 1941–1945," *Register of the Kentucky Historical Society* 100, no. 2 (Spring 2002): 172–173.

37. *Courier-Journal,* August 16, 1942, Section 1, p. 10; John E. Kleber, ed., *The New History of Shelby County Kentucky* (Prospect, KY: Harmony House, 2003), 514–515; *Paducah Sun-Democrat,* December 12, 1941, pp. 1, 15; http://histclo.com/country/us/chron/940/cus40ww2.html.

38. Miller, "The War That Never Came," 14.

39. T. A. Larson, *Wyoming's War Years, 1941–1945* (Laramie: University of Wyoming Press, 1954), 68–71; Lisa L. Ossian, *The Home Fronts of Iowa, 1939–1945* (Columbia: University of Missouri Press, 2009), 14.

40. Miller, "The War That Never Came," 14–15.

41. LCDP, Box 3, Fat Salvage Program File Folder, letter from Shackleton to Dr. J. J. Rice, July 10, 1944; Bulletin no. 163, May 24, 1944; Box 5, Meat Rationing—"Share the Meat" File Folder, Local Release, November 15, 1942.

42. LCDP, Box 2, Clean-Up Campaign File Folder, letter from John B. Kennedy to Shackleton, October 24, 1944; Box 1, File Folder 5, Air Raid Warden letter, September 13, 1944.

43. J. D. Wright, *Lexington,* 190; *Paducah Sun-Democrat,* January 16, 1942, p. 1; December 10, 1941, p. 11; December 12, 1941, p. 1.

44. Kleber, *Encyclopedia of Louisville,* xxvi–xxvii; LCDP, Box 2, Flood Work; Victory Book Drive File Folder, Special Report entitled "The Flood Front," 1; Miller, "The War That Never Came," 15.

45. *Ashland Daily Independent,* January 3, 1943, p. 1; January 2, 1943, p. 5; LCDP, Box 2, Flood Work, "Flood Front" report, 20–21.

46. *Maysville Daily Independent,* January 4, 1943, p. 1; LCDP, Box 2, Flood Work, "Flood Front" report, 25–28.

47. LCDP, Box 2, Flood Work, "Flood Front" report, 25; *Ashland Daily Independent,* January 3, 1943, p. 1.

48. Miller, "The War That Never Came," 10. Miller's contention that Cincinnati's civil defense network was run by middle-class white males seems just as true for Louisville—and for Kentucky as a whole.

49. LCDP, Box 8, Race Relations File Folder, Replies by Dan T. Moore, Director, Fifth Region Office of Civilian Defense to Questions of the National Conference of Christians and Jews, July 1942, 1; *The Encyclopedia of Cleveland History* (http://ech.cwru.edu/ech-cgi/article.pl?id=ccv; http://ech.cwru.edu/ech-cgi/article.pl?id=FOL); *Somerset Journal,* December 25, 1941, p. 1.

50. Miller, "The War That Never Came," 18.

51. LCDP, Box 1, File Folder 7, letter from Shackleton to All Post Building Wardens, August 12, 1943.

52. Ibid., File Folder 5, letter from Shackleton to Harry F. Wagner, November 14, 1944; letter from Shackleton to Mayor Wilson W. Wyatt, June 19, 1944; letter from Sharp to Shackleton, July 6, 1944.

53. Ibid., Box 10, "Winding Down . . ." File Folder, letter from Arthur B. Zubrod to Shackleton, June 19, 1945; letter from H. L. Foster to Shackleton, October 25, 1945; Shackleton letter, May 18, 1945, p. 1.

7. A Black Man's Place and a New Place for Blacks

1. Marion B. Lucas, *A History of Blacks in Kentucky, Vol. 1: From Slavery to Segregation, 1760–1891* (Frankfort: Kentucky Historical Society, 1992), 3–5; Kenneth M. Stampp, *The Peculiar Institution* (New York: Vintage Books, 1956), 64; John E. Kleber, ed., *The Kentucky Encyclopedia* (Lexington: University Press of Kentucky, 1992), 3–4; James Oakes, *The Ruling Race: A History of American Slaveholders* (New York: Vintage Books, 1982), 184–185.

2. James M. McPherson, *Abraham Lincoln* (New York: Oxford University Press, 2009), 48; Kleber, *Kentucky Encyclopedia*, 4; Lowell H. Harrison, "Lincoln and Compensated Emancipation in Kentucky," in Douglas Cantrell, Thomas D. Matijasic, Richard E. Holl, Lorie Maltby, and Richard Smoot, eds., *Kentucky through the Centuries: A Collection of Documents and Essays* (Dubuque, IA: Kendall Hunt, 2005), 191–195. The Thirteenth Amendment was ratified in 1865 despite Kentucky's objections. Only in 1976 did the Kentucky legislature formally ratify the Thirteenth Amendment.

3. Lowell H. Harrison and James C. Klotter, *A New History of Kentucky* (Lexington: University Press of Kentucky, 1997), 237; W. A. Low, "The Freedmen's Bureau in the Border States," in Cantrell et al., *Kentucky through the Centuries*, 226; Kleber, *Kentucky Encyclopedia*, 5.

4. Kleber, *Kentucky Encyclopedia*, 808–810; Harrison and Klotter, *New History*, 247–248.

5. Kleber, *Kentucky Encyclopedia*, 5; James C. Klotter, *Kentucky: Portrait in Paradox, 1900–1950* (Frankfort: Kentucky Historical Society, 1996), 116–117; Harrison and Klotter, *New History*, 385; George C. Wright, *A History of Blacks in Kentucky, Vol. 2: In Pursuit of Equality, 1890–1980* (Frankfort: Kentucky Historical Society, 1992), 83–84, 170–176; Catherine Fosl and Tracy E. K'Meyer, *Freedom on the Border: An Oral History of the Civil Rights Movement in Kentucky* (Lexington: University Press of Kentucky, 2009), 226.

6. Kentucky Oral History Commission Collection, Kentucky History Center, Frankfort, Loraine Mathis interview, August 16, 2000; Mary Northington interview, April 10, 1999; Georgia Davis Powers interview, undated.

7. Sixteenth Census of the United States (1940), Population, Vol. 2: Characteristics of the Population, Part 3, 174–175, 304–305, 313; Harrison and Klotter, *New History*, 167.

8. *Report of the Kentucky Commission on Negro Affairs*, November 1, 1945, Frankfort, KY, 37 (copy available from Morehead State University, Morehead, KY); William T. Turner interview, Hopkinsville, KY, March 27, 2010.

9. *Report of the Kentucky Commission on Negro Affairs*, 38; Arnold H. Taylor, *Travail and Triumph: Black Life and Culture in the South since the Civil War* (Westport, CT: Greenwood Press, 1976), 165–166, 171; Maurice R. Davie, *Negroes in American Society* (New York: McGraw-Hill, 1949), 206–211; Brownie Wallace interview, Jackson, KY, March 16, 2010. The 3.3 figure for the average size of the

black family in Kentucky during World War II seemed too low to this author when he first saw it. Additional research confirmed that 3.3 is indeed reasonable. The 1940 U.S. Census of Housing, Vol. 2, General Characteristics, Part 3, Section 3, Table 1 (p. 217) reveals that the average number of persons in the nonwhite Kentucky family stood at 3.73 in 1930 and 3.55 in 1940. A 3.3 figure for the war years (1941–1945) therefore is in line with that downward trend. The key here is that family size is equated with occupants per dwelling unit, a figure that was certain to fall as the military draft and out-migration subtracted individuals from their places of residence.

10. J. Harvey Kerns, *A Survey of the Economic and Cultural Conditions of the Negro Population of Louisville, Kentucky, and a Review of the Program and Activities of the Louisville Urban League* (New York: National Urban League, 1948), 172; Turner interview, March 28, 2010.

11. Joe William Trotter Jr., *The African American Experience* (Boston: Houghton Mifflin, 2001), 352–353; Wade Hall, *The Rest of the Dream: The Black Odyssey of Lyman Johnson* (Lexington: University Press of Kentucky, 1988), 212–213; Taylor, *Travail and Triumph*, 147; Kerns, *Survey of the Economic and Cultural Conditions of the Negro Population*, 163; Brownie Wallace interview, March 16, 2010.

12. Low, "The Freedmen's Bureau," 225; Alicestyne Turley-Adams, *Rosenwald Schools in Kentucky, 1917–1932* (Frankfort: Kentucky Heritage Council and the Kentucky African American Heritage Commission, 1997), 10; Brownie Wallace interview, March 16, 2010.

13. Peter M. Ascoli, *Julius Rosenwald: The Man Who Built Sears, Roebuck and Advanced the Cause of Black Education in the American South* (Bloomington: Indiana University Press, 2006), 26–27, 82; Turley-Adams, *Rosenwald Schools in Kentucky, 1917–1932*, 3.

14. Turley-Adams, *Rosenwald Schools in Kentucky, 1917–1932*, 15, 25.

15. George C. Wright, *Life behind a Veil: Blacks in Louisville, Kentucky, 1865–1930* (Baton Rouge: Louisiana State University Press, 1985), 262–268; John E. Kleber, ed., *The Encyclopedia of Louisville* (Lexington: University Press of Kentucky, 2001), 16, 103, 575, 645; Kerns, *Survey of the Economic and Cultural Conditions of the Negro Population*, 197; Alice A. Dunnigan, *The Fascinating Story of Black Kentuckians* (Washington, DC: Associated Publishers, 1982), 205.

16. Kleber, *Encyclopedia of Louisville*, 619; G. Wright, *History of Blacks in Kentucky, Vol. 2*, 68.

17. David M. Kennedy, *Freedom from Fear: The American People in Depression and War, 1929–1945* (New York: Oxford University Press, 1999), 763–766.

18. *Courier-Journal*, July 30, 1940, Section 1, p. 7; *Louisville Leader*, December 20, 1941, p. 4; July 8, 1939, p. 4.

19. Kennedy, *Freedom from Fear*, 764–766.

20. Richard Polenberg, *War and Society: The United States, 1941–1945* (New York: J. B. Lippincott Co., 1972), 102–105; Trotter, *African American Experience*, 502–507.

21. John Morton Blum, *V Was for Victory: Politics and American Culture during World War II* (New York: Harcourt Brace Jovanovich, 1976), 188.

22. G. Wright, *History of Blacks in Kentucky, Vol. 2,* 16.

23. Trotter, *African American Experience,* 502–503; "The *Pittsburgh Courier* during World War II: An Advocate for Freedom," http://www.yurasko.net/vv/courier .html; http://www.newsreel.org/guides/blackpress/treason.htm.

24. Fumiko Sakashita, "'Remember Pearl Harbor, but Don't Forget Sikeston': Anti-Lynching Discourse and Transnational Politics of Race," paper presented at the Annual Meeting of the American Studies Association, May 24, 2009; Harriet C. Frazier, *Lynchings in Missouri, 1803–1981* (Jefferson, NC: McFarland & Co., 2009), 180–181; *Louisville Leader,* August 8, 1942, p. 4; March 7, 1942, p. 4.

25. *Report of the Kentucky Commission on Negro Affairs,* 15; Sixteenth Census of the U.S., Population, Vol. 2, 194; Kerns, *Survey of the Economic and Cultural Conditions of the Negro Population,* 22.

26. Kleber, *Encyclopedia of Louisville,* 619.

27. Ibid., 708; *Courier-Journal,* May 15, 1957, p. 16; June 29, 2007, p. A11; Finding Aid, Samuel Plato Papers, Filson Club Historical Society, Louisville.

28. "Samuel Plato," *Kentucky Negro Educational Association Journal* 13, no. 1 (November–December 1942): 27; K. D. Durr, *Behind the Backlash: White Working-Class Politics in Baltimore, 1940–1980* (Chapel Hill: University of North Carolina Press, 2003), 24.

29. *Courier-Journal,* October 20, 1970, p. B3.

30. Kerns, *Survey of the Economic and Cultural Conditions of the Negro Population,* 31; http://www.answers.com/topic/the_carbide_graphite_group_inc; http:// www.cpa.gov/air/ej/conference2007/Arnita_Gaston_Brochure.pdf.

31. Dunnigan, *Fascinating Story,* 424; *Louisville Defender,* September 30, 1976; Kerns, *Survey of the Economic and Cultural Conditions of the Negro Population,* 46.

32. Brownie Wallace interview, January 27, 2010.

33. Ibid.

34. Kentucky Oral History Commission Collection, F. E. Whitney interview, June 7, 2000; Amanda Cooper Elliott interview, Lexington, KY, April 8, 2010; Charles Jewell Francis Jr. interview, Dayton, OH, February 24, 2010. Elliott and Francis interviews in possession of author.

35. Kennedy, *Freedom from Fear,* 771; Polenberg, *War and Society,* 123–124.

36. *Courier-Journal,* June 4, 1940, p. 7.

37. Kennedy, *Freedom from Fear,* 773; Ronald Takaki, *A Different Mirror: A History of Multicultural America* (Boston: Little, Brown and Co., 1993), 395–396.

38. Hall, *Rest of the Dream,* 202; Kennedy, *Freedom from Fear,* 774.

39. Melvyn Dubofsky and Athan Theoharis, *Imperial Democracy: The United States since 1945* (Englewood Cliffs, NJ: Prentice-Hall, 1983), 121–122.

40. Kleber, *Encyclopedia of Louisville,* 34–35; *Louisville Leader,* November 9, 1935, p. 1.

41. *Louisville Leader,* November 16, 1935, p. 4.

42. *Courier-Journal,* November 9, 1935, p. 2; G. Wright, *History of Blacks in Kentucky, Vol. 2,* 158–160.

43. Kleber, *Encyclopedia of Louisville,* 35; G. Wright, *History of Blacks in Kentucky, Vol. 2,* 160–161; *Courier-Journal,* June 15, 1960, p. 16.

44. *Kentucky New Era,* January 31, 1977, p. 1; Fosl and K'Meyer, *Freedom on the Border,* 228; *Courier-Journal,* March 23, 1960, p. 7.

45. *Report of the Kentucky Commission on Negro Affairs;* G. Wright, *History of Blacks in Kentucky, Vol. 2,* 191–192.

46. Kleber, *Kentucky Encyclopedia,* 258–259.

47. Kerns, *Survey of the Economic and Cultural Condition of the Negro Population,* 176.

48. Kleber, *Encyclopedia of Louisville,* 35; *Courier-Journal,* June 15, 1960, p. 1; October 20, 1970, p. B3.

49. Fosl and K'Meyer, *Freedom on the Border,* 19–20; G. Wright, *History of Blacks in Kentucky, Vol. 2,* 161–162; Mary Sudman Donovan and D. Patricia Wagner, *Kentucky's Black Heritage: The Role of Black People in the History of Kentucky from Pioneer Days to the Present* (Frankfort: Kentucky Commission on Human Rights, 1971), 90; Davie, *Negroes in American Society,* 315–316; *Lexington Herald-Leader,* February 21, 1999, pp. B1 and B4.

50. Kerns, *Survey of the Economic and Cultural Conditions of the Negro Population,* 174; Hall, *Rest of the Dream,* x–xi, 202–207.

8. Choosing to Go

1. Although Kentucky migration from 1940 to 1945 can fairly be described as heavy, my estimate of 350,000 migrants over this span (not taking into account military personnel) is a rough one. I was unable to locate exact migration data from U.S. Census records, I reached my figure by using a combination of resources, making 350,000 a highly educated guess. The sources I reviewed include David M. Kennedy, *Freedom from Fear: The American People in Depression and War, 1929–1945* (New York: Oxford University Press, 1999), 747–748; Lowell H. Harrison and James C. Klotter, *A New History of Kentucky* (Lexington: University Press of Kentucky, 1997), 410; Olaf F. Larson, "Wartime Migration and the Manpower Reserve on Farms in Eastern Kentucky," *Rural Sociology* 8, no. 2 (June 1943): 148–161; 1950 U.S. Census of Population, Table 19: Population of Counties in Continental United States, Alaska, Hawaii, and Puerto Rico, 1950 and 1940—Continued, pp. 1–33, 1–34; and Henry S. Shryock Jr., "Redistribution of Population: 1940 to 1950," *Journal of the American Statistical Association* 46, no. 256 (December 1951): 417.

2. Larson, "Wartime Migration and the Manpower Reserve," 148, 151–156; John C. Belcher, "Population Growth and Characteristics," in Thomas R. Ford,

ed., *The Southern Appalachian Region: A Survey* (Lexington: University of Kentucky Press, 1967), 38; 1950 U.S. Census of Population, Table 19, pp. 1–33, 1–34. Since Larson notes that 85,000 rural farming eastern Kentuckians left eastern Kentucky between April 1, 1940, and December 1, 1942, with remaining manpower reserves of 63,000 to 98,000, an estimate of 140,000 migrants from eastern Kentucky alone during World War II seems reasonable. The population figures for western Kentucky were obtained by adding up the county figures for that region for 1940 and 1950.

3. Wayne T. Gray, "Population Movements in the Kentucky Mountains," *Rural Sociology* 10, no. 4 (December 1945): 384, 386; 1950 U.S. Census of Population, Table 19, 1–33, 1–34; James S. Brown and George A. Hillery Jr., "The Great Migration, 1940–1960," in Ford, *Southern Appalachian Region*, 56; Luther Adams, "'Headed for Louisville': Rethinking Rural to Urban Migration in the South, 1930–1950," *Journal of Social History* 40, no. 2 (Winter 2006): 419.

4. Shryock, "Redistribution of Population," 428–430; Brown and Hillery, "Great Migration," 59; 1950 U.S. Census of Population, Vol. 2, Part 1, United States Summary, Table 12, Rank of States according to Amount and Percent Increase in Population between 1940 and 1950, pp. 1–14; W. S. Woytinsky, "Interstate Migration during the War," *State Government* 19 (March 1946): 83.

5. James C. Klotter, *Kentucky: Portrait in Paradox, 1900–1950* (Frankfort: Kentucky Historical Society, 1996), 260–261; Larson, "Wartime Migration and the Manpower Reserve," 153; Henry S. Shryock Jr. and Hope Tisdale Eldridge, "Internal Migration in Peace and War," *American Sociological Review* 12, no. 1 (February 1947): 32.

6. Gray, "Population Movements in the Kentucky Mountains," 383; Klotter, *Kentucky: Portrait in Paradox*, 261.

7. Alan Clive, *State of War: Michigan in World War II* (Ann Arbor: University of Michigan Press, 1979), 173.

8. Shryock and Eldridge, "Internal Migration in Peace and War," 29; Gray, "Population Movements in the Kentucky Mountains," 382; Brown and Hillery, "Great Migration," 63; Kennedy, *Freedom from Fear*, 748.

9. *Jackson Times*, June 8, 1944, p. 6; James D. Cockrum, "Owensboro Goes to War," *Daviess County Historical Quarterly* 2, no. 1 (January 1984): 6; 1950 U.S. Census of Population, Table 19, p. 1–33.

10. *Lexington Herald*, May 27, 1943, pp. 1–2; June 21, 1943, p. 5.

11. *Jackson Times*, December 18, 1941, p. 1; Brown and Hillery, "Great Migration," 61.

12. Adams, "'Headed for Louisville,'" 407.

13. Ibid.

14. Ibid., 420–422.

15. Chad Berry, *Southern Migrants, Northern Exiles* (Champaign: University of Illinois Press, 2000), 87, 90.

16. Ibid., 90–91.

17. *New York Times*, June 2, 1997; *Lexington Herald-Leader*, March 31, 2007, Section B, pp. 1, 5.

18. Berry, *Southern Migrants, Northern Exiles*, 92–93.

19. *Jackson Times*, February 3, 1944, p. 3; Norman Polmar and Thomas B. Allen, eds., *World War II: America at War, 1941–1945* (New York: Random House, 1991), 717.

20. James Russell Harris, ed., "Rolling Bandages and Building Thunderbolts: A Woman's Memories of the Kentucky Home Front, 1941–1945," *Register of the Kentucky Historical Society* 100, no. 2 (Spring 2002): 167–169.

21. Ibid., 168.

22. Polmar and Allen, *World War II*, 610–611; Harris, "Rolling Bandages," 180.

23. Harris, "Rolling Bandages," 181–182.

24. Berry, *Southern Migrants, Northern Exiles*, 95.

25. Ibid., 95–96.

26. Ibid.

27. Ibid., 96–97.

28. Ibid., 89, 92.

29. Clive, *State of War*, 179–180.

30. Berry, *Southern Migrants, Northern Exiles*, 88–92.

31. Clive, *State of War*, 181.

32. Loyal Jones, *Appalachian Values* (Ashland, KY: Jesse Stuart Foundation, 1994), 75, 99; Clive, *State of War*, 181.

33. Luther Adams, "'It Was North of Tennessee': African American Migration to Louisville and the Meaning of the South," *Ohio Valley History* 3, no. 3 (Fall 2003): 46.

34. Berry, *Southern Migrants, Northern Exiles*, 88, 92.

35. Clive, *State of War*, 183; Berry, *Southern Migrants, Northern Exiles*, 212–213.

36. Kennedy, *Freedom from Fear*, 645; John E. Kleber, ed., *The Encyclopedia of Louisville* (Lexington: University Press of Kentucky, 2001), 734.

37. *Courier-Journal*, January 1, 1943, Section 2, p. 7.

38. Ibid., April 15, 1943, Section 2, p. 1.

39. Ibid., February 24, 1943, Section 2, p. 1; Louisville Office of Civilian Defense Papers, Box 10, Winding Down . . . and Returning to Normal File Folder, letter from Walter F. Shackleton to Members of the Jefferson County Fiscal Court and Department of Finance, May 19, 1945, Special Collections, Kentucky Historical Society, Frankfort.

40. Kleber, *Encyclopedia of Louisville*, 532.

41. James Gilbert, *A Cycle of Outrage: America's Reaction to the Juvenile Delinquent in the 1950s* (New York: Oxford University Press, 1986), 24–28; Richard Polenberg, *War and Society: The United States, 1941–1945* (New York: J. B. Lippin-

cott, 1972), 147–148; John W. Jeffries, *Wartime America: The World War II Home Front* (Chicago: Ivan R. Dee, 1996), 87; Kentucky Legislative Research Commission, *Kentucky Youth Problems: A Report to the Governor and the General Assembly* (Frankfort, KY: Legislative Research Commission, Research Publication no. 33, January 1952), 3–5.

42. William M. Tuttle Jr., *"Daddy's Gone to War": The Second World War in the Lives of America's Children* (New York: Oxford University Press, 1993), 74; Jeffries, *Wartime America,* 90.

43. *Ashland Daily Independent,* July 14, 1943, pp. 1–2; July 12, 1943, pp. 1–2; *New York Times,* July 12, 1943, p. 10.

44. *New York Times,* July 12, 1943, p. 10.

45. *Ashland Daily Independent,* July 13, 1943, pp. 1–2.

46. Ibid., July 12, 1943, p. 2.

47. Ibid., July 13, 1943, p. 2.

48. Interview with Jim Short, Olive Hill, KY, March 6, 2008.

49. Negley K. Teeters and John Otto Reinemann, *The Challenge of Delinquency: Causation, Treatment, and Prevention of Juvenile Delinquency* (New York: Prentice-Hall, 1950), 498–500; Herbert A. Bloch and Frank T. Flynn, *Delinquency: The Juvenile Offender in America Today* (New York: Random House, 1956), 429.

50. Interview with Gloria Blakely, Louisville, KY, February 23, 2008; phone interview with August Wheately of Pendleton, KY, February 24, 2008.

51. Interview with Orville Morris, Louisville, KY, February 27, 2008.

52. Woytinsky interview with Albert Lee Cook and Mary Stevens Cook, Louisville, KY, February 23, 2008.

53. Teeters and Reinemann, *Challenge of Delinquency,* 498–500; Bloch and Flynn, *Delinquency,* 429.

54. John Costello, *Virtue under Fire: How World War II Changed Our Social and Sexual Attitudes* (Boston: Little, Brown and Co., 1985), 85; *Courier-Journal,* April 12, 1942, Section 3, p. 8.

55. Kleber, *Encyclopedia of Louisville,* 732, 956.

56. See http://www.bgdailynews.com/bicentennnial/grandma-pauline-tabor -morphed-into-a-madam/ and Pauline Tabor, *Pauline's: Memoirs of the Madam on Clay Street* (Bowling Green, KY: Touchstone Publishing Co., 1971).

57. Costello, *Virtue under Fire,* 85; Polenberg, *War and Society,* 151; Kleber, *Encyclopedia of Louisville,* 956; Jeffries, *Wartime America,* 91.

9. Loved Ones

1. David M. Kennedy, *Freedom from Fear: The American People in Depression and War, 1929–1945* (New York: Oxford University Press, 1999), 636–637; Lowell H. Harrison and James C. Klotter, *A New History of Kentucky* (Lexington: University Press of Kentucky, 1997), 372; Lewis H. Carlson, *We Were Each Other's Prisoners:*

An Oral History of World War II American and German Prisoners of War (New York: Basic Books, 1997), vii; James Russell Harris, "The Harrodsburg Tankers: Bataan, Prison, and the Bonds of Community," *Register of the Kentucky Historical Society* 86 (Summer 1998): 230–277; National Archives, Department of Defense figures, 1947 (www.archives.gov/research/arc/ww2); Charles W. Johnson, "V for Virginia: The Commonwealth Goes to War," *Virginia Magazine of History and Biography* 100, no. 3 (July 1992): 398; U.S. Census Bureau Data, 1940. The numbers I use for Kentuckians who served in World War II, and for those who were either wounded, captured, or killed, are all estimates. The number of Kentuckians who died in the conflict is fairly accurate, but even that estimate is subject to fluctuation depending upon the source consulted. Harrison and Klotter say that nearly 8,000 Kentuckians perished; the Department of Defense (DOD) figure is 6,915; and 9,417 names are listed in Memorial Coliseum at the University of Kentucky. Figures for Kentuckians wounded and captured are even less precise. Apparently, the DOD did not break down wounded by state. The Kentucky Historical Society does not have that information either. Since the figure for Kentucky's dead more or less falls into line with the national figure (when the 400,000 total dead is divided by 48, the number of states at the time), it seems feasible to use the same approach with the wounded and prisoners of war. The DOD lists 671,846 American military personnel wounded during World War II, which yields roughly 14,000 wounded for Kentucky after the math is done. Similarly, some 115,000 Americans were held by Germany and Japan during the war. This translates into approximately 2,000 Kentucky POWs. The estimates for Kentucky wounded and captured are admittedly extremely rough, however; better ones are needed.

2. Michael C. C. Adams, *The Best War Ever: America and World War II* (Baltimore: Johns Hopkins University Press, 1994), 105.

3. Edward M. Coffman, "A Younger Brother of the Greatest Generation," *Register of the Kentucky Historical Society* 100, no. 2 (Spring 2002): 129–138; Jeffrey S. Suchanek and William J. Marshall, eds., *Time on Target: The World War II Memoir of William R. Buster* (Frankfort: Kentucky Historical Society Foundation, 1999), 129, 150.

4. Nancy Disher Baird, "'To Lend You My Eyes . . . ': The World War II Letters of Special Services Officer Harry Jackson," *Register of the Kentucky Historical Society* 88 (Summer 1990): 289, 297.

5. Ibid., 292–302.

6. Ibid., 304.

7. El Hannen Stacy, *A Boy from Appalachia Goes to War* (Lost Creek, KY: Stacy Publications, 1999), 4–5, 235.

8. Ibid., 137–147.

9. Ibid., 164–165, 170–171.

10. Ibid., 197–199.

11. Ibid., 176.

12. Nancy Disher Baird, "An Opportunity to Meet 'Every Kind of Person': A Kentuckian Views Army Life during World War II," *Register of the Kentucky Historical Society* 101 (Summer 2003): 298–299, 314–317.

13. Harris, "Harrodsburg Tankers," 247–249, 267, 271.

14. *Mt. Sterling Advocate,* November 29, 2007, pp. A1, A11.

15. Norman Polmar and Thomas B. Allen, *World War II: America at War, 1941–1945* (New York: Random House, 1991), 657; Carlson, *We Were Each Other's Prisoners,* ix–x.

16. *Mt. Sterling Advocate,* October 18, 2007, p. A18; *Sterling Sentinel* 17, no. 9 (September 2006): 3. (The *Sterling Sentinel* is a newsletter published by the Windsor Care Center, Mt. Sterling, KY.)

17. Frances Jones Gaitskill interview, Mt. Sterling, KY, October 25, 2007.

18. Ibid.

19. Ibid.

20. John E. Kleber, ed., *The Kentucky Encyclopedia* (Lexington: University Press of Kentucky, 1992), 415.

21. Harris, "Harrodsburg Tankers," 251–252.

22. Ibid., 251–265; Cecilia Broadwater interview, Lexington, KY, July 29, 2008.

23. Polmar and Allen, *World War II,* 657–658; Ronald H. Spector, *Eagle against the Sun: The American War with Japan* (New York: Free Press, 1985), 396–400.

24. Harris, "Harrodsburg Tankers," 266. For the significance of U.S. victory over the Axis powers and its meaning for the future, see John Morton Blum, *V Was for Victory: Politics and American Culture during World War II* (New York: Harcourt Brace Jovanovich, 1976).

25. James Russell Harris interview, Frankfort, KY, June 26, 2008; Broadwater interview, July 29, 2008.

26. Larry S. Tabor, "The Rock of Corregidor: The Heroism of Lieutenant Bethel V. Otter," *Filson Club History Quarterly* 68, no. 3 (July 1994): 348–363.

27. Ibid., 360; Spector, *Eagle against the Sun,* 136; John Costello, *The Pacific War* (New York: Rawson, Wade, 1981), 183. For a good account of Kentucky soldiers who saw front-line action in battles like Iwo Jima, see Arthur L. Kelly, *Battlefire! Combat Stories from World War II* (Lexington: University Press of Kentucky, 1997).

28. *Courier-Journal,* April 29, 1949, Section 2, p. 10; Larry L. Arnett, *Call to Arms: A Collection of Fascinating Stores, Events, Personalities, and Facts about Kentucky's Military History* (Frankfort: Kentucky Publishing Co., 1995), 100.

29. Hugh Ridenour, "Wartime Romance and D-Day Tragedy: A Kentucky Flyer's Death and His Wife's Struggle to Cope," *Register of the Kentucky Historical Society* 102 (Winter 2004): 39–67.

30. Ibid., 51–60.

31. Ibid., 64–67.

32. Kenneth G. Maddox Papers, Box 1, December 1944 Letters (with Memorial Service, 1985) File Folder, Western Union telegram, December 20, 1944, Kentucky Historical Society, Frankfort; Keystone Club Program for Memorial Service of Kenneth G. Maddox, April 14, 1985.

33. Maddox Papers, Box 1, October 1943–July 1944 Letters File Folder, letter from Kenny Maddox to Doris and Hunt Maddox, July 25, 1944; October 1944–November 1944 Letters File Folder, letter from Kenny Maddox to Oma Mae and George Maddox, November 15, 1944.

34. Maddox Papers, Box 1, December 1944 Letters File Folder, "Dear Ones" letter (written by Oma Mae Maddox), October 24, 1945.

35. John D. Perrine interview, Lexington, KY, April 23, 2014; Mary Ellen Perrine Massenburg interview, Cary, NC, April 27, 2014.

36. Kleber, *Kentucky Encyclopedia*, 833.

37. Ibid.; James C. Klotter and Freda C. Klotter, *A Concise History of Kentucky* (Lexington: University Press of Kentucky, 2008), 170.

38. Kleber, *Kentucky Encyclopedia*, 136–137.

39. Ibid., 137.

40. *Courier-Journal*, February 6, 1949, Section 1, p. 23; Polmar and Allen, *World War II*, 175.

41. John Keegan, *The Second World War* (New York: Penguin Books, 1989), 567–573; Spector, *Eagle against the Sun*, 532–540; Costello, *Pacific War*, 577–578.

42. "Lieutenant General Simon Bolivar Buckner, Jr.," *Filson Club History Quarterly* 23 (April 1949): 152–157.

43. *New York Times*, June 19, 1945, p. 7; *Courier-Journal*, February 10, 1949, Section 1, pp. 1, 16.

44. *Lexington Herald-Leader*, October 12, 2007, Section A, pp. 1, 10.

45. Ogden, *The Public Papers of Governor Keen Johnson, 1939–1943* (Lexington: University Press of Kentucky, 1982), 476.

46. Coffman, "Younger Brother," 134–135; John Perrine interview, Lexington, KY, March 9, 1999; Henrietta Wallace interview, Jackson, KY, December 11, 2007.

10. Rupp on the Rise and Rubinstein's Wine

1. David M. Kennedy, *Freedom from Fear: The American People in Depression and War, 1929–1945* (New York: Oxford University Press, 1999), 716; Lowell H. Harrison and James C. Klotter, *A New History of Kentucky* (Lexington: University Press of Kentucky, 1997), 372.

2. Tracy Campbell, *Short of the Glory: The Fall and Redemption of Edward F. Prichard Jr.* (Lexington: University Press of Kentucky, 1998), 167; *Courier-Journal*, February 10, 1941, p. 9; Gregory Kent Stanley, *Before Big Blue: Sports at the University of Kentucky, 1880–1940* (Lexington: University Press of Kentucky, 1996), 6.

3. John E. Kleber, ed., *The Kentucky Encyclopedia* (Lexington: University Press

of Kentucky, 1992), 520; Russell Rice, *The Wildcats: A Story of Kentucky Football* (Huntsville, AL: Strode Publishers, 1975), 134.

4. Rice, *Wildcats*, 140–141; *Lexington Herald-Leader*, October 8, 1939, Section 1, pp. 1, 18; *Lexington Leader*, November 19, 1918, p. 5; November 22, 1918, Second Section, p. 2; November 27, 1918. The 1918 University of Kentucky Wildcats football team played just three games. The season ended abruptly after that because of the flu pandemic, which led to cancellation of games with St. Louis University and Fort Benjamin Harrison. Numerous players on the St. Louis team came down with the flu and were too sick to play. The Lexington Health Board ban on public gatherings prevented the Fort Harrison game from being played. The UK Athletic Committee finally decided enough was enough, canceling the only two remaining contests on the football schedule on November 26, 1918.

5. Tony Neely et al., *2005 Kentucky Football Media Guide* (Lexington: Post Printing, 2005), 157; *Courier-Journal*, December 16, 1942, Section 2, p. 8.

6. Rice, *Wildcats*, 142–144.

7. *Courier-Journal*, June 30, 1943, Section 2, p. 4.

8. Neely et al., *2005 Kentucky Football*, 157.

9. Letter from Ab Kirwan to Dr. Herman Donovan, December 1, 1942, Department of Athletics 1940–1942 File Folder, Box 53, Herman Lee Donovan Papers, University Archives and Special Collections, Margaret I. King Library, Lexington, KY.

10. *Courier-Journal*, December 29, 1941, Section 2, p. 2; James C. Klotter, *Kentucky: Portrait in Paradox, 1900–1950* (Frankfort: Kentucky Historical Society, 1996), 262.

11. William E. Ellis, *A History of Eastern Kentucky University* (Lexington: University Press of Kentucky, 2005), 91–92; Donald F. Flatt, *Morehead State University, 1887–1997: A Light to the Mountains* (Ashland, KY: Jesse Stuart Foundation, 1997), 135.

12. Flatt, *Morehead State University, 1887–1997*, 135; *Lexington Herald-Leader*, October 4, 1942, p. 7; *Rowan County News*, October 15, 1942, p. 3; John A. Hardin, *Onward and Upward: A Centennial History of Kentucky State University, 1886–1986* (Frankfort: Kentucky State University, 1987), 85–86; *Chicago Defender*, January 24, 1942; "W. Va. State Topples Kentucky from Undefeated Ranks in 18–15 Grid Upset," newspaper clipping in Clippings—"Scrapbook"—Athletics 1939–1942 File Folder, Center of Excellence for the Study of Kentucky African Americans, Kentucky State University, Frankfort.

13. Robert Snyder, *A History of Georgetown College* (Georgetown, KY: Georgetown College, 1979), 112; John D. Wright Jr., *Transylvania: Tutor to the West* (Lexington: University Press of Kentucky, 1975), 384; Kathryn Jay, *More Than Just a Game: Sports in American Life since 1945* (New York: Columbia University Press, 2004), 13.

14. *Courier-Journal*, September 11, 1939, Section 2, p. 8.

15. Bert Nelli and Steve Nelli, *The Winning Tradition: A History of Kentucky Wildcat Basketball* (Lexington: University Press of Kentucky, 1998), 14–15, 19–20, 36; Kleber, *Kentucky Encyclopedia*, 787; Russell Rice, *Adolph Rupp: Kentucky's Basketball Baron* (Champaign, IL: Sagamore Publishing, 1994), 5.

16. Rice, *Adolph Rupp*, 9–10.

17. Ibid., 14–17; Russell Rice interview of Adolph Rupp, p. 11, Rupp File 960H23 A/F 538, University of Kentucky Library Alumni/Faculty Oral History Project, Special Collections, Margaret I. King Library, University of Kentucky, Lexington.

18. Rice, *Adolph Rupp*, 18.

19. Ibid., 11–12; Nelli and Nelli, *Winning Tradition*, 39.

20. Nelli and Nelli, *Winning Tradition*, 20–21.

21. *Lexington Herald*, February 2, 1943, p. 5.

22. Tom Wallace, *Kentucky Basketball Encyclopedia* (Champaign, IL: Sports Publishing, 2002), 110–111, 385; *Lexington Herald*, March 21, 1942, p. 7; "Aegis," 1942, pp. 58–62, Rauner Special Collections, Dartmouth College Library, Hanover, NH; *101 Years of UK Basketball* (Paducah, KY: Turner Publishing Co., 2004), 89.

23. Russell Rice, *Kentucky Basketball's Big Blue Machine* (Huntsville, AL: Strode Publishers, 1978), 139.

24. Wallace, *Kentucky Basketball Encyclopedia*, 111; Rice, *Adolph Rupp*, 76; *Lexington Herald-Leader*, January 24, 1943, p. 8.

25. *Lexington Herald*, January 29, 1943, p. 4; February 2, 1943, p. 5; January 17, 1943, p. 9.

26. Nelli and Nelli, *The Winning Tradition*, 59.

27. Wallace, *Kentucky Basketball Encyclopedia*, 113–115; Rice interview of Rupp, p. 20, Rupp File 960H30, A/F 545, University of Kentucky Library Alumni/Faculty Oral History Project; *Lexington Herald*, December 14, 1943, p. 6; March 5, 1944, p. 8.

28. Wallace, *Kentucky Basketball Encyclopedia*, 115–117, 386; *Lexington Herald*, March 23, 1945, p. 8; Nelli and Nelli, *Winning Tradition*, 61.

29. Rice, *Adolph Rupp*, 85.

30. Ibid., 62; Rice interview of Rupp, p. 9, Rupp File 960H22, A/F 537, University of Kentucky Library Alumni/Faculty Oral History Project.

31. Kleber, *Kentucky Encyclopedia*, 265–266.

32. Dave Kindred, *Basketball: The Dream Game in Kentucky* (Louisville: Fetter Printing Co., 1976), 115, 118, 126–127; C. Harvey Gardiner, *Coach Diddle, Mister Diddle: Motivator of Men* (Nashville, TN: Parthenon Press, 1984), 138.

33. *Courier-Journal*, February 23, 1941, Section 4, p. 4; Kindred, *Basketball*, 122.

34. *Park City Daily News* (Bowling Green, KY), March 20, 1942, p. 5; Gardiner, *Coach Diddle, Mister Diddle*, 134–135.

35. Kindred, *Basketball*, 131.

36. Ibid., 139.

37. Ellis, *History of Eastern Kentucky University*, 93, 97; Flatt, *Morehead State University*, 137–138; *Ashland Daily Independent*, February 6, 1944, p. 11; goracers .com (Hall of Fame and Media Guide); http://www.hoophall.com/hall-of-famers/ tag/joseph-f-joe-fulks.

38. Robert Markel, ed., *The Baseball Encyclopedia* (New York: Macmillan, 1969), 15; Bruce Chadwick, *When the Game Was Black and White* (New York: Abbeville Press, 1992), 110–111.

39. Markel, *Baseball Encyclopedia*, 2281.

40. Ibid., 334, 338, 342, 351.

41. *Courier-Journal*, October 10, 1944, Section 2, p. 2.

42. *Louisville Leader*, June 19, 1943, p. 3.

43. Brent Kelley, *The Negro Leagues Revisited* (Jefferson, NC: McFarland & Co, 2000), 70–174.

44. See Kleber, *Kentucky Encyclopedia*, 57–58, and Kentucky High School Basketball Hall of Fame, 2012 Inductees, at http://www.khsbhf.com/inductees.asp.

45. Ibid.; *Kentucky Standard*, November 6, 1941, p. 6; October 30, 1941, p. 6. Another source is the Kentucky High School Athletic Association Hall of Fame: kyathletichalloffame.org.

46. Kleber, *Kentucky Encyclopedia*, 442–443.

47. William H. P. Robertson, *The History of Thoroughbred Racing in America* (Englewood Cliffs, NJ: Prentice-Hall, 1964), 339–341; Beverly Bryant and Jean Williams, *Portraits in Roses: 109 Years of Kentucky Derby Winners* (New York: McGraw-Hill, 1984), 82; Joe Hirsch and Gene Plowden, *In the Winner's Circle: The Jones Boys of Calumet Farm* (New York: Mason & Lipscomb, 1974), 49; Bill Doolittle, *The Kentucky Derby: Run for the Roses* (Del Mar, CA: A Tehabi Book, 1998), 8–9.

48. Robertson, *History of Thoroughbred Racing*, 344–345.

49. Ibid., 339; William F. Reed, *Keeneland: A Half-Century of Racing* (Louisville: Harmony House, 1986), 97.

50. Reed, *Keeneland*, 97–99.

51. James C. Nicholson, *The Kentucky Derby: How the Run for the Roses Became America's Premier Sporting Event* (Lexington: University Press of Kentucky, 2012), 26–27; Frank G. Menke, *Down the Stretch: The Story of Colonel Matt J. Winn* (New York: Smith & Durrell, 1945), 1–3, 38; John E. Kleber, ed., *The Encyclopedia of Louisville* (Lexington: University Press of Kentucky, 2001), 946–947.

52. Menke, *Down the Stretch*, 279–280; Lynn S. Renau, *Jockeys, Belles, and Bluegrass Kings* (Louisville: Herr House Press, 1995), 77; Nicholson, *Kentucky Derby*, 116–119.

53. Renau, *Jockeys, Belles, and Bluegrass Kings*, 77; *Paducah Sun-Democrat*, May 2, 1943, p. 12; Menke, *Down the Stretch*, 269.

54. Robertson, *History of Thoroughbred Racing*, 352–353.

55. *Lexington Herald-Leader*, December 12, 2001, p. D7; *Courier-Journal*,

August 11, 1940, Section 5, p. 4; Kleber, *Kentucky Encyclopedia*, 484; *Lexington Herald*, August 15, 1943, p. 8.

56. *Lexington Herald*, August 8, 1943, Yearling Sale Section, p. 1; August 15, 1943, p. 8; Kleber, *Kentucky Encyclopedia*, 484.

57. Menke, *Down the Stretch*, 271.

58. Robertson, *History of Thoroughbred Racing in America*, 356–359, 367.

59. *Courier-Journal*, February 24, 1943, Section 2, p. 9; Rosemary Clooney (with Joan Barthel), *Girl Singer: An Autobiography* (New York: Doubleday, 1999), 17–18.

60. Norman Polmar and Thomas B. Allen, *World War II: America at War, 1941–1945* (New York: Random House, 1991), 744; www.history.navy.mil/photos/pers-us/uspers-f/h-forgy.htm.

61. Polmar and Allen, *World War II*, 745.

62. Glenn Miller, lyrics from "In the Mood," Glenn Miller: Greatest Hits, RCA Victor, Audio CD.

63. Kleber, *Encyclopedia of Louisville*, p. 939.

64. *Courier-Journal*, April 5, 1944, Section 2, p. 2.

65. Ibid.

66. Ibid., November 11, 1942, Section 1, p. 12.

67. Ibid., October 7, 1942, Section 2, p. 12.

68. See the movie theater advertisements in the *Courier-Journal*, the *Lexington Herald*, and the other local newspapers at any time between the attack on Pearl Harbor and the Japanese surrender. The periodicals department of the Young Library at the University of Kentucky has these newspapers on microfilm.

69. Edward F. Dolan Jr., *History of the Movies* (Greenwich, CT: Bison Books, 1983), 223–225; Clayton R. Koppes and Gregory D. Black, *Hollywood Goes to War: How Politics, Profits, and Propaganda Shaped World War II Movies* (New York: Free Press, 1987), 80.

70. Koppes and Black, *Hollywood Goes to War*, 79, 260; Bernard F. Dick, *The Star-Spangled Screen: The American World War II Film* (Lexington: University Press of Kentucky, 1985), 106, 255–256.

71. Kathryn Kane, *Visions of War: Hollywood Combat Films of World War II* (Ann Arbor: VMI Research Press, 1982), 135–144, 165.

72. Meleta Crim Hill interview, Lexington, KY, April 22, 2014; John D. Perrine interview, Lexington, KY, April 23, 2014.

73. Thomas Doherty, *Projections of War: Hollywood, American Culture and World War II* (New York: Columbia University Press, 1993), 182–183.

74. Kane, *Visions of War*, 10; *Movie Trivia Mania* (New York: Beekman House, 1984), 75–76.

75. *Movie Trivia Mania*, 75; *Ride 'em Cowboy*, Universal Studios, 1942.

76. *Movie Trivia Mania*, 75–76.

77. Jay A. Brown and the Editors of *Consumer Guide*, *Rating the Movies* (Lin-

colnwood, IL: Publications International, 1988), 376; *The Road to Morocco*, Paramount Pictures, 1942.

78. *Jackson Times*, January 28, 1943, p. 2; *Talk of the Town*, Columbia Pictures, 1942; *Calling Dr. Death*, Universal Pictures, 1943; *Somerset Journal*, February 10, 1944, p. 3.

Conclusion

1. *Mt. Sterling Advocate*, August 16, 1945, p. 1; H. E. Everman, *Bourbon County since 1865* (Richmond, KY: Book Crafters, 1999), 162; James C. Klotter, *Kentucky: Portrait in Paradox, 1900–1950* (Frankfort: Kentucky Historical Society, 1996), 262.

2. *Kentucky Post*, May 8, 1945, p. 1; Mary Jean Kinsman, "The Kentucky Home Front: World War II," *Filson Club History Quarterly* 68, no. 3 (July 1994): 375; Paul A. Tenkotte and James C. Claypool, eds., *The Encyclopedia of Northern Kentucky* (Lexington: University Press of Kentucky, 2009), 923; John E. Kleber, ed., *The Encyclopedia of Louisville* (Lexington: University Press of Kentucky, 2001), 772. Additional information on the postwar uses of wartime plants can be obtained by searching the Internet.

3. Richard Polenberg, *War and Society: The United States, 1941–1945* (New York: J. B. Lippincott Co., 1972), 235–236.

4. Paul A. C. Koistinen, *Arsenal of World War II: The Political Economy of American Warfare, 1940–1945* (Lawrence: University Press of Kansas, 2004), 446.

5. Meg Jacobs, 'How About Some Meat?': The Office of Price Administration, Consumption Politics, and State Building from the Bottom Up, 1941–1946," *Journal of American History* 84, no. 3 (December 1997): 911–913, 938–941; Laura McEnaney, "Nightmares on Elm Street: Demobilizing in Chicago, 1945–1953," *Journal of American History* 92, no. 4 (March 2006): 1268, 1274–1275, 1289–1291. Jacobs's and McEnaney's sophisticated accounts of Office of Price Administration state-building efforts underscore historian Robert Cuff's insight that there may well be a "constant dialectic between decentralization and centralization in the evolution of social organization." As Jacobs and McEnaney show, OPA regulation of prices and rents represented a high point for state intervention in the immediate postwar civilian economy, and the OPA's defeat became both a symbol of New Deal–Fair Deal retrenchment and a part of that process. As the military-industrial complex grew, regulation of consumers diminished. Decentralization and diminution of state power occurred in some areas, though not others.

6. George Brown Tindall, *America: A Narrative History* (New York: W. W. Norton & Co., 1988), 1235.

7. Hollis B. Gibson interview, Jackson, KY, February 18, 1999; Lizzie B. Watts interview, Jackson, KY, January 20, 1999; *Jackson Times*, September 24, 1992, pp. 1, 8; El Hannen Stacy, *A Boy from Appalachia Goes to War* (Lost Creek, KY: Stacy Pub-

lications, 1999), 164–165, 170–171; Frances Gaitskill interview, Mt. Sterling, KY, October 25, 2007; James Russell Harris interview, Frankfort, KY, February 8, 2012.

8. James Russell Harris, "The Harrodsburg Tankers: Bataan, Prison, and the Bonds of Community," *Register of the Kentucky Historical Society* 86 (Summer 1988): 230–233, 238–253, 260–261, 277; Harris interview, February 8, 2012.

9. Tindall, *America,* 1237–1239; Klotter, *Kentucky: Portrait in Paradox,* 263.

10. U.S. Census of 1950, Population and Housing, Vol. 2, Part 17, Kentucky, 36; Historic Personal and Per Capita Income in Kentucky and U.S., 1940–2003, U.S. Bureau of Economic Analysis, Annual State Personal Income; *Hardin County Enterprise,* June 13, 1946, p. 1.

11. U.S. Census Bureau, Statistical Abstract of the United States: 2003, Mini-Historical Statistics, 67, Chart No. HS-35, Personal Income and Personal Income Per Capita by State, 1929–2001—Continued; Historic Personal and Per Capita Income in Kentucky and U.S., 1940–2003, U.S. Bureau of Economic Analysis.

12. Annual Cash Receipts, 1924–2010, Kentucky, 1940–1944, Table 5 (revised), December 4, 2001, Economic Research Service, United States Department of Agriculture, Washington, DC.

13. Watts interview, January 20, 1999; Gibson interview, February 18, 1999; Daniel Boone Razor Jr. and Elaine Razor interview, Mt. Sterling, KY, June 27, 2009; George H. Yater, *Two Hundred Years at the Falls of the Ohio: A History of Louisville and Jefferson County* (Louisville: Heritage Corporation, 1979), 215–216.

14. Richard E. Holl, *From the Boardroom to the War Room: America's Corporate Liberals and FDR's Preparedness Program* (Rochester, NY: University of Rochester Press, 2005), 40; *Hardin County Enterprise,* October 24, 1946, p. 1; October 1, 1946, p. 1.

15. U.S. Census of 1930, Population, Vol. 4, Occupations, by States, Kentucky, 587 (Table 1); U.S. Census of 1940, Population, Vol. 3, The Labor Force, Part 3, Kentucky, 129 (Table 2), 138; U.S. Census of 1950, Population, Vol. 2, Part 17, Kentucky, 36 (Table 26), 37 (Table 28); U.S. Census of 1960, Population, Vol. 1, Part 19, Kentucky, 155 (Table 52); U.S. Census of 1970, Population, Vol. 1, Part 19, 212 (Table 53). Also see Polenberg, *War and Society,* 146.

16. *Louisville Leader,* December 15, 1945, p. 1.

17. George C. Wright, *A History of Blacks in Kentucky: Vol. 2, In Pursuit of Equality, 1890–1980* (Frankfort: Kentucky Historical Society, 1992), 177–182; Lowell H. Harrison and James C. Klotter, *A New History of Kentucky* (Lexington: University Press of Kentucky, 1997), 385–386.

18. G. Wright, *History of Blacks in Kentucky, Vol. 2,* 189.

19. Malcolm E. Jewell and Everett W. Cunningham, *Kentucky Politics* (Lexington: University of Kentucky Press, 1968), 22–23; U.S. Census of 1950, Population and Housing, Vol. 2, Kentucky, Part 17, 35.

20. Jewell and Cunningham, *Kentucky Politics,* 224–225; http://www.lrc.ky.gov/lrcpubs/IB175a.pdf; James C. Klotter, "Snapshots of a State in Change: An

Overview of Kentucky in the Twentieth Century," *Filson Club History Quarterly* 66, no. 3 (July 1992): 439–440; Tracy Campbell, *Short of the Glory: The Fall and Redemption of Edward F. Prichard Jr.* (Lexington: University Press of Kentucky, 1998), 7–10, 162–168.

21. Harrison and Klotter, *New History*, 374.

22. Koistinen, *Arsenal of World War II*, 8–11; Harrison and Klotter, *New History*, 365, 374.

23. Melvyn Dubofsky and Athan Theoharis, *Imperial Democracy: The United States since 1945* (Englewood Cliffs, NJ: Prentice-Hall, 1983), 20; George C. Herring, *From Colony to Superpower: U.S. Foreign Relations since 1776* (New York: Oxford University Press, 2008), 611; *Hardin County Enterprise*, November 21, 1946, p. 2; James K. Libbey, *Dear Alben: Mr. Barkley of Kentucky* (Lexington: University Press of Kentucky, 1979), 84, 91–92, 100, 111; Robert Schulman, *John Sherman Cooper: The Global Kentuckian* (Lexington: University Press of Kentucky, 1976), 3–4, 83.

24. Bert Nelli and Steve Nelli, *The Winning Tradition: A History of Kentucky Wildcat Basketball* (Lexington: University Press of Kentucky, 1998), 59–68; Harrison and Klotter, *New History*, 338–342. Also consult Russell Rice, *The Wildcats: A Story of Kentucky Football* (Huntsville, AL: Strode Publishers, 1975).

Bibliography

Primary Sources

Manuscript Collections

"Aegis." Rauner Special Collections. Dartmouth College Library, Hanover, NH.

Herman Lee Donovan Papers. University Archives and Special Collections, Margaret I. King Library, Lexington, KY.

Leon Henderson Papers. Franklin D. Roosevelt Presidential Library, Hyde Park, NY.

Keen Johnson Papers. Thomas and Hazel Little Building. Eastern Kentucky University, Richmond.

Louisville Civilian Defense Papers. Special Collections, Kentucky Historical Society, Frankfort.

Kenneth G. Maddox Papers. Kentucky Historical Society, Frankfort.

Samuel Plato Papers. Filson Club Historical Society, Louisville, KY.

Franklin Delano Roosevelt Papers. Franklin D. Roosevelt Presidential Library, Hyde Park, NY.

Edward R. Stettinius Jr. Papers. University of Virginia Library, Charlottesville.

Simeon Willis Papers. Special Collections. Margaret I. King Library, University of Kentucky, Lexington.

Archival Sources

Center of Excellence for the Study of Kentucky African Americans. Athletics 1939–1942 File Folder. Scrapbook. Kentucky State University, Frankfort.

Hagley Museum and Library. DuPont Company Records and Digital Archives, Wilmington, DE.

National Archives. Modern Military Branch. Record Group 107. Records of the Planning Branch, Assistant Secretary of War, Office of the Secretary of War. College Park, MD.

National Archives. Modern Military Branch. Record Group 179. War Production Board Policy Documentation File. College Park, MD.

National Archives. Modern Military Branch. Record Group 389. Office of the Provost Marshal General. Axis Prisoner of War Camp Records (Boxes 2477 through 2665). College Park, MD.

University of Louisville Archives and Records Center. *L&N Employes' Magazine* and James W. Settle Memoir. University of Louisville, Louisville, KY.

Government/Public Documents

Annual Cash Receipts, 1924–2010, Kentucky, 1940–1944, Table 5 (revised), Washington, DC: Economic Research Service, U.S. Department of Agriculture, 2001.

Blue Grass Army Depot, Army Defense Environmental Restoration Program, Installation Action Plan, FY 2008. Richmond, KY.

Census of Agriculture (1945). *State Reports and County Statistics with a U.S. Summary.* U.S. Department of Agriculture. Washington, DC: U.S. Government Printing Office, 1946.

County Data Book, A Supplement to the Statistical Abstract of the United States. U.S. Department of Commerce and U.S. Bureau of the Census. Washington, DC: U.S. Government Printing Office, 1947.

"Guide for Planning the Local Victory Garden Program." Washington, DC: Office of Civilian Defense, 1942.

Historical Statistics of the United States, Colonial Times to 1970, Part 1. Washington, DC: U.S. Department of Commerce and the U.S. Bureau of the Census, 1975.

Hockbaum, H. W. "The 1943 Victory Garden Program." Washington, DC: U.S. Department of Agriculture and the U.S. Department of Civil Defense, 1943.

"Industrial Mobilization Plan" (Revision of 1939). Washington, DC: U.S. Government Printing Office, 1939.

Kentucky Acts (1940 and 1942).

Kentucky General Assembly Membership 1900–2005, Vol. 1, 1900–1949, Informational Bulletin no. 175 (4th rev. ed.). Frankfort: Legislative Research Commission.

Kentucky Legislative Research Commission. *Kentucky Youth Problems: A Report to the Governor and the General Assembly.* Frankfort: Legislative Research Commission, Research Publication no. 33, January 1952.

Report of the Kentucky Commission on Negro Affairs, November 1, 1945. Frankfort. (Copy available from Morehead State University, Morehead, KY.)

Sources of Personal Income by Major Industry Groups for Kentucky, 1930–2003. Washington, DC: U.S. Bureau of Economic Analysis, Department of Commerce.

Statistical Abstract of the United States, 68th ed. Washington, DC: U.S. Government Printing Office, 1947.

Statistical Abstract of the United States: 2003. U.S. Census Bureau, no. HS-29 (Employment Status of the Civilian Population: 1929–2002). Washington, DC: U.S. Census Bureau, 2004.

U.S. Census of 1930. Population, Vol. 4. Washington, DC: U.S. Government Printing Office, 1931.

U.S. Census of 1940. Population, Vols. 2 and 3. Washington, DC: U.S. Government Printing Office, 1941.

U.S. Census of Housing 1940. Vol. 2, General Characteristics, Part 3, Section 3. Washington, DC: U.S. Government Printing Office, 1941.

U.S. Census of 1950. Census of Agriculture. Vol. 1, Part 19, Kentucky (Chapter A: Statistics for the State). Washington, DC: U.S. Government Printing Office, 1952.

U.S. Census of Population 1950. Table 19: Population of Counties in Continental United States, Alaska, Hawaii, and Puerto Rico, 1950 and 1940—Continued. Washington, DC: U.S. Government Printing Office, 1952.

U.S. Census of Population 1950. Vol. 2, Part 1, United States Summary, Table 12, Rank of States according to Amount and Percent Increase in Population between 1940 and 1950. Washington, DC: U.S. Government Printing Office, 1952.

U.S. Census of 1950. Population and Housing, Vol. 2, Kentucky, Part 17, Historic Personal and Per Capita Income in Kentucky and U.S., 1940–2003. U.S. Bureau of Economic Analysis, Annual State Personal Income, Washington, DC.

U.S. Census of 1960. Population, Vol. 1, Part 19, Kentucky. Washington, DC: U.S. Government Printing Office, 1966.

U.S. Census of 1970. Population, Kentucky. Washington, DC: U.S. Government Printing Office, 1971.

U.S. Census Bureau. Statistical Abstract of the United States: 2003, Mini-Historical Statistics, Chart No. HS-35, Personal Income and Personal Income Per Capita by State, 1929–2001—Continued. Washington, DC.

Newspapers

Ashland Daily Independent (1941–1944)
Bowling Green News-Democrat (1939)
Chicago Defender (1942)
Courier-Journal (1935–1945, 1949, 1957, 1960, 1970, 2000, 2003, 2007)
Grant County News (1943)
Hardin County Enterprise (1946)
Harlan Daily Enterprise (1943)
Harrison Heritage News (2005)
Henderson County Gleaner (1941)
Henderson Morning Gleaner (1955)
Henry County Local (1944)
Jackson Times (1939, 1941–1945, 1992)
Kentucky New Era (1977)
Kentucky Post (1939–1945)
Lexington Herald (1941–1945)
Lexington Herald-Leader (1939–1945, 1999, 2001, 2007)
Lexington Leader (1943)
Louisville Defender (1976)
Louisville Leader (1935–1945)
Madisonville Messenger (1939, 1950)
Mayfield Messenger (1942)

Maysville Daily Independent (1943)
Mt. Sterling Advocate (1941–1945, 2007)
News-Enterprise (2012, article online)
New York Times (1939–1945, 1997)
Owensboro Messenger (1943)
Paducah Sun-Democrat (1939–1945)
Park City Daily News (1942–1943)
Richmond Daily Register (1939)
Rowan County News (1942)
Russellville News-Democrat (1939)
Somerset Journal (1939–1945)
Sterling Sentinel (2006)
Washington Post (1939–1945)
Whitesburg Mountain Eagle (1969)

Periodicals

Atlantic Monthly (1946)
Fortune (1939 and 1941)
Kentucky Business (1950)
Nation's Business (1942)
Newsweek (1944)

Oral Histories

Kentucky Oral History Commission Collection. Kentucky History Center, Frankfort.
University of Kentucky Library Alumni/Faculty Oral History Project. Russell Rice
    interview of Adolph Rupp. Special Collections, Margaret I. King Library, University of Kentucky, Lexington.

Interviews

Baird, Nancy. E-mail to author. June 9, 2011.
Baker, Brenda. Louisville, KY. August 11, 2011.
Blakely, Gloria. Louisville, KY. February 23, 2008.
Broadwater, Cecilia. Lexington, KY. July 29, 2008.
Burns, Edward. Georgetown, IN. July 31, 2011.
Cook, Albert Lee, and Mary Stevens Cook. Louisville, KY. February 23, 2008.
Doron, Adron, and Mignon Doron. Lexington, KY. July 20, 1999.
Elliott, Amanda Cooper. Lexington, KY. April 8, 2010.
Francis, Charles Jewell, Jr. Dayton, OH. February 24, 2010.
Gaitskill, Frances Jones. Mt. Sterling, KY. October 25, 2007.
Gibson, Hollis B. Jackson, KY. February 18, 1999.
Harris, James Russell. Frankfort, KY. June 26, 2008.
Hill, Barry. Lexington, KY. March 7, 1999.

Hill, Meleta Crim. Lexington, KY. April 22, 2014.
Ingram, Eileen Wooton Sandlin. Jackson, KY. May 16, 2014.
Lawson, Elizabeth. Lexington, KY. March 20, 1999.
Massenburg, Mary Ellen Perrine. Cary, NC. April 27, 2014.
Morris, Orville. Louisville, KY. February 27, 2008.
Nathan, Robert R. Bethesda, MD, and Arlington, VA. May 20, 1992, and July 10, 1995.
Newton, Patricia Porter. Louisville, KY. August 1, 2011.
Perrine, John D. Lexington, KY. March 9, 1999, and April 23, 2014.
Puckett, Billy Joe, and Sylvia Puckett. Murray, KY. May 11, 2014.
Razor, Daniel Boone, Jr. Mt. Sterling, KY. July 18, 2009.
Razor, Daniel Boone, Jr., and Elaine Razor. Mt. Sterling, KY. June 27, 2009.
Short, Jim. Olive Hill, KY. March 6, 2008.
Turner, William T. Hopkinsville, KY. March 27, 2010.
Wallace, Brownie. Jackson, KY. January 27, 2010, and March 16, 2010.
Wallace, Brownie, and Henrietta Wallace. Jackson, KY. December 11, 2007.
Watts, Lizzie B. Jackson, KY. January 20, 1999.
Wheately, August. Pendleton, KY. February 24, 2008.

Secondary Sources

Books, Articles, Theses, and Dissertations

Adams, Luther. "'Headed for Louisville': Rethinking Rural to Urban Migration in the South, 1930–1950." *Journal of Social History* 40, no. 2 (Winter 2006): 407–430.
———. "'It Was North of Tennessee': African American Migration to Louisville and the Meaning of the South." *Ohio Valley History* 3, no. 3 (Fall 2003): 37–52.
Adams, Michael C. C. *The Best War Ever: America and World War II.* Baltimore: Johns Hopkins University Press, 1994.
Alexander, Thomas G. "Utah War Industry during World War II : A Human Impact Analysis." *Utah Historical Quarterly* 51 (Winter 1983): 72–92.
Anderson, Karen Tucker. "Last Hired, First Fired: Black Women Workers during World War II." *Journal of American History* 69 (June 1982): 82–97.
Ardery, Philip. *Bomber Pilot: A Memoir of World War II.* Lexington: University Press of Kentucky, 1978.
Arnett, Larry L. *Call to Arms: A Collection of Fascinating Stories, Events, Personalities, and Facts about Kentucky's Military History.* Frankfort: Kentucky Publishing Co., 1995.
Arnett, Maralea. *The Annals and Scandals of Henderson County, Kentucky, 1775–1975.* Corydon, KY: Fremar Publishing Co., 1976.
Ascoli, Peter M. *Julius Rosenwald: The Man Who Built Sears, Roebuck and Advanced the Cause of Black Education in the American South.* Bloomington: Indiana University Press, 2006.

Axton, W. F. *Tobacco and Kentucky*. Lexington: University Press of Kentucky, 1975.

Badger, Anthony J. *The New Deal: The Depression Years, 1933–1940*. New York: Hill and Wang, 1988.

Baird, Nancy Disher. "An Opportunity to Meet 'Every Kind of Person': A Kentuckian Views Army Life during World War II." *Register of the Kentucky Historical Society* 101 (Summer 2003): 297–318.

———. "'To Lend You My Eyes . . . ': The World War II Letters of Special Services Officer Harry Jackson." *Register of the Kentucky Historical Society* 88 (Summer 1990): 288–317.

Baker, M. Joyce. *Images of Women in Film: The War Years, 1941–1945*. Ann Arbor: UMI Research Press, 1978.

Ballard, Jack Stokes. *The Shock of Peace: Military and Economic Demobilization after World War II*. Washington, DC: University Press of America, 1983.

Beck, Earl R. *The European Home Fronts, 1939–1945*. Arlington Heights, IL: Harlan Davidson, 1993.

Beckner, Lucien. "Drifting Sands of Politics, 1900–1944." In Hambleton Tapp, ed., *A SesquiCentennial History of Kentucky*. Vol. 2. Hopkinsville, KY: Historical Record Association, 1945.

Belcher, John C. "Population Growth and Characteristics." In Thomas R. Ford, ed., *The Southern Appalachian Region: A Survey*. Lexington: University of Kentucky Press, 1967.

Berk, Gerald. "Corporate Liberalism Reconsidered: A Review Essay." *Journal of Policy History* 3, no. 1 (1991): 70–84.

Berlin, Ira. *Generations of Captivity*. Cambridge, MA: Harvard University Press, 2003.

Bernstein, Irving. *Turbulent Years: A History of the American Worker, 1933–1941*. Boston: Houghton Mifflin, 1970.

Berry, Chad. *Southern Migrants, Northern Exiles*. Champaign: University of Illinois Press, 2000.

Blakey, George T. *Hard Times and New Deal in Kentucky, 1929–1939*. Lexington: University Press of Kentucky, 1986.

Bloch, Herbert A., and Frank T. Flynn. *Delinquency: The Juvenile Offender in America Today*. New York: Random House, 1956.

Blum, John Morton. *V Was for Victory: Politics and American Culture during World War II*. New York: Harcourt Brace Jovanovich, 1976.

Brandes, Stuart A. *American Welfare Capitalism, 1880–1940*. Chicago: University of Chicago Press, 1976.

Brinkley, Alan. *The End of Reform: New Deal Liberalism in Recession and War*. New York: Knopf, 1995.

———. "The New Deal and the Idea of the State." In Steve Frazer and Gary Gerstle, eds., *The Rise and Fall of the New Deal Order, 1930–1980*. Princeton, NJ: Princeton University Press, 1989.

Brody, David. "The Rise and Decline of Welfare Capitalism." In John Braeman, Robert H. Bremner, and David Brody, eds., *Change and Continuity in Twentieth-Century America: The 1920s.* Columbus: Ohio State University Press, 1968.

Brown, James S., and George A. Hillery, Jr. "The Great Migration, 1940–1960." In Thomas R. Ford, ed., *The Southern Appalachian Region: A Survey.* Lexington: University of Kentucky Press, 1967.

Brown, Jay A., and the Editors of *Consumer Guide. Rating the Movies.* Lincolnwood, IL: Publications International, 1988.

Bryant, Beverly, and Jean Williams. *Portraits in Roses: 109 Years of Kentucky Derby Winners.* New York: McGraw-Hill, 1984.

Buchanan, A. Russell. *Black Americans in World War II.* Santa Barbara, CA: Clio Books, 1977.

Burns, James MacGregor. *Roosevelt: The Lion and the Fox.* New York: Harcourt, Brace and World, 1956.

———. *Roosevelt: The Soldier of Freedom.* New York: Harcourt Brace Jovanovich, 1970.

Campagna, Anthony S. *U.S. National Economic Policy, 1917–1985.* New York: Praeger, 1987.

Campbell, D'Ann. *Women at War with America: Private Lives in a Patriotic Era.* Cambridge, MA: Harvard University Press, 1984.

Campbell, Tracy. *Short of the Glory: The Fall and Redemption of Edward F. Prichard Jr.* Lexington: University Press of Kentucky, 1998.

Carlson, Lewis H. *We Were Each Other's Prisoners: An Oral History of World War II American and German Prisoners of War.* New York: Basic Books, 1997.

Catton, Bruce. *The War Lords of Washington.* New York: Harcourt, Brace and Co., 1948.

Cavnes, Max Parvin. *The Hoosier Community at War.* Bloomington: Indiana University Press, 1961.

Chadwick, Bruce. *When the Game Was Black and White.* New York: Abbeville Press, 1992.

Chafe, William H. *The American Woman: Her Changing Social, Economic, and Political Roles, 1920–1970.* New York: Oxford University Press, 1972.

Channing, Steven A. *Kentucky: A Bicentennial History.* New York: Norton, 1977.

Clark, Thomas D. *Clark County, Kentucky: A History.* Winchester, KY: Clark County Heritage Commission and the Clark County Historical Society, 1995.

———. *A History of Kentucky.* New York: Prentice-Hall, 1937.

Clinard, Marshall B. *The Black Market: A Study of White Collar Crime.* New York: Rinehart & Co., 1952.

Clive, Alan. *State of War: Michigan in World War II.* Ann Arbor: University of Michigan Press, 1979.

Clooney, Rosemary (with Joan Barthel). *Girl Singer: An Autobiography.* New York: Doubleday, 1999.

Cockrum, James D. "Owensboro Goes to War." *Daviess County Historical Quarterly* 2, no. 1 (January 1984): 2–9.

Coffman, Edward M. "A Younger Brother of the Greatest Generation." *Register of the Kentucky Historical Society* 100, no. 2 (Spring 2002): 129–138.

Cole, Wayne S. *America First: The Battle against Intervention, 1940–1941.* Madison: University of Wisconsin Press, 1953.

———. *An Interpretive History of American Foreign Relations.* Rev. ed. Homewood, IL: Dorsey Press, 1974.

———. *Roosevelt and the Isolationists, 1932–1945.* Lincoln: University of Nebraska Press, 1983.

Coleman, J. Winston, Jr. *Slavery Times in Kentucky.* Chapel Hill: University of North Carolina Press, 1940.

Collins, Robert M. *The Business Response to Keynes, 1929–1964.* New York: Columbia University Press, 1981.

Connelley, William Elsey, and E. M. Coulter. *History of Kentucky.* Vol. 4. Chicago: American Historical Society, 1922.

Costello, John. *The Pacific War.* New York: Rawson, Wade, 1981.

———. *Virtue under Fire: How World War II Changed Our Social and Sexual Attitudes.* Boston: Little, Brown and Co., 1985.

Crowe-Carraco, Carol. *The Big Sandy.* Lexington: University Press of Kentucky, 1979.

Cuff, Robert D. "An Organizational Perspective on the Military-Industrial Complex." *Business History Review* 52, no. 2 (Summer 1978): 250–267.

———. *The War Industries Board: Business Government Relations during World War I.* Baltimore: Johns Hopkins University Press, 1973.

Dalfiume, Richard M. *Desegregation of the United States Armed Forces: Fighting on Two Fronts, 1939–1953.* Columbia: University of Missouri Press, 1969.

———. "The Forgotten Years of the Negro Revolution." *Journal of American History* 55 (1968): 90–106.

Dallek, Robert. *Franklin D. Roosevelt and American Foreign Policy, 1932–1945.* New York: Oxford University Press, 1979.

Davie, Maurice R. *Negroes in American Society.* New York: McGraw-Hill, 1949.

Dear, I. C. B., and M. R. D. Foot, eds. *The Oxford Companion to World War II.* New York: Oxford University Press, 2001.

Delzell, E., N. Sathiakumar, M. Hovinga, et al. "A Follow-Up Study of Synthetic Rubber Workers." *Toxicology* 113 (1996): 182–189.

Derber, Milton. *The American Idea of Industrial Democracy, 1865–1965.* Urbana: University of Illinois Press, 1971.

Dick, Bernard F. *The Star-Spangled Screen: The American World War II Film.* Lexington: University Press of Kentucky,1985.

Doherty, Thomas. *Projections of War: Hollywood, American Culture, and World War II.* New York: Columbia University Press, 1993.

Dolan, Edward F., Jr. *History of the Movies.* Greenwich, CT: Bison Books, 1983.

Donovan, Mary Sudman, and D. Patricia Wagner. *Kentucky's Black Heritage: The Role of the Black People in the History of Kentucky from Pioneer Days to the Present.* Frankfort: Kentucky Commission on Civil Rights, 1971.

Doolittle, Bill. *The Kentucky Derby: Run for the Roses.* Del Mar, CA: A Tehabi Book, 1998.

Dubofsky, Melvyn, and Foster Rhea Dulles. *Labor in America: A History.* 8th ed. Wheeling, IL: Harlan Davidson, 2010.

Dubofsky, Melvyn, and Athan Theoharis. *Imperial Democracy: The United States since 1945.* Englewood Cliffs, NJ: Prentice-Hall, 1983.

Dubofsky, Melvyn, and Warren Van Tine. *John L. Lewis: A Biography.* New York: Quadrangle, 1977.

Dunnigan, Alice A. *The Fascinating Story of Black Kentuckians.* Washington, DC: Associated Publishers, 1982.

Durr, K. D. *Behind the Backlash: White Working-Class Politics in Baltimore, 1940–1980.* Chapel Hill: University of North Carolina Press, 2003.

Duvall, Jeffery A. "Knowing about the Tobacco: Women, Burley, and Farming in the Central Ohio River Valley." *Register of the Kentucky Historical Society* 108, no. 4 (Autumn 2010): 317–346.

Ehrmann, Henry W. "An Experiment in Political Education: The Prisoner-of-War Schools in the United States." *Social Research* 14, no. 3 (Fall 1947): 304–320.

Eisenhower, Dwight D. *Crusade in Europe.* Garden City, NJ: Doubleday & Co., 1948.

Ellis, William E. *A History of Eastern Kentucky University.* Lexington: University Press of Kentucky, 2005.

Ellis, William E., H. E. Everman, and Richard D. Sears. *Madison County: 200 Years in Retrospect.* Richmond, KY: Madison County Historical Society, 1985.

Ellison, Betty Boles. *Illegal Odyssey: 200 Years of Kentucky Moonshine.* Lexington, KY: First Books, 2003.

Everman, H. E. *Bourbon County since 1865.* Richmond, KY: Book Crafters, 1999.

Farago, Ladislas. *The Game of the Foxes: The Untold Story of German Espionage in the United States and Great Britain during World War II.* New York: David McKay Co., 1971.

Fesler, James W., et al. *Industrial Mobilization for War: History of the War Production Board and Predecessor Agencies, 1940–1945.* Washington, DC: U.S. Government Printing Office, 1947.

Fite, Gilbert C. *American Agriculture and Farm Policy since 1900.* New York: Macmillan Co. for Service Center for Teachers of History, 1964.

———. *Cotton Fields No More: Southern Agriculture, 1865–1980.* Lexington: University Press of Kentucky, 1984.

Flatt, Donald F. *Morehead State University, 1887–1997: A Light to the Mountains.* Ashland, KY: Jesse Stuart Foundation, 1997.

Flynn, Elizabeth Gurley. *Women in the War*. New York: Workers Library Publishers, 1942.

Fosl, Catherine, and Tracy E. K'Meyer. *Freedom on the Border: An Oral History of the Civil Rights Movement in Kentucky*. Lexington: University Press of Kentucky, 2009.

Fowler, Bertram. *Food: A Weapon for Victory*. Boston: Little, Brown, 1942.

Fox-Genovese, Elizabeth. "Mixed Messages: Women and the Impact of World War II." *Southern Humanities Review* 27 (Summer 1993): 235–245.

Frazier, Harriet C. *Lynchings in Missouri, 1803–1981*. Jefferson, NC: McFarland & Co., 2009.

Gabel, Christopher R. *The U.S. Army GHQ Maneuvers of 1941*. Washington, DC: Center of Military History, United States Army, 1991.

Gaddis, John Lewis. "The Corporatist Synthesis: A Skeptical View." *Diplomatic History* 10 (Fall 1986): 357–362.

Galambos, Louis. "The Emerging Organizational Synthesis in Modern American History." *Business History Review* 44, no. 3 (Autumn 1970): 279–290.

Gansberg, Judith. *Stalag: U.S.A.* New York: Thomas Y. Crowell Co,, 1977.

Gardiner, C. Harvey. *Coach Diddle, Mister Diddle: Motivator of Men*. Nashville, TN: Parthenon Press, 1984.

Gilbert, Felix. *The End of the European Era, 1890 to the Present*. 4th ed. New York: W. W. Norton & Co., 1991.

Gilbert, James. *A Cycle of Outrage: America's Reaction to the Juvenile Delinquent in the 1950s*. New York: Oxford University Press, 1986.

Goldfield, David R. *Cotton Fields and Skyscrapers: Southern City and Region, 1607–1980*. Baton Rouge: Louisiana State University Press, 1982.

Goodwin, Doris Kearns. *No Ordinary Time: Franklin and Eleanor Roosevelt; The Home Front in World War II*. New York: Simon & Schuster, 1994.

Gordon, Susan L. "Home Front Tennessee: The World War II Experience." *Tennessee Historical Quarterly* 51 (Spring 1992): 3–18.

Graham, Otis L. *Toward a Planned Society: From Roosevelt to Nixon*. New York: Oxford University Press, 1976.

Gray, Wayne T. "Population Movements in the Kentucky Mountains." *Rural Sociology* 10, no. 4 (December 1945): 380–386.

Hall, Wade. *The Rest of the Dream: The Black Odyssey of Lyman Johnson*. Lexington: University Press of Kentucky, 1988.

Hamby, Alonzo. *Beyond the New Deal: Harry S Truman and American Liberalism*. New York: Columbia University Press, 1973.

Hamilton, David E. *From New Day to New Deal: American Farm Policy from Hoover to Roosevelt, 1928–1933*. Chapel Hill: University of North Carolina Press, 1991.

Hardin, John A. *Fifty Years of Segregation: Black Higher Education in Kentucky, 1904–1954*. Lexington: University Press of Kentucky, 1997.

———. *Onward and Upward: A Centennial History of Kentucky State University, 1886–1986*. Frankfort: Kentucky State University, 1987.

Harmon, Shirley Mae. "A Comparison Study of Black and White Women War Workers in Louisville, Kentucky during World War II." MA thesis, University of Louisville, 1999.

Harris, James Russell. "The Harrodsburg Tankers: Bataan, Prison, and the Bonds of Community." *Register of the Kentucky Historical Society* 86 (Summer 1988): 230–277.

———. "Rolling Bandages and Building Thunderbolts: A Woman's Memories of the Kentucky Home Front, 1941–1945." *Register of the Kentucky Historical Society* 100, no. 2 (Spring 2002): 167–194.

Harrison, Lowell H. *Kentucky's Governors, 1792–1985*. Lexington: University Press of Kentucky, 1985.

———. "Lincoln and Compensated Emancipation in Kentucky." In Douglas Cantrell, Thomas D. Matijasic, Richard E. Holl, Lorie Maltby, and Richard Smoot, eds., *Kentucky through the Centuries: A Collection of Documents and Essays*. Dubuque, IA: Kendall Hunt, 2005.

———. "Memories of Slavery Days in Kentucky." *Filson Club History Quarterly* 47, no. 3 (July 1973): 242–257.

Harrison, Lowell H., and James C. Klotter. *A New History of Kentucky*. Lexington: University Press of Kentucky, 1997.

Harrison, Mark. "Resource Mobilization for World War II: The USA, USSR, and Germany, 1938–1945." *Economic History Review* 41 (May 1988): 171–192.

Hartmann, Susan M. *The Home Front and Beyond: American Women in the 1940s*. Boston: Twayne Publishers, 1982.

Hawley, Ellis W. "The Discovery and Study of a 'Corporate Liberalism.'" *Business History Review* 52 (Autumn 1978): 309–320.

———. *The Great War and the Search for a Modern Order: A History of the American People and Their Institutions, 1917–1933*. New York: St. Martin's Press, 1979.

———. *The New Deal and the Problem of Monopoly*. Princeton, NJ: Princeton University Press, 1966.

———. "The New Deal State and the Anti-Bureaucratic Tradition." In Robert Eden, ed., *The New Deal and Its Legacy: Critique and Reappraisal*. Westport, CT: Greenwood Press, 1989.

Haws, Robert, ed. *The Age of Segregation: Race Relations in the South, 1890–1945*. Jackson: University Press of Mississippi, 1978.

Hays, Samuel P. *The Response to Industrialism, 1885–1914*. Chicago: University of Chicago Press, 1957.

Heckscher, August. *When LaGuardia Was Mayor: New York's Legendary Years*. New York: W. W. Norton & Co., 1978.

Heclo, Hugh. *Modern Social Politics in Britain and Sweden*. New Haven, CT: Yale University Press, 1974.

Heinrichs, Waldo. *Threshold of War: Franklin D. Roosevelt and American Entry into World War II.* New York: Oxford University Press, 1988.

Henderson, Leon, and Donald M. Nelson. "Prices, Profits, and Government." *Harvard Business Review* 19 (Summer 1941): 389–404.

Herr, Kincaid A. *The Louisville & Nashville Railroad, 1850–1963.* Lexington: University Press of Kentucky, 2000.

Herring, George C. *Aid to Russia, 1941–1946.* New York: Columbia University Press, 1973.

———. *From Colony to Superpower: U.S. Foreign Relations since 1776.* New York: Oxford University Press, 2008.

Hirsch, Joe, and Gene Plowden. *In the Winner's Circle: The Jones Boys of Calumet Farm.* New York: Mason & Lipscomb, 1974.

Hogan, Michael J. "Corporatism: A Positive Appraisal." *Diplomatic History* 10 (Fall 1986): 363–372.

Holl, Richard E. *From the Boardroom to the War Room: America's Corporate Liberals and FDR's Preparedness Program.* Rochester, NY: University of Rochester Press, 2005.

———. "German Prisoners of War Visit Henry County, Kentucky, September–October 1944." *Quarterly Review* (Henry County) 22, no. 3 (September 1999): 1–6.

———. "Swastikas in the Bluegrass State: Axis Prisoners of War in Kentucky, 1942–1946." *Register of the Kentucky Historical Society* 100, no. 2 (Spring 2002): 139–166.

Hollingsworth, Randolph. *Lexington: Queen of the Bluegrass.* Charleston, SC: Arcadia Publishing, 2004.

Honey, Maureen. *Creating Rosie the Riveter: Class, Gender, and Propaganda during World War II.* Amherst: University of Massachusetts Press, 1984.

Hopkins, James F. *A History of the Hemp Industry in Kentucky.* Lexington: University of Kentucky Press, 1951.

Howard, Frank A. *Buna Rubber: The Birth of an Industry.* New York: D. Van Nostrand Co., 1947.

Iriye, Akira. *Power and Culture: The Japanese-American War, 1941–1945.* Cambridge, MA: Harvard University Press, 1981.

Jacobs, Meg. "'How About Some Meat?' The Office of Price Administration, Consumption Politics, and State Building from the Bottom Up, 1941–1946." *Journal of American History* 84, no. 3 (December 1997): 910–941.

Janeway, Eliot. *The Struggle for Survival: A Chronicle of Economic Mobilization during World War II.* New Haven, CT: Yale University Press, 1951.

Jay, Kathryn. *More Than Just a Game: Sports in American Life since 1945.* New York: Columbia University Press, 2004.

Jeffries, John W. *Wartime America: The World War II Home Front.* Chicago: Ivan R. Dee, 1996.

Jewell, Malcolm E., ed. *The Politics of Reapportionment.* New York: Atherton Press, 1962.

Jewell, Malcolm E., and Everett W. Cunningham. *Kentucky Politics.* Lexington: University of Kentucky Press, 1968.

Jillson, Willard Rouse. "Governor Simeon S. Willis." *Register of the Kentucky Historical Society* 42, no. 138 (1944): 3–5.

Johnson, Charles W. "V for Virginia: The Commonwealth Goes to War." *Virginia Magazine of History and Biography* 100, no. 3 (July 1992): 365–398.

Johnson, W. M., Jr. *A Survey of Agriculture in Fleming County.* Lexington: Kentucky Utilities Co., 1953.

Jones, Loyal. *Appalachian Values.* Ashland, KY: Jesse Stuart Foundation, 1994.

Kane, Kathryn. *Visions of War: Hollywood Combat Films of World War II.* Ann Arbor: VMI Research Press, 1982.

Karl, Barry D. *The Uneasy State: The United States from 1915 to 1945.* Chicago: University of Chicago Press, 1983.

Keegan, John. *The Second World War.* New York: Penguin Books, 1989.

Kelley, Brent. *The Negro Leagues Revisited.* Jefferson, NC: McFarland & Co., 2000.

Kelly, Arthur L. *Battlefire! Combat Stories from World War II.* Lexington: University Press of Kentucky, 1997.

Kennedy, David M. *Freedom from Fear: The American People in Depression and War, 1929–1945.* New York: Oxford University Press, 1999.

Kentucky Commission on Human Rights. *Kentucky's Black Heritage.* Frankfort, 1971.

Kerns, J. Harvey. *A Survey of the Economic and Cultural Conditions of the Negro Population of Louisville, Kentucky, and a Review of the Program and Activities of the Louisville Urban League.* New York: National Urban League, 1948.

Kimball, Warren F. *The Juggler: Franklin Roosevelt as Wartime Statesman.* Princeton, NJ: Princeton University Press, 1991.

Kindred, Dave. *Basketball: The Dream Game in Kentucky.* Louisville: Fetter Printing Co., 1976.

Kinsman, Mary Jean. "The Kentucky Home Front: World War II." *Filson Club History Quarterly* 68, no. 3 (July 1994): 365–378.

Kirkendall, Richard S. *The United States, 1929–1945: Years of Crisis and Change.* New York: McGraw-Hill, 1974.

Kleber, John E., ed. *The Encyclopedia of Louisville.* Lexington: University Press of Kentucky, 2001.

———, ed. *The Kentucky Encyclopedia.* Lexington: University Press of Kentucky, 1992.

———, ed. *The New History of Shelby County, Kentucky.* Prospect, KY: Harmony House, 2003.

Klein, Maury. *History of the Louisville & Nashville Railroad.* Lexington: University Press of Kentucky, 2003.

Klotter, James C. *Kentucky: Portrait in Paradox, 1900–1950.* Frankfort: Kentucky Historical Society, 1996.

———, ed. *The Public Papers of Simeon Willis, 1943–1947.* Lexington: University Press of Kentucky, 1988.

———. "Snapshots of a State in Change: An Overview of Kentucky in the Twentieth Century." *Filson Club History Quarterly* 66, no. 3 (July 1992): 421–448.

Klotter, James C., and Freda C. Klotter. *A Concise History of Kentucky.* Lexington: University Press of Kentucky, 2008.

Koehler, Franz A. *Special Rations for the Armed Forces: Army Operational Rations; A Historical Background.* Washington, DC: QMC Historical Studies, Historical Branch, Office of the Quartermaster General, 1958.

Koistinen, Paul A. C. *Arsenal of World War II: The Political Economy of American Warfare, 1940–1945.* Lawrence: University Press of Kansas, 2004.

———. "The Hammer and the Sword: Labor, the Military, and Industrial Mobilization, 1920–1945." PhD diss., University of California, Berkeley, 1964.

———. *The Military-Industrial Complex: A Historical Perspective.* New York: Praeger, 1980.

———. "Mobilizing the World War II Economy: Labor and the Industrial-Military Alliance." *Pacific Historical Review* 42 (1972): 443–478.

———. *Planning War, Pursuing Peace: The Political Economy of American Warfare, 1920–1939.* Lawrence: University Press of Kansas, 1998.

Koppes, Clayton R., and Gregory D. Black. *Hollywood Goes to War: How Politics, Profits, and Propaganda Shaped World War II Movies.* New York: Free Press, 1987.

Kramer, Carl E. *Capital on the Kentucky: A Two-Hundred-Year History of Frankfort and Franklin County.* Frankfort: Historic Frankfort, 1986.

Krammer, Arnold. *Nazi Prisoners of War in America.* New York: Stein and Day, 1979.

Krasner, Stephen D. "Approaches to the State: Alternative Conceptions and Historical Dynamics." *Comparative Politics* 16, no. 2 (January 1984): 223–246.

Larson, Olaf F. "Wartime Migration and the Manpower Reserve on Farms in Eastern Kentucky." *Rural Sociology* 8, no. 2 (June 1943): 148–161.

Larson, T. A. *Wyoming's War Years, 1941–1945.* Laramie: University of Wyoming Press, 1954.

Leonard, Stephen J. "Denver at War: The Home Front in World War II." *Colorado Heritage* 4 (1987): 30–39.

Leuchtenburg, William E. *Franklin D. Roosevelt and the New Deal, 1932–1940.* New York: Harper and Row, 1963.

———. "The New Deal and the Analogue of War." In John Braeman, Robert H. Bremner, and Everett Walters, eds., *Change and Continuity in Twentieth-Century America.* Columbus: Ohio State University Press, 1964.

Lever, Harry, and Joseph Young. *Wartime Racketeers*. New York: G. P. Putnam's Sons, 1945.

Lewis, George G., and John Mewha. *History of Prisoner of War Utilization by the United States Army, 1776–1945*. Washington, DC: Department of the Army, 1955.

Lewis, Peter. Review of Lizzie Colingham, *The Taste of War* (London: Allen Lane, 2011). *The Mail Online*, January 27, 2011.

Libbey, James K. *Dear Alben: Mr. Barkley of Kentucky*. Lexington: University Press of Kentucky, 1979.

Lichtenstein, Nelson. *Labor's War at Home: The CIO in World War II*. Cambridge, UK: Cambridge University Press, 1982.

———. *State of the Union: A Century of American Labor*. Princeton, NJ: Princeton University Press, 2002.

"Lieutenant General Simon Bolivar Buckner, Jr." *Filson Club History Quarterly* 23 (April 1949): 152–157.

Lingeman, Richard R. *Don't You Know There's a War On? The American Home Front, 1941–1945*. New York: G. P. Putnam's Sons, 1970.

Link, Arthur S., and Richard L. McCormick. *Progressivism*. Arlington Heights, IL: Harlan Davidson, 1983.

Losey, Philip H. "The Election and Administration of Governor Simeon Willis, 1942–1947." MA thesis, Eastern Kentucky University, 1978.

Low, W. A. "The Freedmen's Bureau in the Border States." In Douglas Cantrell, Thomas D. Matijasic, Richard E. Holl, Lorie Maltby, and Richard Smoot, eds., *Kentucky through the Centuries: A Collection of Documents and Essays*. Dubuque, IA: Kendall Hunt, 2005.

Lucas, Marion B. "African Americans on the Kentucky Frontier." In Doug Cantrell et al., eds., *Kentucky through the Centuries*. Dubuque, IA: Kendall Hunt, 2005.

———. *A History of Blacks in Kentucky, Vol. 1: From Slavery to Segregation, 1760–1891*. Frankfort: Kentucky Historical Society, 1992.

MacFarlane, David L., and Max M. Tharp. "Trends in Kentucky Agriculture, 1929–1940." Bulletin 429 of the Kentucky Agricultural Experiment Station, University of Kentucky, Lexington (June 1942): 1–51.

Markel, Robert, ed. *The Baseball Encyclopedia*. New York: Macmillan, 1969.

Markowitz, Norman D. *The Rise and Fall of the People's Century: Henry A. Wallace and American Liberalism, 1941–1948*. New York: Free Press, 1973.

Marwick, Arthur. *Britain in the Century of Total War: War, Peace, and Social Change, 1900–1967*. Boston: Little, Brown, 1968.

Mathias, Frank F. "A Memoir Is as a Memoirist Does: A Kentucky Bandsman in World War II." *Register of the Kentucky Historical Society* 92, no. 3 (Summer 1994): 288–304.

McCracken County, Kentucky, History. New York: Turner Publishing Co,, 1989.

McEnaney, Laura. "Nightmares on Elm Street: Demobilizing in Chicago, 1945–1953." *Journal of American History* 92, no. 4 (March 2006): 1265–1291.

McIntosh, Woodrow. *A Survey of Agriculture in Bell County.* Lexington: Kentucky Utilities Co., 1953.

——. *A Survey of Agriculture in Knox County.* Lexington: Kentucky Utilities Co., 1954.

McKelvey, Thelma. *Women in War Production.* New York: Oxford University Press, 1942.

McPherson, James M. *Abraham Lincoln.* New York: Oxford University Press, 2009.

McQuaid, Kim. "Corporate Liberalism in the American Business Community, 1920–1940." *Business History Review* 52 (Autumn 1978): 342–368.

McTighe, John W. *The Barefoot Boy on the Parkway: A History of UAW Local 862.* Louisville: UAW Local 862, 1988.

McWilliams, Cary. *Ill Fares the Land: Migrants and Migratory Labor in the United States.* Boston: Little, Brown, 1942.

Mehring, A. L., Hilda M. Wallace, and Mildred Drain. "Nitrogen, Phosphoric Acid, and Potash Consumption in the United States by Years and by States with Preliminary Figures for 1944." *Journal of the American Society of Agronomy* 37, no. 8 (August 1945): 595–609.

Meier, August, and Elliott Rudwick. *CORE: A Study in the Civil Rights Movement, 1942–1968.* New York: Oxford University Press, 1973.

Menke, Frank G. *Down the Stretch: The Story of Colonel Matt J. Winn.* New York: Smith & Durrell, 1945.

Merrill, Frances E. *Social Problems on the Home Front: A Study of Wartime Influences.* New York: Harper & Brothers, 1948.

Metcalf, Evan B. "Economic Stabilization by American Business in the Twentieth Century." PhD diss., University of Wisconsin, 1972.

Miller, Robert Earnest. "The War That Never Came: Civilian Defense in Cincinnati, Ohio, during World War II." *Queen City Heritage* 49, no. 4 (Winter 1991): 2–22.

Milward, Alan S. *War, Economy, and Society, 1939–1945.* Berkeley: University of California Press, 1977.

Moore, John Hammond. "Hitler's Wehrmacht in Virginia, 1943–1946." *Virginia Magazine of History and Biography* 85, no. 3 (1977): 260–273.

Morgan, Hiram A. *A Survey of Agriculture in Fulton County.* Lexington: Kentucky Utilities Co., 1953.

Movie Trivia Mania. New York: Beekman House, 1984.

Mowrer, Ernest R. "War and Family Solidarity and Stability." *Annals of the American Academy of Political and Social Science* 229 (1943): 100–106.

Murphy, E. R. *A Survey of Agriculture in Grayson County.* Lexington: Kentucky Utilities Co., 1952.

——. *A Survey of Agriculture in Muhlenberg County.* Lexington: Kentucky Utilities Co., n.d.

Murphy, E. R., and W. M. Johnson. *A Survey of Agriculture in Bracken County*. Lexington: Kentucky Utilities Co., 1952.

Nash, Gerald D. "Experiments in Industrial Mobilization: W.I.B. and the N.R.A." *Mid-America* 45 (1963): 157–174.

———. *The Great Depression and World War II: Organizing America, 1933–1945*. New York: St. Martin's Press, 1979.

Neely, Tony, et al. *2005 Kentucky Football Media Guide*. Lexington: Post Printing, 2005.

Nelli, Bert, and Steve Nelli. *The Winning Tradition: A History of Kentucky Wildcat Basketball*. Lexington: University Press of Kentucky, 1998.

Nelson, Donald M. *Arsenal of Democracy: The Story of American War Production*. New York: Harcourt, Brace and Co., 1946.

Nevins, Allan, and Frank Ernest Hill. *Ford: Decline and Rebirth, 1933–1962*. New York: Charles Scribner's Sons, 1962.

Nicholson, James C. *The Kentucky Derby: How the Run for the Roses Became America's Premiere Sporting Event*. Lexington: University Press of Kentucky, 2012.

Noble, Annette Chambers. "Utah's Rosies: Women in the Utah War Industries during World War II." *Utah Historical Quarterly* 59 (Spring 1991): 123–145.

Oakes, James. *The Ruling Race: A History of American Slaveholders*. New York: Vintage Books, 1982.

Ogden, Frederic D., ed. *The Public Papers of Governor Keen Johnson, 1939–1943*. Lexington: University Press of Kentucky, 1982.

Ohly, John H. *Industrialists in Olive Drab: The Emergency Operation of Private Industries during World War II*. Washington, DC: Center of Military History, United States Army, 2000.

101 Years of UK Basketball. Paducah, KY: Turner Publishing Co., 2004.

O'Neill, William L. *A Democracy at War: America's Fight at Home and Abroad in World War II*. New York: Free Press, 1993.

Ossian, Lisa L. *The Home Fronts of Iowa, 1939–1945*. Columbia: University of Missouri Press, 2009.

Patterson, James T. *Congressional Conservatism and the New Deal*. Lexington: University of Kentucky Press, 1967.

Pearce, John Ed. *Divide and Dissent: Kentucky Politics, 1930–1963*. Lexington: University Press of Kentucky, 1987.

Perkins, John A. *A Survey of Agriculture in Boyle County*. Lexington: Kentucky Utilities Co., 1954.

Perrett, Geoffrey. *Days of Sadness, Years of Triumph: The American People, 1939–1945*. New York: Coward, McCann & Geoghegan, 1973.

Persico, Joseph E. *Roosevelt's Secret War: FDR and World War II Espionage*. New York: Random House, 2001.

Polenberg, Richard. *War and Society: The United States, 1941–1945*. New York: J. B. Lippincott Co., 1972.

Polmar, Norman, and Thomas B. Allen. *World War II: America at War, 1941–1945.* New York: Random House, 1991.

Purcell, Aaron D. "Bourbon to Bullets: Louisville's Distilling Industry during World War II, 1941–1945." *Register of the Kentucky Historical Society* 96, no. 1 (Winter 1998): 61–87.

Reed, William F. *Keeneland: A Half-Century of Racing.* Louisville: Harmony House, 1986.

Reiss, Matthias. "Bronzed Bodies behind Barbed Wire: Masculinity and the Treatment of German Prisoners of War in the United States during World War II." *Journal of Military History* 69, no. 2 (April 2005): 475–504.

Renau, Lynn S. *Jockeys, Belles, and Bluegrass Kings.* Louisville: Herr House Press, 1995.

Rice, Russell. *Adolph Rupp: Kentucky's Basketball Baron.* Champaign, IL: Sagamore Publishing, 1994.

———. *Kentucky Basketball's Big Blue Machine.* Huntsville, AL: Strode Publishers, 1978.

———. *The Wildcats: A Story of Kentucky Football.* Huntsville, AL: Strode Publishers, 1975.

Ridenour, Hugh. "Wartime Romance and D-Day Tragedy: A Kentucky Flyer's Death and His Wife's Struggle to Cope." *Register of the Kentucky Historical Society* 102 (Winter 2004): 39–67.

Robertson, William H. P. *The History of Thoroughbred Racing in America.* Englewood Cliffs, NJ: Prentice-Hall, 1964.

Roland, Charles P. "Albert Benjamin Chandler." In Lowell H. Harrison, ed., *Kentucky's Governors.* Lexington: University Press of Kentucky, 1985.

Rutherford, H. K. "Mobilizing Industry for War." *Harvard Business Review* 18 (Autumn 1939): 1–10.

Sakashita, Fumiko. "'Remember Pearl Harbor, but Don't Forget Sikeston': Anti-Lynching Discourse and Transnational Politics of Race." Paper presented at the Annual Meeting of the American Studies Association, May 24, 2009.

Salstrom, Paul. *Appalachia's Path to Dependency: Rethinking a Region's Economic History, 1730–1940,* Lexington: University Press of Kentucky, 1994.

"Samuel Plato." *Kentucky Negro Educational Association Journal* 13, no. 1 (November–December 1942): 27.

Sanson, Jerry Purvis. *Louisiana during World War II: Politics and Society, 1939–1945.* Baton Rouge: Louisiana State University Press, 1999.

Schulman, Robert. *John Sherman Cooper: The Global Kentuckian.* Lexington: University Press of Kentucky, 1976.

Schwartz, Charles F., and Robert E. Graham Jr. *Personal Income by States since 1929.* Washington, DC: Department of Commerce, 1956.

Scott, Otto J. *The Exception: The Story of Ashland Oil & Refining Company.* New York: McGraw-Hill, 1968.

Seidman, Joel. *American Labor from Defense to Reconversion.* Chicago: University of Chicago Press, 1953.

Shabecoff, Philip, and Alice Shabecoff. *Poisoned for Profit: How Toxins Are Making Our Children Chronically Ill.* White River Junction, VT: Chelsea Green Publishing, 2010.

Shannon, Jasper B., and Ruth McQuown. *Presidential Politics in Kentucky, 1824–1948: A Compilation of Election Statistics and an Analysis of Political Behavior.* Lexington: Bureau of Government Research, College of Arts and Sciences, University of Kentucky, 1950.

Sharkey, Teresa Cecilia. "The Home Front: The Women of Lexington, Kentucky, during World War II." *Filson Club Historical Quarterly* 68, no. 4 (October 1994): 466–483.

Shryock, Henry S., Jr. "Redistribution of Population: 1940 to 1950." *Journal of the American Statistical Association* 46, no. 256 (December 1951): 417–437.

Shryock, Henry S., Jr., and Hope Tisdale Eldridge. "Internal Migration in Peace and War." *American Sociological Review* 12, no. 1 (February 1947): 27–39.

Skidelsky, Robert. *John Maynard Keynes: Vol. 2, The Economist as Saviour, 1920–1937.* New York: Penguin Books, 1992.

Skocpol, Theda. "Bringing the State Back In: Strategies of Analysis in Current Research." In Peter Evans, Dietrich Rueschemeyer, and Theda Skocpol, eds., *Bringing the State Back In.* Cambridge, UK: Cambridge University Press, 1985.

———. "A Society without a 'State'? Political Organization, Social Conflict, and Welfare Provision in the United States." *Journal of Public Policy* 7 (October–December 1987): 349–371.

Skowronek, Stephen. *Building a New American State: The Expansion of National Administrative Capacities, 1877–1920.* Cambridge, UK: Cambridge University Press, 1982.

Smith, C. Calvin. *War and Wartime Changes: The Transformation of Arkansas, 1940–1945.* Fayetteville: University of Arkansas Press, 1986.

Smith, Jason Scott. *Building New Deal Liberalism: The Political Economy of Public Works, 1933–1956.* New York: Cambridge University Press, 2006.

Smith, R. Elberton. *The Army and Economic Mobilization.* Washington, DC: Office of the Chief of Military History, Department of the Army, 1959.

Smoot, Richard Clayton. "John Sherman Cooper: The Paradox of a Liberal Republican in Kentucky Politics." PhD diss., University of Kentucky, 1988.

Snyder, Robert. *A History of Georgetown College.* Georgetown, KY: Georgetown College, 1979.

Spector, Ronald H. *Eagle against the Sun: The American War with Japan.* New York: Free Press, 1985.

Stacy, El Hannen. *A Boy from Appalachia Goes to War.* Lost Creek, KY: Stacy Publications, 1999.

Stampp, Kenneth M. *The Peculiar Institution.* New York: Vintage Books, 1956.

Stanley, Gregory Kent. *Before Big Blue: Sports at the University of Kentucky, 1880–1940.* Lexington: University Press of Kentucky, 1996.

Stettinius, Edward R., Jr. *Lend-Lease: Weapon for Victory.* New York: Macmillan, 1944.

Stone, I. F. *Business as Usual: The First Year of Defense.* New York: Modern Age Books, 1941.

———. *The War Years, 1939–1945.* Boston: Little, Brown, 1988.

Stone, Richard G., Jr. *Kentucky Fighting Men, 1861–1945.* Lexington: University Press of Kentucky, 1982.

Suchanek, Jeffrey S., and William J. Marshall, eds. *Time on Target: The World War II Memoir of William R. Buster.* Frankfort: Kentucky Historical Society Foundation, 1999.

Tabor, Larry S. "The Rock of Corregidor: The Heroism of Lieutenant Bethel V. Otter." *Filson Club History Quarterly* 68, no. 3 (July 1994): 348–363.

Tabor, Pauline. *Pauline's: Memoirs of the Madam on Clay Street.* Bowling Green, KY: Touchstone Publishing Co., 1971.

Takaki, Ronald. *A Different Mirror: A History of Multicultural America.* Boston: Little, Brown and Co., 1993.

Tallant, Harold D. *Evil Necessity: Slavery and Political Culture in Antebellum Kentucky.* Lexington: University Press of Kentucky, 2003.

Taylor, Arnold H. *Travail and Triumph: Black Life and Culture in the South since the Civil War.* Westport, CT: Greenwood Press, 1976.

Teeters, Negley K., and John Otto Reinemann. *The Challenge of Delinquency: Causation, Treatment, and Prevention of Juvenile Delinquency.* New York: Prentice-Hall, 1950.

Tenkotte, Paul A., and James C. Claypool, eds. *The Encyclopedia of Northern Kentucky.* Lexington: University Press of Kentucky, 2009.

Terkel, Studs. *"The Good War": An Oral History of World War II.* New York: Pantheon Books, 1984.

Thomas, Mary Martha. *Riveting and Rationing in Dixie: Alabama Women and the Second World War.* Tuscaloosa: University of Alabama Press, 1987.

Thompson, Antonio S. *German Jackboots on Kentucky Bluegrass: Housing German Prisoners of War in Kentucky, 1942–1946.* Clarksville, TN: Diversion Press, 2008.

Thomson, Harry C., and Lida Mayo. *The Ordnance Department: Procurement and Supply.* Washington, DC: Office of the Chief of Military History, Department of the Army, 1960.

Tindall, George Brown. *America: A Narrative History.* New York: W. W. Norton & Co., 1988.

Trotter, Joe William, Jr. *The African American Experience.* Boston: Houghton Mifflin, 2001.

Truman, Harry S. *Memoirs of Harry S. Truman.* Vol. 1, *Year of Decisions.* Garden City, NY: Doubleday & Co., 1953.

Turley-Adams, Alicestyne. *Rosenwald Schools in Kentucky, 1917–1932.* Frankfort: Kentucky Heritage Council and the Kentucky African American Heritage Commission, 1997.

Tuttle, William M., Jr. *"Daddy's Gone to War": The Second World War in the Lives of America's Children.* New York: Oxford University Press, 1993.

Unger, Irwin. *These United States: The Questions of Our Past.* Combined concise ed. Upper Saddle River, NJ: Prentice Hall, 1999.

Vatter, Harold G. *The U.S. Economy in World War II.* New York: Columbia University Press, 1985.

Waddell, Brian. "Economic Mobilization for World War II and the Transformation of the U.S. State." *Politics and Society* 22 (June 1994): 165–194.

———. *The War against the New Deal: World War II and American Democracy.* Dekalb: Northern Illinois University Press, 2001.

Wagner, Thomas E., and Phillip J. Obermiller. *African American Miners and Migrants: The Eastern Kentucky Social Club.* Urbana: University of Illinois Press, 2004.

Wallace, Tom. *Kentucky Basketball Encyclopedia.* Champaign, IL: Sports Publishing, 2002.

Walton, Francis. *Miracle of World War II: How American Industry Made Victory Possible.* New York: Macmillan, 1956.

Wiebe, Robert H. *The Search for Order, 1877–1920.* New York: Hill and Wang, 1968.

Wilcox, Warren W. *The Farmer in the Second World War.* Ames: Iowa State College Press, 1947.

Willigen, John van, and Anne van Willigen. *Food and Everyday Life on Kentucky Farms, 1920–1950.* Lexington: University Press of Kentucky, 2006.

Wilson, Stephen Douglas. "The Adjustment Process of Southern Appalachian Whites in Cincinnati, 1940–1979." PhD diss., University of Kentucky, 1983.

Winkler, Allan M. *Home Front U.S.A.: America during World War II.* 2nd ed. Wheeling, IL: Harlan Davidson, 2000.

Wolfe, Margaret Ripley. "Fallen Leaves and Missing Pages: Women in Kentucky History." *Register of the Kentucky Historical Society* 90 (1992): 64–89.

Woytinsky, W. S. "Interstate Migration during the War." *State Government* 19 (March 1946): 81–84.

Wright, George C. *A History of Blacks in Kentucky, Vol. 2: In Pursuit of Equality, 1890–1980.* Frankfort: Kentucky Historical Society, 1992.

———. *Life behind a Veil: Blacks in Louisville, Kentucky, 1865–1930.* Baton Rouge: Louisiana State University Press, 1985.

Wright, John D., Jr. *Lexington: Heart of the Bluegrass.* Lexington, KY: Lexington-Fayette County Historic Commission, 1982.

———. *Transylvania: Tutor to the West.* Lexington: University Press of Kentucky, 1975.

Wrobel, Art. "'The Fuss I Had with Sam Dudley': Robert Wickliffe and Slavery in Mid-Nineteenth Century Lexington, Kentucky." In Doug Cantrell et al., eds., *Kentucky through the Centuries*. Dubuque, IA: Kendall Hunt, 2005.

Wynn, Neil A. *The Afro-American and the Second World War*. New York: Holmes & Meier, 1976.

Yater, George H. *Two Hundred Years at the Falls of the Ohio: A History of Louisville and Jefferson County*. Louisville: Heritage Corp., 1979.

———. *Waterworks: A History of the Louisville Water Company*. Louisville: Louisville Water Co., 1996.

Yellin, Emily. *Our Mothers' War: American Women at Home and at the Front during World War II*. New York: Free Press, 2004.

Young, Erin Michelle. "Revival of Industrial Hemp: A Systematic Analysis of the Current Global Industry to Determine Limitations and Identify Future Potentials within the Concept of Sustainability." Master's thesis, Lund University (Sweden), 2005.

Zieger, Robert H. *John L. Lewis: Labor Leader*. Boston: Twayne Publishers, 1998.

Zwicky, John F. "A State at War: The Home Front in Illinois during the Second World War." PhD diss., Loyola University, Chicago, 1989.

Encyclopedias

Current Biography (1939–1941).
Dictionary of American Biography (1946–1950).
National Cyclopaedia of American Biography (1943–1946, 1953, 1955).
The New Encyclopaedia Britannica (Volume 7, 2005 edition).

Videos

Kentucky at War (World War II). Kentucky Educational Television. Creation Films. Louisville. 2007.

Index

Abbott and Costello, 291, 293
Abwehr, 160
acetylene gas, 28
Acheson, Dean, 312–13
Adenauer, Konrad, 299
Adolphus, J., 197–98
African Americans, 2, 5, 7, 61–64; and church, 188; employment, 200–201; family, 186; newspapers, 194, 200; political positions, 204–6; school, 188–90; segregation, 181–185, 189; slavery, 181–82, 208; social clubs, 186–88; sports, 267, 280–81, 289–90, 295; 309–11, 314
Agricultural Adjustment Administration, 80, 82
Air Force (film), 291–92
airplane industry, 56–57, 59–60
air raid drills, 159, 162, 165–67, 171–72, 178–79
Akron, Ohio, 30
Alabama, 85, 264–66
Allen, Ermal, 273
Allen, Forrest ("Phog"), 269
Alsab (horse), 283, 287
Aluminum Company of America, 160
Alumni Gym, 264
American Distillery, 120
American Federation of Labor, 64–65, 67–69
American Radiator and Standard Sanitary Company, 185
American Rolling Mill Company, 27
Anderson, Charles W., 202–6
Anderson, Marian, 289–90

Anderson, W. D., 176–77
Andrews Steel Company, 39
A New History of Kentucky (Harrison and Klotter), 1
Angus cattle, 97
anti-Chandlerites, 2, 6, 129–31, 155, 311
Anzio (battle), 240
Ardery, Philip, 111
Arkansas, 5, 47, 197
Armour Creameries, 67
Arnold School, 176
"arsenal of democracy" (slogan), 5, 140
artillery shells, 153
Ashby, Everylee, 62
Ashland, Kentucky, 6, 14, 27, 97, 116, 149, 151
Ashland Oil Company, 41
Ashley, Polly, 217, 219, 221
Assault (horse), 313
Atmospheric Nitrogen Corporation (Allied Chemical & Dye Corporation), 22
Atwell, C. V., 18
Atwood, Rufus, 184, 191
Austria, 3, 10
automobile industry, 24
Auxiliary Coast Guard (Louisville), 165, 168
auxiliary firemen, 161, 164, 176
auxiliary policemen, 161, 164–65, 176
aviation gasoline, 41

B-24 bomber, 54, 59
B-25 Mitchell (bomber), 53–55
B-29 Superfortress (bomber), 53–55

baby boom, 308, 310
Backus, Mrs. B. H., 42
Badeau, Carroll, 68–69
Ballard, Robert, 198
bank earnings assets, 126
Barber, William E., 111
Barkley, Alben W., 17, 23, 82, 122, 130–31, 142–44, 313
baseball, 279–81, 295
basketball, 263–64, 268–78, 295, 313
Bass, Bill, 267
Bataan Death March, 246
Bates and Moore, 117
Battle of the Bulge, 239, 256, 297
Beard, Ralph, 281–82
"Beardless Wonders" (basketball squad), 273–74
Beatty-Cummins, 62, 64
Beauchamp, L., 56
Beer Hall Putsch, 9
Belgium, 201, 239, 253, 297
Bell County, Kentucky, 41, 88–89, 98, 217, 222
Benham, Kentucky, 55
Bennett, Millard, 52, 54
Bernberg, Germany, 260
Bevin, Ernest, 82
Bill of Rights, 100, 108
Bishop, W. T., 283
bituminous coal strike (1943), 70–75
Black, Robert, 202, 206
black market, 115–16, 118, 128
Black Market Rustlers (film), 294
Blakely, Gloria, 230
Blanton. A. F., 116
Blevins, Ray, 277
blitzkrieg (1940), 15
blood drives, 173
Blue Grass Ordnance Depot, 34–35, 43, 68
bombs, 153
Bonesteel, Hartwell, 259

borrowing, 107, 122
Bourbon County, Kentucky, 89, 300
Bowling, Sherman, 67
Bowling Green, Kentucky, 31, 40, 69, 146, 232
Bowman Field, 15, 112, 285
Boyle County, Kentucky, 86–87
Boy Scouts, 31, 167, 231, 252
Bracken County, Kentucky, 98
Bradley, Mildred, 217
Bradley, Omar, 259
Bragg, Mrs. W. C., 260
Brandon's Chapel (Kentucky), 139
Brannum, Bob, 273–74
Breathitt County, Kentucky, 93, 121, 127, 219, 238
Brewer, Mel, 275
Brooks, Robert, 207–8
brothels, 231–32
Brown, John Y., 131–37
Brown v. Board of Education decision, 310
Bryant, Paul ("Bear"), 266, 313
Buckner, Adele, 259
Buckner, Simon B., Jr., 257–59
Bullitt County, Kentucky, 15
Buna-S (synthetic rubber product), 30, 38, 46
Burlew, Roy, 68–69
Burns, Shelby, 52–55
Burns, Virginia, 57, 60
Buster, William R., 236–37
butadiene, 30, 38, 45–47
Butler County, Kentucky, 220–21

C-46 Commando, 22, 59
calcium carbide, 28, 55, 197
California, 85, 301
Calling Dr. Death (film), 294
Calumet Farm, 283, 288
Campbell County Civilian Defense Council, 176

Camp Breckinridge, 34, 102, 111, 143
Camp Cabanatuan (Philippines), 247
Camp Campbell, 34, 102, 111, 143, 232, 307
Camp O'Donnell (Philippines), 246–47
Camp Tyson, Tennessee, 43
cannabis, 92, 141
Canton, Ohio, 21
Capitol Cleaners, 62
Carbide and Carbon Chemical Company, 30, 45–46
carburetor diaphragms, 28
Carpenter, James, 229–30
Carr, Charles V., 177
Carr Creek, 281–82
Carroll, Alfred, 183–84
Carroll County, Kentucky, 90
Carrollton (KY) News-Democrat, 90
cash-and-carry policy, 3, 24
Catlettsburg, Kentucky, 176–77
cattle, 86–87, 97–99, 104
celebration (of victory), 260, 300
Central College (Missouri), 139
Central State Hospital, 145
Chamberlain, Neville, 10
Chandler, Albert Benjamin, 2, 17, 23, 93, 138, 156, 311
Chandlerites, 2, 6
Chaney, Lon, Jr., 294
charcoal, 41
Charlestown, Indiana, 19–20, 41, 160, 227, 301; bag loading plant, 20–21, 41, 301; rocket propellant plant, 20–21, 301; smokeless powder plant, 19–21, 41, 301
chickens, 83, 97
children, 227–28, 230–33
China, 3–4, 157
Chisholm, Gary, 46
Christian, Maude, 61
Churchill Downs, 282–86

cigarettes, 90–91
Cincinnati, Ohio, 6, 178–79
Cincinnati Milling Machine Company, 160
Cincinnati Reds, 279
Citation (horse), 313
City College of New York, 277
City Hide and Tallow Company, 173
civil defense, 157–59, 161–64, 168–75, 177–79
Civilian Conservation Corps, 110
civil rights crusade, 208–9, 310
Civil War, 181–82
Claiborne, Jerry, 282
Clark, I. B., 22
Clark, Sylvia, 122, 124
Clark County, Kentucky, 31
Clayton, Eugene, 202–6
Clements, Earle Chester, 136, 155, 259, 311
Cleveland, Horace, 100
Clinard, Marshall, 121
Clive, Alan, 214, 317n1
Clooney, Rosemary, 288, 313
coal, 13–14, 27, 49, 55–56, 64, 70–75, 218
Coca-Cola Bottling Company, 31, 90
Cochran, A. P., 35–36
Cochran Foil Company, 36
Coffman, Edward, 260
Coffman, Howard, 236, 238, 240, 260
coke (coal product), 27–28
Cold War, 300, 313–14
Cole, I. Willis, 191
Collins, Warnie, 198
Commission on Interracial Cooperation, 190
Commodity Credit Corporation, 92–93
concentration camps, 242
Congress of Industrial Organizations, 64, 67–68, 71, 135–37

Connecticut, 216
Consolidated Aircraft Corporation, 54
Constitution (U.S.), 107–8, 182
Constitution of 1891 (Kentucky), 129, 154
Controlled Materials Plan, 26
convicts, 101–2
Cooper, John Sherman, 137–38, 313
Cooper, Thomas P., 97
Cooper, Warren, 278
corn, 79, 83, 86–88, 94, 104
corporatism, 76
Corregidor (Philippines), 249–50, 304
Corrigan, Ray, 294
Corrupt Practices Act (1944), 153
cost-plus contracts, 36
cotton, 87–88
Count Fleet, 284, 286–87, 313
Covington, Kentucky, 13, 39, 159–60
Cowden Manufacturing Company, 38–39
C-rations, 90
Cravens, Bill, 274
Creason, Joe, 265
Crosby, Bing, 293–94
Crum, Denny, 277
Cumberland Falls, 224
Cumberland Manufacturing Company, 39, 41
Curd, Ed, 264
Curtiss-Wright Corporation, 22, 59, 62
Curtiss-Wright Technical Institute, 54
Cynthiana, Kentucky, 96
Czechoslovakia, 10–11

Dalton, Neil, 162, 178
Darfork, Kentucky, 117
Davis, Chester, 81, 96
Dawson, Charles I., 138
Day Law, 205, 207
Dayton, Kentucky, 39
Dean, Gerald, 309

Decatur, Alabama, 196
Defense Plant Corporation, 28, 92
demobilization, 300–303
denazification, 299
desegregation, 5, 206, 209, 310
De Sylva, B. G., 293
Detroit, Michigan, 6, 21, 42, 120, 159, 214–15, 218, 221–24, 227, 258, 279
Dewey, Thomas, 44
Dexheimer, Paul, 170
Diddle, Ed, 275–78
distilleries, 18–19, 30, 37–38
District of Columbia, 44
Donaldson, J. Lyter, 146–50
Donovan, Herman L., 139, 265
Doolittle, Jimmy, 250
Doran, Mignon, 32
Dorsey, Jimmy, 288–89
Dorsey, Tommy, 288
Dosker, Nicholas, 226–27
"Double V" campaign, 194, 206
Downs, John, 62
Downs, Nova Hays, 62
Dresden, Germany, 299
Dummit, Eldon S., 155
Dunlap, Turner, 93
DuPont, 18, 21, 28–30
DuPont Paint Service Store, 166
dynamite, 32, 229

Eastern Kentucky State Teachers College, 139, 275
Eastern State Hospital, 145
Eastman, Joseph, 285
economic recovery, 14
Edwards, Leroy ("Cowboy"), 270
eggs, 84, 86, 99, 104
Eisenhower, Dwight D., 37, 205, 251, 311
El Alamein, 99
electrification, 143, 146

Elizabethtown, Kentucky, 6, 44, 98, 305, 307
Elkhorn, Kentucky, 14
Elkton, Kentucky, 136
Elliott, Amanda Cooper, 199–200
Ellis, Tom, 282
Emancipation Proclamation, 182
Emergency Medical Service (Louisville), 168
Eminence, Kentucky, 102
Employment Act (1946), 75
England, Kenny, 272, 275
Eubanks, Charles, 183–84
Evans, R. M., 82
Evansville, Indiana, 59–60, 216
Executive Order 8802, 193
explosives, 23–24, 46
exposure suits, 28

factory/plant conversion, 18
Fair Employment Practices Committee (FEPC), 193
farm block, 312
farming: farm income, 104; labor, 100–103; prices of agricultural products, 80, 104
Fasig-Tipton Sales Company, 287
Fayette County, Kentucky, 159
Federal Bureau of Investigation (FBI), 117, 160–61, 169–70
fertilizers, 84, 89, 105
Firestone Tire and Rubber Company, 68
Fleming County, Kentucky, 86–87, 257
Flemingsburg, Kentucky, 116, 119
Florida, 85
Florida Gators (University of Florida football team), 265
Floyd County, Kentucky, 137
Food for Freedom, 82, 85, 96–97
Ford, Ernest, 67

Ford, Henry, 17, 218
Ford Motor Company, 14, 36–37, 306
Forgy, Howell M., 288
Fort Knox, 15, 34, 231, 285, 307
Fort Nelson, 33
Fort Thomas, 15, 111
Fortune Magazine Roundtable, 125
Foster, Willard, 247
Fourteenth Amendment, 183
Fowler, Earl, 247
France, 3, 141, 237, 251
Francis, Charles Jewell, 200
Frankfort, Kentucky, 38, 160, 259
Frankfort Cemetery, 259
Freedmen's Bureau, 182, 189
French, Morgan, 247
Frost, W. A., 102
Fulks, "Jumping Joe," 278
Fulton County, Kentucky, 88

Gaines v. Canada case, 183
Gaitskill, David, 243–46, 303–4
Gaitskill, Frances, 244–45
Galvin, Maurice, 137
gasoline, 32, 38, 114
Gayle & Son, 38
General Maximum Price Regulation (1942), 114
General Motors, 11, 17, 306
General Shoe Company, 54
Geneva Convention (1929), 103, 247–48
Gentry, William H., 248–49
Germany, 3, 9–10, 99–100, 141, 157, 159–61, 191, 207, 237–40, 243–46, 253–54, 257, 260, 297–300
GI Bill of Rights, 154
Gibson, Hollis, 121, 127, 303, 306
Gilbertsville Dam, 143–44
Givens, J. E., 197–98
Glasgow, Kentucky, 152
Glass, James, 217

Glenmore Distillery Company, 41
glycerin, 32
Goforth, Jim, 275
Goodman, Bill, 98–99
Goodman, George H., 115, 118
Goodrich Company, 28, 30, 32, 301
Goodyear Engineering Corporation,
    20–21
Goodyear Tire and Rubber Company,
    20
Graves County, Kentucky, 22, 32
Grayson County, Kentucky, 62
Great Britain, 3, 25, 47, 80–82, 253,
    297–98
Great Depression, 1, 48, 305
Great Lakes Navy basketball team,
    272–73
Green, William, 64
Greendale, Kentucky, 231
Greenleaf, John J., 142, 158–59
Greenup County, Kentucky, 101, 151
Greenwood, Clifford, 238
Griffey, Woolford, 55–56
Griswold, Dwight, 124
Groza, Alex, 274–75, 313
Guadalcanal Diary (film), 291–92
gun mounts, 21

Hall, Allen, 116, 119–20
Hamilton County National Defense
    Council (Cincinnati, Ohio), 178
Hammittee, Jim, 217–19, 221–24
Hansley Mills, 102
Hardin County, Kentucky, 15, 98, 307
Hardin County Enterprise, 313
Harlan, Kentucky, 148, 281
Harlan County, Kentucky, 116
Harlan Daily Enterprise, 72
Harris, Hillious, 56
Harris, Mildred, 57, 59–60, 219–20
Harrison, Lowell H., 1, 317n1
Harrison County, Kentucky, 96

Harrodsburg, Kentucky, 241, 246–49,
    304
Harsh, Robert S., 166
Hart County, Kentucky, 258
Hatch, John Wesley, 207
Haun, Robert D., 115
Havely, T. Ward, 159
Hayden, Basil, 268
Hayden, Margaret Peyton Lutes, 62
Hazard, Kentucky, 51, 198
Helm Meadows, 305
hemp, 91–94, 104, 306
Henderson, Kentucky, 22, 142
Henderson, Leon, 114–15, 119
Henderson ammonia plant, 22
Henderson County, Kentucky, 22
Hendrickson, Roy F., 99–100
Henry County, Kentucky, 102–3
Hereford cattle, 97
Hickman, Kentucky, 119
Hickman, Bernard ("Peck"), 277
Higgins, Andrew Jackson, 317n1
high school sports, 263, 281–82, 295
Hill, Barry, 167
Hill, Meleta Crim, 292
Hillerich John A., III, 35
Hillerich & Bradsby Company, 35, 37
Hiram, Kentucky, 116
Hirohito (emperor), 124, 194
Hiroshima, 48, 299
Hitler, Adolph, 3, 9–10, 48, 124, 142,
    191, 194, 214, 253, 257, 292, 297,
    299, 309
hoarding, 116
Hoffman, Herbert F., 34
hogs, 83, 85–87, 97, 99, 104
Holland, Ty, 281
Hollywood, 290–95, 313
Hoover, Herbert, 151
Hope, Bob, 293–94
Hopkinsville, Kentucky, 31, 111, 136,
    186–88, 282, 307

horses: and horse industry, 282, 284, 288; horse racing, 282–88; horse sales, 263, 287
hosiery, 32, 117
housing, 41–45, 224–27, 302–3, 307
Houston, Texas, 30
Howard Shipyards, 112
Hub Tool Company, 60
Huggett, Howard L., 251–52
Hungate, Wesley, 247
Hutti, Philip, 30

Ickes, Harold, 73, 75
Illinois Central Railroad, 13–14, 170
Indiana, 19–20, 166–67
Indiana Army Ammunition Plant, 20–21
industrial alcohol, 4, 18, 30, 37–38, 301
industrial mobilization for war, 10–13, 110
Industrial Mobilization Plan (1939), 11
inflation, 113–15, 121–22, 128
Ingram, Eileen Wooton Sandlin, 117
Internal Revenue Service, 93
International Harvester, 55
internationalism, 312
International Shoe Company, 39, 41
Interstate Commerce Commission, 108
Iowa, 85, 93, 172
iron ore, 27
Irvine, John W., 101
Irvine, Kentucky, 198, 260
Irving Air Chute Company, 38, 60
isolationism, 312
Italy, 153, 239, 275
Iwo Jima, 257, 260, 297

Jackson, Harry L., 236–38
Jackson, Kentucky, 111, 186–87, 260–61, 291, 307
Jackson Purchase, 87–88
Jackson Times, 1, 3, 10, 214

Japan, 3–4, 142, 157, 192, 246–49, 258–61, 288, 291–92, 297, 299–300, 304
Jarvis, Vickie, 57
Jaxon Theatre, 294
jeeps, 36–37, 48, 301
Jeffboat, 64
Jefferson County, Kentucky, 31, 167, 178
Jefferson County Fiscal Court, 178
Jeffersonville, Indiana, 41
Jeffersonville Boat & Machine Company, 37
Jenkins, Kentucky, 217
Johnson, A. J., 51
Johnson, Keen, 31–32, 65, 67, 72, 101, 129, 131–147, 156, 205
Johnson, Lyman, 201–2, 309–10
Johnson, Walter, 274–75
Jones, D. C., 148
Jones, Loyal, 223
Jones, Marvin, 96
Jones, Wallace ("Wah-Wah"), 281
jute, 93
juvenile delinquency, 227–31, 233

Kansas, 268–69
Kean, Henry Arthur, 267
Keeneland, 283–84, 287
Kelley-Koett Manufacturing Company, 13
Kemper, L. C., 118
Kennedy Military Hospital (Tennessee), 241
Ken-Rad Company, 13, 39–41, 68–70, 215
Kentucky Agricultural Defense Board, 84
Kentucky Commission on Negro Affairs, 204–6
Kentucky Department of Education, 153
Kentucky Department of Vocational Education, 49–50

Kentucky Derby, 283–86, 288
Kentucky General Assembly, 152–53
Kentucky Highway Patrol, 229
Kentucky Horticultural Society, 100
Kentucky Houses of Reform, 231
Kentucky Institution for the Education
   of the Blind, 182
Kentucky Intercollegiate Athletic
   Conference (KIAC), 276–78
Kentucky National Guard, 246
Kentucky Negro Education Association
   (KNEA), 2, 190
Kentucky Ordnance Works, 23–24, 43,
   112, 301
Kentucky Retail Food Dealers'
   Association, 117
Kentucky Senate, 153
Kentucky Shell Manufacturing
   Company, 300–301
Kentucky State Bar Association, 151
Kentucky State University, 184,
   266–67
Kentucky Unemployment
   Compensation Commission, 126
Kentucky Utilities Company, 23
Kentucky Wesleyan College, 278
Keynes, John Maynard, 124–25
Kidd, Mae Street, 311
Kilgore, Ben, 146–47
King, Jim, 273, 275
Kinney, E. J., 92
Kirwan, Albert, 264–66
Klotter, James C., 1, 317n1
Knott County, Kentucky, 121
Knox County, Kentucky, 88–89, 212
Knudsen, William, 16–17, 25
Korean War, 301
K-rations, 91
Kraus, Albert, 231
Kroger, 85
labor: black female workers, 61–64;
   black male workers, 55–56; labor

shortages, 56, 195; summation of
   changes to Kentucky workforce
   as a result of war, 308–9; unions,
   64–67; white female workers,
   56–61; white male workers, 51–55
lambs, 86
L&N Strawberry Yards, 21
Lane, Fannie, 62
Lanham Act, 228
Larkin, George E., Jr., 250
Laughlin, Donald and Edward, 42
Lawson, Elizabeth, 62
Lawson, Kentucky, 219
Leatherwood, Kentucky, 4, 307
Lees College, 219, 240
Leitchfield, Kentucky, 62
LeMaster, Luther, 228
lend-lease policy, 3, 24
lespedeza, 86–87, 94
Lewis, Alec, 198–99, 208
Lewis, John L., 49, 70–75, 77, 135, 304
Lewis, John W., 116, 119–20
Lexington, Kentucky, 6, 120–21, 159–
   61, 264, 284, 287, 291, 307
Lexington Civilian Defense Council,
   159, 161
Lexington Herald-Leader, 72
Lexington Signal Depot (Avon Signal
   Depot), 34–35, 43, 61
Lexington Telephone Company, 159
Lexington Water Company, 159
Lexington Yellow Cab Company, 61
lime, 28, 197
limestone, 27
Lincoln, Abraham, 182, 208
Lions Club (Bowling Green), 31
Litchfield, P. W., 20–21
Logan, M. M., 138
Logan County, Kentucky, 129, 137
London, Kentucky, 50
Los Angeles, California, 42
Louisiana, 5, 145

Louisiana State University Tigers, 274
Louisville, Kentucky, 1, 6, 15, 18–19,
    21, 28–32, 35–37, 41–48, 50–53,
    64, 72, 96, 112, 121, 133, 136–37,
    150, 155, 159–69, 173, 175, 178–
    79, 183, 185–87, 190, 193, 195–98,
    202–5, 212, 216–17, 224–27, 232–
    33, 249, 252, 277, 281–82, 284–85,
    288–89, 291, 301, 307, 309
Louisville & Nashville Railroad,
    13–14, 56, 198, 217
Louisville Black Colonels, 279–81
Louisville Community Chest, 206
Louisville Courier-Journal, 50, 72,
    200–201
Louisville Defender, 194
Louisville Gas & Electric Company,
    217
Louisville Leader, 191, 194
Louisville Metropolitan Area Defense
    Council, 161–62, 164–68, 178
Louisville Naval Ordnance Station, 21,
    60–61
Louisville Tin & Stove Company, 67
Louisville Urban League, 190, 207
Louisville Water Company, 169, 227
Luxembourg, 201, 253, 297
lynching, 182–83, 194, 208
Lyon County, Kentucky, 139

MacArthur, Douglas, 249, 299
machine guns, 39
Maddox, Doris, 253
Maddox, George, 253–54
Maddox, Hunt, 253
Maddox, Kenneth, 252–54, 297
Maddox, Oma Mae, 252–56, 261
Madisonville, Kentucky, 152
Madisonville Messenger, 10
Madisonville Sanatorium, 152
Majo, Mount (Italy), 239
management, 49, 74–76, 197

Manchuria, 247
Mansbach Metal Company, 32
March on Washington, 193
Marijuana Tax Act (1937), 92
Maritime Commission, 25, 37, 112
Marshall, George C., 200
Martin, Emma, 219–21
Martin, Jesse, 220–21
Martin, Lawrence, 246
Marx, Jack, 173
Massachusetts, 216
Massenburg, Mary Ellen Perrine,
    255–56
Massie, Dan, 203–4
Mathias, Frank F., 111
Mathis, Loraine, 184
Mauer, John, 268, 270
May, Andrew Jackson, 120
May Act (1941), 232
Mayfield, Kentucky, 50, 136
Maysville, Kentucky, 103, 170, 176, 255
McCarthy, Joe, 54
McCormick, Frank, 279
McCracken County, Kentucky, 23
McDevitt, Anna, 57, 60
McGlore Stove Company, 41
McKesson and Roberts, 120
McLean County News, 252
McMurtrey, G. H., 93
Meade County, Kentucky, 15
Mengel Company, 22, 32
mental hospitals, 138, 140
Metals Reserve Company, 32
Metropolitan Sportsman's Club, 280
Meyer, Agnes E., 228
Meyzeek, Albert Ernest, 190–91, 196
Michigan, 4, 214, 217, 301, 310
migration, 5–6, 211–17, 220–21, 223–
    24, 226–28, 232–33, 310
military-industrial complex, 26, 77, 307
milk, 81, 83–85, 97, 104
milkweed pods, 94

Miller, Glenn, 288–90
Miller, "Junior," 280–81
Mills, L. H., 228–30
Mississippi, 5
Mississippi Rebels, 265
Mississippi State Bulldogs, 265
Modern Welding Company, 41
Monarch Tool and Manufacturing
    Company, 39
Monroe, Rose Will, 57–58, 217–19
Montgomery, Ben, 185
moonshiners and moonshining, 121,
    303
Moore, D. C., 147
Morehead State Teachers College,
    266–68, 276, 278
Morganfield, Kentucky, 111, 225
Morris, Orville, 231
Mount Sterling, Kentucky, 47, 120
Mount Sterling Gazette and Kentucky
    Courier, 138
movies, 290–95, 313
Muhlenberg County, Kentucky, 86,
    94
Munich Conference, 10
Murray State Teachers College, 266–
    67, 276, 278
music, 288–90, 295, 313
Mussolini, Benito, 147, 153, 194, 214
mustard gas, 35
Myers, Billy, 279
Myers, Rodes K., 146–47

Nagasaki, 48, 247, 299
Naismith, James, 269–70
National Association for the
    Advancement of Colored People, 2,
    183, 190–91, 200
National Carbide Corporation, 28, 30,
    32, 55, 197, 206, 301
National Collegiate Athletic
    Association, 272, 274–75

National Defense Advisory
    Commission (NDAC), 3, 12,
    15–17, 23–24, 81–82, 110
National Distillery, 120
national farm policy, 80–84
National Fireworks Company, 22
National Invitational Tournament
    (NIT), 272–74, 277
National Labor Relations Act, 65, 109
National Socialist Party, 9
National Synthetic Rubber Company,
    30
National Urban League, 190, 195
National Wage Stabilization Board
    (NWSB), 76
National War Labor Board (NWLB),
    65, 68–69, 71–72, 76, 114–15
National Youth Administration (NYA),
    49–50, 110
Nation's Business, 35
naval guns, 21, 48
Neal, Gerald, 311
Nebraska, 124
Nelson, Donald, 16–17, 26–27, 36,
    302
neoprene, 28–29
Newcastle, Wyoming, 172
New Deal, 1, 108–10, 155–56, 202,
    311; New Dealers, 302–3
Newell, Doug, 255
Newport, Kentucky, 39, 176–77, 233
Newton, Creighton, 52, 54
Newton, Patricia Porter, 61
New York City, 158–60
nitric acid, 22
nitrogen, 84, 89
Noble, Thelma Jo, 216, 219, 221
Nolan, Lloyd, 291
Norfleet, Carl, 170
North Carolina, 85
Northington, Mary, 184–85
no-strike pledge, 49, 65, 77

Notre Dame Fighting Irish, 271, 272, 274
nylon, 18, 32

Office of Civilian Defense (OCD), 157–59, 173, 177
Office of Defense Transportation (ODT), 285
Office of Price Administration (OPA), 76, 107, 113–21, 128, 196, 302–3
Office of Production Management (OPM), 12–13, 24–26, 110, 141
Office of the Provost Marshal General (OPMG), 102
Office of War Information, 96, 221
Ohio River flood (1943), 174, 176–77
Ohio Valley Conference (OVC), 268
Okinawa, 258–60, 299
Oklahoma, 212–13
Oklahoma A&M, 274
old-age pensions, 133–34, 140–41
Oldham County, Kentucky, 171
Olive Hill Uprising (1943), 228–30
Operation Pastorius, 160
Oregon, 160, 216
organizational society (concept), 48
Ormsby Village, 230–31
Osborne Association, 231
Ossian, Lisa L., 317n1
Otter, Bethel V., 249–50
Owen County, Kentucky, 102
Owensboro, Kentucky, 13, 68–69, 116, 121

P-47 fighter (Thunderbolt), 60
Paducah, Kentucky, 6, 23–24, 169–70, 301
Paducah airport, 23, 143
Paducah Municipal Defense Council, 169–70
Paris, Kentucky, 102, 152, 259
Parker, Glen, 274

Parkinson, Jack, 274
Parkway Field, 280
patronage, 2, 6, 151–52, 311
Pearl Harbor, Hawaii, 4, 30, 115, 231, 288, 299
Peavler, William Lee, 246
Pennington, J. J., 177
Pennyrile, 85–86
pentaerythritol tetranitrate (PETN), 24
per capita income (Kentucky), 126, 305
Perguson, Dee Carl, Jr., 240–42
Perrine, John Dixon, 103, 255–56, 260
Perrine, Sam, 255–56
Perry, John H., 102
Perry County, 121
phosphoric acid, 89
Piatt, Thomas, 287
Pidgeon, Walter, 57, 218
Pitino, Rick, 277
Pittsburgh, Pennsylvania, 30
Plato, Samuel, 196–97, 208
Plessy v. Ferguson, 189
Poland, 3, 10–11
political corruption, 133, 311
Porter, Patsie, 61, 64
Port Neches, Texas, 45–46
post-traumatic stress disorder, 242, 304
postwar planning, 148
Postwar Planning Commission, 154
potash, 84, 89
Potts Lumber Company, 171
Poundstone, Bruce, 215
powder bags, 20, 32, 56
Powell, Dorothy Louise, 57, 59
Powell County, Kentucky, 31
Powell-Hackney Company, 198
Powers, Georgia, 311
Powleit, Alvin, 247
preparedness measures for World War II, 3, 10–13, 35
price controls, 107, 113–15, 121, 128, 302–3

Prichard, Edward, 311
Princeton, Kentucky, 41
priorities, 24–26, 112
prisoners of war, 101–3
prostitution, 231–33
Providence, Kentucky, 59, 220
PT boats, 292
Pulaski County, Kentucky, 57, 169–70, 218
Purchasing Department (Kentucky state government), 145–46, 149

Quinn Chapel AME Church, 188, 202

radar equipment, 34, 68
Radcliff, Kentucky, 44
radio tubes, 13, 39–40, 68–70
Raibert, R. H., 117–18
railroad industry, 13–14, 108
Ralph the Riveter, 5, 49, 51–52, 77
Ramsey, Lloyd, 272
Randolph, A. Philip, 191–93, 200
rationing (of goods), 113–14, 128
Rat Menace (Louisville), 173–74
Rayburn, J. E., 230
Razor, Daniel Boone, Jr., 120, 128, 306
Razor, Daniel Boone, Sr., 127–28, 306
Reagan Revolution, 314
recovery (economic), 125–27, 305
Red Cross, 165, 174, 176
redistricting, 143
Reed, Donna, 292
Remember Pearl Harbor (film), 291
Republic Aviation, 59
Reynolds Metal Company, 23, 37, 64, 214
Rhea, Thomas, 129–30, 134–37, 311
Rhineland, 10
Richmond, Kentucky, 6, 35, 41, 43, 139, 225
Richmond Daily Register, 10, 139
Ripple, Jimmy, 279

Road to Morocco, The (1942 film), 294
Roberts, Herman, 52–53
Robinson, Major, 199–200
Robsion, John M., 138, 148
Roosevelt, Franklin D., 1, 3, 5, 11–12, 15–17, 24–26, 35, 48, 68–69, 71–74, 80–81, 104–5, 108–10, 121–22, 131, 134, 157, 159, 192–93, 290
Rosenstiel, Lewis S., 37
Rosenwald, Julius, 189
Rosie the Riveter, 5, 49, 56–58, 77, 308–9
Rott, Art, 117
rubber (natural), 27–28, 115–16
Rubber Reserve Company, 31–32
Rubbertown, 28
Rubinstein, Artur, 289
Rue, Arch B., 241
Rue, Edwin, 240–42, 246, 249
Rupp, Adolph, 264, 268–76, 278, 295, 313
Russia, 82, 172, 297

Sadler, John, 247
Sale, Aggie, 270
Salmon, Walter J., 287
Sampson, Flem, 165, 177, 179
Sanson, Jerry Purvis, 317n1
Saratoga, New York, 287
savings, 126–28
savings bonds, 122–24
Sawyer, Charles, 169–70
Scandinavia, 76
Schenley Distillers Corporation, 37, 120
Schmelzle, George, 269
Schuler Koster Motor Company, 179
Scott, James, 229
Scottsville, Kentucky, 136
scrap drives, 30–32, 48, 173
Seabiscuit (horse), 283

Sears, Roebuck, and Company, 17
Secretariat (horse), 286
segregation, 2, 182–83, 206–9, 309–10
Selective Service, 72
Settle, James W., 52, 54
Shackleton, Walter, 162, 178–79
sheep, 86, 97, 99
Sheffield, Alabama, 23
Shepherd, Joe, 264
Shively, Bernie, 265
shoes, 39, 41
Short, Jim, 230
shortages, 100–105, 113–14, 116, 120, 127
Shouse, S. Headley, 103
Sicily, 99
silk, 20
Simms, Alfonso, 55
Sims, Cecil, 247, 249
slavery, 181–82, 208
Smith, Bert, 278
Smith, C. Calvin, 317n1
Smith, H. L., 102
Smith, Larry, 61
Smith, Milton Hannibal, 108
Smith, Rebecca, 217
Smith-Connally Act, 75
smokeless powder, 18–20, 48, 301
Social Security Act (1935), 109
soil conservation districts, 140
Somerset, Kentucky, 169–70, 291, 294
Sousley, Franklin R., 123, 257, 297, 299
South Carolina, 47, 85
Southeastern Conference (SEC), 271–75, 313
Southern Railroad, 14
soybeans, 83, 86, 104, 306
Sparks, Mrs. C., 101
Springfield, Kentucky, 53, 60
Stacy, El Hannen, 111, 236, 238–40
Stagg Distillery, 38

Stalag 17-B, 243–44
Stalingrad, 99
Standard Oil, 64
Standiford Field, 21
Stanford, Kentucky, 116
state building (concept), 15–17, 107–11
state debt, 140, 145
State Defense Council, 142
state income tax, 148, 154
state parks, 154
State Personnel Board, 206
State Trucking Association, 145, 147, 149
Stearns, Kentucky, 61
steel, 14, 27
Steel, Herbert, 247
Stettinius, Edward R., Jr., 11–12, 16–17, 25, 82–83
Stevenson, Adlai E., 311
Stewart Iron Works Company, 39
St. John's University, 274
stills, 121
Stimson, Henry, 36, 200
Stone, Jeptha Carl, 269
Stone, Kathleen, 60–61
Stout, Rufus, 55, 205–6, 208
Streetcar Derby, 285
St. Xavier High School (Louisville), 281
subcontracts, 21, 26
Sudetenland, 10
sweet potatoes, 88
Swope, King, 130, 132, 137–39
Sydnor, Buck, 277
synthetic rubber, 4, 18, 26, 28, 30, 197, 301

Tabor, Pauline, 232
Tafel, Arthur G., 226
Taft-Hartley Act, 75–76
Talk of the Town (film), 294
taxation, 11, 107, 122, 128, 133, 148, 154

Taylor, L. N., 189–90
Teachers' Retirement Act (1938),
  140–41
Tennessee, 4, 85, 145, 214, 220–21,
  273–74
Tennessee Valley Authority, 109–10, 143
Terry, Peggy, 46, 57, 60
tetryl, 24, 46
tetrytol, 24
Texas, 4–5, 45–46, 85, 199
textiles, 38–39
They Were Expendable (1945 film), 292
Thirteenth Amendment, 182
Thomas, Frank, 273
Thompson, James G., 194
Thornton on the Law of Oil and Gas (ed.
  Willis), 151
tires, 30, 32, 61
tobacco, 1, 79–80, 83, 86–91, 102–4,
  135–36, 306
Tobacco Control Act (1934), 80
Todd, Jouett Ross, 138, 148
Tojo, Hidecki, 214, 257, 292, 299, 309
Tokyo, 250, 297
torpedo tubes, 21
toys, 31
tractors, 84, 89, 105
Transylvania College, 268
Travis, Onis M., 153
Trawick, Herb, 267
trinitrotoluene (TNT), 23–24, 43, 46,
  48, 144, 301
Truman, Harry, 76, 202, 299, 312
tuberculosis hospitals, 151–52
Tube Turns, Incorporated, 37, 53, 60
Tucker, C. Eubank, 203
Tulane University, 274

unemployment, 1, 4, 124–25, 305
Union Underwear Company, 38
United Automobile Workers–American
  Federation of Labor Local 783, 69

United Automobile Workers Local 862,
  52–53
United Mine Workers of America
  (UMW), 49, 70–75, 77, 135, 304
United Nations Relief and
  Rehabilitation Administration, 99
United Service Organizations (USO),
  44–45
United States Army, 4, 13, 15, 19, 26,
  68–70, 73, 90–91, 105, 200–202,
  236–40, 246, 252–53, 258–59, 285,
  297, 299, 303
United States Army Air Corps, 15, 54,
  112, 220, 251
United States Army Corps of
  Engineers, 46
United States Army Signal Corps, 112
United States Coast Guard, 165
United States Department of Agriculture,
  81–86, 88, 92, 96–97, 104
United States Employment Service, 51,
  100–101
United States Environmental
  Protection Agency, 45
United States Navy, 13, 15, 22, 25, 38,
  201–2, 250, 272, 303
United States Treasury Department,
  122–24
United States War Department, 13, 17,
  69–70, 251, 254
United States War Food Supply
  Program, 100, 104
University of Florida, 265
University of Kentucky: 183–84, 202,
  309–10; basketball program, 268–
  75, 295, 313; College of Agriculture
  and Home Economics, 92, 96, 215;
  football team, 263–66, 295, 313
University of Notre Dame, 271, 272, 274

Vanderbilt Commodores, 264–65
venereal disease, 232

Versailles, Kentucky, 184
Versailles Treaty, 9
victory gardens, 94–97
Victory Loan Drive, 122
Vine Grove, Kentucky, 50
vinyl chloride, 47
Viola, Kentucky, 22, 46, 60, 143
Viola shell-loading plant, 22, 60
Virginia, 6, 214, 235
Virginia Theatre of Somerset, 294
V-J day, 21
Vogt Manufacturing Company, 32, 37
Vultee Aircraft, 216

Wadsworth Watchcase Company, 39
Waggoner, Raymond, 228–30
Wainright, Jonathan, 249
Wallace, Brownie, 186, 188–89
Wallace, Henrietta, 186–89, 260–61
Wallace, Henry A., 82
war bonds, 122–24, 174
War Food Administration, 96, 302
War Industries Board, 11–12
War Loan drives, 122
War Manpower Commission, 50–51, 101, 103
War Production Board, 12–13, 26, 31–32, 107, 110, 112, 225, 302
War Resources Administration, 11–12
War Resources Board, 11–12, 16, 110
Washington, DC, 44
Watts, Lizzie, 4, 127
Watts, Von, 127, 303–4, 306–7
Wayne, John, 292
Weimar Republic, 9
Wells, Millard C., 259–60
Wells, Virgie, 96–97
Western Kentucky State Teachers College, 275–78
Western Union, 63
Westinghouse Electric & Manufacturing Company, 21

Westover subdivision, 196
West Virginia, 213, 277
Weyler, Edward H., 68
Whalen, Clarence and Dean, 96
WHAS (radio), 133–34, 288
wheat, 79, 83–84, 86, 94, 101, 104
Wheatley, Gus, 230–31
Wheeler, Alma, 250–52, 256, 261
Wheeler, Gene, 250–52
Whirlaway, 283, 287, 313
whiskey, 18, 37–38, 120–21
White Engineering Corporation, 21
White, Robert F., 197–98
White, Walter, 191, 200
Whitehead, Don, 274
Whitney, Francis E., 199
Whittaker, B. H., 56
Wickard, Claude, 81–82, 96
Wickliffe, Kentucky, 119
Wilder, Kentucky, 39
Wilkins, Ray, 169–70
Williams, David, 159
Williams, John Fred, 155
Willis, Simeon, 100, 129, 146–56, 311
Willow Run, 218
Wilson, Brown, 260–61
Winchester, Kentucky, 43, 93, 184
Winn, Matt J., 282, 284–86
Winstead, Edna, 57, 59
Wisconsin, 93
Witt, Paul, 240–42
Wolfe County, Kentucky, 212
Woman's Land Army, 101
Woods, Ralph, 50
Woolridge, Sandy, 54, 56
Works Department (Louisville), 162, 166
Works Progress Administration, 1, 43, 110, 164
World War I, 3, 11, 13, 113, 139, 258, 281

World War II, 1–7, 9–10, 25–26,
28, 30, 34–35, 37–39, 44–49,
53–54, 56–57, 59, 62–64, 74,
79, 86, 89, 91, 94, 103–4, 107,
109–10, 116, 120, 127–29, 140,
142, 145, 151, 153–57, 162, 170,
184–86, 189, 200, 206–8, 211,
231–33, 235–36, 240, 255–59,
261, 263–64, 268, 271–73, 275,
277–85, 287–93, 295, 297, 299–
2, 305–14
Wright, Cleo, 194
Wright, James, 216–17

Wright, Warren, 288
Wyatt, Wilson, 161–62, 166
Wyoming, 172

x-ray equipment, 13, 301

York, Laura Gay, 117
Young Men's Christian Association
(YMCA), 184, 186–88
Young Women's Christian Association
(YWCA), 186–88
Youngblood, Clete W., 118
Ypsilanti, Michigan, 57, 218

Topics in Kentucky History

James C. Klotter, Series Editor

Books in the Series

The Family Legacy of Henry Clay: In the Shadow of a Kentucky Patriarch
Lindsey Apple

George Keats of Kentucky: A Life
Lawrence M. Crutcher

A History of Education in Kentucky
William E. Ellis

Madeline McDowell Breckinridge and the Battle for a New South
Melba Porter Hay

Committed to Victory: The Kentucky Home Front during World War II
Richard E. Holl

Henry Watterson and the New South: The Politics of Empire, Free Trade, and Globalization
Daniel S. Margolies

Murder and Madness: The Myth of the Kentucky Tragedy
Matthew G. Schoenbachler

How Kentucky Became Southern: A Tale of Outlaws, Horse Thieves, Gamblers, and Breeders
Maryjean Wall

Madam Belle: Sex, Money, and Influence in a Southern Brothel
Maryjean Wall

CPSIA information can be obtained at www.ICGtesting.com
Printed in the USA
BVOW08*1638280815

415267BV00001B/1/P